Network Systems Design

Using Network Processors

Intel IXP version

Other Books In the Internetworking Series
from Douglas Comer and Prentice Hall

Internetworking With TCP/IP Volume I: Principles, Protocols and Architectures, 4th edition: 2000, ISBN 0-13-01830-6

The classic reference in the field for anyone who wants to understand Internet technology and the TCP/IP protocol suite.

Internetworking With TCP/IP Volume II: Design, Implementation, and Internals (with David Stevens), 3rd edition: 1999, ISBN 0-13-973843-6

Volume II continues the discussion of Volume I by using code from a running implementation of TCP/IP to illustrate all the details.

Internetworking With TCP/IP Volume III: Client-Server Programming and Applications (with David Stevens)
> **Linux/POSIX sockets version: 2000, ISBN 0-13-032071-4**
> **AT&T TLI Version: 1994, ISBN 0-13-474230-3**
> **Windows Sockets Version: 1997, ISBN 0-13-848714-6**

Volume III describes the fundamental concept of client-server computing used to build all distributed computing systems. The text discusses various server designs as well as the tools and techniques used to build clients and servers. Three versions of Volume III are available for the socket API (Linux/POSIX), the TLI API (AT&T System V), and the Windows Sockets API (Microsoft).

Computer Networks And Internets (with a CD-ROM by Ralph Droms), 3rd edition: 2001, ISBN 0-13-091449-5

The text provides a broad introduction to data communication, networking, internetworking, and client-server applications, including both hardware and software components that make up computer networks. The CD-ROM features animations and data sets.

The Internet Book: Everything you need to know about computer networking and how the Internet works, 3rd edition: 2000, ISBN 0-13-030852-8, paperback

A gentle introduction to networking and the Internet that does not assume the reader has a technical background. The text explains both the terminology and concepts

Hands-On Networking With Internet Technologies, 2002, ISBN 0-13-048003-7, paperback

The text describes a set of networking testbed facilities that vary from a single computer to an extensive protocol development lab, and lists experiments that the reader can perform using each facility.

To order, visit the Prentice Hall Web page at www.prenhall.com/
or contact your local bookstore or Prentice Hall representative.
In North America, call 1-515-284-6751, or send a FAX to 1-515-284-6719.

Network Systems Design

Using Network Processors

Intel IXP version

DOUGLAS E. COMER

Department of Computer Sciences
Purdue University
West Lafayette, IN 47907

PEARSON

Prentice
Hall

Upper Saddle River, New Jersey 07458

Library of Congress Cataloging-in-Publication Data

CIP DATA AVAILABLE.

Vice President and Editorial Director,ECS: *Marcia Horton*
Publisher: *Alan Apt*
Associate Editor: *Toni Holm*
Editorial Assistant: *Patrick Lindner*
Vice President and Director of Production and Manufacturing, ESM: *David W. Riccardi*
Executive Managing Editor: *Vince O'Brien*
Assistant Managing Editor: *Camille Trentacoste*
Production Editor: *Irwin Zucker*
Manufacturing Manager: *Trudy Pisciotti*
Manufacturing Buyer: *Lisa McDowell*
Director of Creative Services: *Paul Belfanti*
Creative Director: *Carole Anson*
Art Director: *Heather Scott*
Cover Art: *Illustration by Steve Lefkowitz*
Executive Marketing Manager: *Pamela Shaffer*
Marketing Assistant: *Barrie Reinhold*

 © 2004 Pearson Education, Inc.
Pearson Prentice Hall
Upper Saddle River, New Jersey 07458

The author and publisher of this book have used their best efforts in preparing this book. These efforts include the development, research, and testing of the theories and programs to determine their effectiveness. The author and publisher make no warranty of any kind, expressed or implied, with regard to these programs or the documentation contained in this book. The author and publisher shall not be liable in any event for incidental or consequential damages in connection with, or arising out of, the furnishing, performance, or use of these programs.

TRADEMARK INFORMATION: Company and product names used in this text may be trademarks or registered trademarks ofthe individual companies, and are respectfully acknowledged. A detailed list is included on page vi.

Printed in the United States of America

10 9 8 7 6 5 4 3 2 1

ISBN 0-13-141792-4

Pearson Education Ltd., *London*
Pearson Education Australia Pty. Ltd., *Sydney*
Pearson Education Singapore Pte. Ltd.
Pearson Education North Asia Ltd. *Hong Kong*
Pearson Education Canada Inc., *Toronto*
Pearson Educación de Mexico, S.A. de C.V.
Pearson Education—Japan, Inc., *Tokyo*
Pearson Education—Malaysia Pte. Ltd.
Pearson Education Inc., *Upper Saddle River, New Jersey*

To The Power Of Programmability

TRADEMARK INFORMATION

Contents

Chapter 3   Review Of Protocols And Packet Formats   **15**

PART I   Traditional Protocol Processing Systems

Chapter 4   Conventional Computer Hardware Architecture   **29**

Chapter 5   Basic Packet Processing: Algorithms And Data Structures   **43**

Chapter 6   Packet Processing Functions   67

Chapter 7   Protocol Software On A Conventional Processor   83

Chapter 8   Hardware Architectures For Protocol Processing   97

Chapter 9   Classification And Forwarding   115

Chapter 12   The Complexity Of Network Processor Design   165

Chapter 13   Network Processor Architectures   177

Chapter 14   Issues In Scaling A Network Processor   195

Chapter 17   Design Tradeoffs And Consequences   261

PART III   Example Network Processor

Chapter 18   Overview Of The Intel Network Processor   273

Chapter 19   Embedded RISC Processor (StrongARM Core)   289

Chapter 20   Packet Processor Hardware (Microengines And FBI)   301

Chapter 21   Reference System And Software Development Kit (Bridal   325
Veil, SDK)

Chapter 22   Programming Model (ACE)   335

Chapter 23   ACE Run-Time Structure And StrongARM Facilities   **349**

Chapter 24   Microengine Programming I   **371**

Foreword

With *Network Systems Design*, Doug Comer has written the book I wish I had written. He gives a step-by-step account of how to build the bridges, switches, routers, firewalls, NAT-boxes, and proxies that serve as the building blocks of today's Internet, and he has done it with the clarity for which his books are famous. This book is required reading for anyone who wants to understand what goes on inside the plethora of magic boxes that make the Internet work.

The first part of the book outlines the packet processing functionality common to all network systems. From packet classification to buffer management to queuing disciplines to scheduling algorithms, the book walks the reader through everything that happens to a packet from the moment it arrives on an incoming link until the moment it is transmitted on an outgoing link. A major strength of the book is that it describes the mechanisms and techniques in an application-neutral way, that is, independent of whether one is building a firewall, an intrusion detection system, or a router (or better yet, all three at the same time).

The second and third parts of the book focus on an emerging hardware technology — *network processors* — that is being used to construct network systems. These devices are unique in two respects. First, they are designed to process packets (or more precisely, fixed-sized chunks of packets) in parallel, thereby allowing them to keep pace with ever-increasing link speeds. Second, they are software programmable, thereby allowing the system designer to customize their behavior for the task at hand; i.e., program them to be a bridge, a firewall, or a proxy. In fact, many of the network processors on the market today provide primitives that directly support the classification, buffering, queuing, and scheduling functions common to all network systems. The book surveys the capabilities of network processors from several vendors (e.g., Agere, IBM), but to make the discussion concrete, focuses on a specific chip — Intel's IXP1200.

The Internet is enormously large and complex, and it is understandable that we often focus on global functions such as routing, security, and congestion control. We must remember, however, that each of the global functions has a localized implementation — the Internet is composed of thousands of individual systems that each operate independently. This book describes all aspects of the design and implementation of the individual systems — it explains the general-purpose and special-purpose hardware, protocol software, and design tradeoffs.

Larry Peterson

January, 2003

Preface

This book describes the design of network systems such as routers, bridges, switches, firewalls, and other equipment used in the Internet. It considers the functionality required for protocol processing, and explains how the functionality has been implemented on a range of hardware architectures. The book focuses on network processor technology, a recent development that has quickly become one of the standard tools designers use. In addition to discussing the motivation and use of network processors, the text provides an overview of network processor architectures, examines programming languages for network processors, and considers the many design tradeoffs.

The text is intended for both professionals who are building network systems and students who are learning about network systems design. To aid professionals, the text discusses design decisions, both for network processors and for network systems. In addition, all examples used in discussions have been taken from commercially available products, and the code in the book has been tested on network processor hardware. To aid students, the book presents concepts without presuming a working knowledge of the jargon used in the industry. Both students and professionals will appreciate the glossary of terms that helps the reader navigate the maze of acronyms.

Following a three-chapter review of protocols and an introduction to network systems, the main text is divided into three parts. The first part, Chapters 4 - 10, considers protocol processing, and covers implementations on a range of hardware architectures used in traditional network systems. The range extends from a conventional, uniprocessor system, used in low-end network systems, to a high-end, multiprocessor architecture that uses intelligent network interface cards to handle higher-speed networks. In addition, chapters in Part 1 discuss the important topics of classification and switching fabric architectures.

The second part, Chapters 11 - 17, explores network processor technology. It examines the economic motivation for network processors, explains the possible roles that network processors fill in network systems, and discusses network processor architecture. To make the discussion concrete and demonstrate the variety of designs, Chapter 15 surveys commercially-available architectures. Chapter 16 considers languages used to program network processors, giving examples from two commercially-available classification languages: NCL and FPL.

The third part of the text examines one network processor in detail. This version of the book uses Intel's IXP1200 as the example. The text presents details of both the multi-processor hardware architecture and software development environment that Intel supplies. After explaining the fundamental components on the Intel chip, chapters examine the programming paradigm, and describe how the software written for the IXP1200 uses the onboard processors and other components. Most important, the book contains the complete code for an example bump-in-the-wire network system.

A Web site has been created to accompany the text:

http://www.npbook.cs.purdue.edu

The site, which is managed by Robert Dusek, contains all the program examples from the text as well as a set of course notes for professors. In addition, I invite network processor vendors to submit example code for their chips. In particular, I encourage each vendor to show how the example system from Chapter 26 is implemented on their network processor.

I thank the many individuals and groups who have helped with this text and deserve credit. Agere, IBM, and Intel provided network processor hardware and software for my lab at Purdue. Chris Telfer worked tirelessly to set up the lab facilities, and wrote the code for the wwbump example. Other students, including Jing Liu, Xiaodong Li, Fan Zhang, and Shireen Javali searched literature, checked details, and commented on drafts. Om Prakash Pitta, Vasudeva Nithyananda Pai, and students in two graduate seminars inspired me by using network processors to create a variety of projects. Colleague Sonia Fahmy reviewed material on switching fabrics.

I am also grateful for the comments and criticism from many professionals who either participate in the creation of network processors or use them to build network systems. Craig Partridge of BBN and Paul Phillips of Nauticus Networks provided general comments; Craig provided an insight on switching fabrics. Mike Hathaway of Austin Ventures gave valuable background, and suggested the division of second and third generation architectures. Dale Parson and Rob Munoz of Agere Systems offered extensive reviews, and provided details about both FPL and the Agere architecture. Mohammad Peyravian of IBM commented on the presentation of the IBM architecture. Matt Tryzna of IBM came to Purdue to conduct two classes on the IBM architecture, and also provided comments on a draft of the text. Erik Johnson and Aaron Kunze of Intel provided comments, including a critique of the example code. Paul Schmitt of Calix Networks filled in many background and hardware details, and helped me understand the history of the industry. T. Sridhar of Future Communications Software and John Lin of Bell Labs provided comments on chapters. Robert Dusek of Saint Joseph's College volunteered to manage the web site.

Finally, I thank my wife, Chris, for her patient and careful editing and valuable suggestions that improve and polish each book.

Douglas E. Comer

January, 2003

What Others Have Said About
Network Systems Design

"Finally, a book that helps reunite the disciplines of computer engineering and network engineering."

— Michael Hathaway, Austin Ventures

"A sturdy and clear explanation of the intricacies of designing and using network processors. I expect it to become the standard textbook on the subject."

— Craig Partridge, Chair, ACM SIGCOMM

"Professor Comer has done it again. This is another comprehensive book from him — this time on designing network systems with a specific focus on the emerging area of network processors. Engineers and students will definitely find this book valuable."

— T. Sridhar, FutureSoft

"This book is required reading for anyone who wants to understand what goes on inside the plethora of magic boxes that make the Internet work."

— Larry Peterson, Princeton University

"The author shows an amazing understanding of the subtle issues."

— Paul Schmitt, Calix Incorporated

"This book is excellent: clearly written, easy to understand, and comprehensive."

— John Lin, Bell Labs

"*Network Systems Design Using Network Processors* is the right book at the right time. Upon seeing the book, friends who have recently entered the field of network processors invariably say something like, 'I wish I'd had this book nine months ago!' It is an excellent fusion of network processing design principles, current architectures, and architectural directions. It is sure to become the standard text for this field the minute it hits the shelves."

— Dale Parson, Agere Systems

"Comer discusses all of the crucial architectural and economic decisions that drive modern network systems design today. *Network Systems Design* will be extremely helpful to engineers building those systems, as well as anyone interested in understanding how they work."

— Paul Phillips, Nauticus Networks

About The Author

Dr. Douglas Comer is an internationally recognized expert on TCP/IP protocols, computer networking, and the Internet. One of the researchers who contributed to the Internet as it was being formed in the late 1970s and 1980s, he was a member of the Internet Architecture Board, the group responsible for guiding the Internet's development. He was also chairman of the CSNET technical committee and a member of the CSNET executive committee.

Comer consults for industry on the design and implementation of network systems. In addition to talks in universities, he teaches onsite courses to networking professionals around the world. Comer's operating system, Xinu, and implementation of TCP/IP protocols (both documented in his textbooks) have been used in commercial products.

Comer is a professor of computer science at Purdue University, where he develops and teaches courses and does research on computer networking, internetworking, and operating systems. Comer has created networking laboratories in which students can build and measure network systems such as IP routers, NAT boxes, and bridges; all of Comer's courses include hands-on lab work. Students in his network processor course have access to facilities from Agere, IBM, and Intel.

In addition to writing a series of highly acclaimed technical books on computer networks and TCP/IP, Comer serves as the North American editor of the journal *Software — Practice and Experience*. He is a Fellow of the ACM.

Additional information can be found at:

www.cs.purdue.edu/people/comer

and information about Comer's books can be found at:

www.comerbooks.com

Chapter Contents

1

Introduction And Overview

1.1 Network Systems And The Internet

The Internet has become so pervasive that it influences all networking. New networking architectures build on the Internet paradigm. New communication technologies are evaluated by assessing their potential role in the Internet. New network components and systems are engineered to extend or replace facilities used in the Internet. New applications are built to use the Internet.

More important, the rapid global Internet expansion has fueled development of a wide variety of new networking systems and technologies. Much of the justification is economic: the market for networking is both large and growing. Thus, companies perceive that the potential for profits is enormous.

1.2 Applications Vs. Infrastructure

The Internet is designed to accommodate arbitrary applications and communication technologies; the design has proven to be extremely effective. Indeed, many of the applications currently in use over the Internet were invented long after the basic technology had been established. In particular, the World Wide Web, streaming media, and IP telephony were all developed after the Internet was in place. Furthermore, although the new applications differed dramatically from their predecessors, the fundamental infrastructure remained unchanged.

A similar situation has occurred with communication technologies. Because the Internet can accommodate arbitrary, heterogeneous networks, new communication technologies can be incorporated in the Internet without requiring changes to the protocols or applications. For example, 10 Mbps Ethernet emerged at the same time as the Internet protocols. Later generations of Ethernet, which operate at speeds of 100 Mbps and 1 Gbps, are now used throughout the Internet. More important, the Internet accommodates technologies such as Packet Over SONET (POS) that had not been invented when the Internet was designed.

The question arises: if the existing Internet has sufficient functionality to support all possible applications, why should we consider the design of new systems? In other words, why should we be interested in architecture and infrastructure? The answer lies in extension and growth: although the existing Internet allows arbitrary applications to communicate, performance may not be optimal and further expansion may not be possible — changes in infrastructure and architecture are required to improve performance and to accommodate growth in traffic. For example, to work well, IP telephony requires low delay or users complain. However, low delay can only be achieved by improving the underlying infrastructure to reduce congestion.

1.3 Network Systems Engineering

The term *network engineering*† refers to the macroscopic design of a network or intranet (i.e., choice of topology), and the term *network systems engineering* refers to the design of individual systems such as bridges and routers. In the broadest sense, of course, network systems encompass all aspects of digital communications, ranging from high-level applications that provide services users desire to low-level components that transfer bits over copper or optical fiber. In practice, the engineers who engage in systems design seldom need to consider either extreme. Instead, they use off-the-shelf hardware components and concentrate on finding new and better ways to employ the hardware.

If network systems engineering does not involve the creation of new ways to transfer bits, what does it involve? We will see that the central activity is protocol implementation — to ensure that the resulting system interoperates correctly with other systems, a designer must follow published standards that specify all the details of digital communication. The challenge in network systems design consists in devising implementations that operate at high speed, have low initial cost, and are easy to maintain.

1.4 Packet Processing

Because the Internet is built on packet switching technologies, packet processing is fundamental to all network systems. Each network system device has one or more inputs over which packets arrive, and one or more outputs to which packets can be sent. The network system examines each packet that arrives, performs a set of operations on the packet, and then forwards the results. The operations may be straightforward (e.g., count packets as they pass through the system), or complex (e.g., divide each incoming packet into several smaller packets and forward the small packets).

---

†Throughout this text, we follow the widespread industry practice of using the term *engineering* to refer to the process of designing, building, measuring, and testing; we will not distinguish between Engineers and Computer Scientists.

Part of the challenge in network systems design arises from concurrent events. For example, we will see that packets can arrive simultaneously on two or more inputs, and that a network system must be able to handle simultaneous events correctly. Furthermore, we will see that packet processing may require storing packets in memory because the actions to be performed on a packet can depend on previous or subsequent packets. In addition to storing packets, a network system must store auxiliary data structures that maintain information about the packets.

1.5 Achieving High Speed

Our goal is to devise network systems that can achieve high performance at low cost. That is, the system should be able to process packets at high speed, but should not be expensive to build, operate, or maintain. There are several aspects to high performance. For example, the hardware must have sufficient memory and bus bandwidth to handle packets as fast as the network hardware delivers them. The system must also have sufficient capability to process and forward packets as fast as they arrive.

Higher hardware speed is often achieved through parallelism. For example, high-speed network systems have multiple processing units because a single processor does not have sufficient power to handle packets that arrive from multiple interfaces. In addition, to avoid an I/O bottleneck, the underlying system is usually designed with sufficient bus capacity to ensure that all processors can access memory without blocking.

Raw hardware speed does not guarantee that a network system will perform well because processing can become a bottleneck. Higher speed processing requires clever data structures and algorithms as well as attention to detail. For example, when a packet arrives, the network system must search its auxiliary data structure to determine whether the packet is related to previous packets. Unless it has been optimized carefully, the search can require significant processing.

1.6 Network Speed

How fast is a "high speed" network system? The definition continues to change. As the Internet was begin devised, Local Area Network (LAN) speed increased from 3 Mbps to 10 Mbps. Thus, a network system with two inputs (e.g., a bridge or a small IP router) needed to handle data at an aggregate rate of 20 Mbps. A network system with 16 inputs needed to handle an aggregate rate of 160 Mbps. By the mid 1990s, a single LAN operated at 100 Mbps, which meant that a network system with 16 inputs could deliver data at an aggregate of 1.6 Gbps. The current generation of LAN hardware operates at 1 Gbps, which means that a network system with 16 inputs must handle data at 16 Gbps.

In addition to network systems that connect LANs, some network systems handle digital circuits such as T1 and OC-3 lines. Similar speed increases have occurred in digital circuits. For example, a T1 line, which was once considered high speed, operates at 1.544 Mbps. During the early 1990s, large enterprises used OC-3 circuits to connect to the Internet; OC-3 operates at approximately 155 Mbps. In the early 2000s, ISPs use OC-48 circuits that operate at 2.4 Gbps.

What speeds will be needed in the future? Large ISPs have already begun to use OC-192 circuits that transmit data at approximately 10 Gbps, and commercial LAN hardware may emerge that runs even faster. Thus, 10 Gbps has become the goal for the next generation of network systems. Although such data rates may not seem overwhelming, they pose a challenge for network systems design because systems must accommodate multiple simultaneous connections. For example, a router that interconnects four OC-192 circuits must be capable of receiving, processing, and forwarding data at an aggregate rate of 40 Gbps.

Later chapters consider high data rates in more detail and examine the consequences for network systems design. In particular, we will see that some network system architectures are incapable of handling packets that arrive at such high speeds.

1.7 Hardware, Software, And Hybrids

One of the fundamental questions surrounding network systems design focuses on hardware vs. software: should network systems consist of conventional hardware with all the processing encoded in software, or should network systems be built entirely with special-purpose hardware? On one hand, software solutions offer flexibility — the software can be modified or upgraded at almost no cost. The basic system can survive major changes (e.g., a change in a protocol). Furthermore, the underlying hardware speed can increase without requiring new software. On the other hand, custom hardware solutions offer highest speed — special-purpose hardware can be built for each function. Internal data paths can be engineered to move packets between I/O devices and memory without delay, and the architecture can be design to avoid the bottleneck of a conventional CPU.

Unfortunately, both hardware and software designs have disadvantages. Software designs have low performance; hardware designs are inflexible and expensive to modify or upgrade. Consequently, hardware designers have devised a compromise: a hardware device known as a *network processor*. Like a conventional CPU, a network processor can be programmed. But unlike a conventional CPU, a network processor has been optimized for packet processing. The goal of the network processor approach is a technology that combines the speed advantages of a custom hardware design and the flexibility of a software implementation.

1.8 Scope And Organization Of The Text

This book is intended for anyone who is interested in learning how to design and build network systems such as packet switches, bridges, and routers. It describes hardware architectures and explains how software uses each. More important, the book explains the architecture and use of programmable devices known as network processors.

After a brief review of basic networking components and protocols, the main body of the text is divided into three parts. The first part describes the implementation of networking systems in software that runs on a conventional processor. It explains algorithms for tasks such as bridging and IP forwarding.

The second part of the text introduces network processors. It describes possible architectures, characterizes their use, and considers specific hardware functions. It also examines the economic motivations that underlie network processors.

The third part of the text focuses on an example — Intel's IXP1200 network processor. The text examines the hardware, considers the vendor's software development facilities and programming paradigm, and provides examples of how the Intel chip can be used to build network systems.

1.9 Summary

The text considers the design and implementation of networking system components such as packet switches, bridges, and routers that form the basic building blocks of the Internet. Early chapters discuss traditional software implementations; later chapters focus on network processor implementations.

FOR FURTHER STUDY

RFC 1958 considers the architectural principles underlying the Internet. Clark [1988] gives design goals of the Internet, and attempts to capture some of the early reasoning that shaped the Internet architecture and protocols.

Chapter Contents

2

Basic Terminology And Example Systems

2.1 Introduction

What systems are used in the Internet? This brief chapter begins to answer the question. It defines terminology used throughout the remainder of the text, and lists example systems with a brief description of each. Later chapters in this part of the text expand the descriptions and explain how the systems described here process packets.

2.2 Networks And Packets

We use the term *computer network* (*network*) to refer to a digital communication system that connects two or more computers and allows them to exchange information, and we use the term *internet* to refer to an interconnection of networks that functions as a seamless communication system. In particular, the global *Internet* is composed of many individual networks.

We will restrict our attention to *packet switching networks* that divide all transfers into small units called *packets*. We will see that a packet is divided into two parts: the *header* contains auxiliary information such as the identification of the computer for which the packet is destined, and the *payload* contains the data being carried.

The term *packet* is generic — it refers to the general concept without giving details. Protocol standards define the exact form of packets used with specific network and Internet technologies. When defined by hardware-layer standards, packets are

7

known as *frames* or *layer 2 packets*. Packets sent across the Internet are known as *IP datagrams*, and fixed-size packets used by technologies such as ATM are called *cells*.

2.3 Connection-Oriented And Connectionless Paradigms

Networks adhere to one of two basic paradigms: *connection-oriented* or *connectionless*. A connection-oriented system is analogous to a telephone — two computers first request that a "connection" be established, use the connection to exchange data, and then terminate the connection. A connectionless system is analogous to postal mail — a computer creates a packet that includes identification of the intended recipient, and sends the result without establishing or terminating any connection. We distinguish between the external paradigm a networking system offers and the internal paradigm used to achieve it. For example, TCP offers a connection-oriented interface to applications, but uses a connectionless paradigm to communicate internally.

2.4 Digital Circuits

Long-distance connections in the Internet (i.e., connections that span several kilometers) consist of *digital circuits* leased from a telephone company. Figure 2.1 lists a few of the digital circuit standards available in North America and the data rate of each†.

Standard Name	Bit Rate	Voice Circuits
–	0.064 Mbps	1
T1	1.544 Mbps	24
T3	44.736 Mbps	672
OC-1	51.840 Mbps	810
OC-3	155.520 Mbps	2430
OC-12	622.080 Mbps	9720
OC-24	1,244.160 Mbps	19440
OC-48	2,488.320 Mbps	38880
OC-192	9,953.280 Mbps	155520
OC-768	39,813.120 Mbps	622080

Figure 2.1 Examples of digital circuits available in North America.

Digital circuits are classified as *point-to-point* because each circuit connects directly between two systems. Digital circuits were originally designed to interconnect pairs of telephone offices, which explains why data rates are multiples of the data rate required for a single voice telephone call.

---

†As an alternative to fixed circuits, phone companies also lease *virtual circuits* that use technologies such as *Frame Relay* and *ATM*.

Because it was designed to transport voice telephone calls, digital circuit hardware does not accept and deliver packets. Instead, a digital circuit transfers 8-bit units known as *octets*†. Because the digital circuit hardware does not impose any packet format, additional protocols are used to define packet framing when sending packets over a digital circuit. Computers on each end of the circuit must agree on the frame format and encoding used.

2.5 LAN And WAN Classifications

Packet switching technologies can be divided into two broad categories: *Local Area Networks* (*LANs*) and *Wide Area Networks* (*WANs*). The most widely used conventional LAN technology is *Ethernet* (IEEE standard 802.3); the most widely used wireless LAN technology is *IEEE 802.11b*, which adheres to the same packet format and addressing scheme as wired Ethernet.

Ethernet LAN technology has evolved over three generations. Although the physical wiring and data rates vary among the three generations, the packet format and addressing scheme have remained unchanged‡. The first commercial version of Ethernet transmitted data at 10 Mbps, a version known as *Fast Ethernet* operates at 100 Mbps, and the latest version, *Gigabit Ethernet*, transmits data at 1 Gbps.

2.6 The Internet And Heterogeneity

The Internet is a global communication system that provides seamless, high-speed communication among hundreds of millions of computers around the world. Although programmers and users view it as a single monolithic networking system, the Internet consists of tens of thousands of individual computer communication networks that have been interconnected and configured to interoperate. The resulting architecture can be viewed as a ''network of networks''.

The chief strength of the Internet architecture lies in its support for heterogeneity. Because it can accommodate arbitrary types of networks, the Internet can include a wide variety of underlying network technologies. For example, constituent networks that comprise the Internet can consist of an inexpensive network suitable for use in a single building or a network capable of spanning a long distance. Similarly, the Internet can use both high-speed and low-speed networks.

2.7 Example Network Systems

We use the term *network system* to refer to an electronic component that handles data. Although computer networks contain many electronic components, we are only interested in those that process packets. For example, we will not be concerned with a

---

†Although the term *byte* is commonly used as a synonym for *octet*, a byte's size is defined for each computer.

‡The next chapter examines Ethernet addressing and packet format in detail.

hub, *repeater*, or *modem* because such devices operate on electrical signals. Instead, we will focus on systems that send and receive packets. Specifically, we will concentrate on systems that use addresses when deciding how to handle a packet. We can group such systems into two broad categories: systems used to construct a single computer network and those used to construct an internet. Examples of systems used in a network include:

- **Bridge.** A network system that connects two individual networks and forwards packets between them. To be precise, a bridge forwards frames. The next chapter explains how a bridge uses the addresses in each incoming frame when deciding how to forward the frame. Bridges are often used to interconnect Ethernet networks.

- **Switch.** A network system that connects two or more computers and forwards frames among them. Network switches are also called *layer 2 switches*. Conceptually, a switch can be viewed as providing the bridge functionality among a set of computers. The physical connections between computers and a switch resemble the physical connections between computers and a hub, but a switch offers higher throughput. As with bridges, switches are often used with Ethernet.

- **VLAN Switch.** A layer 2 switch that can emulate multiple network segments. Like a conventional switch, a VLAN switch connects multiple computers and forwards frames among them. Unlike a conventional switch, a network administrator can configure a VLAN switch to emulate multiple, smaller switches. That is, the administrator divides computers into subsets, and the VLAN switch then provides communication as if each subset were connected to an independent switch.

2.8 Broadcast Domains

Informally, we use the term *broadcast* to refer to communication with "all computers". On early networks the meaning was obvious — a broadcast on a given network reached all computers on that network. For example, if a computer broadcasts a packet to an Ethernet hub, each computer connected to the hub receives a copy.

VLAN switches give rise to a new interpretation of broadcasting. In essence, when a network administrator configures separate virtual LANs, the administrator partitions the computers into separate *broadcast domains*. The VLAN switch restricts all broadcast and multicast traffic to the domain in which the packet originates. For example, suppose computers A, B, C, and D connect to a switch, and the administrator has configured A and B to be on VLAN 1 and C and D to be on VLAN 2. If A sends a broadcast, only B will receive it. Similarly, if D sends a broadcast, only C will receive it.

2.9 The Two Key Systems Used In The Internet

Because the Internet consists of many computer networks, the network systems mentioned above are all used in the Internet. In addition, the Internet contains special network systems used to provide communication across multiple, interconnected networks. The two most important Internet systems consist of:

- **Host.** A conventional computer attached to the Internet that can communicate with other computers on the Internet. A host can be a large, mainframe computer, desktop system, hand-held personal digital assistant, or an embedded control system. Large, powerful hosts are usually chosen to run server software, and less powerful host computers are usually chosen to run client software.

- **Router.** A network system used to interconnect physical networks and forward Internet traffic among them. The terms *IP router*, *IP gateway*, *Internet router*, and *Layer 3 Switch* are synonymous with *router*. The main conceptual difference between a host and a router lies in the protocol software required — a host needs transport protocol software that applications use, and a router needs software to propagate routing information.

Routers form the basic building blocks of the Internet. Each router interconnects two or more networks and passes Internet traffic among them. Figure 2.2 illustrates the concept.

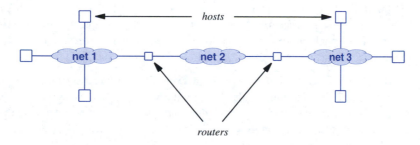

Figure 2.2 Illustration of the basic Internet architecture with IP routers interconnecting networks. Networks *1* and *3* have host computers attached.

Routers differ from bridges or layer 2 switches in two significant ways. First, a router understands Internet protocols while a bridge or switch only understands lower layer protocols such as Ethernet. Second, although a bridge or switch only provides interconnection for one type of network, a router can interconnect heterogeneous networks†. Figure 2.2 uses a cloud to denote each network because the network can con-

---

†Although it requires homogeneous frames, a bridge can accommodate heterogeneous physical media (e.g., a bridge can connect Ethernet over copper wire to Ethernet over optical fiber).

sist of any technology. For example, networks 1 and 3 might be Ethernets, and network 2 might be a digital circuit.

2.10 Other Systems Used In The Internet

The Internet includes other systems that understand and process Internet packets. Examples include:

- **Firewall.** A system that provides security according to a policy given by an administrator. A typical firewall checks for unauthorized access (intrusion detection), and blocks incoming or outgoing packets that do not adhere to the policy. Although firewall functionality can be embedded in a router or a computer operating system, it is also possible to implement a firewall as a stand-alone network system†.

- **Virtual Private Network (VPN).** A system that uses encryption to provide private communication over the Internet. VPN systems are used in pairs — two sites each install a VPN system between the site and the Internet, and configure the systems to know about each other. Once a VPN has been installed, computers at the two sites can communicate with one another privately. That is, even if an outsider intercepts packets traveling across the Internet between the two sites, the outsider will not be able to decode or interpret the contents.

- **Network Address Translation (NAT).** A system that allows multiple computers at a site to share a single, globally valid IP address. The NAT system, which is inserted on the connection between the site and the Internet, rewrites packets to change addresses and other information in the headers. One variant of NAT is also known as *TCP splicing*.

- **Load Balancer.** A system used at large web sites to increase performance and availability by allowing multiple computers each to run a copy of a web server. A load balancer accepts incoming requests and sends each to the server that has the least load. The terms *Layer 4+ Switch* and *Layer 7 Switch* are synonyms for Load Balancer.

- **Set-Top Box.** A system used with digital entertainment systems that allows a subscriber to select from a set of broadcast programs or to request customized content. A set-top box communicates with the provider's equipment by sending requests, decrypting the data stream from the provider, and forwarding the stream to the local audio/video system.

---

†Security experts often separate the concept of a firewall, which blocks some packets, from an intrusion detection system, which merely monitors packets and reports potential problems.

2.11 Monitoring And Control Systems

The examples listed above describe the most important systems used in the Internet. Although many other systems exist, they are usually reserved for special purposes, and are not universally deployed. For example, consider the following:

- **Traffic Monitor.** A system that can measure the peak and average traffic from or to a set of destinations. An ISP that bases fees on use needs a traffic monitor to measure the traffic for each customer.

- **Traffic Policer.** A system used to discard traffic that exceeds a predetermined threshold according to a specification given by the network administrator. An ISP that charges for levels of service can use a traffic policer to ensure that a given customer does not transmit more data than authorized.

- **Traffic Shaper.** A system that delays some packets and allows others to pass through quickly according to a set of specifications. Some routers offer traffic shaping. ISPs use traffic shaping to prevent congestion and to give priority to customers who pay more. By forcing traffic to adhere to specifications, a shaper can ensure that packets will pass through a downstream policer without being discarded.

- **Packet Analyzer.** A system that attaches to a network and captures copies of packets to measure network performance. Packet analyzers are used to detect problems and measure load.

2.12 Summary

We have defined basic terminology used in computer networks and the Internet, and have described some of the underlying systems. Examples of networking systems that process packets include bridges and switches; examples of Internet systems include hosts, routers, firewalls, VPNs, NATs, and load balancers. Less important Internet systems include packet analyzers and traffic monitors, policers, and shapers.

FOR FURTHER STUDY

Comer [2001] covers general principles and terminology used in computer networks and internets. Perlman [2000] discusses bridges and routers.

Chapter Contents

3

Review Of Protocols And Packet Formats

3.1 Introduction

The previous chapter reviews basic terminology and lists examples of network systems that process packets. This chapter reviews important communication protocols and shows the packet format. The next chapter explains how protocol processing can be implemented on a conventional hardware architecture. Later chapters extend the discussion of protocol processing to newer architectures.

3.2 Protocols And Layering

To ensure that network systems can interoperate correctly and efficiently, all communication facilities are implemented according to written standards documents known as *protocols*. Protocols specify all aspects of communication, including syntactic details such as the format of packets and semantic details such as how a receiver processes an incoming packet and how it responds if the packet contains an error.

Because communication involves many details, humans have found it impossible to devise a single protocol that solves the problem completely. Instead, to keep protocol specifications manageable, engineers divide the communication problem into separate pieces and devise a protocol for each piece. Once individual protocols have been formulated and studied in isolation, they are combined into a coordinated set known as a *suite*.

We use the term *layering* to refer to the division of the communication problem into separate pieces, and refer to each piece as a *layer*. Before the Internet became prominent, the *International Standards Organization* (*ISO*) devised a 7-layer reference model known as the *Open System Interconnect* (*OSI*). The researchers who devised the Internet replaced the older ISO model with a 5-layer reference model that includes an explicit internet layer. Figure 3.1 illustrates Internet layering.

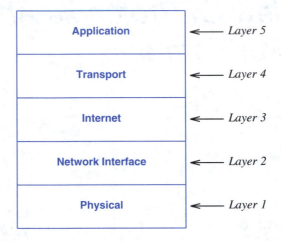

Figure 3.1 The Internet 5-layer reference model. Layer 2 is also known as the *link layer, data link layer*, or *MAC layer*.

When a layered protocol system is implemented, the resulting software is known as a *stack*. In the most straightforward implementation, outgoing data must pass down through all layers of the stack between the application and the physical network. Similarly, incoming data must pass up through all layers of the stack. We will learn that optimizing communication among layers is an important aspect of building high-speed network systems. Throughout this text, we will assume that physical interface hardware exists to handle layer 1, and we will concentrate on layers 2 and higher.

A given layer can contain more than one protocol. In some cases, multiple protocols work together in a layer; in other cases, one particular protocol must be chosen for a given communication. Later chapters consider the consequences of multiple protocols and discuss demultiplexing.

3.3 Layers 1 And 2 (Physical And Network Interface)

3.3.1 Ethernet

Ethernet protocol standards specify details for both layers 1 and 2. Layer 1 standards specify details such as the voltage used on copper wires. The standards specify *Carrier Sense Multiple Access* with *Collision Detection* (CSMA/CD). Layer 2 standards specify details such as the format of frames and addresses. We will assume that hardware exists to handle layer 1 and focus on layer 2.

Ethernet uses *variable-size frames*. That is, although the standard specifies a minimum and maximum frame size, Ethernet allows a sender to choose the exact size of a frame for the data being sent. For example, if an application generates a 200-octet message, the sending computer generates a frame that carries 200 octets of data. If another application chooses to send a larger size message (e.g., 1024 octets of data), the sending computer generates a larger frame.

3.3.2 Ethernet Frame Format

Each Ethernet frame begins with a header that identifies the sending computer, the computer to which the frame is destined, and the contents of the frame. Figure 3.2 illustrates the frame format.

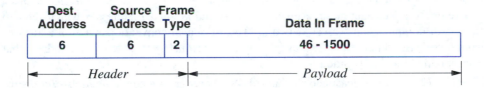

Figure 3.2 The Ethernet frame format as seen by a network system. Numbers give the size of each field measured in 8-bit octets.

As the figure shows, the payload area can be as small as 46 octets or as large as 1500 octets. When transferring a large quantity of data over Ethernet, header overhead is minimized when each frame contains as much data as possible. Thus, frames containing 1500 octets of data are common.

When transmitted across an Ethernet network, an Ethernet frame is preceded by a 64-bit *preamble* of alternating 1's and 0's, and followed by a 32-bit *Cyclic Redundancy Check* (*CRC*) used to verify that the frame is not damaged in transit. The physical interface hardware adds the preamble and CRC to outgoing frames and removes them from incoming frames. Thus, the preamble and CRC remain transparent to network systems that process the frame after it arrives.

3.3.3 Ethernet Addresses

The Ethernet standards specify layer 2 addressing. Each computer attached to an Ethernet is assigned a unique 48-bit value known as an *Ethernet address*, *MAC address* or *station address*. The address is configured into the physical interface hardware such as a *Network Interface Card* (*NIC*). Each frame that travels across an Ethernet contains the address of the system that sent the frame (the *source address*) and the address of the system to which the frame has been sent (the *destination address*).

The destination address in an Ethernet frame can be one of three types. Figure 3.3 lists the types and the meaning of each.

Type	Meaning
unicast	frame destined for a single station
multicast	frame destined for a subset of computers in the broadcast domain
broadcast	frame destined for all computers in the broadcast domain

Figure 3.3 The three types of addresses that can be specified in the destination address field of an Ethernet frame.

In addition to a unique address for each station, Ethernet supports a *broadcast* address that refers to all computers on a given network, and *multicast* addresses which refer to subsets of computers on a given network. To distinguish conventional station addresses from broadcast and multicast, we use the term *unicast address* to denote an address that corresponds to a single station.

The Ethernet broadcast address has all 48 bits set to 1; a single *multicast bit* distinguishes between broadcast and unicast addresses. Figure 3.4 shows the location of the multicast bit.

Figure 3.4 The multicast bit in a 48-bit Ethernet address is the low-order bit of the high-order octet. Unicast addresses have the bit set to 0, and multicast addresses have the bit set to 1.

3.3.4 Ethernet Type Field

The *Frame Type* field in an Ethernet frame specifies the contents of the payload area. The sending system sets the type in each outgoing frame, and the receiving system interprets the value in each incoming frame. For example, a frame carrying an IP datagram has the type field set to 0800_{16}, and a frame carrying an ARP message has value 0806_{16}.

3.4 Layer 3 (Internet)

3.4.1 The Internet Protocol

The *Internet Protocol* (*IP*) is the primary protocol used at layer 3. IP defines the basic packet delivery service available throughout the Internet, including the format of packets, addresses, and delivery semantics. IP is especially important for network systems design because the protocol specifies how both intermediate and end systems process packets.

3.4.2 IP Datagram Format

An Internet packet is known as an *IP datagram*. Like most packets, a datagram consists of a fixed-size *header* followed by a variable-size *payload*. Figure 3.5 illustrates the version 4 datagram header. As the figure shows, extracting fields from the header is straightforward because each field is allocated to a fixed location†. Frame encapsulation (which is discussed in Section 3.7) extends the concept by placing a datagram at a fixed location in the underlying frame.

0	4	8	16	19	24	31
VERS	HLEN	SERVICE	TOTAL LENGTH			
ID			FLAGS	F. OFFSET		
TTL		TYPE	HDR CHECKSUM			
SOURCE						
DESTINATION						
IP OPTIONS (MAY BE OMITTED)					PADDING	
BEGINNING OF PAYLOAD ⋮						

Figure 3.5 The IPv4 datagram header. Each field occupies a fixed position

---

†If a datagram contains multiple IP options, successive options after the first do not reside at a fixed location.

Figure 3.6 lists individual fields of the IP header and gives the meaning of each. Chapter 6 explains the header fields used in datagram fragmentation†.

Field	Meaning
VERS	Version number of IP being used (4)
HLEN	Header length measured in 32-bit units
SERVICE	Level of service desired
TOTAL LENGTH	Datagram length in octets including header
ID	Unique value for this datagram
FLAGS	Bits to control fragmentation
F. OFFSET	Position of fragment in original datagram
TTL	Time to live (hop countdown)
TYPE	Contents of payload area
HDR CHECKSUM	One's-complement checksum over header
SOURCE	IP address of original sender
DESTINATION	IP address of ultimate destination
IP OPTIONS	Special handling parameters
PADDING	To make options a 32-bit multiple

Figure 3.6 The interpretation of each field in the IP datagram header.

3.4.3 IP Addresses

The source and destination addresses in a datagram each consist of a 32-bit value known as an *Internet address* or *IP address*. An IP address is divided into a *prefix* that specifies a network and a *suffix* that specifies a computer on that network. In most datagrams, the source address refers to the original source, and the destination address refers to the ultimate destination. Thus, the addresses remain unchanged as the datagram passes across the Internet (i.e., the addresses of intermediate routers do not appear in the datagram header). However, the rule is not absolute because network systems such as NAT can rewrite a source or destination address.

3.5 Layer 4 (Transport)

3.5.1 UDP And TCP

The Internet suite of protocols includes two protocols at layer 4: the *Transmission Control Protocol (TCP)* and the *User Datagram Protocol (UDP)*. Both are end-to-end protocols that allow applications to communicate. TCP is the more widely used because it provides full reliability by handling the problems of loss, duplication, delay, and out-of-order delivery. TCP provides full-duplex, connection-oriented stream service

---

†Chapter 5 explains fragmentation and reassembly.

to a pair of applications — the connection must be established before data is sent and shutdown when no longer needed. Chapter 5 provides more detail about TCP connection creation and termination.

3.5.2 UDP Datagram Format

UDP allows applications to send and receive individual packets called *user datagrams*. A user datagram consists of an 8-octet header followed by a payload containing the data being sent. Like most transport protocols, UDP is classified as *end-to-end*, meaning that a UDP datagram does not change as the datagram passes through the Internet. Because each user datagram is encapsulated in an IP datagram for transport across the Internet, the UDP header does not contain fields that identify the source or destination computers or the length of the payload. Figure 3.7 illustrates the user datagram format.

0	16	31
SOURCE PORT	DESTINATION PORT	
MESSAGE LENGTH	CHECKSUM	
BEGINNING OF PAYLOAD		
⋮		

Figure 3.7 UDP user datagram format.

As the figure shows, a UDP header contains eight octets. Figure 3.8 summarizes the contents of the header fields.

Field	Meaning
SOURCE PORT	ID of sending application
DESTINATION PORT	ID of receiving application
MESSAGE LENGTH	Length of datagram including the header
CHECKSUM	One's-complement checksum over entire datagram

Figure 3.8 The interpretation of fields in the UDP datagram header.

Header fields labeled *SOURCE PORT* and *DESTINATION PORT* each contain a sixteen-bit integer; the source port number identifies the sending application, and the destination port identifies the receiving application. The *MESSAGE LENGTH* field specifies the total size of the UDP datagram measured in octets, and the *CHECKSUM* field contains a one's complement checksum over the UDP datagram plus a *pseudo header* that includes source and destination IP addresses.

3.5.3 TCP Segment Format

TCP on a computer attached to the Internet communicates with TCP on another computer attached to the Internet by sending packets known as *TCP segments*. Each segment is encapsulated in an IP datagram for transmission across the Internet. Except in special cases such as NAT, the segment remains unchanged during transit. Each segment begins with a *segment header* followed by a *payload*. Figure 3.9 illustrates the TCP segment format.

0	4	10	16	24	31

SOURCE PORT		DESTINATION PORT
SEQUENCE		
ACKNOWLEDGEMENT		

HLEN	NOT USED	CODE BITS	WINDOW

CHECKSUM	URGENT PTR
OPTIONS (MAY BE OMITTED)	PADDING

BEGINNING OF PAYLOAD
⋮

Figure 3.9 The TCP segment format.

As the figure shows, each field in the TCP header occupies a fixed location. Figure 3.10 lists individual fields and gives the meaning of each.

Field	Meaning
SOURCE PORT	ID of sending application
DESTINATION PORT	ID of receiving application
SEQUENCE	Sequence number for data in payload
ACKNOWLEDGEMENT	Acknowledgement of data received
HLEN	Header length measured in 32-bit units
NOT USED	Currently unassigned
CODE BITS	URGENT, ACK, PUSH, RESET, SYN, FIN
WINDOW	Receiver's buffer size for additional data
CHECKSUM	One's-complement checksum over entire segment
URGENT PTR	Pointer to urgent data in segment
OPTIONS	Special handling
PADDING	To make options a 32-bit multiple

Figure 3.10 The interpretation of fields in the TCP segment header. A later chapter explains how systems use header fields to perform splicing.

3.6 Protocol Port Numbers And Demultiplexing

Although they rely on IP to identify the sending and receiving computers, UDP and TCP need to identify specific application programs. To do so, they arrange for applications to use 16-bit values known as *protocol port numbers*. Each UDP user datagram and each TCP segment carries the protocol port number of the sending application (*SOURCE PORT*) and the port number of the receiving application (*DESTINATION PORT*). However, the port spaces of the two protocols are completely independent — the application that uses a given TCP port number may have no relationship to a UDP application that uses the same value.

UDP or TCP software on a destination computer uses port numbers to *demultiplex* incoming packets, sending each to the intended application program. UDP demultiplexing uses a straightforward selection procedure that depends on the destination IP address and destination protocol port number. Unlike UDP, TCP uses four items to identify a specific TCP connection: the source IP address, destination IP address, source port number, and destination port number.

3.7 Encapsulation And Transmission

Both TCP and UDP use IP to send packets across the Internet. To do so, they place a message in the payload area of an IP datagram. The IP datagram, in turn, is placed in the payload area of a frame. We use the term *encapsulation* to describe the concept. Figure 3.11 illustrates encapsulation by showing an example of a UDP user datagram encapsulated in an IP datagram, which is encapsulated in an Ethernet frame.

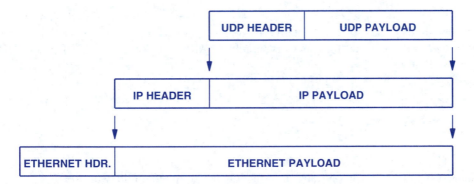

Figure 3.11 Illustration of encapsulation. A UDP datagram travels in an IP datagram, which is encapsulated in an Ethernet frame during transport across one network.

3.8 Address Resolution Protocol

The *Address Resolution Protocol* (*ARP*) is a layer 2 protocol that translates the IP address of a computer on a local network to an equivalent layer 2 address. ARP is never used to obtain the address of a remote computer; it can only be used across one network at a time. Although it can work over a variety of network technologies, ARP is most often used to map the IP address of a computer to an Ethernet address. Figure 3.12 illustrates the ARP packet format when used with Ethernet.

0	8	16	24	31
ETHERNET ADDRESS TYPE (1)			IP ADDRESS TYPE (0800)	
ETH ADDR LEN (6)	IP ADDR LEN (4)		OPERATION	
SENDER'S ETH ADDR (first 4 octets)				
SENDER'S ETH ADDR (last 2 octets)		SENDER'S IP ADDR (first 2 octets)		
SENDER'S IP ADDR (last 2 octets)		TARGET'S ETH ADDR (first 2 octets)		
TARGET'S ETH ADDR (last 4 octets)				
TARGET'S IP ADDR (all 4 octets)				

Figure 3.12 The format of an ARP packet when ARP is used over an Ethernet.

3.9 Summary

Protocol standards define the semantics of computer communication and specify the details of packet formats. Internet protocols are divided into five conceptual layers. We reviewed the packet formats of Ethernet and ARP at layer 2, IP at layer 3, and TCP and UDP at layer 4.

FOR FURTHER STUDY

The *Institute of Electrical and Electronic Engineers* (*IEEE*) defines the Ethernet standards in standard 802.3; more information can be found on the web site:

http://grouper.ieee.org/groups/802/3/

For a list of Ethernet type values and the meaning assigned to each, visit:

http://www.iana.org/assignments/ethernet-numbers

TCP/IP protocols standards are published in a series of documents known as *Request For Comments* (*RFCs*), which are available from the *Internet Engineering Task Force* (*IETF*) at the web site:

http://www.ietf.org/rfc.html

The protocol standard for IP is given in RFC 791, and the protocol standard for TCP is given in RFC 793. Both standards are updated in RFC 1122.

Numeric values assigned for use with TCP/IP protocols were originally published in an RFC entitled *Assigned Numbers*. In 2002, the Internet Assigned Numbers Authority discontinued publication of the Assigned Numbers RFCs and switched to an online database. Thus, official values used in TCP/IP header fields can be found at:

http://www.iana.org

Comer [2000] provides a general overview of TCP/IP protocols, including a description of header formats and protocol operation.

Traditional Hardware And Software Architectures For Network Systems

Chapter Contents

4

Conventional Computer Hardware Architecture

4.1 Introduction

Previous chapters review network systems and protocol fundamentals, including packet header formats. This chapter begins a discussion of network systems implementation. It examines the architecture of a conventional computer system and discusses the operation of a network interface. The chapter introduces concepts like the fetch-store paradigm that are key to understanding hardware architectures covered in later chapters. The next chapter discusses software, and shows how conventional hardware architectures can be used to build a packet processing system.

4.2 A Conventional Computer System

The least expensive packet processing systems are created by using conventional computer hardware. We define a conventional computer system to consist of four basic components: a single CPU, a memory, one or more I/O devices, and a mechanism known as a *bus* that interconnects the other components and allows them to communicate. For example, an inexpensive PC meets our definition of a conventional computer system because it includes all four components.

To transform a conventional computer into a network system that can process packets, it must be augmented with additional hardware and software. Additional hardware is needed to transmit and receive packets; additional software is needed to process packets. We will consider the hardware first.

4.3 Network Interface Cards

A hardware device that connects a computer system to a network is known as a *Network Interface Card* (*NIC*). To the computer, a NIC appears to function like other I/O devices — the NIC attaches to the computer's bus, and is controlled by the CPU similar to the way the CPU controls a device such as a disk. To the network, the NIC appears to function like an attached computer — the NIC can send or receive packets. Figure 4.1 illustrates the architecture.

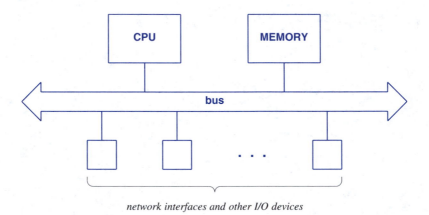

network interfaces and other I/O devices

Figure 4.1 Illustration of conventional computer architecture when used for a network system. Network interface hardware attaches to the computer's bus.

Because a host computer or a packet analyzer only attaches to one network, such systems only need one network interface card. However, more complex systems such as bridges and routers require multiple network connections. There are two possible implementations. On one hand, it is possible to plug multiple NICs into a bus and attach each to a network. On the other hand, commercial NIC hardware is available that supplies several independent network interfaces on one printed circuit card. From the computer's point of view, the two styles operate the same. Physically, however, having multiple interfaces on a single card reduces the number of bus slots occupied by network interfaces, which is advantageous because bus slots are limited. All information in the text regarding multiple network interfaces applies to either implementation.

4.4 Definition Of A Bus

To understand how hardware is organized, one must know how a bus works. We will see later that several of the concepts discussed here apply to hardware interfaces in general. Thus, we explain the conceptual organization and operation of a bus now, and refer back to the concept in later chapters.

We think of a *bus* as a parallel set of wires over which hardware units communicate; the wires in a bus are often called *lines*. In practice, a bus must be built according to an exact standard that specifies details such as the meaning of each line, the signals and voltage to be used, and the timing of operations. For our purposes, it will be sufficient to abstract away many of the details and look at general concepts. To do so, we imagine that the wires of a bus are divided into three groups. One group of wires is used to communicate *address* information, another is used to communicate a *data* value, and the third is used to communicate *control* information. Figure 4.2 illustrates the organization.

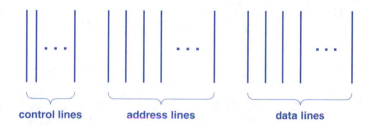

control lines   address lines   data lines

Figure 4.2 The wires of a bus partitioned into three conceptual groups. An individual wire carries one bit, and all wires operate in parallel.

Values pass across the bus in parallel, meaning that all the data lines are used during a transfer and that each transfer carries exactly the same amount of information. To send a data value, for example, the sending hardware unit places each bit of the value on one of the data lines. Similarly, the sender places bits of the address on the address lines. When the address and data are ready, the sender uses one of the control lines to indicate that the values are ready for transfer. The transfer completes after another hardware unit makes a copy of the item being sent and uses a control line to signal the sender†.

The amount of data that can be sent across the bus in one operation is determined by the number of data lines, which is known as the *bus width*. The amount of time required for a transfer is determined by the bus hardware clock, and is known as the *bus cycle time*. For example, a bus might have a width of 64 bits, and the clock for the bus might operate at 1 GHz, which results in a maximum data rate of 64 Gbps (assuming one transfer per clock cycle). A wider bus or a bus with a faster clock rate (i.e., a lower cycle time) can transfer more data per unit time.

---

†In practice, a bus often contains hardware for burst transfers (to optimize access to sequential locations), caching (to optimize repeated access of an address), and split transactions (to allow a bus and CPU to proceed in parallel).

4.5 The Bus Address Space

A bus is a shared communication medium — multiple hardware units attach to the bus and communicate in pairs. To guarantee that only the intended recipient receives a communication, each hardware unit is assigned a unique set of *addresses*. The number of addresses assigned to a given hardware unit depends on its purpose. For example, a serial line device only needs a few addresses, but a memory controller may need several million. When a command passes over the bus, all functional units attached to the bus examine the command. If the address in the command lies within the range of addresses assigned to a given device, the device responds; otherwise, the device ignores the command.

The assignment of addresses defines an *address space*. If a bus has k address lines, the address space contains 2^k possible values. All addresses on a bus do not need to be assigned. If the address space contains unassigned addresses, we say that it contains *holes*. Figure 4.3 illustrates an example address assignment.

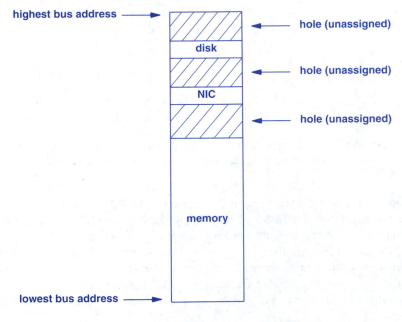

Figure 4.3 An example bus address space occupied by a disk device, a network interface device, and memory. Holes occur when no hardware device has been assigned to an address.

4.6 The Fetch-Store Paradigm

Bus hardware uses a *fetch-store paradigm*, which is sometimes called a *load-store paradigm*. That is, the bus only supports two basic operations: a *fetch* moves data from another hardware unit to the unit that issued the request, and a *store* moves data from the unit that issued the request to another unit.

The easiest way to understand the fetch-store paradigm is to imagine a CPU communicating with memory over a bus that is 32 bits wide. To store a 32-bit value into memory, the CPU places the value on the data lines, places the memory address on the memory lines, and then uses a control line to request a *store* operation. Like other functional units, the memory watches the bus continuously. When it detects that the address in the store operation corresponds to one of its addresses, the memory hardware extracts the address and data item from the bus, stores the data value in the specified memory location, and uses a control line to indicate that the operation was successful. Similarly, to fetch an item from memory, the CPU places a memory address on the address lines, and uses a control line to request a *load* operation. Because the address corresponds to one of its memory addresses, the memory hardware fetches a 32-bit value from the specified memory location, places it on the data lines, and uses a control line to signal the CPU. The CPU makes a copy of the data item, and then uses a control line to signal that the operation is complete.

All operations on a bus must be cast in the fetch-store paradigm, even if they do not involve fetching or storing values. For example, suppose an engineer wishes to build an I/O device that requires a *reset* operation (e.g., the device must be reset by the CPU before it can be used). Because a bus only supports fetch or store operations, the engineer must use one of the two operations to trigger a reset.

How can a reset be encoded as a *store*? The idea is straightforward: the device is built to watch the bus and use the occurrence of a certain bit combination to trigger the reset operation. For example, the device can watch for a *store* to occur with the address of the device and a data value of 0. When it finds such a combination, the hardware triggers a reset. In later chapters, we will see that the concept applies broadly to hardware.

> *Many hardware devices use a fetch-store paradigm for control. A* store *operation causes the device to perform an action and a* fetch *or* load *operation causes the device to return status information.*

In practice, of course, bus hardware is more complicated than suggested above. Before it can use the bus, a unit must wait for any previous operation to complete. Furthermore, multiple devices may attempt to use the bus simultaneously. To solve the problem of simultaneous access, the hardware includes a *bus arbiter*. Each unit is assigned a priority, and the arbiter determines which of the units has highest priority and grants the bus to that unit.

4.7 Network Interface Card Functionality

Like other I/O devices, a network interface is operated by the CPU, meaning that the CPU controls all packet transmission and reception. To send a packet, the CPU first assembles the packet in memory. When the packet is ready, the CPU transfers the packet to the NIC, which then transmits the packet over the network. The CPU also controls packet reception. Before the system can receive a packet, the CPU must enable the NIC and specify exactly where the packet is to be stored. The NIC waits for a packet from the network, places the packet in the specified location, and informs the CPU.

A NIC must follow exact specifications. When it interacts with the CPU, the NIC follows standards for the computer's bus. When it transmits or receives packets over the network, the NIC adheres to network protocols. For example, a NIC usually contains physical interface chips that implement layer 1 network standards. The interface chips ensure that each outgoing packet has the correct format and that the generated signals adhere to the precise waveforms specified by the protocol standards. Similarly, the interface chips verify each incoming frame to ensure that the frame is valid according to the layer 1 protocol standards.

4.8 NIC Optimizations For High Speed

A typical bus is not wide enough to transfer an entire packet at one time. Thus, a packet must be passed to the NIC in small pieces (e.g., 64 bits). The description above implies that the CPU is involved in such transfers. Indeed, early NIC hardware did rely on the computer's CPU. During packet reception, for example, the CPU repeatedly accessed the NIC to retrieve the next piece of the packet and place it in memory. Similarly, during packet transmission, the CPU repeatedly passed the NIC pieces of the packet. The primary advantage of using the CPU for packet transfer is low cost — the NIC hardware can be inexpensive because it does not do much of the work. The primary disadvantages are overhead and limits on scale — using the CPU to handle I/O means it is not available for other tasks. More important, a single CPU cannot keep up with high-speed networks, especially on systems that have multiple network interfaces.

To achieve scale, it is necessary to decouple I/O from packet processing and avoid using the CPU whenever possible. Consequently, modern NICs contain sophisticated hardware that operates independently from the CPU. Four techniques are used to optimize data transfers and reduce overhead:

- Onboard address recognition and filtering

- Onboard packet buffering

- Direct memory access (DMA)

- Operation chaining

The next sections explain each of these optimizations. Later chapters in the text will explain how the general concepts apply to other architectures.

4.9 Onboard Address Recognition

4.9.1 Unicast And Broadcast Recognition And Filtering

Technologies such as Ethernet use a shared medium for transmission; each station receives all transmissions and then discards any frame intended for another station. That is, at the lowest level, each station makes a copy of each frame that passes across the network. The station then examines the destination address field in the header to determine whether to handle the frame. If the address matches the station's unicast address or the network broadcast address, the frame is processed; if not, the frame is discarded.

The idea of onboard address recognition and filtering is straightforward: instead of using the computer's CPU to check the frame's destination address, arrange for the NIC hardware to perform the test. That is, build NIC hardware that can operate independently and that has the ability to test the destination address field in the header of incoming frames. The NIC tests the destination address as the frame header arrives, before the frame is passed to the CPU. If the destination address does not match the station's unicast address or the network broadcast address, the NIC discards the frame without interrupting the CPU. Onboard address recognition can reduce the load on the CPU dramatically because a shared network may transfer many frames that are not destined for a given computer.

4.9.2 Multicast Recognition And Filtering

Onboard recognition of multicast addresses increases NIC complexity. Each multicast address corresponds to a multicast group. Unlike the station address or the network broadcast address, which remain unchanged, the set of multicast addresses that a station recognizes is dynamic. An application running on a computer may choose to join or leave a multicast group at any time, a given application may join more than one group, or multiple applications on a computer may join the same group. A computer accepts a multicast frame if at least one application on the computer is participating in the group, and discards the frame otherwise.

How can a NIC provide onboard recognition for multicast addresses if the set of addresses changes over time? Early NICs did not filter multicast. Instead, the NIC accepted all multicast frames and required the CPU to examine each. Unfortunately, accepting all multicast frames can result in significant overhead because multicast is often used for applications like audio or video that stream data continuously. More important, all computers on a network experience overhead, even if they do not choose to participate in any multicast.

To reduce overhead, modern NICs do provide onboard multicast recognition and filtering. Because multicast groups are dynamic, however, the NIC must allow the CPU to specify or change the set of multicast addresses. When it first receives power, a NIC only recognizes the station's unicast address and the network broadcast address. At any time, the CPU can instruct the NIC to begin accepting packets destined to a specific multicast address or to stop accepting packets for a specific address. Once the CPU specifies an address, the NIC handles all recognition. The NIC accepts and delivers frames that match the specified addresses and discards other frames.

A computer cannot specify an arbitrary number of multicast addresses because NIC hardware limits the size of the set. In fact, many NICs limit multicast recognition to 32 or 64 addresses. In practice, such limits are seldom important. To understand why, observe that a typical application only participates in one or two multicast groups at any time (e.g., to receive a stream of video and audio). Furthermore, only a few applications participate in multicast at any time. Thus, most computer systems only use a few multicast addresses simultaneously.

Can a NIC compare the address in an incoming frame to 64 addresses before another frame arrives? Few NICs have sufficient computational power to do so. Instead, NIC hardware often uses an optimization: the NIC keeps a vector of 64 bits, and uses a hash function to map a multicast address into the range 0 through 63. In essence, the NIC divides the set of all possible multicast addresses into 64 groups. When a multicast packet arrives, the NIC computes a hash of the address, and checks the corresponding group bit when deciding whether to accept the packet. The scheme means a NIC never rejects a packet that should be accepted, but the NIC may accept a multicast packet even if the address does not match one of the specified addresses. Although the probability is low, the CPU must be prepared to handle a false acceptance (i.e., check the address and discard the frame).

4.10 Onboard Packet Buffering

Another NIC optimization involves placing sufficient memory on the NIC to allow onboard packet buffering. To understand why onboard buffering helps, it is important to know that:

- Packets do not arrive over a network at a steady rate.
- The bus to which the NIC is attached is shared by other devices.

We use the term *bursty* to describe network traffic because the packet arrival rate varies rapidly and widely. A packet network can experience a period of no traffic (i.e., an idle condition) followed by an abrupt transition to a period of continuous traffic. A NIC must be able to handle continuous arrivals because all the packets in a burst may be destined for a given computer. If NIC hardware cannot accommodate continuous arrivals, some packets will be lost.

Bus sharing and CPU interaction both impact the speed with which a NIC can transfer packets. A NIC may need to wait for bus access because multiple devices share the bus and each has an assigned priority. More important, a transfer can require many cycles (e.g., a NIC may need to wait while a higher priority device transfers a block of data into memory). CPU interaction can be delayed because the CPU honors interrupts in order of priority. Thus, if a NIC interrupts the CPU for each packet, the NIC can experience delay and lose packets.

Onboard buffers allow a NIC to handle bursty traffic because the NIC can accept packets without waiting for the bus or the CPU. NIC hardware for onboard buffering permits two simultaneous operations: the NIC can accept and store a new packet in an onboard buffer at the same time it uses the bus to transfer an existing packet to the computer. Thus, the NIC can continue to accept packets from the network even if the bus is temporarily unavailable for transfer or the CPU is busy handling a higher priority device. Having a large onboard memory is important — if the memory is sufficient to accommodate the entire burst, no packets will be lost.

4.11 Direct Memory Access

Although onboard buffers help handle packet bursts, further optimization is needed to provide high-speed transfer from a NIC to the computer's memory. One optimization is known as *direct memory access* (*DMA*). Originally invented to optimize disk transfers, DMA can be used with any I/O device that transfers large amounts of data over a bus to memory.

To understand DMA, observe that even a 128-bit wide bus is not wide enough to transfer an entire packet at one time. Consequently, a packet must be divided into pieces, and a separate bus transfer must be used for each piece. Many early I/O interfaces used a technique known as *Programmed I/O* (*PIO*) that required the CPU to handle each transfer across the bus. DMA gives an I/O device direct access to the computer's memory without an intermediary. In particular, a DMA device operates in parallel with the CPU, and can perform transfers across the bus without using the CPU. To do so, the NIC must divide a packet into pieces and perform a series of bus operations to transfer each piece into memory. Once the entire packet has been transferred, the NIC interrupts the CPU to inform it that the transfer is complete. DMA optimizes performance because it overlaps I/O with processing — while a DMA transfer is in progress, the CPU can perform a (possibly unrelated) computation.

How does a NIC that uses DMA know where to place items in the computer's memory? It does not; only the CPU knows. Thus, the NIC waits for instructions from the CPU. The CPU uses the bus to send the location of a buffer in memory and to enable packet reception. The NIC transfers the packet to the specified location in the computer's memory, and then generates an interrupt to inform the CPU that the operation has completed.

DMA works equally well for packet output. The CPU assembles a packet in memory, and uses the bus to pass the memory address of the packet to the NIC. The CPU can proceed with other tasks. The NIC uses DMA to access the packet (i.e., to fetch each piece of the packet). Once it has fetched all the pieces, the NIC transmits the packet over the network. Finally, once transmission is complete, the NIC generates an interrupt to inform the CPU.

4.12 Operation And Data Chaining

We said that DMA permits a NIC to handle the transfer of a packet between the network and the computer's memory without using the CPU. Some NICs provide a mechanism known as *data chaining* or *buffer chaining*. When using data chaining, the CPU can provide the NIC with a linked list of small buffers instead of a single, large buffer. As it delivers a large frame, the NIC starts placing octets of the frame in the first buffer. If the first buffer fills, the NIC automatically moves to the next buffer, and so on.

As a further optimization, the highest speed NICs use a technique known as *operation chaining* or *command chaining* that allows the NIC to perform a series of packet transfers. Operation chaining can be combined with data chaining, or used independently. To initiate operation chaining, the CPU creates a linked list of ''commands'' in memory and passes the address to the NIC. The NIC proceeds to execute each command, and only stops when it reaches the end of the command list. For example, Figure 4.4 illustrates a linked list that contains a series of transfer commands.

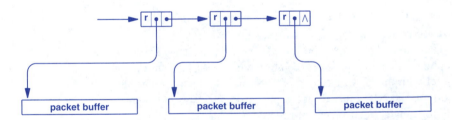

Figure 4.4 An example linked list of commands in memory. Each node on the list specifies an operation (*transmit* or *receive*), a pointer to a buffer in memory (or a list of buffers if data chaining is used), and a pointer to the next command.

If a NIC proceeds to execute commands independently, how does the CPU know which input buffers the NIC has filled or which output buffers the NIC has emptied? Each entry in the command list contains an extra bit (not shown in Figure 4.4) that is used for *synchronization*. When it creates the command list, the CPU clears the synchronization bit in each entry (i.e., sets the bit to zero). After it finishes with an opera-

tion, the NIC sets the synchronization bit (i.e., sets the bit to one) and interrupts the
CPU. If the CPU does not process the interrupt fast enough, the NIC may finish another command. Thus, when an interrupt occurs, the CPU must examine the synchronization bits along the list to determine how many entries the NIC has completed.

4.13 Data Flow Diagram

Throughout the text, we will use *data flow diagrams* to depict the path of data
through a processing system. As an example, Figure 4.5 illustrates the flow of packets
directly into and out of memory through a network interface that uses DMA.

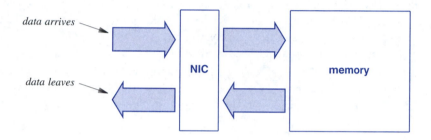

Figure 4.5 A data flow diagram with large arrows showing the flow of packets through a DMA interface. Input arrives at the NIC from the
network and flows directly into memory; output flows directly
from memory to the NIC and then to the network.

4.14 Promiscuous Mode

The NIC optimizations described above cannot be used in all network systems.
For example, consider a packet analyzer that generates statistics about packets on a network. An analyzer must capture all packets that traverse the network. Thus, onboard
address recognition and filtering, normally used to optimize NIC performance, is incompatible with a packet analyzer.

To accommodate special-purpose network systems, most NICs offer a way to disable one or more optimizations. For example, even if the NIC offers onboard multicast
address recognition, it may be possible to configure a NIC to accept all multicast packets. Most NICs provide a facility known as *promiscuous mode* that disables onboard
address recognition. Once a NIC has been placed in promiscuous mode, the NIC will
accept any packet that traverses the network. Promiscuous mode allows a NIC to be
used with any network system, including a packet analyzer.

4.15 Summary

A conventional computer system consists of a single CPU, memory, and I/O devices interconnected by a bus. A computer bus consists of wires that allow parallel data transfer, and the amount of data that can be transferred in one operation is known as the bus width. A bus uses a fetch-store paradigm; each operation must be formulated as the result of storing a value into an address or fetching a value from an address.

Like any other I/O device, a network interface card (NIC) attaches to the computer's bus and provides a connection to a computer network. Also, like other I/O devices, a NIC operates under control of the CPU.

Several optimizations improve the performance of network interfaces: onboard address recognition, onboard packet buffering, direct memory access (DMA), and operation chaining. DMA is especially important because a bus is not wide enough to send a complete packet in one transfer operation. With DMA, the NIC operates independently. The NIC repeatedly transfers pieces of a packet across the bus, and only informs the CPU when the entire packet has been transferred.

The optimizations available on NICs are incompatible with some uses. To accommodate special needs such as packet analyzers, most NICs offer a way to disable optimizations. In particular, promiscuous mode disables onboard address recognition and filtering.

FOR FURTHER STUDY

Hennessy and Patterson [2002] provides a broad introduction to computer architecture, and explains concepts such as DMA.

Chapter Contents

5

Basic Packet Processing: Algorithms And Data Structures

5.1 Introduction

The previous chapter describes the architecture of a conventional computer system, including network interface cards that attach to the computer's bus. This chapter describes packet processing software for such an architecture. After considering issues of packet size and examining the details of byte ordering, the chapter considers algorithms and data structures used in basic packet processing. Later chapters consider alternative implementations designed for special-purpose hardware.

5.2 State Information and Resource Exhaustion

Information stored indefinitely in memory is known as *state information*. For example, a packet analyzer that counts broadcast and unicast packets keeps two pieces of state information: an integer for each counter. In some systems, the amount of state information depends on traffic. For example a NAT box must keep state information for each TCP connection that is currently active. Thus, as more connections are formed, the amount of state information increases.

Because a network system is designed to run for an arbitrary length of time without being rebooted or reinitialized, the entire system must be engineered so it never exhausts resources. All memory must be recycled. Furthermore, the designer should guarantee that no combination of input will cause state information or packet buffers to exceed the resources available. Throughout this text, we make a fundamental assumption:

> *To allow it to run arbitrarily long, a network system must be designed with limits on all resources, and the limits must be fixed independent of arriving traffic; designs that violate this principle will not be considered.*

5.3 Packet Buffer Allocation

Memory is perhaps the most obvious resource that must be limited because memory is used to buffer packets. Thus, the amount of memory needed depends on traffic: if more packets arrive than depart, available memory will eventually be exhausted. Unfortunately, asymmetric traffic is common. As an example, consider a bridge between a 100Base-T network and an 802.11b wireless LAN. Traffic can arrive over the 100Base-T network much faster than it can be sent across the wireless LAN. To avoid memory exhaustion, the total amount of memory allocated to packet buffers must be limited; when the limit is reached, the network system cannot accept any incoming packets.

How much memory should be allocated to packet buffers? The question is not easy to answer. Buffers must be sufficient to handle traffic at wire speed. In the extreme case where a continuous stream of traffic arrives faster than it departs, no amount of memory will suffice. Recall, however, that data traffic is bursty. Thus, it may seem that the amount of memory allocated to buffers should be chosen to be sufficiently large to contain all packets in a burst. Interestingly, buffer management is closely related to quality of service. Research shows that buffer size can be used to provide guarantees on both bandwidth and delay. In fact, some research suggests that when combined with a straightforward scheduling policy, intelligent buffer management can be used to provide per-flow bandwidth and delay guarantees. Unfortunately, data traffic does not follow easily predictable patterns. Furthermore, the amount of time a packet remains in memory depends on the speed with which the packet is processed. Thus, most network systems designers do not use an analytical approach. Instead, they choose an initial size for buffer memory, and measure the resulting system to determine whether it can handle bursts.

How should buffers be allocated? As we have seen, high-speed NICs require the CPU to preallocate packet buffers and create a linked list of commands for the NIC to execute. Except for networks that use cells, a system designer must choose a size for each buffer. For output, the exact size of the buffer is known because the packet must be created before it can be transmitted. For input, although the exact size of the next arriving packet may be unknown, the maximum size is fixed. Thus, it may seem that a system can allocate variable-size buffers for output and fixed-size buffers for input. Unfortunately, variable-size buffer allocation does not work well in a network system because it leads to *memory fragmentation*, a situation in which free memory is divided into many small blocks interspersed with larger blocks of allocated memory. To avoid memory fragmentation, network systems usually allocate fixed-size buffers.

How large should an individual packet buffer be? In a network system that handles only one network technology, the decision is trivial: choose a size appropriate for the technology. For example, an Ethernet bridge only needs to handle a maximum-size Ethernet frame. A network system that handles frames from multiple technologies can choose a single buffer size equal to the largest frame size, or can divide buffer memory into multiple regions and allocate buffers in each region appropriate to a particular technology. As a variation of the idea, a designer can choose to divide buffer memory into N regions, where each region corresponds to a network interface†.

5.4 Packet Buffer Size And Copying

Whether to share buffers among network interfaces depends on the protocols used and how packets are processed. For example, a system such as a bridge forwards frames from one interface to another. In such cases, it makes sense to have a single set of packet buffers that are shared among all interfaces. More important, using a single set of buffers helps avoid an inefficiency: *packet copying*. To understand why copying increases overhead dramatically, observe that most protocols are designed so that processing decisions only need to examine the packet header. Furthermore, headers are usually arranged in fixed locations to make field extraction efficient. By contrast, copying a packet from one buffer to another requires processing time proportional to the entire packet, which is inefficient because memory is much slower than a processor. The point is:

> *Because copying an entire packet from one location to another requires time proportional to the entire packet and because memory speed is often a bottleneck, network systems avoid copying whenever possible.*

5.5 Protocol Layering And Copying

Higher layer protocols also affect the buffer allocation decision. In particular, a network system that handles IP must allocate buffers that can hold an IP datagram. As we have seen, the 16-bit total length field in the IP header specifies the overall datagram size, including the header. As a consequence, a maximum-size datagram contains 64K octets, which means a system that implements IP must allocate buffers sufficient to hold datagrams of up to 64K octets. Designers have observed, however, that Internet traffic contains few maximum-size datagrams. Instead, datagram size spans a large range, starting with a minimum-size datagram of 20 octets (a header with no op-

---

†Another alternative involves using smaller fixed-size buffers, with multiple buffers chained together to hold a large packet.

tions and no payload). Datagrams carring telnet messages occupy only 41 octets. More important, most large datagrams in the Internet occupy only 1500 octets because they passed across an Ethernet†. Although memory is relatively inexpensive, it may not make sense to allocate all datagram buffers to be maximum size. Thus, some systems have two sets of datagram buffers: many of 1500 octets and fewer buffers of 64K octets. The system examines each datagram and chooses a buffer size that is appropriate.

Protocol layering also affects buffer decisions because layering implies encapsulation. That is, each layer adds a header as an outgoing packet passes down the stack, and each layer removes a header as an incoming packet passes up the stack. Two buffer allocation schemes have been devised for layered systems that avoid copying:

> *Large buffer.* On input, place the incoming frame in a buffer, pass the buffer address among layers, and arrange for each layer to locate the appropriate header in the buffer. On output, leave sufficient space in the buffer before the payload, pass the address of the buffer among layers, and allow each layer to prepend another header.

> *Linked List.*‡ On output, allocate a separate buffer for each header and for the data; construct a packet by forming a linked list where each node on the list points to one of the header buffers or the data buffer. On input, create an initial list of one node that points to the frame buffer; as the packet passes up the stack, append a node to the list that points to the next header.

Although the details differ, each of these approaches has the same effect: once written to memory, neither protocol headers nor data is copied. The large buffer approach works best when the exact layering is known in advance because the location of a header in the packet is fixed. For example, if each packet contains TCP, IP, and Ethernet headers, the location of the TCP header is the same in each packet. If the set of protocol headers varies from packet to packet, however, the linked list approach works better because a layer does not need to know about the headers from other layers.

5.6 Heterogeneity And Network Byte Order

To ensure interoperability among heterogeneous computers, many protocols specify representation and transmission details. For example, TCP/IP protocols specify that integer values in headers are represented in *network byte order*. A sending computer must convert integer fields from the local computer's native byte order to network byte order before transmitting a datagram, and a receiving computer must convert integer fields in a datagram from network byte order to the local native byte order.

Several integer representations exist. The two most popular are known as *little endian* and *big endian*. TCP/IP defines network byte order to be big endian, but many computers, including PCs that follow the Intel architecture, use little endian representation. Figure 5.1 illustrates the difference.

---

†A datagram encapsulated in an Ethernet frame must fit in the Ethernet payload limit of 1500 octets.

‡A linked list of buffers is also known as a *buffer chain*.

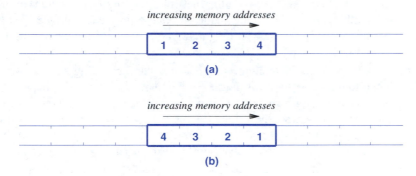

Figure 5.1 The arrangement of a 32-bit integer in (a) little endian and (b) big endian byte order. Bytes of the integer are numbered, with 1 representing the least significant byte and 4 representing the most significant byte.

As the figure shows, the easiest way to understand the two representations consists of viewing bytes of the integer arranged in either increasing significance from left to right or decreasing significance. On a little endian machine, the address used for an integer corresponds to the least significant byte of the integer. On a big endian machine, the address used for an integer refers to the most significant byte of the integer.

In practice, most systems include library routines that perform the necessary byte order translation. Figure 5.2 lists a popular set.

Function	data size	Translation
ntohs	16 bits	Network byte order to host's byte order
htons	16 bits	Host's byte order to network byte order
ntohl	32 bits	Network byte order to host's byte order
htonl	32 bits	Host's byte order to network byte order

Figure 5.2 Examples of library functions used to translate byte order. Each takes an integer of the size specified as an argument and returns the translated value.

5.7 Bridge Algorithm

This section begins an examination of algorithms and data structures for common packet processing tasks, starting with an Ethernet bridge. For low-speed or medium-speed Ethernets, a bridge can be built from a conventional hardware architecture. Indeed, commercial Ethernet bridges are often implemented in software on conventional hardware — the code runs from ROM on an embedded system that consists of a microprocessor, memory, and two network interfaces. Because the bridge needs to receive a copy of any frame that passes across either network, the interfaces operate in promiscuous mode. Furthermore, unlike a conventional NIC, a physical interface on a bridge must not change the source address in outgoing frames because the bridge must replicate an exact copy of the frame.

An Ethernet bridge uses a straightforward rule when forwarding frames: copy each incoming frame to the other segment unless the destination is known to lie on the segment over which the frame arrives. When it boots, a bridge does not know which computers lie on each segment, so the bridge begins by forwarding all frames. As time goes on, the bridge watches source addresses in incoming frames to learn the location of computers†. Algorithm 5.1 lists the steps a bridge takes when forwarding frames.

Algorithm 5.1

Assume: two network interfaces each operating in promiscuous mode.

Create an empty list, L, that will contain pairs of values;

Do forever {

    Acquire the next frame to arrive;

    Set I to the interface over which the frame arrived;

    Extract the source address, S;

    Extract the destination address, D;

    Add the pair (S, I) to list L if not already present.

    If the pair (D, I) appears in list L {

        Drop the frame;

    } Else {

        Forward the frame over the other interface;

    }

}

Algorithm 5.1 Bridge Forwarding. This is the basic algorithm used by a learning bridge.

Although it outlines basic steps, the algorithm omits implementation details that depend on the underlying system. For example, does the bridge need multiple frame buffers? If so, how many? What code does the CPU execute during an idle period when no frames have arrived? How is the CPU informed when a frame arrives? Is information about the interface over which a frame arrived stored with the frame in memory, or does the system use a separate buffer in memory for each interface? If two

---

†The bridge described here is sometimes called a *learning bridge*.

network interfaces each compete for service from the CPU, how does the software guarantee that each interface receives fair access? Can the bridge operate fast enough to process packets as they arrive?

5.8 Table Lookup And Hashing

Algorithm 5.2 provides an example of an important aspect of protocol processing: table lookup. Many network systems use a table to store state information or auxiliary data needed for processing, and lookup must be optimized because it lies on the critical path — the system must search one or more tables for each packet. Thus, even when optimizations are applied, table lookup can account for a significant percentage of the CPU time.

To ensure that lookup does not become a bottleneck, most systems allocate a large table and use a form of *hashing*. In particular, *double hashing* works well if the hash table contains many empty slots.

Algorithm 5.2

Given: a key, a table in memory, and the table size N.

Produce: a slot in the table that corresponds to the key
 or an empty table slot if the key is not in the table.

Method: double hashing with open addressing.

Choose P_1 and P_2 to be prime numbers;

Fold the key to produce an integer, K;

Compute table pointer Q equal to $(P_1 \times K)$ modulo N;

Compute increment R equal to $(P_2 \times K)$ modulo N;

While (table slot Q not equal to K and nonempty) {

 $Q \leftarrow (Q + R)$ modulo N;

}

At this point, Q either points to an empty table slot or to the
 slot containing the key.

Algorithm 5.2 An Example Hash Table lookup.

The intuition behind Algorithm 5.2 is straightforward: hash the key using prime P_1 to produce an initial table slot. If the slot is occupied by a different key, compute another hash using P_2 to find the next slot. Computing a second hash helps spread the entries — even if two keys hash to the same initial entry in the table, the second hash will point them to different slots.

Many computers use 32-bit arithmetic. How can we convert a 48-bit Ethernet address into a 32-bit value? There are several possibilities. We could choose 32 bits from the 48 and ignore the others, or we could use a mathematical function to map the 48-bit value into a 32-bit value. Algorithm 5.2 suggests *folding*, a process that partitions the address into a 32-bit section and a 16-bit section, and then uses an *exclusive or* operation to combine the two. An exercise suggests exploring an alternative; Chapter 20 discusses special-purpose hardware that assists in hashing.

5.9 IP Datagram Fragmentation And Reassembly

Recall that the Internet consists of multiple networks and that an IP datagram is encapsulated in a frame as it crosses each network. Because the Internet contains heterogeneous networks, some networks limit the maximum packet size to a smaller size than others. We use the term *Maximum Transmission Unit* (*MTU*) to refer to the largest payload a given network can accommodate. To accommodate heterogeneous MTUs, IP uses the technique of *fragmentation and reassembly* — a router can divide a large datagram into a set of smaller datagrams called *fragments*†. Each fragment travels independently, and the ultimate destination *reassembles* fragments to reproduce the original datagram.

Depending on the desired speed and cost, all or most of IP, including code for fragmentation and reassembly, can be implemented in software. Indeed, most low-end routers consist of software that runs on a conventional CPU. How difficult is it to build such software? The task is straightforward, but requires us to understand a few protocol details. The following summarizes the important points, which are expanded below‡.

- Each fragment is a datagram that begins with a datagram header.

- Header fields in a fragment are derived from the original datagram.

- In a fragment, the following fields differ from the original datagram:

    TOTAL LENGTH
    FLAGS
    FRAGMENT OFFSET
    HEADER CHECKSUM

- The size of a fragment is determined by the MTU of the outgoing network.

- The *FLAGS* and *FRAGMENT OFFSET* fields together identify a datagram as a fragment; if both contain zero the datagram is not a fragment.

---

†Network systems that implement ATM employ an analogous technique known as *segmentation and reassembly* to divide an AAL5 message into cells.

‡The datagram header format appears on page 19.

5.9.1 Interpretation Of The Flags Field

The *FLAGS* field in a datagram header contains three bits, two of which are used to control fragmentation. Figure 5.3 explains the meaning of each of the FLAGS bits.

Figure 5.3 Bits in the FLAGS field of an IP datagram and their use in fragmentation. Most datagrams start with the three bits all set to
zero.

As the figure shows, one bit is used to grant permission and the other is used to mark the last of the fragments. The *DO NOT FRAGMENT* bit (labeled *D*) allows the sender to specify that a datagram should not be fragmented. If the datagram reaches a point that requires fragmentation and the *D* bit is set, the datagram is discarded and an error message is sent back to inform the source. The *MORE FRAGMENTS* bit (labeled *M*) specifies whether additional fragments follow. When a datagram is divided into fragments, all fragments have the *M* bit set to 1 except the fragment that contains the tail of the original datagram in which the *M* bit is set to 0. Similarly, a datagram that has not been fragmented carries an *M* bit of 0.

5.9.2 Interpretation Of The Fragment Offset Field

The *FRAGMENT OFFSET* field tells the relationship between data in the fragment and data in the original datagram. More specifically, the *FRAGMENT OFFSET* speci-fies how far into the original payload the data in the fragment belongs. For example, the initial datagram has a *FRAGMENT OFFSET* value of zero as does the first frag-ment. A receiver uses the offset during reassembly to put data from each fragment in its original position.

Recall that the *TOTAL LENGTH* field in a datagram contains 16 bits, which means the datagram can be 64K octets long. Because it contains only 13 bits, the *FRAGMENT OFFSET* field cannot represent all possible octet positions in the datagram. Instead, the value in the *FRAGMENT OFFSET* field is interpreted as multiples of eight octets. As a consequence:

The amount of data in a fragment must be a multiple of eight octets.
The limit is imposed even if the network MTU allows extra octets.

5.9.3 IP Fragmentation Algorithm

Typical routers use a *greedy* heuristic to determine fragment size: the router sends fragments that are as large as possible. The datagram size is rarely an exact multiple of the size chosen for fragments, which means that the last piece of data will be smaller than the others. As a result, the final fragment is usually smaller. Algorithm 5.3 outlines the greedy approach.

Algorithm 5.3

Given: an IP datagram, D, and a network MTU.

Produce: a set of fragments for D.

If the *DO NOT FRAGMENT* bit is set {

    Stop and report an error;

}

Compute the size of the datagram header, H;

Choose N to be the largest multiple of 8 such
        that $H+N \leq MTU$;

Initialize an offset counter, O, to zero;

Repeat until datagram empty {

    Create a new fragment that has a copy of D's header;

    Extract up to the next N octets of data from D and place
        the data in the fragment;

    Set the *MORE FRAGMENTS* bit in fragment header;

    Set *TOTAL LENGTH* field in fragment header to be H+N;

    Set *FRAGMENT OFFSET* field in fragment header to be O;

    Compute and set the *CHECKSUM* field in fragment header;

    Increment O by N/8;

}

Algorithm 5.3 IP Datagram Fragmentation. The last fragment may contain fewer than N octets of data.

5.9.4 Fragmenting A Fragment

Fragments themselves can be fragmented. The situation can arise in practice because a datagram may pass over many networks with various size MTUs. The first fragmentation produces fragments small enough for the next network along the path. If the fragments later reach a network with an MTU that is smaller, they need to be fragmented again. Fortunately, because all offsets refer to the original datagram, a router does not reassemble a datagram before performing another fragmentation. Instead, each fragment is handled independently.

When fragmenting the original datagram the *MORE FRAGMENTS* bit follows the description above: the final fragment has an M bit of 0 and each of the other fragments has an M bit of 1. When fragmenting a fragment, however, the situation is more complex. Assume a fragment F arrives and must be further fragmented. If F does not contain the tail of the original datagram (i.e., the M bit is set to 1), all fragments of F must have an M bit of 1. If F does contain the tail of the original datagram, however, the last fragment of F will have an M bit of 0 and all other fragments will have an M bit of 1. The table in Figure 5.4 shows that the above discussion reduces to only two cases.

M bit in original	M bit in last fragment	M bit in other fragments
0	0	1
1	1	1

Figure 5.4 The assignment of the MORE FRAGMENTS bit in fragments. The same rules apply to fragmenting a fragment or a datagram.

5.9.5 IP Reassembly

In most cases, the ultimate destination performs IP reassembly†. The destination accepts incoming fragments and collects the fragments from a given datagram. When all fragments of a datagram arrive, the system reassembles them to produce the original datagram, which it then processes.

The best-effort delivery semantics of IP complicate reassembly and influence the choice of algorithms and data structures. Four semantic items are especially important:

- *Out-Of-Order Delivery.* Routes can change at any time. As a result, fragments may arrive out-of-order. In particular, because some routers give priority to short packets, the fragment carrying the tail of the datagram may arrive first.

---

†Network Address Translation provides a notable exception; NAT systems may need to reassemble fragments because protocol port numbers are carried only in the first fragment.

- *Duplication.* The original datagram or any fragment can be duplicated during its trip through the Internet. More important, if a duplicate datagram is routed along a different path than the original, fragmentation along the paths may differ, which produces fragments that overlap.

- *Loss.* One or more fragments from a datagram may be lost. IP does not retransmit lost datagrams or lost fragments.

- *Concurrent Reception.* A receiving system must be prepared to accept incoming fragments from multiple datagrams concurrently.

The next sections discuss the algorithms and data structures used in reassembly, and consider the effect of each of the semantic items.

5.9.6 Grouping Fragments Together

As a computer system creates datagrams, it assigns a unique value to the 16-bit identification field (*ID*) in the datagram header†. Most systems assign successive datagrams sequential ID values to maximize the time before an ID value is reused. Thus, if a computer transmits a datagram with ID value *k*, the next datagram emitted by the computer may have ID value *k+1*.

Recall that fragmentation replicates the ID field from the original header, which means that all fragments generated from a datagram will have the same ID field. Unfortunately, datagrams generated by two separate computers may have the same identification value. Therefore, reassembly uses two fields in the header of a fragment when grouping fragments together: the ID field and the IP Source Address field. The point is:

> *Because the ID field in a datagram header is only unique to a given source, a receiving system uses both the ID and IP source address fields to determine whether two fragments came from the same datagram.*

5.9.7 Fragment Position

Because fragments that result from duplicate datagrams can overlap, a receiving system cannot assume that one fragment will begin exactly where another ends. Instead, the receiver must be able to accommodate a fragment that carries an arbitrary amount of data with an arbitrary offset. That is, instead of merely expecting a set of fragments to carry disjoint information, the receiver must record the data octets carried in each fragment.

Conceptually, reassembly maintains two pieces of information: the data octets themselves and information about which data has been received. One possible imple-

---

†The datagram header diagram can be found on page 19.

mentation uses a *reassembly buffer* to hold the data, and a separate linked list to specify which data items have been received. Figure 5.5 illustrates the structure.

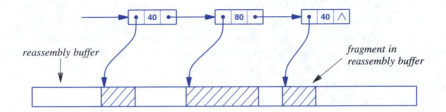

Figure 5.5 Illustration of the data structure used during reassembly after three fragments have arrived. Each node in the linked list contains the data length and a pointer to data in the reassembly buffer.

When a fragment arrives, the reassembly code copies data from the fragment into the buffer and updates the linked list. The position of data in the buffer is computed by multiplying the offset field in the header by 8. Updating the linked list may involve creating a new node or changing existing nodes (in case the new data overlaps or is contiguous with existing data).

5.9.8 IP Reassembly Algorithm

Algorithm 5.4 summarizes the steps in reassembly.

Algorithm 5.4

Given: a fragment, F, add to a partial reassembly.
Method: maintain a set of fragments for each datagram.

Extract the IP source address, S, and ID fields from F;

Combine S and ID to produce a lookup key, K;

Find the fragment set with key K or create a new set;

Insert F into the set;

If the set contains all the data for the datagram {
         Form a completely reassembled datagram and process it;
}

Algorithm 5.4 IP Datagram Reassembly. A receiver must be prepared for a fragment that overlaps existing fragments.

5.10 IP Datagram Forwarding

We will now consider an important function in network systems: IP forwarding. Like an Ethernet bridge, an IP forwarder uses the address in each incoming packet to determine how to forward the packet. However, IP forwarding differs from bridge forwarding in several ways. A bridge operates in layer 2, forwards frames, and uses layer 2 (e.g., Ethernet MAC) addresses to make forwarding decisions; IP forwarding operates in layer 3, forwards IP datagrams, and uses layer 3 (i.e., IP) addresses to make forwarding decisions. A bridge begins with no information and learns the location of computers by watching incoming frames; IP assumes a routing table is in place before any datagrams arrive, and uses the table for each forwarding decision. A bridge uses an implicit *default* action of forwarding frames for which the bridge has no information; IP forwarding uses an explicit default in which the action is specified by a *default route* in the routing table. The forwarding decision in a bridge selects an outgoing interface; the IP forwarding decision chooses a next hop IP address as well as an interface over which to reach the next hop. Thus, IP forwarding can be characterized as a function that returns two values:

$$(\text{next hop, interface}) \leftarrow f(\text{datagram, routing table})$$

We will see that because IP forwarding differs from bridge forwarding, the algorithms and data structures used for IP forwarding differ from those used in a bridge.

One of the most important differences between bridge and IP forwarding arises in the IP routing table. Conceptually, a routing table contains an entry for each possible destination along with a next hop used to reach the destination. Because all IP routing decisions use the network prefix rather than the complete address, the entry in a routing table contains two 32-bit fields: an IP destination address and a bit mask that specifies which bits of the address comprise the prefix. Figure 5.6 shows an example routing table with three entries†.

Destination Address	Address Mask	Next-Hop Address	Interface Number
192.5.48.0	255.255.255.0	128.210.30.5	2
128.10.0.0	255.255.0.0	128.210.141.12	1
0.0.0.0	0.0.0.0	128.210.30.5	2

Figure 5.6 An example IP routing table with three entries. The last two fields in each entry specify the IP address of the next hop and the interface used to reach the next hop.

Given an IP address, A, we must find the first entry in the table that provides a route to A. The most straightforward algorithm searches the table sequentially as the algorithm in the next section shows.

---

†Following the standard, we use dotted decimal to represent a 32-bit address; the values of the four octets are written in decimal separated by dots.

5.11 IP Forwarding Algorithm

Algorithm 5.5

Given: destination address A and routing table R.
Find: a next hop and interface used to route datagrams to A.

For each entry in table R {

　　Set MASK to the Address Mask in the entry;

　　Set DEST to the Destination Address in the entry;

　　If (A & MASK) == DEST {

　　　　Stop; use the next hop and interface in the entry;

　　}

}

if this point is reached, declare error: no route exists;

Algorithm 5.5 Basic IP Route Table Lookup.

Algorithm 5.5 assumes that entries in the table are arranged in order from most specific to least specific. Thus, a route that lists a specific host must precede a route that lists the network to which the host connects. The order of entries can be determined by the size of the address mask — a mask that covers more bits of the address is more specific than a mask that covers fewer bits.

Note that the last entry in the example table in Figure 5.6 has both a destination and address mask equal to zero. Such an entry corresponds to a *default route* that is taken if no other route matches. To see why, observe that the logical *and* of the zero mask with any address is zero, which will compare equal to the zero destination. Thus, if the routing table contains a default route, Algorithm 5.5 will stop before the iteration completes (i.e., the algorithm will never declare an error).

5.12 High-Speed IP Forwarding

Because it searches the routing table sequentially, Algorithm 5.5 can only be used in cases where the table is small or where speed is not an issue. For example, Algorithm 5.5 can be used in a host that only has two entries in a routing table, but it does not suffice for a router that has thousands. To forward at higher speeds, IP route lookup must be optimized. Unfortunately, hashing does not work well for IP route lookup because we need to ensure that (1) all addresses with the same network prefix hash to the same slot in the table, and (2) we cannot know where the prefix ends without consulting the mask in the table entry. Thus, high-speed IP lookup needs an alternative to hashing.

The most popular high-speed IP route lookup scheme uses a tree structure known as a *binary trie*†. A trie search uses individual bits of the lookup key to navigate through the trie — the search starts at the root and proceeds toward the leaves. At each node, a bit of the lookup key specifies whether to follow the left subtree or the right subtree. Figure 5.7 illustrates a trie search.

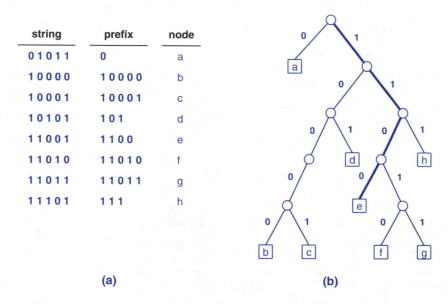

string	prefix	node
0 1 0 1 1	0	a
1 0 0 0 0	1 0 0 0 0	b
1 0 0 0 1	1 0 0 0 1	c
1 0 1 0 1	1 0 1	d
1 1 0 0 1	1 1 0 0	e
1 1 0 1 0	1 1 0 1 0	f
1 1 0 1 1	1 1 0 1 1	g
1 1 1 0 1	1 1 1	h

(a)   (b)

Figure 5.7 (a) A table of binary strings, their unique prefixes, and a node in the trie, and (b) a binary trie for the prefixes with the path corresponding to 1100 (e) darkened. Strings used in an IP routing table are 32 bits long.

In practice, a trie is more complex than the figure shows. For example, although branches of the trie in the figure are pruned to eliminate long sequences that lead to a single leaf, each terminal node must contain a complete IP address, or must point to a complete IP address in a routing table. In addition, the figure distinguishes between internal and external nodes, with external nodes corresponding to a string. Because route lookup needs to return the most specific match, however, a trie used for routing may have some nodes that serve as both the end of one path and the intermediate node on a longer path.

---

†Pronounced ''try''.

5.13 TCP Connection Recognition Algorithm

Network systems such as traffic monitors, firewalls, and NAT boxes must recognize individual TCP connections, which means that the system must keep information about the state of each connection (i.e., whether the connection is being established, is completely established, or is being terminated). To do so, the system examines each segment that passes between two endpoints. A segment used to start a connection has the *SYN* bit set in the code field, and a segment that is used to terminate a connection has the *FIN* bit set. Before a connection is established, each end must send a SYN segment.

Recall that TCP uses a combination of four items to identify a connection: the source IP address, the source protocol port number, the destination IP address, and the destination protocol port number. Thus, to monitor connection status, it is necessary to extract the source and destination IP addresses from the header of the IP datagram that carries the segment, and to extract the protocol port numbers from the segment. Algorithm 5.6 lists the steps required to monitor connections.

Algorithm 5.6

Given: a copy of traffic passing across a network.

Produce: a record of TCP connections present in the traffic.

Initialize a connection table, C, to empty;

For each IP datagram that carries a TCP segment {

    Extract the IP source, S, and destination, D, addresses;

    Extract the source P_1, and destination, P_2, port numbers;

    Use (S,D,P_1,P_2) as a lookup key for table C and
        create a new entry, if needed;

    If the segment has the RESET bit set, delete the entry;

    Else if the segment has the FIN bit set, mark the connection
        closed in one direction, removing the entry from C if
        the connection was previously closed in the other;

    Else if the segment has the SYN bit set, mark the connection as
        being established in one direction, making it completely
        established if it was previously marked as being
        established in the other;

}

Algorithm 5.6 TCP Connection Monitoring.

Once it identifies a particular connection, a connection monitor uses the presence of SYN or FIN bits to determine whether the connection is being formed or being terminated. To start a connection, each side must send a SYN. Therefore, Algorithm 5.6 records the source of a SYN and waits to see a SYN from each side before declaring that the connection is established. Similarly, the algorithm waits to see a FIN from both sides before declaring that the connection has been terminated.

In addition to checking FIN and SYN code bits, Algorithm 5.6 examines the RESET bit. A reset indicates that an error has occurred in which one end has no record of a TCP connection for which the other end has sent a segment. Thus, Algorithm 5.6 uses the presence of a RESET bit to delete its entry for the connection as if both sides had sent FINs.

5.14 TCP Splicing Algorithm

TCP splicing, which is used in systems such as web load balancers and NAT boxes, refers to the interconnection of two independent TCP connections by segment translation. That is, after two connections are open, a splicer is able to rewrite segments that arrive on one connection so they are accepted on the other, and vice versa.

The rules for TCP sequence numbers complicate splicing. TCP allows full-duplex communication, which means that both endpoints of a connection can send data. When a connection is formed, each endpoint chooses a random starting sequence number that it will use for the data it sends; each end acknowledges the initial sequence number that the other end will use. When data is transferred across the connection, each octet is assigned one number in the sequence space, so the sequence numbers in segments increase each time new data is transferred. A sequence number consists of a 32-bit unsigned integer, and the sequence space wraps around (i.e., all arithmetic is performed modulo 32).

Sequence number translation lies at the heart of TCP splicing. A splicer must map the sequence number in a segment that arrives on one connection to an equivalent sequence number for the other connection. Similarly, a splicer must translate acknowledgement numbers between the two. To visualize the mapping, it is easiest to imagine that two connections have just been formed, and that they are currently idle (i.e., no new segments are being sent, and all segments have been acknowledged). Figure 5.8 illustrates the two TCP connections that are in place when a pair of hosts communicate through a splicer.

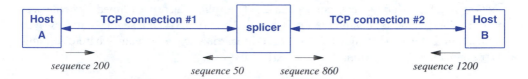

Figure 5.8 Illustration of TCP splicing. Labels show the initial sequence numbers that each side of a connection have chosen for outgoing data.

As the figure shows, splicing begins with two, independent TCP connections. Each of the four connection endpoints has chosen a sequence number to use for outgoing data. As an example, consider the sequence values for TCP connection 1 between the splicer and host *A*. When it sends data, host *A* will use an initial sequence value of 200. When the splicer sends data to host *A*, the splicer will use an initial sequence value of 50.

From the splicer's perspective, segments must be forwarded between the two connections. A segment that arrives over connection 1 will be forwarded over connection 2, and vice versa. Thus, the splicer must perform a mapping on segments that arrive on connection 1 to prepare them to be sent over connection 2. Figure 5.9 lists the changes that must be made in sequence values.

Connection & Direction	Sequence Number	Connection & Direction	Sequence Number
Incoming #1	200	Incoming #2	1200
Outgoing #2	860	Outgoing #1	50
Change	660	Change	-1150

Figure 5.9 Example TCP splicing with the sequence numbers used on two connections and the change required. Segments arriving over connection 1 will be sent out connection 2, and vice versa.

Because both sides exchange sequence information when a connection is created, the splicer learns the sequence values that hosts *A* and *B* will use. Thus, information from Figure 5.9 is available at the splicer. To perform the mapping, the splicer computes the difference between the initial sequence numbers of the outgoing and incoming connections, and then adds that value to the sequence number in each segment.

According to the values in Figure 5.9, the first segment that arrives from host *A* on connection 1 must have a sequence number of 200. Before the splicer can forward the segment over connection 2, the sequence number must be changed to 860. To make the change, the splicer merely adds 660, the difference in the initial values. The splicer must also add 660 to the sequence values in subsequent segments that arrive over connection 1 before sending over connection 2. The splicer also performs a similar mapping for data segments traveling in the opposite direction. When a segment arrives over connection 2, the splicer adds the difference in starting sequence values before sending over connection 1. Algorithm 5.7 summarizes the steps.

Algorithm 5.7

Given: two TCP connections.
Produce: sequence translations for splicing the connection.

Compute D1, the difference between the starting sequences
    on incoming connection 1 and outgoing connection 2;

Compute D2, the difference between the starting sequences
    on incoming connection 2 and outgoing connection 1;

For each segment {

    If segment arrived on connection 1 {
        Add D1 to sequence number;
        Subtract D2 from acknowledgement number;
    } else if segment arrived on connection 2 {
        Add D2 to sequence number;
        Subtract D1 from acknowledgement number;

}

Algorithm 5.7 TCP Splicer.

As the algorithm indicates, a splicer must also translate acknowledgements. When an acknowledgement arrives over connection 1, the acknowledgment value will be given with respect to the outgoing connection 1 sequence space. The acknowledgement must be translated into the sequence values sent over connection 2. In Figure 5.9 and in Algorithm 5.7, differences are computed for the forward direction. Thus, to map a sequence number from connection 1 to connection 2, the splicer adds the computed difference. For an acknowledgement (which travels in the opposite direction), however, the splicer must reverse the action by subtracting the difference instead of adding it. For example, consider an acknowledgement for the values that Figure 5.9 lists. If the acknowledgement arrives on connection 2, it will be given relative to the outgoing sequence on connection 1 (i.e., 860), and must be translated to the incoming sequence on connection 1 (i.e., 200). Thus, the splicer must subtract 660.

5.15 Summary

Network systems implement a variety of algorithms at layers 2, 3 and 4. We have considered algorithms for bridging, hash table lookup, IP fragmentation and reassembly, IP forwarding, TCP connection recognition, and TCP splicing. In addition, we have examined techniques used throughout network systems, including issues of packet size and buffer allocation, copy avoidance, and network byte ordering.

FOR FURTHER STUDY

RFC 791 defines the standard for IP. RFC 894 specifies the transmission of IP datagrams across an Ethernet, and RFC 815 explains datagram reassembly. RFC 793 contains the standard for TCP. The IP and TCP standards are updated by RFC 1122; RFC 1812 provides further information and requirements. RFC 2663 defines NAT terminology; more information can be found in the Internet Draft repository at:

http://www.ietf.org/ID.html

RFC 1191 specifies a standard for *path MTU discovery*, a technique that avoids fragmentation by having a sending host manufacture datagrams that are no larger than the smallest MTU along the entire path. Textbooks such as Aho et. al. [1986] and Knuth [1998] discuss hashing and analyze algorithms.

EXERCISES

5.1   The text suggests using hash table lookup to implement Algorithm 5.2. Should the interface number be used as part of the key for lookup? Why or why not?

5.2   Algorithm 5.1 may fail to perform correctly if a computer moves from one segment to another while the bridge is operating. Find an example to demonstrate the failure, and rewrite the algorithm to correct the flaw.

5.3   Algorithm 5.2 misbehaves when every slot in the hash table is occupied. Identify and correct the problem.

5.4   Collect a set of Ethernet addresses from your local network, and test Algorithm 5.2 with various prime numbers to determine how many addresses map to the same table slot (known as *collisions*).

5.5   Read about the IEEE standard for Ethernet address assignment, and devise a scheme to produce a hash key by extracting 32 bits from the address. Does your choice perform better or worse than folding?

5.6   Implement a procedure that performs datagram fragmentation according to Algorithm 5.3.

5.7   Modify the data structure in Figure 5.5 to embed the linked list in the reassembly buffer (i.e., observe that the linked list can be kept in areas for which no data has been received).

5.8   Implement IP reassembly according to Algorithm 5.4.

5.9   Build and measure the performance of an IP routing table that uses sequential search according to Algorithm 5.5.

5.10 Find an upper bound on the amount of memory needed for a binary trie that corresponds to N binary strings. Assume that each node in the trie requires at least five 32-bit values.

5.11 Extend Algorithm 5.6 to handle errors such as a second SYN that never receives an ACK.

5.12 Implement Algorithm 5.6, and observe TCP connections.

5.13 Extend Algorithm 5.6 to handle duplicate segments and to handle the case where the monitor begins execution after TCP connections have been established.

5.14 Build an implementation of Algorithm 5.7 that can map two TCP connections.

5.15 Extend the implementation in the previous exercise to handle multiple, simultaneous TCP connections.

5.16 Extend Algorithm 5.7 to count the number of data octets sent across each connection.

Chapter Contents

6

Packet Processing Functions

6.1 Introduction

The previous chapter considers algorithms and data structures for tasks that network systems perform at various layers, including bridging at layer 2, fragmentation and reassembly at layer 3, and connection splicing at layer 4. Although the algorithms assume network interfaces use DMA and onboard buffering to overlap processing and I/O, the algorithms themselves are sequential — they are intended for a conventional hardware platform that consists of a single CPU. Each algorithm specifies the steps taken to perform a complete task.

This chapter takes another approach to the subject. Instead of considering algorithms that list a series of macroscopic steps, we analyze the underlying functionality. We strive to identify important themes that arise again and again across many network systems and many processing steps. Our ultimate goal is to define concepts that will help us understand and discuss various hardware architectures. Once the basic functions have been pinpointed, we will be able to assess how a given type of hardware accommodates each function. More important, as we explore hardware architectures in later chapters, we will be able to understand the motivation for some of the design decisions and to see how the functions listed here map onto network processors.

6.2 Packet Processing

The functionality found in network systems falls into ten broad categories:

- Address lookup and packet forwarding
- Error detection and correction
- Fragmentation, segmentation, and reassembly
- Frame and protocol demultiplexing
- Packet classification
- Queueing and packet discard
- Scheduling and timing
- Security: authentication and privacy
- Traffic measurement and policing
- Traffic shaping

The next sections consider each of these categories by defining the broad concept and giving examples.

6.3 Address Lookup And Packet Forwarding

We have already discussed two examples of *address lookup* and seen how it is used in network systems. Lookup of a MAC address occurs when an Ethernet bridge decides whether to forward a copy of a frame. Lookup of an IP address occurs in an IP router. In each case, the system maintains a table, and uses the table to look up the destination address in a packet. Other instances of address lookup also occur. For example, the ARP protocol maintains a small cache that must be searched when sending an IP datagram.

Address lookup is often related to *forwarding*, the process of sending a packet on toward its destination. We have already seen two forwarding schemes that differ. In the case of a bridge, the forwarding table is formed automatically by extracting header information from incoming frames. Lookup requires an *exact match* of an item in the table. In the case of an IP router, however, the table must be built by a separate entity; each entry contains an address mask that cannot be deduced from the packets. More important, instead of an exact match, IP lookup uses a *longest prefix match*. IP multicast forwarding introduces yet another variant of address lookup because the output path(s) selected during forwarding depend on a datagram's source as well as the destination address. Thus, the forwarding employs several forms of address lookup, including exact match lookup for layer 2 and a longest prefix match for layer 3. We can summarize:

Although packet forwarding occurs at many layers, exact match look-up does not suffice in all cases. IP unicast forwarding uses a longest-prefix match, and multicast forwarding uses another scheme.

6.4 Error Detection And Correction

Basic error detection ranks among the most studied and optimized aspects of protocol processing. The need for error detection is universal: as packets traverse a network, *bit errors* can be introduced in which one or more bits in the packet are corrupted. Typical cases include random corruption of bits caused by electromagnetic noise. Regular patterns of corruption caused by malfunctioning hardware can also occur. For example, every N^{th} bit can be set to one, or a contiguous section of bits in the packet can be set to zero. To detect corruption, the sender includes additional error detection information in the packet that the receiver uses to verify correctness. Error detection is statistical; the most common forms are a *Cyclic Redundancy Check (CRC)* or a *checksum*.

Although error checking information is small compared to the packet and does not add significant transmission overhead, error checking can cause significant computational overhead. To understand why, observe that a checksum or CRC requires both the sender and receiver to process the data covered. In particular, an error detection scheme that covers all bits in the packet must process the entire packet. The important observation is:

The cost of an operation is proportional to the amount of data processed. An operation such as checksum computation that requires examination of all the data in a packet is among the most expensive.

To lower costs, error detection is often optimized. For example, most CRC computation is relegated to hardware — a special-purpose Ethernet chip is used to compute the CRC for each outgoing frame and check the CRC on each incoming frame. Checksum computation offers an alternative optimization: incremental update. If an intermediate system changes one field in a packet header, the system can update the original checksum without scanning all the data.

A variant of error detection known as *error correction* provides additional redundancy that can be used to correct corrupted bits. Values sent to perform error correction are known as *Error Correcting Codes (ECCs)*. Error correcting codes are most important for applications like audio and video; they are not widely used in the protocols that most network systems handle. There at least two reasons why error correction is not used for individual packets. First, layering models place more responsibility for error correction at transport layers, and techniques such as retransmission have proved effective. Second, error correcting codes have significant overhead: they occupy more space in a packet and require more computation than error detection mechanisms.

6.5 Fragmentation, Segmentation, And Reassembly

Many protocols contain facilities that allow a sender to divide a large packet into smaller units for transfer, and a receiver to reassemble the units to reproduce the original packet. For example, we have seen that IP defines a *fragmentation and reassembly* mechanism that is used when a large datagram must be sent across a network that has a small MTU. Similarly, ATM defines a *segmentation and reassembly* mechanism used to divide a large AAL5 data packet into cells for transfer across an ATM network.

Although they consume both time and space in a network system, fragmentation and segmentation are each straightforward because the system begins with all the information needed: a packet to be divided and a maximum size for each piece. The system can bound the amount of memory used and the delay. Reassembly is more complex, however, because pieces of the packet arrive asynchronously. While it awaits the arrival of the entire set, the receiving system must hold pieces in memory. Furthermore, a receiving system must implement a mechanism to handle the case where one or more pieces are lost. Finally, a system performing reassembly does not usually know the final packet size until reassembly has been completed. As a consequence, a system that does not use chained buffers may need to allocate a maximum-size buffer to hold each packet that is being reassembled. Thus, reassembly can consume large amounts of resources.

6.6 Frame And Protocol Demultiplexing

Demultiplexing consists of choosing from among several possible alternatives a single protocol that will be used to process a given packet. The concept pervades packet processing, and occurs at each layer of the stack. For example, when a frame arrives, the frame type is used to demultiplex the frame among a set of protocol modules such as ARP and IP. Exactly one module at the next layer is chosen to handle the frame. The process of demultiplexing is repeated at each layer. For example, if a frame contains an IP datagram, the IP module uses type information in the datagram to demultiplex among transport protocols such as UDP and TCP. Transport protocols, in turn, use information in the packet to demultiplex among multiple applications.

To achieve demultiplexing on input, a packet must contain type information for each layer. Thus, insertion of type information on output is closely related to demultiplexing on input. Type information is inserted when a protocol encapsulates its packet in the payload of a protocol at the next lower layer. For example, when it encapsulates a datagram in an Ethernet frame for transmission, an IP module sets the frame type to 800_{16}, which allows the receiver to demultiplex when the frame arrives.

6.7 Packet Classification

6.7.1 Static And Dynamic Classification

We use the term *packet classification* to refer to the process of mapping a packet to one of a finite set of *flows* or *categories*†. The concept is both broad and important: it encompasses classification into a static set of categories that have been determined a priori or into a dynamic set of categories that change over time. The intuition is that packets with similar characteristics will flow along the same logical path (either through the packet processing procedures on one system or across a network through multiple systems). For example, consider an IP router that segregates traffic into four flows that are each routed to a separate network: TCP, UDP, ICMP, and other. We can describe the flows by specifying packets that are assigned to each:

1. A frame containing an IP datagram that carries a TCP segment.

2. A frame containing an IP datagram that carries a UDP datagram.

3. A frame containing an IP datagram that carries an ICMP message.

4. A frame that contains something other than the above.

The set of four flows is *static* because the set never changes and can be defined before any packets arrive. As an alternative, it is possible to assign flows *dynamically*. For example, a classification system can use the IP source address in a packet to determine the flow, with all packets from a given IP source address assigned to the same flow.

6.7.2 Demultiplexing Vs. Classification

Classification differs from demultiplexing in several ways. First, demultiplexing is always a stateless operation in the sense that the set of possible choices is fixed and the choice for a given packet depends only on the contents of that packet. Second, demultiplexing uses a global type system. That is, both the sender and receiver must participate and agree on the interpretation of values — the sender stores a value in a type field, and the receiver consults the value to determine packet disposition. Third, demultiplexing operates one layer at a time.

Unlike demultiplexing, a classification system is not guaranteed to be stateless. The classification is said to be *stateless* if the system determines the flow for a packet from the packet contents alone, and it is said to be *stateful* if the system derives information from the packets that arrive, and uses both the state information and the contents of the packet when assigning the packet to a flow. Stateful classification systems have the property that reordering the sequence of packets can result in changes to flows (i.e., the classification of a packet depends on the history of previous packets). In the sim-

---

†This chapter provides a brief introduction to classification; Chapter 9 expands the definition and gives details.

plest cases, only flow numbers are affected by reordering packets; in other cases, the set of packets in each flow changes.

Unlike demultiplexing, a stateful classification system does not need to use a global type system, and it does require the sender to participate. As we saw in the source address example above, flow numbers can be determined dynamically from items in the packets; the sender can remain completely unaware of the classification. Furthermore, a classifier can use packets from many sources to determine flows.

Finally, classification differs from demultiplexing because classification can span multiple layers of the stack. That is, a classifier takes a complete packet as input, examines header fields of various protocol layers, and produces a classification. We can summarize:

> *Packet classification assigns each packet to a* category *or* flow. *Classification differs from demultiplexing because classification allows stateful as well as stateless operation, does not require a global type system, does not require the sender to participate, allows flows to be created dynamically, and spans multiple layers.*

6.7.3 Optimized Packet Processing

Proponents of classification claim that its ability to bypass traditional layering gives classification potential for higher performance. Chapter 9 explores the topic further by considering both hardware and software implementations. For the present, it is sufficient to understand that classification introduces *layer compression* by examining fields from multiple layers in a single step. For example, consider an incoming TCP segment. A traditional demultiplexing system examines the frame type to determine that the frame contains a datagram, and then uses the protocol field in the datagram header to determine that the datagram contains a TCP segment. Classification compresses the steps by examining the frame type and IP protocol field at the same time. The point is:

> *Unlike a traditional layering scheme, where processing is restricted to a sequential tour through the layers, classification spans multiple layers in one step.*

6.7.4 Classification Languages

Classification is so fundamental to high-speed packet processing that hardware vendors have investigated special-purpose programming languages to describe classification. Known informally as *classification languages*, the languages are designed to allow engineers to write packet classification rules that are precise and unambiguous.

Furthermore, if a classification language is designed well, it is possible to build a translator analogous to a conventional compiler. Like a compiler, a classification translator will check the specification for syntactic correctness and then perform a translation. If a classification language is designed carefully, a compiler can produce code that is more effectively optimized than the code produced for a procedural language like C. Unlike a compiler, however, the translation will not produce code for a conventional processor. Instead, the output will either consist of code that runs on a special-purpose hardware device or a specification that can be used to build new hardware.

Several network processor vendors have investigated classification languages. For example, Agere Systems has designed a classification language named *Functional Programming Language* (*FPL*); Intel has adopted the *Network Classification Language* (*NCL*). Chapter 16 describes classification languages, and provides concrete illustrations of their use.

6.8 Queueing And Packet Discard

6.8.1 Basic Queueing

Packet processing systems are characterized as *store-and-forward* because such systems store packets in memory while the packets await processing. We use the term *queueing* to refer to the policies, data structures, and algorithms related to storing and selecting packets†.

In the simplest case, a queue is literally a *First-In-First-Out* (*FIFO*) data structure. That is, arriving packets are added to the queue at one end, and packets are removed from the other end. The data structure used for a FIFO must be arranged to make access efficient, to notify the receiver when packets are present, and to handle extreme cases such as an empty queue (i.e., no packets can be extracted) or a full queue (i.e., no packets can be added). However, a designer has only two important choices regarding FIFOs: where to place FIFOs and how large to make each queue.

When a FIFO is associated with input, the speed of the network, expected burst size, and available memory determine the size of the FIFO. However, variations arise among input FIFOs. For example, on a system that has multiple interfaces, a designer must choose whether to allocate a single, common FIFO for all interfaces or to allocate a separate FIFO for each interface. Each alternative requires an additional mechanism. The former means that input devices must contend for access to the shared FIFO, so a mechanism is needed to arbitrate access. The latter means that packet processing must choose a packet from among many FIFOs, so a mechanism is needed to make the selection.

---

†Some authors use the term *buffering* in place of *queueing*.

6.8.2 Priority Mechanisms

Queueing becomes more complex in network systems that implement *priorities*. A priority policy favors some packets over others; priorities may depend on packet contents, the sender's identity, or packet size. Priority processing is usually implemented with multiple queues — an incoming packet is placed in the queue appropriate to its priority. Output processing is arranged to give higher levels of service to higher priority queues.

A *queueing discipline* consists of an algorithm and a data structure used to select packets for processing according to a priority. Three queueing disciplines are popular among network system designers:

- Priority Queueing
- Weighted Round Robin
- Weighted Fair Queueing

In each case, the system maintains a set of queues, with a priority assigned to each queue. When it is ready to process a packet, the system invokes the queueing discipline to select a queue to service. The discipline only needs to choose a queue; the system always extracts the packet at the head of the queue.

Priority Queueing (*PQ*) is the most straightforward. Queues are serviced in strict priority order: the discipline chooses the packet at the head of the highest priority, nonempty queue. Although it is trivial to implement, strict priority queueing has the disadvantage of *starvation*: as long as packets remain in higher priority queues, a low priority queue receives no service at all.

Weighted Round Robin (*WRR*) attempts to avoid starvation. To do so, WRR sequences through the set of queues, servicing one queue and then going on to the next. To implement priorities, WRR selects more than one packet from a queue before moving to the next queue; the number of packets selected depends on the queue's priority and the average packet size. Of course, a given queue may not contain sufficient packets. Therefore, if a given queue becomes empty before the target number of packets has been selected, WRR moves to the next queue. Unlike priority queueing, WRR isolates queues from one another — excessive traffic in one queue will not deprive another queue of service. Despite its advantages, WRR does have a drawback that arises from its estimation of average packet size: if packet sizes vary from the estimated mean, a queue can receive more or less service than the ideal.

Weighted Fair Queueing (*WFQ*) avoids starvation, and attempts to allocate service more accurately than WRR. To do so, WFQ simulates a CPU timeslicing discipline known as *Generalized Processor Sharing* (*GPS*). GPS assigns a given CPU p/T of the available time, where p is the processor's priority and T is the sum of the priorities of all processors. The chief difference between CPU timeslicing with GPS and packet processing with WFQ arises because time is continuous and packets are discrete: a system must process an entire packet before moving on to another packet. Thus, WFQ cannot specify processing of partial packets. Instead, WFQ assigns each packet a *finish number* equal to the virtual time that the packet should be finished processing if partial packets could be handled according to the GPS algorithm. WFQ then selects the packet with the smallest finish number.

WFQ has both advantages and disadvantages. Like WRR, WFQ isolates queues to prevent starvation. In addition, WFQ operates without a priori knowledge of traffic or assumptions about packet size, and can be used to guarantee performance (i.e., limit the total delay a packet experiences). The chief disadvantage of WFQ lies in its use of resources: the algorithm stores state information and requires computation for each packet that arrives. As a result, WFQ does not scale well for large numbers of queues or high aggregate packet rates.

6.8.3 Packet Discard

Because a network system has finite buffer capacity, the system cannot accept an arbitrary number of packets. *Packet discard* refers to the policies and mechanisms used to handle the problem.

The most straightforward discard mechanism is known as *tail drop*: discard an arriving packet when memory is full and accept an incoming packet if memory is not full. The *Random Early Detection* (*RED*) technique uses a probabilistic approach that increases the probability of discard as the memory fills. RED works better than tail drop for TCP because it avoids global synchronization of retransmission†.

Other discard schemes exist that are intended to optimize performance in cases where a packet has been divided into smaller pieces (especially when using small cells). For example, when discarding an ATM cell, the *Early Packet Discard* (*EPD*) technique identifies other cells that are part of the same packet, and discards all pieces at the same time.

6.9 Scheduling And Timing

The term *scheduling* is used to characterize the coordination of concurrent and parallel activities in a network system. Scheduling is related to timer management, traffic shaping, and queueing. It is needed to coordinate packets arriving over multiple interfaces, and to ensure that multiple output interfaces are kept active. If the system implements layers of a protocol stack, scheduling may entail management of threads or processes that implement individual protocols or layers.

Scheduling is especially important in systems that implement priorities because a scheduling mechanism must ensure fairness. For example, in most network systems, some amount of processing and bandwidth is reserved for low-priority traffic. Rather than allowing high-priority traffic to completely block low-priority traffic, the scheduler in such systems must apportion resources.

---

†RED can also be used to *mark* packets for later discard. In particular, an *Explicit Congestion Notification* (*ECN*) bit has been proposed for IPv6.

6.10 Security: Authentication And Privacy

Network systems such as firewalls and secure connection terminators handle security protocols and mechanisms. The term *authentication* refers to security mechanisms that allow a receiver to validate the identity of a sender and the integrity of the data; the term *privacy* refers to mechanisms that ensure confidentiality.

Protocols for both authentication and privacy rely on a fundamental underlying technology: *encryption*. The relationship between encryption and privacy is obvious. A sender encrypts data before sending, and a receiver decrypts data to reproduce the original message. The encryption scheme transforms bits in the message in such a way that only the receiver can perform decryption. Thus, even if the message is intercepted, an outsider cannot understand the content.

Authentication mechanisms also rely on encryption. Information about the sender and the packet is encrypted and sent along with the packet. The receiver decrypts the additional information and uses it to validate both the sender's identity and that the information in the packet has not been changed in transit.

Although the amount of extra information carried in a packet to handle authentication is relatively small, the processing required for authentication or privacy can be substantial. There are two reasons. First, either mechanism requires a computation that covers large amounts of data (e.g., an entire packet). Second, cryptographic protocols require more intense computation than mechanisms such as checksums. Thus, network systems that implement security mechanisms often require additional processing power.

6.11 Traffic Measurement And Policing

Network systems such as traffic analyzers perform basic *traffic measurement*. To do so, the system obtains a copy of each frame that traverses the network, examines the frame contents, and updates counters and other statistical information. For example, traffic measurement may produce a count of packets, an average number of packets per unit time, an estimate of the current network utilization, the percentage of broadcast frames, the number of frames carrying IP messages, or the average duration of a TCP connection.

Traffic measurement often arises in the context of *service level agreements* (*SLAs*). A service level agreement is a legal contract between two entities in which one entity agrees to provide a network service for another to use. For example, an ISP may offer a corporation a connection to the Internet. The service agreement may specify the maximum and average data rates, or a maximum number of data bytes that can be transferred each month.

Each participant in an SLA can benefit from traffic measurement. A customer can benefit because the cost of service is related to the level of service needed. Thus, a customer can use traffic measurement to determine the category of service into which actual traffic falls; if a less expensive category of service suffices, the customer can renegotiate the contract. The supplier can use traffic measurement to monitor the customer's traffic. As the customer's traffic increases, the supplier can use the measurements to convince the customer to move to a more expensive category of service†.

The concept of *traffic policing* is closely related to traffic measurement and the more general concept of *traffic management*. As the name implies, traffic policing refers to active enforcement in which traffic that exceeds specified bounds is marked as a candidate for discard or explicitly dropped. Policing requires measurement because enforcement uses the results to determine whether traffic falls within specified parameters. Traffic policing often requires finer granularity measurements than measurements used for billing because policies are designed to control specific types of traffic. For example, a policer may need a separate measurement for each individual TCP connection or for traffic destined to a specific protocol port rather than an aggregate sum.

Suppliers use traffic policing to ensure that customers do not obtain more service than their contract allows. For example, consider a customer who pays for a data rate of 1 Mbps and then attempts to transmit traffic at 2 Mbps. The supplier can use a traffic policer to drop all packets from the customer that exceed 1 Mbps averaged over a short period of time.

One aspect of traffic policing is important in systems design: speed. Policing decisions must be made rapidly because a policing system needs to decide how to handle packets in real-time. That is, the policing system cannot spend a long time to reach a decision. The point is:

> *An operation lies on the critical path if the operation must be performed in real-time. Traffic policing operations lie on the critical path because the policer must finish before the disposition of the packet is known.*

6.12 Traffic Shaping

The term *traffic shaping* refers to the process of conforming traffic to stated statistical bounds. Shaping may be applied to aggregate traffic (e.g., all traffic from a given site or all traffic destined to a given TCP port) or to an individual flow (e.g., traffic on a specific TCP connection). Shaping is related to policing, but the two differ in both the overall goal and the mechanisms used. As we have seen, policing implies hard boundaries — when traffic exceeds the bound, traffic policing discards packets. Shaping generally implies soft boundaries. Thus, a traffic shaper attempts to change traffic until it meets the desired bounds, but does not usually discard packets.

Shapers are needed because packet switching tends to produce nonuniform traffic. The problem is well-known: instead of steady streams, packet switching systems tend to generate bursts of packets. From a network provider's point of view, traffic bursts make it difficult to assess capacity needs or to provide service guarantees. For example, suppose a provider agrees to offer service at an average transmission rate of N Mbps.

---

†Traffic measurement will become especially important if ISPs move from the current *flat rate billing* to a form of *measured service*.

The provider cannot assume a maximum rate of *N* Mbps because a transmission can include bursts. Thus, the customer may send a 1 second burst at a rate of *4N* Mbps followed by 3 seconds of silence. The problem becomes more severe if traffic from multiple customers is aggregated because all customers may choose to send a burst at the same time.

Even if an application injects traffic into a packet network at a steady rate, the traffic may not arrive at a steady rate. To see why, observe that unlike an isochronous network, a packet switching network tends to have random latency — a given packet may experience more or less delay than previous or subsequent packets. For example, transmission of a packet over a Local Area Network can be delayed if other stations contend for access simultaneously; transmission is not delayed if no other stations contend for access. As a result, packet networks exhibit high *jitter*, a measure of the variation in latency.

Unfortunately, when one packet is delayed, subsequent packets may also be affected. Thus, instead of arriving in a continuous stream, packets tend to arrive in *clumps* known as *packet trains*. Once a train forms, the packets in the train tend to remain together until they are delivered in a burst.

To reduce bursts, a packet shaper smooths packet rates. Because a shaper cannot ''speed up'' packets that have experienced long delays, the only way a shaper can smooth rates is to guarantee that packets are injected at a steady rate and that all packets experience equal delay. Thus, the overall effect of shaping is to ''slow down'' packets that have not experienced long delay.

One of the earliest mechanisms used for traffic shaping became known as *leaky bucket*, an analogy to a bucket of water with a small hole through which water drips. Figure 6.1 illustrates the leaky bucket concept.

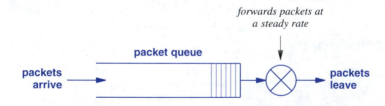

Figure 6.1 Illustration of a leaky bucket traffic shaper. As they arrive in bursts, packets are deposited in a queue. The leaky bucket mechanism then forwards one packet at a time.

The analogy with a water bucket is appropriate. Like the drips from a water bucket, packets leave the bucket at a steady rate. Furthermore, like water dripping from a bucket, the exact rate depends on the number of packets in the queue (which is analogous to the depth of the water in a leaking bucket). Finally, packets arrive at a leaky bucket shaper in bursts, which is analogous to someone adding water to the bucket one pitcherful at a time. Although the packet rate changes as the bucket fills, the output of a leaky bucket is much smoother than the input.

A leaky bucket tends to smooth bursts, but it does not guarantee a steady data rate. To see why, observe that although leaky bucket sends a fixed number of packets per second, the amount of data sent each second varies because packet size can vary. A modified shaping mechanism known as *token bucket* refines the leaky bucket algorithm to better control the data rate. Instead of forwarding a packet every N time units, a token bucket shaper forwards up to *K* octets of data every time unit. In essence, the shaper examines the size of the next packet in the queue to determine how long to hold the packet before forwarding. Interestingly, in cases where the token bucket has accumulated sufficient tokens for multiple packets, the output can consist of a burst.

6.13 Timer Management

Timer management is a fundamental part of packet processing. We have seen that timers are needed for activities such as traffic shaping. In addition, even protocols that seem trivial often require a system to time operations. For example, consider the address binding protocol ARP, which is among the most straightforward of the TCP/IP protocols. ARP uses timers for two reasons: retransmission and cache management. Retransmission is needed because Ethernet employs best-effort delivery, which means a packet can be lost. Before it declares a system is unreachable, ARP software retransmits a request. Thus, when ARP sends a request, it must start a timer. If a reply arrives before the timer expires, ARP cancels the timer; if the timer expires before the reply arrives, ARP retransmits the request. Finally, if the timer expires after a retransmission, ARP declares the target system unreachable. ARP also uses a timer to manage entries in an ARP cache. ARP software starts a timer when it adds an entry to the cache, and restarts the timer if the entry is updated or revalidated. If the timer expires, ARP removes the entry from the cache.

Layer 3 protocols also use timers. For example, although it is connectionless and does not retransmit lost datagrams, IP uses timers to handle reassembly. A timer is started when the first fragment arrives for a datagram. If all fragments arrive before the timer expires, the timer is cancelled; if the timer expires before all fragments arrive, the fragments are discarded and an error message is sent.

Because it must handle packet loss, a reliable transport protocol makes extensive use of timers. For example, TCP uses a timer to control segment retransmission. If an acknowledgement arrives before the timer expires, the sending TCP cancels the timer. Otherwise, the sender retransmits the segment. TCP also uses timers for connection setup and long-term maintenance of connection state.

The wide range of timeout values, concurrent protocol activities, and the dynamic nature of timeouts makes timer management complex. For example, IP can reassemble multiple datagrams concurrently, and must maintain a separate reassembly timer for each. TCP can send data over multiple connections concurrently, and must maintain a separate retransmission timer for each connection. Timeout granularity spans a large range, with some events requiring seconds (or even minutes) and others requiring accuracy to milliseconds or less. Furthermore, timers are created on demand and are often cancelled. We can summarize:

> *Timer management is complex because a system must accommodate multiple independent timers, timers span a wide range of granularities, and protocols create and cancel timers dynamically.*

6.14 Summary

Although protocol processing can be expressed as algorithms that specify steps to perform on a packet, each algorithm requires support from the underlying system. Thus, we seek to understand common themes that arise in many algorithms. To help focus attention on the basic functionality needed in networking systems, we have defined ten categories that provide a basis for all network systems. Each category corresponds to a fundamental aspect of protocol processing that arises in many situations.

The relevance of some categories is obvious. For example, many protocols include error detection mechanisms, and the use of timers is fundamental in most protocols. Other categories relate more to the system hardware architecture than to protocols. In particular, classification is a key idea in high-speed hardware design because parallel hardware can perform classification across many layers of protocols quickly.

FOR FURTHER STUDY

Standard texts in computer networking cover basic packet processing. RFC 1071 examines IP checksum computation. Keshav [1997] describes queueing disciplines and provides a mathematical analysis of each. Romanow and Floyd [1995] discusses early packet discard.

EXERCISES

6.1 Examine the algorithms in Chapter 5 and decide which of the functions in this chapter are needed for each.

6.2 For each category of functionality discussed in this chapter, decide whether the category is relevant to input, internal packet processing, and / or output.

6.3 Examine a set of protocols and determine the range of timeout values. Suppose a timer runs at a rate equal to one tenth the smallest timeout; determine how many bits are required to represent the largest timeout using that rate.

6.4 Is it possible to implement classification in software? In hardware? Explain.

6.5   What is the chief disadvantage of early packet discard? The chief advantage?

6.6   Read about the token bucket scheme for traffic shaping and develop an algorithm.

6.7   Build an implementation of token bucket traffic shaping and measure the performance on a set of simulated packets. What operations consume most of the CPU?

6.8   Read more about Weighted Fair Queueing. How does the algorithm use a virtual clock?

6.9   Examine protocols and protocol implementations. What additional functionality can you find that is not covered by the categories in this chapter?

Chapter Contents

7

Protocol Software On A Conventional Processor

7.1 Introduction

Earlier chapters give algorithms for common protocol processing tasks, and the previous chapter describes the basic functionality needed. This chapter considers the architecture of protocol software for a conventional processor. It discusses both concepts (e.g., processing priority) and mechanisms (e.g., software interrupts and threads). The chapter also considers the organization of software for layered systems. The next chapter considers special-purpose hardware architectures that have been created to optimize performance.

7.2 Implementation Of Packet Processing In An Application

Although seldom used in practice, it is possible to implement a network system as an application program. The application runs on a standard computer system and handles packets one at a time. The application waits until a packet arrives, and then processes the packet. As part of the processing, the application may generate a new packet or forward packet(s) that arrived previously.

Using an application program to implement protocol processing has several advantages. Building application software is straightforward because tools exist that make such software easy to write, compile, and debug. An application program runs in a private virtual address space, which simplifies allocation of data structures and buffers. An application only requires basic I/O support from the underlying system — the computer system does not need to provide networking facilities beyond the ability to send or receive packets. Because an application program is self-contained, all the code required to handle packets is bound together. Finally, many library routines are available to application programmers that offer convenient ways to access services and facilities such as the computer's file system.

7.3 Fast Packet Processing In Software

Despite the ease of programming, few network systems are implemented with an application program. The primary reason is lack of speed. Most network systems are optimized so they can process packets at *wire speed* (i.e., the speed at which they arrive from the network). Unfortunately, an application program introduces overhead that lowers the overall performance considerably. For example, because an application program runs in a private virtual address space outside the computer's operating system, data transfer between an I/O device and an application usually requires copying data from one address space to another. Only the operating system can instruct a NIC to perform chained I/O operations because only the operating system interacts with the NIC. Thus, even if an application allocates many packet buffers, the NIC will not be able to chain operations unless the operating system allocates its own packet buffers. Finally, virtual memory systems can add significant delay to memory access.

To achieve the highest speed, packet processing software must interact directly with network interface devices, control buffer allocation, optimize bus utilization, and avoid packet copying. Two high-speed implementations are possible:

- A stand-alone embedded system

- Software that is part of an operating system kernel

7.4 Embedded Systems

An *embedded system* consists of a programmable hardware device dedicated to a specific task. The hardware for a typical embedded system consists of a processor, software in *Read Only Memory* (*ROM*), *Random Access Memory* (*RAM*), and one or more I/O interfaces. The software has complete control of the processor. Furthermore, an embedded system is usually designed to restart without delay when it receives power, which means that the system can operate automatically without human interaction.

An embedded system implementation is ideal for a *stand-alone* network device such as a bridge that operates unattended. The software can be optimized to achieve the maximum performance of the hardware. In addition, because an embedded system restarts automatically and quickly when it receives power, a bridge that is designed as an embedded system can recover automatically after a power failure.

7.5 Operating System Implementations

In later chapters, we will see that embedded systems are used for higher speed. The lower-cost alternative to an embedded system consists of building packet processing software in a computer's operating system. We use the term *operating system kernel* to refer to the complex software system that manages resources such as memory and I/O devices. A kernel is loaded when a computer starts, and remains resident in the computer's memory at all times. Kernel software executes in a separate address space, has highest privilege, and can control all hardware resources. In particular, for each I/O device, the kernel contains device driver software that controls the device and performs all transfer operations.

Building packet processing software inside a kernel has several advantages over an embedded system. First, operating systems offer programming abstractions that raise the level of the code, making it easier to understand and debug complex protocol software. Second, an operating system offers facilities such as device drivers that allow a programmer to concentrate on protocol software without spending inordinate amounts of time on hardware details. Third, a designer can choose to divide protocol processing into two parts — packet processing that requires high speed can be placed in the operating system, and portions such as the human interface that do not require optimization can be placed in an application program. Fourth, protocol software in the operating system can be shared by all applications that run on the computer.

7.6 Software Interrupts And Priorities

One of the primary differences between an application program and code in the operating system kernel concerns *interrupt processing*. Knowledge of interrupts permeates the kernel; when writing code, the programmer must understand whether the processor is currently executing an interrupt and, if so, bound the time the computer executes with interrupts disabled.

Protocol software often relies on a *software interrupt* mechanism. Unlike a hardware interrupt, a software interrupt is caused by an executing piece of code rather than an I/O device. To generate a software interrupt, a program executes a special instruction. Once requested, a software interrupt is processed the same way as a hardware interrupt: the CPU executes a designated handler in the kernel and then returns to the point at which the interrupt occurred.

It may seem that requesting a software interrupt is equivalent to calling a subroutine — as soon as the request is made, the CPU executes the handler. However, software interrupts introduce processing priorities. A software interrupt has higher priority than an application program (i.e., a user process), but has lower priority than a hardware interrupt. That is, a software interrupt can only occur when no hardware interrupts are being serviced.

A software interrupt mechanism provides three levels of priority: application programs have the lowest priority; a software interrupt handler has medium priority; and hardware interrupt handlers have highest priority†. Furthermore, software interrupts can be used to change priorities. For example, an application program can prepare data and then schedule a software interrupt that causes the operating system to process the data. That is, the software interrupt causes control to pass to a handler in the operating system kernel; the handler code executes at higher priority than the application. Similarly, software interrupts can be used to schedule lower priority events. In particular, a hardware interrupt executes at highest priority. If the device driver schedules a software interrupt, the software interrupt will only execute after all hardware interrupts have been serviced.

Network systems designers reserve the highest priority for handling network interfaces, and use the medium level(s) of priority for protocol processing. To understand why, consider an IP router that forwards IP datagrams among multiple Ethernet interfaces. When a frame arrives, an interrupt invokes the device driver and further interrupts are temporarily disabled. The driver must service the device and return from the interrupt quickly, however, because keeping interrupts disabled denies service to other interfaces, which will eventually cause them to drop packets. In particular, a driver cannot keep interrupts disabled long enough to reassemble IP fragments or search a large routing table.

To ensure that hardware interrupts are not disabled for significant amounts of time, designers arrange for protocols like IP to execute at lower priority than hardware interrupts. Thus, whenever an interface receives a packet and signals an interrupt, the system executes the device driver. When no devices need service, IP protocol processing can continue. When IP finishes processing and neither hardware nor software interrupts are pending, the CPU executes application programs (i.e., applications have the lowest priority).

Although it is necessary to assign hardware interrupts the highest priority, a designer must be careful to avoid *livelock*, a condition that arises when the CPU does not have sufficient power to handle a higher interrupt load. Livelock occurs when devices interrupt frequently because the CPU does not process or forward packets while it handles interrupts. Eventually, if the interrupt load is high enough, the CPU becomes saturated, and does not have time to forward any packets. Throughout the rest of the discussion, we will assume that the CPU has sufficient power to avoid livelock.

Because a device driver cannot perform all protocol processing on an incoming packet, the driver must store the packet. To make a priority scheme work, the system must maintain a packet queue between each priority level. Figure 7.1 illustrates the concept.

In the figure, packets arrive via the network interfaces at the bottom of the diagram. A NIC uses DMA to place a packet in the next available memory buffer, and then generates a high-priority interrupt. The device driver extracts a frame from the memory buffer and (assuming the frame contains an IP datagram), enqueues the frame for TCP/IP software‡. Before returning from the interrupt, the driver requests a

---

†On some computers, software interrupts are further subdivided into multiple priority levels.

‡Although the figure shows only one packet queue at each boundary, multiple queues may be used if the protocol system assigns some packets higher priority than others.

software interrupt. As soon as all hardware interrupts have been serviced, the CPU honors the software interrupt and runs the TCP/IP code, which processes waiting packets. If the incoming packet is destined for an application on the local system, protocol software may enqueue the data for the application program.

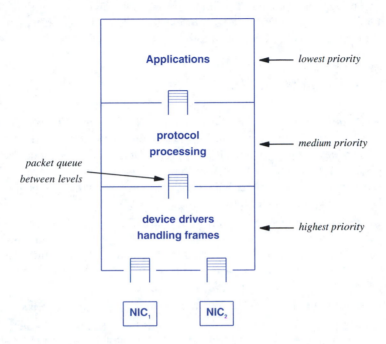

Figure 7.1 Conceptual processing priorities when using a software interrupt mechanism. A packet queue provides the interface between each priority level.

7.7 Multiple Priorities And Kernel Threads

Although a software interrupt mechanism allows a programmer to run protocol software at lower priority than hardware interrupts, the mechanism may not provide additional levels of processing priority†. Many operating systems offer an alternative mechanism that programmers can use to assign processing priority to pieces of software: concurrent *threads of execution*. Specifically, protocol software uses *kernel threads*.

A kernel thread is an independent unit of execution; multiple threads proceed *concurrently*. That is, each thread has an independent program counter and a private execution stack, and the execution of two threads appears to proceed at the same time. Because a kernel thread executes in the kernel address space, the thread has access to all kernel data structures and to I/O devices.

_____

†Some computers offer multiple levels of software interrupts, but the number of priorities may be fixed at 4 or 8.

The operating system defines a *scheduling policy* that uses assigned priorities to determine how to allocate CPU service among threads. If a high-priority thread is ready to execute, the CPU runs the thread. If a thread blocks for any reason (e.g., to wait for a packet to arrive), the CPU selects and runs the next highest priority thread. If no kernel thread remains ready to execute (i.e., all kernel threads are blocked), the CPU is given to an application program. The chief advantage of threads arises from the granularity they offer — to build software with K levels of processing priority, a programmer creates K threads and assigns a unique priority to each.

7.8 Thread Synchronization

Kernel threads share the address space, which allows a thread to examine or modify any data structures. Because each thread executes independently, a programmer must coordinate activities among all threads to prevent interference. Without coordination, for example, two threads may both attempt to place a packet on the queue for IP to process; concurrent modifications to a linked list can leave pointers corrupted or a thread can nullify the actions of another thread.

To allow a programmer to coordinate thread execution, an operating system that supports threads provides mechanisms for thread *synchronization*. There are two main uses of synchronization: *mutual exclusion* that guarantees only one thread modifies a data structure at any time, and *notification* that allows a thread to block until an event occurs (e.g., a packet arrives in a queue)†.

Protocol software that uses kernel threads relies on mutual exclusion for each shared item. For example, if one thread deposits packets on a list and another thread extracts packets from the list, both threads must use the mutual exclusion mechanism to guarantee that only one will modify the list at any time.

7.9 Software For Layered Protocols

How should a stack of layered protocols be organized into separate threads? Computer scientists and engineers have investigated several approaches; each has advantages in some circumstances:

- One thread for each layer

- One thread for each protocol

- Multiple threads for each protocol

- Threads for protocols plus timer management threads

- One thread for each packet

---

†Thread synchronization introduces the possibility of *priority inversion* in which a low-priority thread gains access to a resource, thereby blocking any high-priority thread that arrives later.

7.9.1 One Thread Per Layer

We said that hardware and software interrupts allowed a programmer to partition software into a three-level priority scheme. Threads allow a programmer to extend the scheme by devoting one thread to each of the layers in a stack. To ensure that basic I/O operations receive CPU service, lower-layer threads are assigned higher priority. The thread for layer 2 has highest priority, the thread for layer 3 has the next highest priority, and so on.

With one thread per layer, each thread must handle both incoming and outgoing packets. Figure 7.2 illustrates the organization.

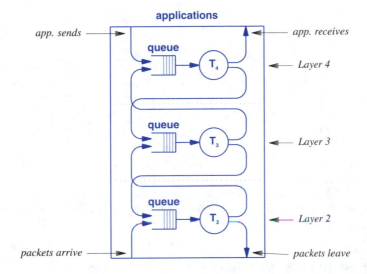

Figure 7.2 Illustration of a system using one thread per layer. Each layer has a queue for packets that arrive from the next higher layer or next lower layer.

How does a packet pass from a thread in one layer to a thread in another? As the figure indicates, each layer has a packet queue that can be accessed by threads in adjacent layers. Thus, if the IP thread operating in layer 3 processes a datagram that contains TCP, the IP thread enqueues the packet in the layer 4 queue.

In addition to enqueueing packets for service, threads at various layers must synchronize. If a thread processes all packets in its queue, the thread blocks. Thus, whenever a packet is enqueued for service at layer N, the software unblocks the thread at layer N. If the thread is already executing, unblocking has no effect; if the thread is blocked waiting for packets to process, the thread becomes ready to run.

7.9.2 One Thread Per Protocol

In addition to allowing a programmer to assign priority levels, threads offer a way to structure code to make it easier to create and modify. To impose structure, a programmer associates all the code related to a single processing task with a single thread. For example, layered protocol stacks include more than one protocol at each layer. Even if the protocols at a given layer have equal processing priority, a programmer can associate a thread with each protocol to make the code easier to understand.

At layer 4, for example, a programmer can use two independent threads to implement TCP and UDP; doing so keeps the code for the two protocols separate. Each protocol uses a separate queue for incoming packets. Figure 7.3 illustrates the organization.

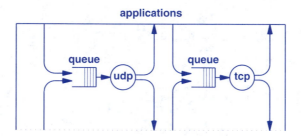

Figure 7.3 An illustration of one thread per protocol at layer 4. Software in adjacent layers must choose one of the two queues when depositing a packet.

7.9.3 Multiple Threads Per Protocol

Using one thread per protocol solves two conceptual problems: it allows a designer to assign lower layer protocols higher priority, and reduces the complexity of software by keeping the code for each protocol separate. A programmer can assign multiple threads to a single protocol to further reduce the complexity of the software. For example, many protocols specify asymmetric I/O handling — the processing of incoming and outgoing packets are almost unrelated. Furthermore, a designer may wish to give higher priority to packets in one direction. In such cases, the designer can use multiple threads to divide the work.

7.9.4 Separate Timer Management Threads

As we pointed out, timer management is fundamental in protocols. In addition to retransmission timers used by transport protocols, timers are needed for tasks such as reassembly and route update. Implementations that assign multiple threads to a protocol often use one of the threads to manage timed events. A thread works well for timers because the thread can delay until the next event should occur, allowing other threads to proceed. For example, Figure 7.4 shows how a timer thread can be used with TCP.

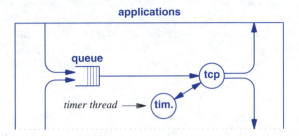

Figure 7.4 Illustration of a separate timer thread used with TCP. The timer manages events such as segment retransmission and maximum segment lifetime timeout, and notifies the TCP thread whenever an event must occur.

Because timer management occurs in protocols at many layers, an alternative design coalesces all timer management into one timer thread for software at any layer to use. The timer maintains a set of events. The code consists of an infinite loop that delays until an event should occur, notifies whichever thread requested the event, and then continues by delaying until the next event.

In practice, one timer thread may not be sufficient for all purposes. To understand why, observe that protocols specify timeouts in a range from microseconds to minutes. Large timeouts that are associated with cleaning up state information usually have lower priority than microsecond timeouts. Furthermore, timer mechanisms generate overhead that depends on the timeout granularity. As a result, it may be better to have at least two timer threads, one to manage large granularity timeouts (e.g., seconds) and another to manage fine granularity timeouts (e.g., microseconds).

7.9.5 One Thread Per Packet

Despite their advantages, threads do introduce additional overhead in a layered system. To understand why, consider the common case of a packet arriving destined for an application. Once the interrupt has been serviced and the packet has been placed on a layer 2 queue, the layer 2 thread is awakened. The layer 2 thread demultiplexes the frame, moves the packet to the appropriate layer 3 queue, and awakens the layer 3 thread. The layer 2 thread blocks, which allows the layer 3 thread to run. The situation continues at each layer — once the packet has been moved to the queue in the next highest layer, the thread at that layer is awakened.

When a thread blocks, the operating system performs a *context switching* operation to move the CPU from one thread to another. As part of the context switch, the system performs a *thread scheduling* operation to select a highest priority thread that is ready to execute. From a programmer's point of view, scheduling and context switching are considered overhead because they use the CPU but do not execute code from the program. In the case of a packet that passes through all layers of a stack, the operating system must switch context at least once for each layer. More than one context switch per layer can occur if the software uses multiple threads for a given protocol (e.g., one thread reads the packet and another thread sends an acknowledgment).

Researchers have devised a scheme that reduces context switching overhead for layered protocols: assign one thread per packet. The design assumes many threads are available, that thread assignment does not incur much overhead, and that each packet tends to pass through layers of the stack without being divided (e.g., fragmented). When a packet arrives, the system assigns a thread. As the packet progresses up the stack, the same thread executes code in each layer. Thus, in the case where the packet passes through the entire stack, no context switch is needed.

7.10 Asynchronous Vs. Synchronous Programming

Software interrupts and threads lead to different styles of programming. Structuring a program around interrupts tends to make the program *asynchronous*. That is, the programmer views input as a series of events that can occur at any time (e.g., a packet arrives, or a timer expires). The code is structured as a set of modules that each handle one of the possible events. More important, the CPU can be preempted to handle a higher-priority event at any time.

Structuring a program around the thread abstraction tends to make the program *synchronous*. That is, the programmer views a set of threads as each acting independently. A thread handles one item at a time. For example, if the first item on the queue consists of an incoming packet, the thread will process the header and send the packet to the next layer. If the next item on the queue is a message that specifies a timer has expired, the thread will take appropriate action. A thread completes one action before starting another.

Synchronous code is usually easier to write and understand than asynchronous code. As a consequence, a program devised using a synchronous abstraction reduces the accidental complexity and is therefore less prone to errors†. However, because it does not match the underlying hardware well, a synchronous program often incurs more overhead. We can summarize:

> *The kernel thread abstraction, which can be used in a variety of ways, leads to synchronous programs. The software is easier to write, but the resulting system may be less efficient than asynchronous systems in which the software more closely matches the hardware.*

---

†Brooks [1995] describes *accidental complexity* as complexity that is caused by the programming environment as opposed to complexity that is inherent in the problem being solved.

7.11 Summary

Although it is possible to implement protocol processing in an application program, doing so increases overhead. Because they are designed for high speed, most network systems either use a stand-alone embedded system or place protocol processing in the operating system kernel.

To guarantee that packets will continue to be forwarded, protocol software must execute at higher priority than application programs. To guarantee that hardware devices receive service, however, protocol software must execute at lower priority than hardware interrupts. Two mechanisms are available to control processing priority: a software interrupt mechanism and a kernel thread abstraction. Threads can incur more overhead than software interrupts, but offer the programmer a synchronous paradigm and more options for structuring protocol software. A programmer can choose one thread per layer, one thread per protocol, multiple threads per protocol, any of the above with separate timer threads, or one thread per packet.

FOR FURTHER STUDY

Clark [1985] describes protocol implementation using an upcall mechanism. Druschel [1996] considers high-speed implementation in an operating system, and Birrel [1989] explains programming using threads.

EXERCISES

7.1   Build an application that echoes packets, and measure the maximum rate at which the application can process packets.

7.2   What commonplace office device runs as an embedded network system?

7.3   Read the vendor's manuals for common processors to determine how many levels of software interrupts are available.

7.4   Given a computer with four levels of software interrupts, how would you partition the protocols from a TCP/IP stack into four priority classes? Explain why.

7.5   Read about the kernel thread synchronization primitive available in your local operating system, and devise pseudo code that shows which synchronization primitives are needed when a thread at layer N enqueues a packet for a thread at layer $N+1$.

7.6   You are assigned to structure IP software using kernel threads. How many threads do you use, and what does each do?

7.7   Argue for or against: when using kernel threads to implement a layered stack, an additional (i.e., separate) thread should be used to handle errors at each layer.

7.8 Argue for or against: although Figure 7.2 shows a thread at layer 2, it would be better to handle layer 2 using interrupts; protocols like ARP do not require a separate thread.

7.9 Write and compare pseudo code for an asynchronous and synchronous version of a reliable protocol that includes timeout and retransmission.

Chapter Contents

8

Hardware Architectures For Protocol Processing

8.1 Introduction

The previous chapter considers the architecture of software used to process protocols. The chapter assumes software is being designed for a conventional computer, and examines the relationship between processing priority and layered protocols. In addition, the chapter discusses two abstractions, software interrupts and kernel threads, and shows how they can be used to organize protocol software.

This chapter begins a discussion of hardware architectures for protocol processing. It discusses packet rates, and shows why a conventional computer is insufficient for protocol processing. The chapter describes hardware architectures, assesses the advantages and disadvantages of each, and describes ways that the facilities have been used. The next chapters expand the discussion by focusing on classification and switching fabrics; later chapters extend the discussion to network processors.

8.2 Network Systems Architecture

Like early computer designers, network systems builders are experimenting with functional units and interconnection strategies. An excess of exuberance and a lack of experience has produced a wide variety of approaches and architectures. As a result, packet processing architectures do not fall into a clean taxonomy, nor is there general consensus about a best architecture for networking hardware. However, we can identify basic approaches and see how each can be used.

8.3 The Traditional Software Router

The first network systems consisted of packet switches. Experimentation with packet switching began in the 1960s and 1970s at the same time that companies such as Digital Equipment Corporation introduced the minicomputer as a smaller, less powerful, and less expensive alternative to a mainframe. Minicomputer hardware was widely adopted, and offered several advantages for use as a packet switch. Because early networks operated at low speed, a minicomputer CPU was sufficient to handle the task of switching packets. The minicomputer's smaller physical size allowed packet switches to be added to existing machine rooms; its less complex I/O interface simplified building network interfaces; and its lower cost made it economically feasible to build a network with multiple packet switches.

By the time Internet technologies emerged, inexpensive small computers were available commercially, and engineers understood how they could be used in network systems. CPU speeds, which increased each year, had become fast enough to handle tasks such as IP forwarding. That is, a small computer's CPU had sufficient power to perform an IP route table lookup before another packet arrived. Consequently, the first commercial IP routers used conventional computer hardware; low-end routers still do.

To characterize an IP router that uses conventional hardware, engineers say that the router has a *general-purpose processor* (GPP), and refer to the entire system as a *software router*. The terminology is important because it highlights a fundamental concept:

> *It is possible to build a network system by adding special-purpose software to general-purpose hardware.*

One can imagine the hardware of a traditional software-based network system to consist of a CPU surrounded by network interface cards. Figure 8.1 illustrates the architecture, and shows the functionality associated with each piece.

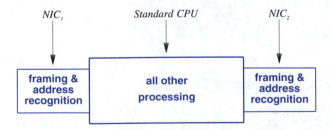

Figure 8.1 The hardware architecture used with a software-based network system. The CPU handles all protocol processing tasks except for framing and onboard address recognition.

8.4 Aggregate Data Rate

The chief advantage of a software router is low cost; the chief disadvantage is low processing speed. Processing speed is an issue for two reasons. First, because a router must be able to handle packets as they arrive from a given network, the processing speed determines the maximum data rate of a network that can be attached to the router. Second, because a router must be able to handle packets arriving from multiple networks, the processing speed limits the possible topologies with which the router can be used.

As an example of the two limitations, consider a software router with two Ethernet interfaces. Assume the router's CPU is operating near capacity. On one hand, the limited processor speed can make it impossible to upgrade one of the Ethernets to a higher data rate (e.g., from 100 Mbps to 1 Gbps). On the other hand, limited processor speed can make it infeasible to add additional Ethernet interfaces.

We use the term *aggregate data rate* to refer to the total rate at which data can arrive or leave a network system. Sometimes, we will only be concerned with the aggregate flow in a single direction. For example, when considering route table lookup in an IP router, we only need to consider packets that arrive. Thus, the aggregate data rate is the sum of the data rates on all interfaces. Similarly, for hardware that uses simplex transmission, we will only consider the data rate in one direction. For hardware that operates in full duplex mode or for an operation that has equal cost for input or output, we will consider the data rate in both directions. The maximum aggregate data rate of a system is especially important because it determines the possible utility of the system. For example, a router that has an aggregate data rate of 400 Mbps can handle up to four networks that run at 100 Mbps. We can summarize:

> *The aggregate data rate is defined to be the sum of the rates at which traffic enters or leaves a system. The maximum aggregate data rate of a system is important because it limits the type and number of network connections the system can handle.*

8.5 Aggregate Packet Rate

Although it is easy to calculate and provides a measure of system capability, aggregate data rate can be misleading. To understand why, remember that although packets vary in size, many protocol processing operations require a fixed amount of CPU time per packet. For example, the time required for IP routing table lookup does not depend on the datagram size. Thus, we observe that for many tasks, the *per-packet overhead* is more significant than the per-bit overhead. The point is:

For protocol processing tasks that have a fixed cost per packet, the number of packets processed is more important than the data aggregate rate.

How many packets arrive per second over a network? The answer depends on the network's throughput rate and the size of the packets. For example, Figure 8.2 lists the packet rate of a single network for various technologies. The rate is measured in *Kilo packets per second* (*Kpps*), where one Kpps equals one thousand packets per second.

Technology	Network Data Rate In Gbps	Packet Rate For Small Packets In Kpps	Packet Rate For Large Packets In Kpps
10Base-T	0.010	19.5	0.8
100Base-T	0.100	195.3	8.2
OC-3	0.156	303.8	12.8
OC-12	0.622	1,214.8	51.2
1000Base-T	1.000	1,953.1	82.3
OC-48	2.488	4,860.0	204.9
OC-192	9.953	19,440.0	819.6
OC-768	39.813	77,760.0	3,278.4

Figure 8.2 Approximate packet rates in thousands of packets per second for a single network using various technologies. Rates assume a small packet size of 64 octets and a large packet size of 1518 octets, but do not account for framing overhead, interpacket gaps, or preambles†.

As the figure shows, packet rates vary several orders of magnitude between the slowest to fastest technologies. At the low end, a single 10Base-T Ethernet delivers large frames at less than 1000 per second. Near the high end, a single OC-192 line delivers small packets at a rate of approximately 20 million per second. Because a network system usually connects to multiple networks, the system's aggregate packet rate, equal to the sum of the packet rates for individual networks, can be much higher than the values listed in the figure.

The bar chart in Figure 8.3, graphically illustrates the surprising range of packet rates. The figure shows the rates for both large and small packets for each of the technologies.

---

†Framing and interpacket gaps are more significant on small packets; an exercise suggests recomputing values in the figure to account for such details.

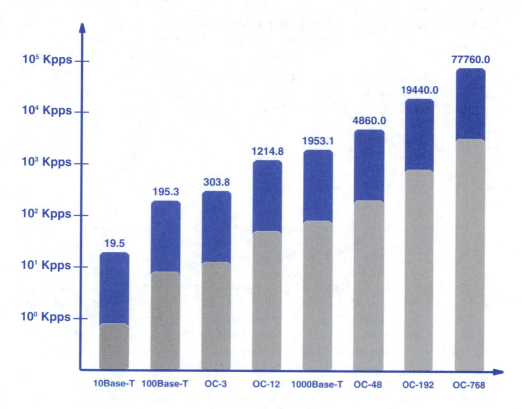

Figure 8.3 Illustration of packet rates on log scale for technologies listed in Figure 8.2. The gray portions show the rates for large packets.

8.6 Packet Rate And Software Router Feasibility

How many packets per second can a software system handle? Anecdotal evidence suggests that a typical PC running the Linux kernel can route up to 50,000 IP datagrams per second if each requires minimal processing, but the number drops to around 8,000 packets per second if each must be processed by firewall code. The exact rate depends on the CPU speed, bus bandwidth, and memory latency as well as the amount of processing. To achieve an aggregate packet rate of N packets per second, the CPU cannot spend more than $1/N$ seconds processing each packet. Figure 8.4 summarizes the maximum time a CPU can spend per packet for each of the technologies listed in Figure 8.2.

Technology	Time per packet for small packets (in μs)	Time per packet for large packets (in μs)
10Base-T	51.20	1,214.40
100Base-T	5.12	121.44
OC-3	3.29	78.09
OC-12	0.82	19.52
1000Base-T	0.51	12.14
OC-48	0.21	4.88
OC-192	0.05	1.22
OC-768	0.01	0.31

Figure 8.4 Maximum per-packet processing time in microseconds of small and large packets for various technologies.

In reality, the time to process a packet includes the time required to service an interrupt and move the packet into memory as well as the time to process the packet. Because we seek an approximation, we will ignore interrupt service times and focus on protocol processing by the CPU. The amount of processing required depends on the packet contents (i.e., the protocols used). Processing times vary widely because a protocol such as ARP requires significantly less computation than a protocol such as TCP, which is higher in the stack. As an upper bound, protocol processing on a typical CPU requires fewer than 10,000 instructions per packet; many packets require fewer than 5,000 instructions.

To understand when a software router is feasible, consider a pair of 10Base-T Ethernets, each delivering a maximum of 19,500 packets per second. The CPU has only 25.60 μs to process each packet. To handle the load from two 10 Mbps Ethernets, a CPU must be able to execute between 5,000 and 10,000 instructions in 25.60 μs. That is, the CPU must perform between 195 and 390 *million instructions per second* (*Mips*). Many commercial CPUs are available that execute at rates higher than 400 Mips. Therefore, we conclude that it is feasible for a software router to handle at least two 10 Mbps Ethernets.

At the other extreme, a software router is unable to handle a 10 Gbps network. To see why, consider an OC-192 line. At the maximum packet rate, the line will deliver approximately 20 packets every microsecond. To perform 10,000 instructions twenty times every microsecond, a CPU must execute at a rate of 2×10^{11} instructions per second†. Even if we consider a device such as a layer 2 switch that only needs a few hundred instructions per packet, it should be obvious that the packet rate exceeds the processing power of a single CPU. The point is:

---

†Engineers have developed a rule of thumb that says a CPU needs approximately 1 GHz of clock speed for each 1 Gbps of network data rate.

> *Software running on a general-purpose processor is an insufficient architecture to handle high-speed networks because the aggregate packet rate exceeds the capabilities of current CPUs.*

8.7 Overcoming The Single CPU Bottleneck

Software designers have invented special algorithms and data structures that optimize performance of network systems. For example, a router must decrement the *time-to-live* field in an IP header, and then recompute the header checksum. Instead of performing the computation from scratch, a high-speed software router performs an incremental update — it begins with the old checksum, subtracts the original value of the *time-to-live* field, and adds the value of the new *time-to-live* field.

Higher performance software-based network systems require changes to the hardware. Engineers have used a variety of hardware mechanisms, techniques, and architectures to optimize performance, including:

- Fine-grain parallelism (instruction-level parallelism)
- Symmetric coarse-grain parallelism (symmetric multiprocessors)
- Asymmetric coarse-grain parallelism
- Special-purpose coprocessors (ASICs)
- NICs with onboard processing
- Smart NICs with onboard stacks
- Cell switching
- Data pipelines

The next sections discuss each of the approaches. We will see that some optimizations are generic (i.e., they work well with most packet processing systems); others apply only to specific network systems. Some improve performance uniformly across many types of network systems; others only improve performance in specific cases. Interestingly, an optimization that improves the performance of one network system may lower performance of another. Similarly, an invention that improves performance for certain types of packets may lower performance for other types.

Of course, an ideal solution is generic, and produces uniform improvements across all possible network systems and all possible inputs. In practice, however, no solution is perfect — each represents a tradeoff among efficiency, generality, and cost. Later chapters will examine how the techniques are used in network processors, and will point out that cost can override other aspects.

8.8 Fine-Grain Parallelism

In theory, the idea of parallelism seems straightforward: to overcome the limitation of a single CPU, arrange for multiple CPUs to work together on the problem. A system that can perform operations in parallel should be able to handle a much higher packet rate than a system that performs one operation at a time.

Parallelism is usually employed for computationally intensive tasks. For example, the most expensive protocol processing operations involve computation over a large volume of data (e.g., a checksum computation over an entire packet). Engineers building graphics systems discovered that they could optimize performance with *fine-grain parallelism*, which is also known as *instruction-level parallelism*. In essence, a parallel CPU has special instructions that apply to an array of values instead of a single value. For example, some CPUs contain parallel instructions that operate on eight consecutive locations in memory at the same time.

Although it has been used in a few network systems, experimental and simulation studies have shown that instruction-level parallelism does not achieve significantly higher performance. There are several reasons. First, few packet processing functions are amenable to fine-grain optimization. In particular, because the processing performed on a packet depends on the contents, a system cannot easily execute a single sequence of instructions on N packets. Second, a program must spend time setting up the parallel instruction; for small packet sizes, the setup cost is a significant fraction of the overall cost. Third, fine-grain parallelism only improves CPU performance; in many cases the bottleneck is I/O. Fourth, fine-grain parallelism is expensive because it requires modifications to the CPU.

8.9 Symmetric Coarse-Grain Parallelism

An alternative to fine-grain parallelism involves the use of *symmetric multiprocessors* that offer a set of *N* identical CPUs. Because each CPU executes independently, a symmetric multiprocessor can operate on multiple packets or can handle multiple protocols simultaneously. For example, while one CPU executes code that reassembles IP fragments, another can execute code to send a TCP segment.

Symmetric multiprocessors were among the earliest optimizations for software-based network systems because they offered two primary advantages. First, network systems designers did not need to invent new symmetric multiprocessor hardware because general-purpose systems were available commercially. Second, vendors such as Sequent Corporation (now IBM) had ported a conventional Unix operating system to their multiprocessor hardware. As a result, programmers working on multiprocessor network systems found much of the operating system familiar — the programmer only needed to learn about the special features used to control and schedule multiple processors.

One might expect that N processors could handle approximately N times as many packets per second as a single processor. In practice, however, performance of symmetric multiprocessor network systems has been disappointing. Processing capability does not scale linearly as the number of processors increases; there are several reasons. First, most multiprocessor systems use a shared memory paradigm where all processors share a kernel address space. Shared memory allows a packet to be passed from one processor to another quickly, but each memory access introduces contention because only one processor can access memory at a time. Second, packet processing software must coordinate access to data structures such as packet queues. Although necessary, coordination reduces the overall processing rate. For example, consider a set of processors that repeatedly extract a packet from an input queue and then handle the packet. The processors must synchronize to ensure that only one of them modifies the queue at any time. In the worst case, $N-1$ processors can delay waiting for one processor to access the queue. Third, although it provides a way to increase the processing capability, a multiprocessor architecture does not automatically increase the I/O bandwidth.

8.10 Asymmetric Coarse-Grain Parallelism

A form of parallelism known as *asymmetric multiprocessing* uses multiple, heterogeneous processors that can operate simultaneously. The advantage of asymmetry arises from the ability to specialize: each processor in an asymmetric system can be optimized for a specific task. For example, one processor might have instructions optimized to handle layer 3 functions (e.g., IP fragmentation), and another might have instructions optimized to handle layer 2 functions (e.g., frame forwarding).

An asymmetric multiprocessor has four drawbacks. First, in addition to specialized instructions optimized for a specific task, the processor needs general-purpose instructions. Second, an asymmetric system is more difficult to program than a symmetric system. Third, a processor optimized for a specific task or a specific protocol may not perform well when used with other tasks or other protocols. Fourth, asymmetric multiprocessors are expensive to design and build.

8.11 Special-Purpose Coprocessors

How can we combine the advantages of a general-purpose processor with the advantages of an asymmetric system? The answer lies in an architecture that contains a general-purpose CPU plus one or more special-purpose processors that are known as *coprocessors*. Each coprocessor is designed to perform a specific function; all coprocessors function under control of the CPU.

The chief advantage of using coprocessors lies in the freedom it gives a designer. Although a coprocessor can be a powerful computational engine, it can also be a small logic circuit that performs one operation. Thus, coprocessors are unlike asymmetric multiprocessors in which each processor must operate independently. The coprocessor does not need general-purpose instructions, and does not need a fetch-execute cycle. For example, consider a coprocessor designed to verify an IP header checksum. The CPU passes two values to the coprocessor (the address of the datagram in memory and the length of the header), and the coprocessor returns a value to indicate whether the checksum is valid. As another example, consider a coprocessor that performs byte swapping on integer fields in an IP header. We can summarize:

> *A coprocessor is a piece of hardware that operates under control of the CPU. A coprocessor need not be sophisticated; the coprocessor only needs to perform one specific task.*

If a coprocessor can compute a result in less time than the general-purpose CPU, overall throughput will be increased. However, more substantial increases are possible if coprocessors function simultaneously. That is, the hardware must allow the CPU to start a second coprocessor before the first coprocessor finishes. Asynchrony allows a programmer to work on multiple packets at the same time or to perform multiple, independent operations on one packet simultaneously.

What additional facilities should be added to augment a conventional CPU for packet processing? Obviously, we should target operations that consume the most CPU time. Thus, we choose operations that each require extensive computation or operations that are performed most frequently†. The observation leads to a fundamental principle in network systems design:

> *To optimize computation, move operations that account for the most CPU time from software into hardware.*

8.12 ASIC Coprocessor Implementation

The term *Application Specific Integrated Circuit* (*ASIC*) refers to an integrated circuit (*IC*) that has been custom-designed for a specific need. ASIC production technology is commercially available, and it is possible to hire engineers who can design an ASIC chip. The availability of ASIC technology is especially pertinent to coprocessors because a company can design and build a coprocessor that meets a specific need.

Because ASIC hardware is expensive to design and build, engineers strive to make each chip as general as possible. Thus, instead of designing a coprocessor that understands one packet format or one protocol, designers attempt to make the coprocessor general enough to work with many protocols. In later chapters, we will discuss network processors, an alternative to ASIC hardware that offers more generality and makes systems less expensive to design.

---

†The idea is attributed to computer architect Gene Amdahl. His principle, which is known as *Amdahl's law*, states that the performance improvement from faster hardware technology is limited to the fraction of time the faster technology can be used.

8.13 NICs With Onboard Processing

The hardware mechanisms in previous sections are each intended to improve computational performance. However, network systems designers have discovered that computation is not the only bottleneck. Many protocol processing tasks are I/O bound. Furthermore, the movement of packets through a system is often more important than the processing applied to a packet. The point is:

> *Because many protocol processing tasks are inherently I/O bound, high-speed network systems must optimize the flow of data through the system.*

Chapter 4 discusses techniques used to improve the speed of traditional I/O interfaces: DMA, onboard buffering, and operation chaining. The chapter also discusses the concept of onboard address recognition and filtering. Even the earliest network interface cards needed such optimizations because CPU clock rates were relatively slow compared to network data rates.

As network speeds increase, designers need ways to accommodate higher packet rates. An obvious optimization consists of moving processing onto the NIC. For example, a NIC can contain additional hardware that allows the NIC to validate an IP checksum or extract fields from the IP header. A NIC can also perform functions such as packet encryption or compression.

The chief advantage of onboard processing lies in reduced CPU load. More important, instead of handling the aggregate packet rate, a NIC only needs to handle packets from a single interface. Thus, the hardware onboard a smart NIC does not need to process packets as rapidly as the CPU in a traditional software-based system. Figure 8.5 illustrates the resulting architecture, and shows the division of functionality.

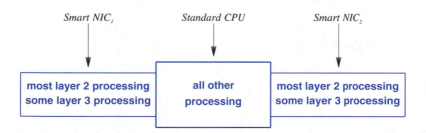

Figure 8.5 Hardware architecture of an optimized system with smart network interface cards. Because each NIC performs more processing, the CPU load is reduced.

What components are used to create smart NICs? Two implementations have become popular:

- ASIC hardware

- Embedded RISC hardware

The ASIC hardware approach uses custom hardware: a company designs a set of special-purpose chips that work together, and engineers incorporate the chips into a NIC. Each ASIC chip performs one protocol processing task.

The RISC approach replaces custom hardware with a standard RISC processor. In addition to a RISC processor, the smart NIC contains an onboard RAM used for packet buffering and an onboard ROM that contains protocol processing software. A RISC processor costs less than an ASIC to design, and makes systems easier to change.

8.14 Smart NICs With Onboard Stacks

How far can we extend the paradigm of onboard processing? A RISC processor makes it possible to add more protocol processing functionality to a NIC. Can we place an entire protocol stack on a NIC? More important, if we do so, does it eliminate the CPU bottleneck and allow us to build systems that scale to handle an arbitrary number of networks? Engineers have indeed developed NICs that handle most of layer 3. As a practical matter, however, constraints arise that limit the scalability of a system that uses smart NICs in a conventional computer. In particular, because a typical network system must forward packets from one network to another, the data path between NICs becomes a bottleneck†. In a traditional computer system, the data path includes the bus to which the NIC attaches and the memory. Chapter 10 continues the discussion of data paths by considering nontraditional architectures that have been developed to provide higher bandwidth interconnections among smart I/O boards.

8.15 Cells And Connection-Oriented Addressing

Some groups have taken a different approach to high-speed networking: instead of designing new hardware to handle existing protocols, they propose redesigning protocols to accommodate high-speed hardware and new applications. Two aspects of existing protocols have been identified as targets for change: variable-size packets and absolute addresses.

Variable-Size Packets. Although popular protocols such as Ethernet or IP specify a maximum packet size, the protocols allow a sender to choose a size up to the maximum. Variable-size packets make hardware design more difficult, and are not well-suited to applications like voice that require bounded latency. A system cannot make

---

†We assume that each NIC connects to a single network. Vendors use the term *blade* to refer to a single physical card. Although it is possible for a blade to contain multiple network interfaces, such designs are usually restricted to networks with low data rates (e.g., a small set of 100Base-T Ethernets), and do not usually provide onboard interconnections among interfaces.

guarantees about latency because the time required to transmit a packet depends on the length.

Absolute, Connectionless Addressing. The two most popular networking technologies, Ethernet and IP, are both connectionless. Connectionless systems use *absolute addressing* in the sense that each address is globally known (i.e., the destination address in a packet does not change as the packet traverses the network). Because they are globally unique, absolute addresses are larger than relative addresses. The chief disadvantage of absolute addressing arises from forwarding overhead: a network system must maintain a large routing table, and must search the table for each packet. For example, an IP routing table in the core of the Internet includes over 85,000 entries.

One technology designed to eliminate both of the difficulties described above is *cell switching*. To eliminate problems with variable-size packets, cell switching systems require all packets to be the same size. To avoid absolute addresses, cell switching systems use a *connection-oriented* paradigm that allows *relative addressing*; in place of an address, each cell contains a *label* that changes at each hop (i.e., a label is only valid across one link).

As an example, consider the *Asynchronous Transfer Mode (ATM)* technology. ATM uses a fixed cell size of 53 octets and relative addressing. An ATM network consists of one or more switches that are interconnected, and the label on a cell changes at each switch. As a result, instead of remaining globally unique and absolute, each label is relative to a given link. Of course, to ensure sensible behavior, switches must be configured to rewrite labels in a meaningful way.

Although it allows designers to build faster hardware, cell switching is not merely a hardware architecture used to build network systems. Instead, cell switching is an alternative approach: it requires new protocols and new packet formats. Most important, relative addressing dictates a connection-oriented paradigm. We can summarize:

> *Unlike hardware architectures described previously, cell switching is not merely used to implement packet processing systems for existing protocols. Instead, cell switching requires new protocols, new packet formats, and a connection-oriented paradigm.*

8.16 Data Pipelines

The term *data pipeline* refers to a hardware architecture in which a packet flows through a series of hardware *stages*, each of which performs one operation. For example, we can imagine IP processing arranged as a series of stages. An arriving datagram enters the first stage, which verifies the header checksum. The second stage decrements the time-to-live field, and the third processes options. When the datagram reaches the fourth stage, the hardware looks up the destination address in the routing table. Later stages perform operations such as fragmentation, computing the outgoing checksum, and encapsulating the datagram for transmission.

Using a pipeline architecture offers two main advantages. First, because each stage performs one operation, the hardware for a stage is much less complex and runs faster than hardware that handles an entire protocol. Second, because each stage is implemented by independent hardware, all stages can operate at the same time. That is, while stage k operates on one packet, stage $k-1$ can operate on the next packet. Of course, parallel execution of all stages only occurs when packets arrive in rapid succession — a pipeline remains full only if a new packet is ready to enter each time a packet leaves.

Although it may be tempting to think of a data pipeline as an assembly line, the analogy is incorrect. Unlike an assembly line, packets do not necessarily move through a data pipeline in lock step. First, because the time required to handle packets can vary, pipeline architectures usually employ packet queues between stages. Thus, a given stage can place a packet in an output queue and begin working on the next packet, even if the succeeding stage remains busy. Second, the number of packets emitted by a given stage is not always identical to the number of packets received. Any stage can drop packets that contain errors. Furthermore, a stage that performs fragmentation or segmentation divides a single input packet into multiple output packets, and a stage that performs reassembly collects multiple input packets. When the final piece of data arrives, the stage reassembles the input packets and passes the reassembled packet on to the next stage. Figure 8.6 illustrates the concept of a data pipeline with packet buffers between stages.

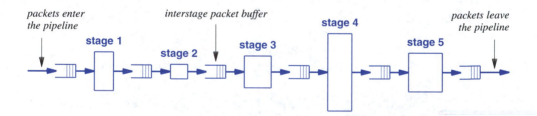

Figure 8.6 Illustration of a 5-stage data pipeline. The size and complexity of hardware varies among stages because the processing performed by a given stage differs from the processing performed by other stages.

As the figure shows, a data pipeline can contain heterogeneous stages. A stage that performs an operation such as IP reassembly, for example, contains more sophisticated hardware than a stage that verifies an IP header checksum.

8.17 Summary

A variety of hardware architectures, mechanisms, and techniques have been used with network systems. The aggregate data rate, aggregate packet rate, and packet processing to be performed determine the hardware needed. Although a traditional software-based system that uses a single CPU can handle the aggregate packet rate created by a few low-speed networks, such an architecture is insufficient for higher-speed networks. Higher speeds require architectures that include: multiprocessor systems, ASIC coprocessors, smart NICs with onboard processing, cell switching, and/or data pipelines.

FOR FURTHER STUDY

Koufopavlou, et. al. [1994] describes gigabit router architecture, and Keshav and Sharma [1998] discusses trends in router design. Partridge [1998] describes facilities needed in a 50 Gbps router. Hennesey and Paterson [2002] discusses computer architecture in general and cites Amdahl's law.

EXERCISES

8.1   Connect a Linux system to a traffic generator, and measure the maximum number of packets per second the system can handle.

8.2   What aggregate packet rate does a processor need to forward IP datagrams from an OC-768 circuit to a 10Base-T Ethernet? From a 10Base-T Ethernet to an OC-768 circuit?

8.3   Read about IP telephony, and compute the aggregate packet rate for IP telephone calls multiplexed over a Gigabit Ethernet.

8.4   Compute the aggregate packet rate for a 56 Kbps dialup connection sending minimum-size TCP segments in PPP framing.

8.5   Compare the data rates and aggregate packet rates for a stream of TCP ACKs arriving over an OC-19 line (assuming one exists) to an identical stream arriving over a Gigabit Ethernet. Explain the anomaly.

8.6   Can the CPU found in a typical PC handle the aggregate packet rate of four 100Base-T Ethernets?

8.7   Recompute the packet rates in Figure 8.2 to account for interpacket gaps and preambles (Ethernet) and framing overhead (all types).

8.8   If a cell switch handles 53-octet cells and connects four OC-192 circuits, what is the aggregate packet rate?

8.9   If the cell switch in the previous exercise executes 120 instructions per cell, at what instruction rate must the processor execute?

8.10 Let O be the number of instructions executed per octet, and P be the number of instructions per packet. What ratio of P/O makes per-packet overhead dominate for ATM cells? for minimum-size IP datagrams? for maximum-size IP datagrams? Assume each datagram carries a TCP segment.

8.11 Consider a network system that processes IP datagrams. Assume the system executes 5,000 instructions per datagram, each instruction occupies 4 octets, each datagram consists of 1500 octets, a lookup examines 1000 4-byte values in an IP routing table, and a datagram arrives and leaves in an Ethernet frame. Compute the total number of memory locations accessed to process one datagram. Assume no memory caching.

8.12 Devise a data pipeline for a layer 2 bridge.

8.13 Devise a data pipeline for a TCP splicer.

Chapter Contents

9

Classification And Forwarding

9.1 Introduction

The previous chapter describes a set of hardware architectures used for protocol processing. This chapter continues the discussion by examining a concept that has gained wide acceptance: classification. The chapter explains the motivation for classification, describes software and hardware implementations, and discusses the relationship between classification and high-speed forwarding. The next chapter continues the discussion by considering interconnection mechanisms used with classification to achieve high throughput. A later chapter explains languages used for classification.

9.2 Inherent Limits Of Demultiplexing

Recall that in a layered protocol system, an outgoing packet passes down the stack and an incoming packet passes up the stack. Because each layer can contain multiple protocols, an incoming packet must be *demultiplexed* as it moves from one layer to the next. To permit protocol software on the receiving system to demultiplex, protocol software on the sending system stores a value in the *type* field of each encapsulating header. For example, when an ICMP message is encapsulated in an IP datagram, the value *1* is stored in the type field of the IP header. Similarly, when an IP datagram is encapsulated in an Ethernet frame, the value 800_{16} is stored in the type field of the Ethernet header.

Protocol software on the receiving system uses the type value in each header to determine which protocol will be used next. For example, when a frame arrives that contains type 800_{16}, frame demultiplexing software passes the contents of the frame to the IP module. Similarly, if it finds the value 1 in the type field, IP software passes the contents of the datagram to ICMP.

The chief advantages of demultiplexing lie in transmission efficiency and flexibility. Demultiplexing improves transmission efficiency by omitting header fields that are irrelevant to a given packet — instead of creating a single, large header for all layers or a single header for all the protocols at a given layer, demultiplexing allows us to define a header for each individual protocol and to choose the exact set of headers needed for a packet. As an example, UDP and TCP both reside at layer 4, and each protocol requires header fields that the other does not. Demultiplexing allows us to define separate headers for the two protocols, and allows a sender to include one of the two headers in a packet.

Demultiplexing provides flexibility because it allows designers to create a new protocol or to change an existing protocol without affecting other protocols. Because each protocol defines a header independently, fields are not shared. Thus, although TCP and UDP each define a *source port* field and both protocols reside at layer 4, the two definitions remain independent.

Despite its advantages, a traditional implementation of demultiplexing for layered protocols is slow because it operates sequentially. Each layer performs demultiplexing as a packet passes through. More important, demultiplexing among layers cannot proceed in parallel — layer N must wait for layer $N-1$ to demultiplex the packet. Thus, if a network system moves a packet through L layers of protocol software, the system performs L demultiplexing operations. We can summarize:

> *Although it provides freedom to define and use arbitrary protocols without introducing transmission overhead, demultiplexing is inefficient because it imposes sequential processing among layers.*

9.3 Packet Classification

How can we retain the advantages of demultiplexing and improve the overall efficiency of a network system? We can use *packet classification* in place of demultiplexing. The concept of classification is straightforward: retain a layered protocol design and have the sending system encode type values in outgoing headers as usual, but arrange for the receiver to optimize processing by compressing demultiplexing from a sequence of many operations at each layer into an operation at one layer.

An example will help clarify the concept and show how classification uses headers from multiple protocol layers. In our example, we will assume that each incoming packet consists of an Ethernet frame and that we wish to identify traffic destined to a web server. Web traffic can be defined as follows: the Ethernet frame contains an IP datagram, the IP datagram contains a TCP segment, and the destination protocol port number in the TCP segment specifies a web server. Figure 9.1 illustrates the encapsulated headers, and highlights the pertinent header fields.

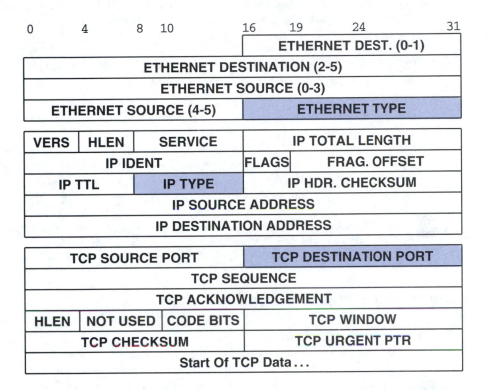

Figure 9.1 Illustration of encapsulated headers at the beginning of a packet shown with extra space between Ethernet, IP, and TCP headers. Highlighted fields are used to determine if the packet is destined for a web server.

9.4 Software Implementation Of Classification

In the case of web traffic, the classification is *static*, which means that values for header fields can be determined a priori. Three *classification rules* are needed to define web traffic:

- The 2-octet type field in the frame contains 0800_{16}

- The 1-octet type field in the IP datagram contains 6

- The 2-octet destination port field in the TCP segment contains 80

Conceptually, a classifier needs to compute a *logical and* of the three conditions specified in the rules. The most straightforward implementation of a classification system uses a series of tests to examine one header field at a time. As soon as it finds a field that does not match the specified value, the classifier stops and declares that the packet is not a match. Only after all tests are completed does the classifier assert that the packet matches. Using a C-like notation, the test is:

```
if  ( (frame type == 0x0800) && (IP type == 6) && (TCP port == 80) )
        declare the packet matches the classification;
else
        declare the packet does not match the classification;
```

Sequential examination of fields is popular for software-based classifiers because the tests can be expressed succinctly. In the worst case, a software-based classifier needs to test all the fields specified by the classification rules. For the example given above, the software makes up to three comparisons. The point is:

> *To classify a packet, a software-based classifier makes at most one comparison for each field specified in the classification rules.*

9.5 Optimizing Software-Based Classification

Consider the number of comparisons a software classifier makes. Although the worst case is fixed, the average case can be optimized. To understand how, recall that the pseudocode above uses sequential testing that terminates as soon as a comparison is negative. The code can be optimized by ordering the tests to ensure that the first test is the least likely to succeed. For example, suppose we know that 95% of all frames carry IP, 92% of all IP datagrams carry TCP, and 85% of all TCP segments have a destination port of 80. In terms of total packets, one can expect:

- 95.0% of all frames have frame type 0800

- 87.4% of all frames have IP type 6†

- 74.3% of all frames have TCP port 80

If a classifier tests the frame type first, 95% of all frames will pass the test (i.e., 5% of the frames will be rejected after a single comparison). However, if it tests the port number first, a classifier will reject over one quarter of all frames after a single comparison. Thus, to minimize the average number of comparisons, the conditional statement in the pseudocode above should be rewritten as:

---

†For purposes of this example, we assume that non-IP traffic does not have 6 in the field that corresponds to an IP type. Similarly, we assume that non-TCP traffic does not have 80 in the field that corresponds to a TCP port.

```
if ((TCP port == 80) && (IP type == 6) && (frame type == 0x0800))
        declare the packet matches the classification;
else
        declare the packet does not match the classification;
```

We can generalize the concept to an arbitrary set of comparisons:

> *Although the maximum number of comparisons in a software classif-*
> *ier is fixed, the average number of comparisons is determined by the*
> *order of the tests; minimum comparisons result if, at each step, the*
> *classifier tests the field that eliminates the most packets.*

9.6 Software Classification On Special-Purpose Hardware

What we have said about software classification applies to the typical case in which the classification software runs on a conventional processor (i.e., a processor that has a general-purpose instruction set). As we will see in Chapters 15 and 16, some network processors include a special-purpose, programmable processor (or coprocessor) optimized for classification. Special-purpose hardware can reduce the time required for software classification without requiring the programmer to handle explicit parallelism.

9.7 Hardware Implementation Of Classification

How can we further optimize classification? One approach uses parallel hardware to avoid testing header fields sequentially: the classifier extracts pertinent fields, concatenates the fields into a multi-octet value, and compares the resulting value to a constant. For example, to test for web traffic, the classifier concatenates the fields into a five-octet value, and then compares the value to the dotted hexadecimal constant†:

$$08.00.06.00.50_{16}$$

The value of the constant is derived directly from the classification rules. The hexadecimal constants 08.00 and 06 are specified explicitly; the value 00.50, in the fourth and fifth octets, is the 2-octet hexadecimal equivalent of the decimal value 80.

Classification is faster than demultiplexing because it avoids sequential processing among layers. Static classification implemented in high-speed hardware can be faster than classification implemented in software because it avoids sequential processing of individual fields. That is, instead of examining each field, it is possible to build a high-speed classifier that uses hardware to perform field extractions and comparisons in parallel. Figure 9.2 illustrates one possible architecture.

---

†To improve readability, *dotted hex notation* separates octet values with a dot.

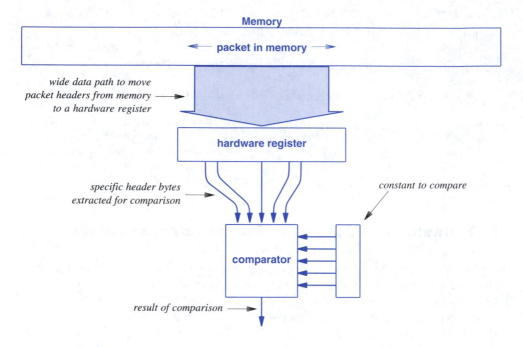

Figure 9.2 A hardware architecture for optimized classification. Packet headers are moved to a register; selected octets are extracted and compared to a constant value.

As the figure shows, hardware moves a packet header across a wide data path from memory to a dedicated register. Once the header has been moved, hardware extracts specific octets and passes them to a comparator circuit. If it finds a match between values from the header and the predefined constant, the comparator sets an output line high (i.e., true); otherwise, the comparator sets the output line low (i.e., false).

9.8 Optimized Classification Of Multiple Rule Sets

The discussion above focuses on packet selection rather than classification. That is, we saw how a classifier decides whether a packet matches a given set of classification rules. To understand the broader issues, consider classifying packets into three disjoint flows†:

- Traffic destined to a web server
- Traffic carrying ICMP echo request messages
- All other traffic

---

†We loosely define a *flow* to be a set of packets that share common characteristics (e.g., have the same destination).

The set of packets carrying ICMP echo request messages can also be identified by the header contents. The frame must carry an IP datagram, the datagram must carry an ICMP message, and the ICMP message must be an echo request. The following three classification rules give specific values for the header fields.

- The 2-octet type field in the frame contains 0800_{16}

- The 1-octet type field in the IP datagram contains 1

- The 1-octet type field in the ICMP message contains 8

As with web traffic, it is possible to build an optimized classifier that uses a single comparison to make all tests in parallel. The classifier extracts the four octets from the headers and compares them to the constant:

$$08.00.01.08_{16}$$

Although we have described hardware that tests for a single set of classification rules, it is also possible to extend a hardware-based classifier to test two or more sets of classification rules in parallel. Thus, instead of sequentially testing for N possible categories, the hardware can perform all tests at the same time.

A software-based classifier can also be optimized to recognize multiple rule sets. For example, consider a software-based classifier that needs to recognize web traffic and ICMP echo traffic. In each case, the classifier must test the frame type to ensure that the frame contains an IP datagram. A software-based classifier does not need to repeat the test for each rule set. Instead, the tests can be factored and performed once. For example, a classifier can execute the following†:

```
if  (frame type != 0x0800)  {
        send frame to flow 3;
}  else  if  (IP type == 6  &&  TCP destination port == 80)  {
        send packet to flow 1;
}  else  if  (IP type == 1  &&  ICMP type == 8)  {
        send packet to flow 2;
}  else  {
        send frame to flow 3;
}
```

---

†An exercise explores further optimization of multiple rule sets.

9.9 Classification Of Variable-Size Headers

The simplistic description of classification given above omits several important details that complicate the architecture. For example, in addition to binding a packet to a flow, a classifier must check for errors such as an invalid IP checksum. Consider how demultiplexing and classification handle a protocol with variable-size headers. Demultiplexing uses sequential computation to solve the problem: before it demultiplexes, software at each layer parses the header and extracts the payload. Thus, demultiplexing can handle a variable-size header as easily as a fixed-size header. Software-based classification follows a similar approach of computing the location of encapsulated headers as it extracts fields.

In contrast, variable-size headers pose a serious challenge for hardware. On one hand, if classification hardware employs sequential header parsing, the system will not execute faster than a software-based classification system. On the other hand, if it always assumes fields lie at fixed offsets, a hardware classifier can extract incorrect fields, which can cause misclassification.

How can a hardware classifier handle variable-size headers without sacrificing speed? In theory, the problem can be solved with additional parallelism. To understand how, consider an IP datagram. The datagram contains twenty octets unless IP options are present, in which case the header is longer. Parallel classification hardware can use the header length field as part of its verification, and parallel hardware can be built for each possible header size.

For example, we can extend the classifier that tests whether an IP datagram contains a TCP segment destined for a web server. Hardware can be added to test multiple header sizes in parallel. To see how, consider the following two sets of classification rules:

Set 1

- The 2-octet type field in the frame contains 0800_{16}

- The 1-octet field at the start of the datagram contains 45_{16}

- The 1-octet type field in the IP datagram contains 6

- The 2-octet field located 22 octets from the start of the datagram contains 80

Set 2

- The 2-octet type field in the frame contains 0800_{16}

- The 1-octet field at the start of the datagram contains 46_{16}

- The 1-octet type field in the IP datagram contains 6

- The 2-octet field located 26 octets from the start of the datagram contains 80

Both sets match a frame that carries an IP datagram and a datagram that carries a TCP segment. Each set also specifies a value for the datagram header length: the first set only matches datagrams in which the header length is 5, and the second set only matches datagrams in which the header length is 6†. Furthermore, the offset of the TCP destination port in each set is correct for the header size (e.g., if the header length is 5‡, the destination port will be located 22 octets beyond the start of the datagram).

As an alternative to parallelism, it is possible to build hardware that computes variable header offsets sequentially like a software classifier. To move to an encapsulated header, the hardware extracts the size of the current header and uses the size to move to the next encapsulated header. Although not as fast as a parallel solution, hardware that computes header offsets dynamically is much less expensive.

9.10 Hybrid Hardware / Software Classification

We have seen that it is possible to build parallel hardware that performs static classification even for protocols that have variable header size. Unfortunately, high cost makes parallel hardware impractical for most situations. Thus, parallel hardware is only used in situations where the packet rate exceeds software capabilities. More important, hardware is unsuitable for many applications because it is inflexible — any modification of the classification rules requires a hardware change.

In cases where speed is important, it is possible to combine high-speed hardware classification with the low cost and increased flexibility of software classification. To do so, one builds a hybrid classifier that contains a hardware stage for standard cases and a software stage for exceptions. In essence, a hybrid design uses hardware as a filter. If it recognizes a packet, the hardware classifier diverts the packet into an appropriate flow; unrecognized packets are passed to the software classifier. Figure 9.3 illustrates the concept.

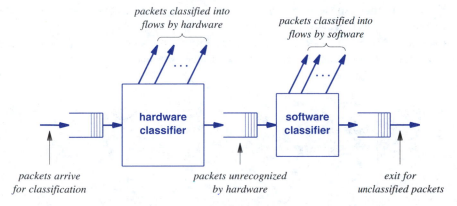

Figure 9.3 Conceptual architecture of a hybrid classification system. In general, the hardware stage handles standard packets and the software stage handles exceptions.

---

†Recall that the first four bits of the octet specify the IP version, 4, and the second four bits specify the header length, 5 or 6 in the above rule sets.

‡The header length is given in 32-bit multiples, so a length of 5 is equivalent to twenty octets.

9.11 Dynamic Vs. Static Classification

Our discussion has focused on static classification in which the set of flows and the classification rules for each flow are determined a priori. Static classification is primarily used to segregate flows determined by the type of service (e.g., IP's *Differentiated Services*, *DiffServ*) or by application (e.g., web traffic). Service providers can use static classification to segregate voice and video service from other traffic. The alternative to static classification, known as *dynamic classification*, allows the set of flows to change over time. Dynamic classification is required for short-term traffic engineering because it allows a new flow to be created or old flows to be combined. Typically, dynamic classification uses a combination of source and packet type to segregate traffic. For example, consider an ISP that offers a premium service in which up to twenty simultaneous TCP connections from a customer are given priority. When a customer upgrades to the premium service, the ISP uses dynamic classification to direct the first twenty connections from the customer into a flow that has higher priority; traffic on additional connections or traffic from customers who do not pay for the premium service is directed into the standard flow. An ISP can also define dynamic classification in which the source, traffic type, or current network conditions determine the classification. For example, dynamic classification makes it possible for an ISP to offer a customer a choice of premium or standard service for each traffic type. Thus, one customer might choose premium service for voice traffic, while another customer chooses premium service for voice, FTP, and web traffic.

In each of the examples above, a network system that performs classification needs an interface that allows classification to be specified and managed. An ISP must be able to add classification information when a new customer subscribes or alter information when an existing customer changes the level of service to which they subscribe.

How can an ISP scale software-based classification to handle traffic from an arbitrary number of customers? The most straightforward implementation of dynamic classification uses a software-based system. Although it cannot handle an arbitrarily high packet rate, a single software-based classifier is inexpensive. Therefore, the solution lies in replicating classifiers in the same way an ISP replicates access routers. Customers are added to existing classifiers until the traffic approaches the system's capacity. The ISP then acquires another classifier, and divides the load among the set of classifiers. We can summarize:

> *The most straightforward implementation of dynamic classification uses a software-based system; classifier replication is needed to handle a load from many sources.*

9.12 Fine-Grain Flow Creation

An interesting aspect of dynamic classification arises from the ability of a classifier to establish flows automatically. The capability is especially important if the underlying network is connection-oriented because classification can map each transport-layer connection into a connection in the underlying network. For example, consider using TCP over an ATM network. A dynamic classification system can be used to map each TCP connection to a separate flow, and each flow can be mapped to a separate network connection.

How can such a mapping be established? In essence, the system builds a table that specifies the items for each flow. For example, to map a TCP connection to a flow, the classifier builds a table in which each entry specifies the TCP connection along with the flow identifier that should be assigned to a packet. For TCP, the table entry contains a flow identifier plus the four header values that identify a TCP connection:

> – Source IP address
> – Destination IP address
> – Source protocol port number
> – Destination protocol port number
> – Flow identifier corresponding to this table entry

When a packet arrives, the classifier examines header fields to verify that the frame contains an IP datagram and the datagram contains a TCP segment. The classifier then extracts the four fields listed above (i.e., the four fields that identify a TCP connection), and uses them to search the table. If an entry in the table matches, the classifier assigns the packet to the corresponding flow.

To manage entries in the table, a classifier must watch for TCP *SYN* and *FIN* segments. When it encounters a SYN, the classifier chooses a new flow identifier and creates a new entry in the table. Similarly, when it encounters a pair of FIN segments that close an existing TCP connection, the classifier removes the corresponding entry from the table.

The advantage of dynamic classification lies in flexibility. A dynamic classifier can assign packets to a fixed set of flows or it can automatically create flows as needed. The disadvantage of dynamic classification lies in greater overhead: the hardware cannot be optimized as much as in the static case. We can summarize:

> *Although dynamic classification permits the automatic creation of flows, including the possibility of one flow per transport connection, dynamic classification incurs more overhead than static classification.*

9.13 Flow Forwarding In A Connection-Oriented Network

Conceptually, classification is the first of a two-step process. The second step, *forwarding*, consists of using the flow to determine how to dispose of the packet. The two steps can be expressed as a pair of bindings, where classification binds a packet to a specific flow and forwarding binds the flow to a specific disposition:

$$classification:\ packet\ \rightarrow\ flow$$

$$forwarding:\ flow\ \rightarrow\ packet\ disposition$$

The second binding can be 1-to-1 or many-to-1. That is, forwarding can choose a separate disposition for each flow or can combine many flows into a single disposition. In the case of a connection-oriented network, forwarding binds a flow to a network connection. A designer can choose to direct each flow to a separate connection or to direct multiple flows to a single connection. For example, consider an ATM network. Forwarding can be arranged to bind multiple flows to a single ATM *virtual circuit* (*VC*)† or to bind each flow to a separate VC.

If ATM *switched virtual circuits* (*SVCs*) are used, the forwarder and classifier work together. The forwarder creates a new SVC each time the classifier creates a new flow. More important, the binding can be optimized by arranging for the classifier to choose a flow identifier equal to the *VPI/VCI* value that ATM uses to identify the virtual circuit. With the optimization, forwarding becomes trivial: once the classifier produces a flow identifier, the forwarder merely passes the identifier to the ATM network. No additional computation or lookup is needed to map the flow identifier to a disposition. The point is:

> *In a connection-oriented network, flow identifiers assigned by classification can be chosen to match connection identifiers used by the underlying network. Doing so makes forwarding more efficient by eliminating one binding.*

9.14 Connectionless Network Classification And Forwarding

Classification can also be used to optimize forwarding in a connectionless network. We think of traditional connectionless forwarding as mapping a destination address to a pair (next_hop, interface), where *next hop* denotes the address of the next hop (e.g., the next IP router) and *interface* denotes the local interface to the next hop. The binding can be described as:

$$forwarding:\ destination\ address\ \rightarrow\ (next\_hop,\ interface)$$

---

†Although ATM uses the term *virtual connection*; we prefer the more generic term *virtual circuit*.

Because it maps each packet to a flow, classification introduces an intermediate binding. Thus, instead of using the destination address as the key, forwarding uses the flow; the binding becomes:

$$forwarding:\ flow\ \rightarrow\ (next\_hop,\ interface)$$

Although it may seem minor, the difference is important because it allows us to place pertinent routing information in a separate *forwarding cache*† where the information can be extracted at high speed. In particular, because a dynamic classification system allows arbitrary values for flow identifiers, a classifier can use the integers from *0* through *N-1*, where *N* is the number of flows currently assigned. When a packet is classified, the classifier maps the packet to flow number, *F*. The forwarder does not need to search the routing table. Instead, the forwarder uses *F* as an index into the forwarding cache where a copy of the route information is stored:

$$(next\_hop,\ interface)\ =\ forward\_cache\,[\,F\,];$$

Indexing is much faster than routing table lookup, and classification is much faster than demultiplexing. As a result, the entire process of classification and indexing is faster than the traditional process of demultiplexing and table lookup. However, the higher speed involves a tradeoff: forwarding efficiency is achieved by early route binding (i.e., caching). The disadvantage is that a cached entry may become stale. Thus, to ensure accuracy, an additional mechanism is required that updates an entry in the forwarding cache when the routing table changes. We can summarize:

> *When classification is used with a connectionless network, a forwarding cache can make forwarding efficient. To prevent cache entries from becoming stale, the system must update the cache when the routing table changes.*

9.15 Second Generation Network Systems

Classification has become a key technology used to achieve high-speed protocol processing. The adoption of classification occurred early in the 1990s as network systems architecture evolved beyond the first generation of software-based routers. Technologies, such as FDDI, emerged that operate at data rates of 100 Mbps. In addition, technologies, such as ATM, emerged that use small cells. Higher data rates and smaller packet sizes each increase packet rates, which means less time is available to process a packet. Although conventional computer systems had sufficed for low packet rates, designers realized that software-based systems and demultiplexing could not handle the new networks that were being built.

---

†Some literature uses the term *route cache*; the two terms are interchangeable.

To accommodate higher packet rates, engineers designed a second generation of networking hardware that uses special-purpose protocol processing hardware. Second generation network systems have three salient features:

- The use of classification instead of demultiplexing to handle the majority of packets.

- A decentralized architecture with classification and forwarding capability on each interface card.

- A high-speed internal interconnection mechanism that provides a *fast data path* to move data among interfaces.

All three features permit scaling. The use of classification allows designers to increase the data rates of connected networks because classification can handle a higher packet rate than traditional demultiplexing. The use of a decentralized architecture and a high-speed interconnect among interfaces makes it possible to add more network connections to the system than a centralized architecture. Because each interface contains separate classification facilities, interfaces can classify and forward packets in parallel. To enable parallel operation of the interfaces, the architecture must also include a high-speed interconnection mechanism that permits packets to move from one interface to another†.

Second generation network systems include a conventional CPU to manage and control the system, provide an interface for the system administrator, and run routing propagation protocols. Thus, the CPU updates routing tables, and the interfaces use the routing tables to forward packets. In addition to updating tables, the conventional CPU handles exceptions and errors, including incoming ICMP messages and packets that do not match any classification. In practice, it is not necessary to have a special case to test for errors and exceptions. Instead, the classification and forwarding mechanism on each interface is configured with a *default flow* that is forwarded to the local CPU. Packets that do not match any of the classification rules automatically fall into the default flow.

Figure 9.4 illustrates the conceptual organization of a second generation network system with a conventional CPU and a fast data path between each pair of interfaces.

9.16 Embedded Processors In Second Generation Systems

We said that it is possible to build optimized hardware for classification. In practice, however, custom ASIC designs are extremely expensive and cannot be reused with other systems. As a result, companies tend to avoid building custom classification hardware. Most second generation systems, for example, use a software implementation of classification. That is, each network interface card contains an *embedded processor* that classifies and forwards packets.

---

†The next chapter discusses mechanisms used to provide high-speed interconnection.

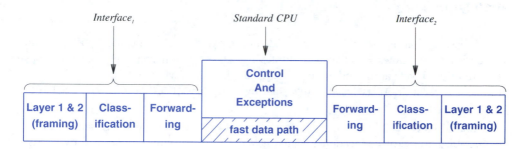

Figure 9.4 The conceptual organization of a second generation network system with more powerful interfaces. An input interface forwards most packets across a fast data path to the appropriate output interface; the central CPU is used to handle exceptions and errors.

Vendors often choose a *Reduced Instruction Set Computer* (*RISC*) for use as an embedded processor on a network interface card. A RISC chip is small, fast, inexpensive, easy to integrate with other hardware, and easy to program. Thus, a typical interface card contains layer 1 framing chips, a RISC processor, ROM that contains software, RAM used for onboard buffer memory, and a bus interface. Later chapters describe how the same basic architecture has been extended by network processors.

9.17 Classification And Forwarding Chips

Several commercial vendors sell classification hardware. Known informally as *classifier chips*, most of the chips provide a limited form of dynamic classification. Unlike the optimized parallel hardware described earlier, a classifier chip does not have a set of classification rules wired in and does not use a conventional software approach (i.e., the chip does not execute instructions from memory). Instead, the chip allows classification rules to be configured (e.g., to be placed in Programmable Read-Only Memory, *PROM*, or a Programmable Gate Array, *PGA*).

Some vendors sell a classifier *chip set*, a group of multiple chips that are designed to work together. For example, an engineer who is building an interface might choose a chip set that performs both classification and forwarding. Often, a chip set includes additional chips that connect the classifier/forwarder to other parts of the system. For example, some additional chips are designed to provide the interface between an Ethernet port and the classifier; others provide the interface between the forwarder and the fast data path mechanism.

9.18 Summary

Classification is an alternative to demultiplexing that segregates packets into categories called flows. Unlike demultiplexing, classification examines header values from multiple layers at the same time. Static classification, which requires classification rules to be set a priori, is less flexible than dynamic classification, but is amenable to more optimization.

Classification can be used with connectionless or connection-oriented network protocols. In the case of connection-oriented networks, forwarding is optimized by choosing each flow identifier to have the same value as the identifier of the network connection over which the flow is forwarded. In a connectionless network, a forwarding cache is used to optimize the binding from a flow identifier to a next hop.

To accommodate higher packet rates, second generation network systems perform classification and forwarding on each network interface, often with an embedded RISC processor. The system includes a fast data path that allows packets to move from an input interface to an output interface without using the CPU.

FOR FURTHER STUDY

Feldmeier [1988] and Partridge [1996] discuss locality of reference and route caches. Waldvogel et. al. [November 2001] summarizes trends.

EXERCISES

9.1   Extend the classification rules for web traffic so they apply to traffic in either direction (i.e., from the browser to the server or from the server to the browser).

9.2   Write classification rules that direct Domain Name System (DNS) traffic to one flow and all other traffic to a second flow. Be careful to include all possibilities.

9.3   Devise a mechanism that allows a software-based classifier to automatically minimize average comparisons without requiring a priori knowledge of the traffic characteristics (i.e., neither the programmer nor the network administrator needs to specify the percentages of packets expected to have certain values in header fields).

9.4   Consider a software-based classifier that must handle multiple rule sets. How should tests be reordered to minimize average comparisons? Why?

9.5   Consider a software classifier that must perform an IP checksum computation on packets assigned to a given flow. Should the computation be performed before or after classification? Why?

9.6   Consider a second generation network system that forwards IP datagrams. If the system has 16 interfaces that each connect to an OC-48 line, what aggregate bandwidth is needed on an internal mechanism that interconnects the 16 interfaces? Assume a 4-octet identifier is transferred with each packet.

9.7 Read about commercially available classifier chips. How is each configured?

9.8 An ISP that connects 500 small industries needs a network system that connects 500 T1 lines to an OC-12 connection. If the ISP uses classifier chips on each interface, how many rule sets will each classifier need to accept? Explain.

Chapter Contents

10

Switching Fabrics

10.1 Introduction

Earlier chapters describe a variety of hardware and software architectures used in network systems. The previous chapter discusses the important concepts of classification and forwarding, and shows how they form the basis of second generation network systems. This chapter continues the discussion by focusing on data flow inside the system. It analyzes bandwidth requirements, and examines interconnection mechanisms that can be used to create a fast path over which packets move from one interface to another. Later chapters show how the concepts apply to network processors.

10.2 Bandwidth Of An Internal Fast Path

As the previous chapter points out, a decentralized hardware architecture allows a network system to be scalable. Because each interface can classify and forward packets without using a central CPU, the CPU speed does not limit the system performance — additional interfaces can be added to accommodate additional network connections. However, unless the internal data path provides sufficient bandwidth, moving packets among interfaces can become a bottleneck. In particular, the bus found in a conventional computer does not provide sufficient bandwidth to handle forwarding packets among high-speed networks.

How fast is a fast data path? As with other aspects of network systems, two measures are used: aggregate data rate and aggregate packet rate. The aggregate data rate of the system provides the primary requirement for an interconnect mechanism, which is known informally as the *system backplane*. A backplane must have sufficient bandwidth to transport all the data that arrives at the system. Thus, a network system that connects sixteen Ethernets that each operate at 100 Mbps requires a backplane with at least 1.6 Gbps†. Similarly, a network system that connects sixteen OC-192 lines must have a backplane with a bandwidth of at least 160 Gbps.

Because network systems use an internal interconnect to move packets, the aggregate packet rate may also be important. That is, if a packet transfer corresponds to an operation, the number of packets transferred will determine the number of separate operations that must be invoked. The bandwidth of an interconnect and the maximum packet rate that the interconnect supports may be related. For example, it is possible to design hardware that offers a high aggregate data rate, but is only able to achieve the high rate when transferring large packets.

10.3 The Switching Fabric Concept

Conceptually, a *switching fabric* is a hardware mechanism that fills the role of a backplane by providing a path for data to move among a set of input ports, a set of output ports, and the CPU. Switching fabrics can also be used to interconnect small network systems to form a larger system. Figure 10.1 illustrates the basic architecture.

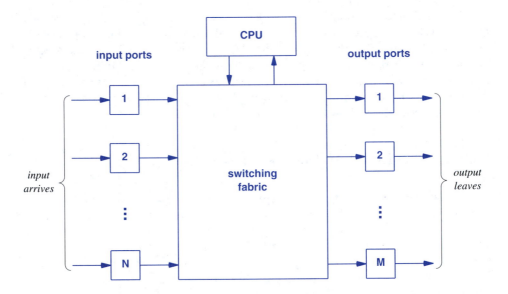

Figure 10.1 The switching fabric concept. The fabric is an internal hardware interconnection mechanism that allows any input port to send to any output port.

---

†In addition to bandwidth for data, a backplane may need a small amount of additional capacity to accommodate control or intertransfer delays.

Although many mechanisms satisfy the general concept, a switching fabric used in network systems must have the following specific properties:

- Designed for use inside a single network system.

- Provides interconnection among the CPU† and smart I/O ports.

- Supports the transfer of unicast, multicast, and broadcast packets.

- Scales to handle an arbitrary data rate on any input or output port.

- Scales to handle an arbitrary packet rate on any input or output port.

- Scales to handle an arbitrary number of input or output ports.

- Has low overhead.

- Has low cost.

10.4 Synchronous And Asynchronous Fabrics

No mechanism fulfills all properties on our list. For example, cost is proportional to bandwidth, so a mechanism that provides high bandwidth will also have high cost. Thus, instead of seeking a mechanism that exhibits all the properties, designers have investigated mechanisms that represent tradeoffs appropriate for a given situation. For example, to achieve lower cost, some switching fabrics limit the aggregate data rate. Others lower cost by limiting the number of ports.

Because many tradeoffs are possible, a myriad of switching fabric designs have been explored and implemented including: shared bus, shared memory, crossbar switch, and Banyan switch; each is appropriate for some situations. Early work on switching fabrics, which predates their use in network systems, arose from two distinct sources and produced two basic architectures. Engineers building telephone systems investigated switching fabrics as a mechanism that could be used to build telephone switches. Computer architects building general-purpose multiprocessors investigated switching fabrics as an interconnection mechanism that allows multiple processors to communicate efficiently.

Fabrics developed for use with telephone switches tend to follow a *synchronous* design, which means that the fabric uses fixed-size blocks of data and transfers occur at regular intervals. To understand why synchronous designs work well for telephone switching, consider the data being switched. Inside a digital telephone switch, all traffic consists of digitized voice calls. The data for a given call must be sent to the output port that leads to the phone at the other end of the call. Digitizing a voice call produces a steady stream of data at a constant rate. Because the data stream arrives at a constant rate, dividing the stream into fixed-size blocks results in blocks being generated at a fixed rate. Furthermore, each voice call produces blocks at exactly the same rate.

---

†Although an extra input and output port can be used to connect the CPU to the switching fabric, systems designed for highest performance use a separate connection fabric for the CPU.

Thus, a synchronous fabric can be designed that accepts blocks of data at exactly the rate they are produced.

Fabrics developed for use with general-purpose multiprocessors tend to follow an *asynchronous* design in which data can be sent across the fabric at arbitrary times. To understand why, observe that processors operate independently. Thus, the fabric is only used when software running on one processor communicates with software running on another processor.

10.5 A Taxonomy Of Switching Fabric Architectures

When switching fabrics are applied to network systems, designers concentrate on mechanisms that transfer packets; variations arise to handle special cases. Most network switching fabrics are synchronous — each packet is divided into fixed-size blocks which are transferred across the fabric at regular intervals. The block size depends on the intended use. For example, some switching fabrics are specifically engineered to forward ATM cells, and others are engineered to forward Ethernet frames. Similarly, some switching fabrics are designed to handle many low-speed ports, and others are designed to handle a few high-speed ports.

To help understand the tradeoffs among approaches, we will divide the designs into two broad categories:

- *Time division approach* in which a single internal path or a small number of paths are shared among many ports.

- *Space division approach* in which many paths are used to reduce the delay.

The next sections each describe an architectural approach. We start by considering a space division architecture that is not generally practical, but which helps us understand the problems of port contention and the need for buffering: a full interconnection. We then go on to discuss time division designs that use a shared path and hybrids that employ sharing on multiple paths.

10.6 Dedicated Internal Paths And Port Contention

The extreme case of a multipath architecture consists of a fully interconnected fabric. That is, the fabric provides a separate hardware path from each input port to each output port. A path might consist, for example, of a single wire or a set of parallel wires. Figure 10.2 illustrates the concept.

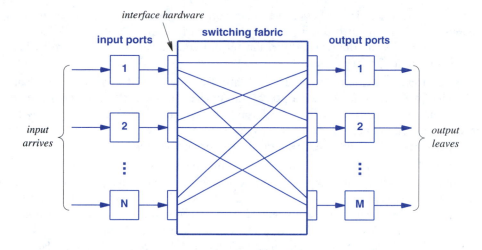

Figure 10.2 Illustration of a fabric that contains a separate physical data path
for each interconnection. Interface hardware is needed to allow
a port to specify the path for data being sent.

When it has a packet to transfer, an input port must first select the path that leads
to the correct output port, and then use the path to transfer the packet. Interface
hardware located between the port and the switching fabric handles the details of path
selection.

Does a complete interconnection of ports with separate physical paths allow all
packets to flow without constraint? Unfortunately, it does not because a problem occurs
when two input ports both attempt to send to the same output port simultaneously.
Each output interface contains additional circuitry to handle *port contention*. Contention circuitry ensures that only one transfer proceeds at any time. Thus, a packet may
be blocked waiting for a port until a previous transfer completes.

10.7 Crossbar Architecture

The chief disadvantage of using a separate physical path for each interconnection
arises from high cost. For example, in Figure 10.2 each interface on an input port must
contain contention circuitry for M output ports, or each interface on an output port must
contain contention circuitry for N input ports. A *crossbar switching fabric* takes a different approach to the contention problem: the interconnection between an input port
and an output port is *switched*. That is, each port attaches to a single physical path, and
the fabric consists of an $N \times M$ array of switches that each connect the path of an input
port to the path of an output port. When a switch is active, data can flow between the
two paths; otherwise, the paths remain unconnected. Figure 10.3 illustrates the design.

In addition to an array of switches, a crossbar fabric includes controller hardware
that handles port contention by ensuring that only one input port accesses each output
port at any time. For example, suppose input port i is ready to transfer a packet to out-

put port j. Interface circuitry associated with port i communicates with the controller to request a path be established to port j. If port j is currently idle, the controller activates the switch connecting the two and the transfer proceeds; otherwise, the controller keeps port i waiting until port j is free.

To provide maximum throughput, a controller allows transfers to proceed in parallel. That is, while port i divides a packet into blocks and sends them to port j, the controller can allow port k to divide a packet into blocks and send them to port l. A controller can establish up to P simultaneous paths, where $P = min(N, M)$ (i.e., at most one path per port). As a result, up to P transfers can occur simultaneously.

Crossbar designs have advantages and disadvantages. The ability to establish simultaneous paths means that the design can scale to handle many pairs of ports and aggregate throughput can be high. Because a path is not shared among multiple transfers, hardware along the path only needs to accommodate a single data transfer, which means the design can scale to a higher data rate on each input port†. Furthermore, a crossbar design is more economical than a fully connected fabric. However, because a crossbar requires $N \times M$ components, cost is higher than alternative designs.

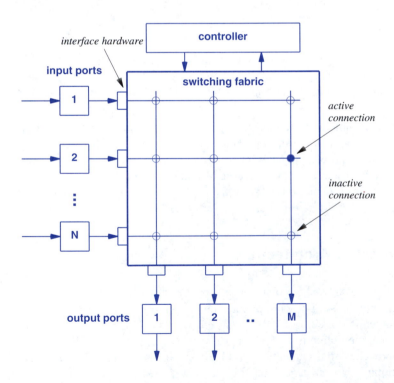

Figure 10.3 Illustration of a crossbar switching fabric shown with an active switch connecting input port 2 and output port M. The controller determines whether a switch is active or inactive.

---

†High-speed commercial switches, which have an aggregate throughput of one terabit per second, use a crossbar architecture.

10.8 Basic Queueing

In addition to a mechanism that handles port contention, switching fabrics use queueing†. There are two basic types from which a designer can choose:

- Input queueing

- Output queueing

To understand the motivation for queueing, recall that packet traffic is bursty, and aggregate throughput is maximized when the fabric permits simultaneous transfers.

Input queueing. If a burst of packets arrives at an input port, the port must send each packet quickly or packets will be lost. However, the port may block waiting for access to an output port. To prevent blocking from affecting subsequent packets, an input queue can be placed between each input port and the fabric. The queue allows subsequent packets to arrive while the packet at the head of the queue is blocked waiting for access to an output port.

If the packet at the head of the queue blocks for an extended period, the queue will fill and arriving packets can be lost. Furthermore, when the packet at the head of a queue blocks waiting for access to a particular output port, s, packets in the queue destined for ports other than s are also blocked. The problem, known as *head of the line blocking*, can be solved by changing the queue to a randomly accessible list and adding hardware that handles each packet on the list independently. The problem can also be solved by using multiple queues, one per output port. Multiple hardware queues has the advantage of allowing hardware associated with each input interface to determine which queues have packets waiting without needing to keep separate records. However, the high cost of additional hardware for either implementation makes input queueing economically unattractive. As an alternative, a system can use *virtual queueing*. When a packet arrives, the system estimates the time that the packet will reach the switching fabric, and uses the estimate to assign the packet a position in the output queue. The system then continues to process the packet. If the estimate is accurate, the packet will arrive at the queue exactly when the previous packet leaves. Thus, if estimates are correct, a packet that requires a long time to process will be assigned a later estimate, and will not block packets that require less time to process.

Output queueing An output queue, which is located between the fabric and the output port, allows bursts from two or more input ports to arrive at a single output port. The queue absorbs and holds the traffic burst until the output port can transmit the packets. After a burst subsides, the output queue drains, making it ready for the next burst. Figure 10.4 illustrates the location of input and output queues in a crossbar architecture.

The main challenge in output queueing centers on queue size. If it is too small, a queue cannot absorb a burst of packets, which means that packets will be dropped‡. If it is too large, a queue will introduce excessive delay by keeping packets that are no longer valid (e.g., keeping voice packets that will arrive at their destination too late to

---

†Some authors refer to queueing as *buffering*; the terms *input buffering* and *output buffering* are used interchangeably with *input queueing* and *output queueing*.

‡The problem of queue size is not as important for input queues because the size of a queue can be computed from the data rate of the physical interface.

be played or data packets that have already been retransmitted by a transport protocol). The optimal output queue size also depends on the protocols being used. One early ATM switch became infamous because its output buffers held less than 64 Kbytes each, which meant that the switch could not handle back-to-back packets totaling 64 Kbytes. The problem was especially severe for IP traffic — when a full-size IP datagram was transferred through the switch, at least one of the cells carrying part of the datagram was lost, which meant that large datagrams were always corrupted.

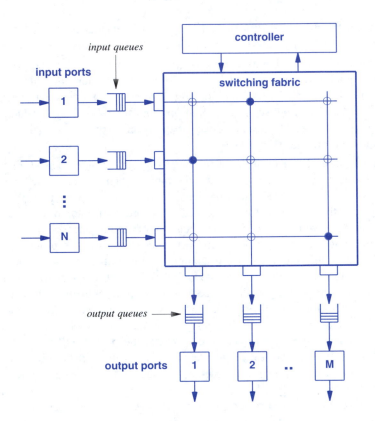

Figure 10.4 Illustration of a crossbar architecture. Although the location of both input and output queues is shown, a given switch usually includes one or the other, but not both. A solid dot indicates a connection (e.g., input port 1 connects to output port 2).

10.9 Time Division Solutions: Sharing Data Paths

An architecture, such as a crossbar switch, relies on space division because the architecture allows a separate data path to be established between a pair of ports. Architectures that rely on time division take a different approach: internal communication paths are shared. At the extreme, time division uses a single, shared data path for all communication. The chief advantage of fewer paths arises from lower cost — instead of $N \times M$ pieces of hardware, a single shared path uses $N + M$. The chief disadvantage of shared paths arises from the lower aggregate throughput and the resulting inability to handle arbitrary scale. The point is:

Switching fabrics employ time division approaches if low cost is more important than performance, and space division approaches if high performance is more important than low cost.

The next sections each discuss one possible shared architecture. We begin by examining designs that have a single data path shared for all communication, and then consider hybrid designs that provide paths with partial sharing.

10.10 Shared Bus Architecture

A switching fabric that uses a *shared bus* has a central hardware facility similar to the bus in a conventional computer. Figure 10.5 illustrates the architecture.

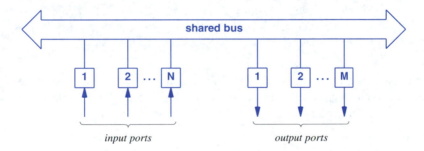

Figure 10.5 Illustration of a shared bus architecture. Each port attaches to the bus over which all transfers occur.

Like a conventional bus, a switching fabric bus has lines for addresses, control, and data. Also like a conventional bus, the switching fabric bus has an attachment for each input and output port, with each port assigned a unique address. A port uses the bus hardware to transfer data to another port; the bus protocol prevents two ports from attempting to transfer at the same time.

At what granularity should a bus operate? A bus that uses *packet granularity* allows a port to transfer an entire packet before allowing any other transfer to proceed. A bus that operates at *cell granularity* chooses a transfer size equal to the network cell size (e.g., a fabric designed for use in an ATM switch uses the ATM cell size). Finally, a bus that operates at *block granularity*† divides all transfers into small blocks, and arranges for senders to take turns transferring one block apiece; each sender is allowed to transfer a block before any sender has the opportunity to transfer a second block.

The chief advantage of packet granularity lies in straightforward operation and simplicity of hardware. The chief disadvantage of packet granularity lies in the delay — transferring a long packet requires the use of the bus for a long time. Thus, a short packet can be blocked waiting for a long packet. Block granularity avoids long delays by forcing a port to relinquish the bus after transferring a single block. Thus, multiple transfers proceed concurrently, and the transfer of a short packet completes before the transfer of a long packet. The disadvantage of block granularity arises from the overhead involved in changing from one sender to another. Cell granularity resembles block granularity, but optimizes the fabric for a particular protocol.

We said that a time division mechanism, such as a shared bus, cannot scale to handle as much data as a space division approach, such as a crossbar. To understand why, consider the speed of hardware. In a space division fabric with separate paths, the hardware along each path needs to transfer bits at the same data rate as the input or output port. In a shared bus, each input port receives approximately $1/N$ of the bus bandwidth, where N is the number of input ports. Thus, to handle additional ports, bus hardware must operate faster. We can summarize:

> *For a shared bus fabric to provide the same aggregate data rate as a crossbar fabric, the bus hardware must operate* N *times faster than the crossbar hardware, where* N *is the number of input ports.*

The consequence should be obvious. The maximum rate of any hardware system is limited by such factors as the underlying technology. Therefore, a shared bus cannot easily scale to accommodate an arbitrary number of ports.

10.11 Other Shared Medium Architectures

In addition to a shared bus, other mechanisms have been explored that employ time sharing to provide access across a single, shared medium. Shared memory, described in the next section, is popular. A technology, known as *Distributed Queue Dual Bus* (*DQDB*), has been defined that uses a pair of unidirectional buses and a multiplexing scheme that assigns a time slot to each sender. DQDB has cell granularity, which means that a large packet must be divided into cells for transport‡.

---

†Although it is possible to build bus hardware that uses octet granularity, the additional overhead makes block granularity the finest grain that is practical for most situations.

‡Few commercial products have adopted DQDB.

In addition to technologies specifically designed to serve as switching fabrics, some engineers have adopted standard networking technologies. For example, some fabrics have been built using *Fiber Distributed Data Interconnect* (*FDDI*) as a shared medium†. FDDI uses a ring topology and *token passing* to control access. One of the advantages of using a standard technology lies in lower cost: inexpensive chip sets are available that implement the interface and access functions. Although it is much less expensive than alternatives, an FDDI fabric can only be used at low speeds — because an FDDI network operates at 100 Mbps, the total bandwidth of the fabric is limited to 100 Mbps.

10.12 Shared Memory Architecture

A *shared memory* architecture uses memory as the shared medium connecting input and output ports. When it has a packet to send, an input port deposits the packet in memory and informs the appropriate output port. The output port extracts the packet from memory. Figure 10.6 illustrates the architecture.

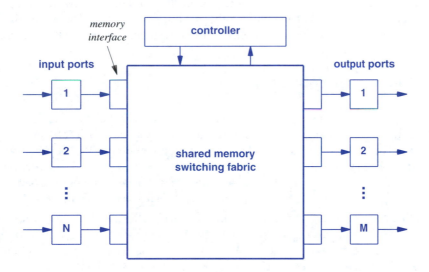

Figure 10.6 Illustration of a switching fabric that uses shared memory. The memory is used to pass data; a separate hardware controller is used to pass coordination and control information.

As the figure shows, each port needs *memory interface* hardware that connects the port to the memory system. Memory interface hardware is expensive. Although we have depicted a separate memory interface for each port, it is possible to lower cost by arranging for multiple I/O ports to share a single memory interface. For example, some

---

†FDDI switches were used early in the Internet in Network Access Points (NAPs), the interconnection points for ISPs.

shared memory designs use a *dual ported memory* that has two interfaces — all input ports share one of the interfaces and all output ports share the other. The amount of sharing determines performance as well as cost: shared memory interfaces lower cost, but also lower overall throughput. The point is:

> *In a shared memory fabric, performance and cost depend on the number of memory interfaces. A designer must choose a compromise between low cost and high performance.*

In addition to memory interface hardware, the figure shows a controller that is used to pass control information among ports. Typically, a controller provides a separate, high-speed bus; ports use the bus to coordinate activities. For example, after an input port places a packet in memory, the hardware associated with the port sends a message through the controller to inform the output port that the packet is ready. The message specifies the address in memory where the packet resides. When it receives a message over the control bus, an output port retrieves the packet from the specified memory location. It may seem that the presence of a controller makes the shared memory unnecessary because packets could be sent through the controller. However, the shared memory has much higher bandwidth than the bus used for control. Therefore, placing a packet in memory and using the controller for short messages optimizes throughput.

10.13 Multistage Fabrics

A set of architectures lie at intermediate points between the extremes of a single, shared path (e.g., a shared bus) and separate paths for each pair of ports (e.g., a crossbar). The intermediate designs have arisen as a compromise of performance and cost. Because they provide multiple data paths, the designs have better performance than a design that uses a single path. Because they do not provide a separate path between all pairs of ports, the designs are not as expensive as designs that do.

Unlike the architectures considered in previous sections (which are classified as *single stage*), intermediate designs are classified as *multistage*. The name arises because the hardware is arranged in sets, and a transfer involves sending a packet through multiple sets. In most multistage designs, hardware is arranged in a *tree*†.

One of the key questions about multistage fabrics centers on queueing and buffering: does the fabric include queues at each stage so that packets can be forwarded through one stage at a time, or does the fabric first establish a path through all stages and then send the packet directly from start to finish? Both approaches have been proposed. Using queues has higher throughput because queues allow more transfers to proceed at the same time. A design that does not use queues has lower cost because less hardware is needed. Thus, the number of queues in a multistage design is determined as a compromise between performance and cost.

---

†We use the term ''tree'' in the graph theoretic sense.

10.14 Banyan Architecture

Among multistage designs, one underlying scheme emerges as especially practical and has been used in commercial products. Known as a *Banyan* architecture, the design offers several advantages.

- Scalability
- Self routing
- Internal packet queues allowed, but not required

Scalability in Banyan designs arises because the hardware can operate at lower rates than a shared bus and the general technique can be applied to an arbitrary number of input ports. More important, the design is modular: a large Banyan switch is created by interconnecting smaller Banyan switches. In fact, we will see that an arbitrary Banyan switch can be built by interconnecting small, inexpensive 2-input switching elements.

A Banyan switch is *self routing* because each output port is identified by a unique binary label, and switches along the path know how to reach a given output port. That is, an individual switching element can make a decision about how to reach a destination without depending on a central controller. To send a packet through a self-routing fabric, the sender prefixes the appropriate label on the packet. At each stage, switching hardware extracts the next bit of the label and uses the bit to determine the path. The chief advantage of a self-routing scheme lies in the low cost: the fabric does not require a complex controller to coordinate transfers or establish paths.

To understand the Banyan architecture and self routing, we begin with a 2-input switching element that forms the basic building block of larger switches. Figure 10.7 illustrates an element that switches between two paths.

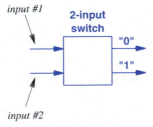

Figure 10.7 Illustration of a 2-input Banyan switching element with the labels associated with output shown. The element extracts the first bit of the label on an input packet, and uses the bit to decide which of the two outputs will receive the packet.

As with other switching fabrics, a Banyan switching fabric can be *synchronous* or *asynchronous*. In the case of an asynchronous Banyan fabric, packets arrive at arbitrary times. Thus, one packet may start before another arrives. A synchronous Banyan fabric requires scheduling hardware that ensures packets are scheduled at regular intervals. Overall, a synchronous Banyan fabric offers twice the effective throughput of an asynchronous Banyan, but the additional scheduling hardware adds cost.

10.15 Scaling A Banyan Switch

To construct a large Banyan switch, switching elements are combined. At each step, a new stage is added to the switch, which allows the number of input lines to double. For example, 2-input switching elements can be used to construct a 4-input Banyan switch, 4-input switches are used to build an 8-input switch, and so on. As a result, the number of inputs on a Banyan switch is a power of two.

To understand how a large Banyan switch is constructed, consider a 4-input switch. As Figure 10.8a shows, the switch can be constructed by interconnecting four 2-input switches. The interconnection produces two stages, and each stage uses one bit of a label to select a path. For example, when an input arrives at switching element SW_1, the first bit of the label is extracted. If the bit is zero, the packet will be forwarded to SW_3; otherwise, the packet will be forwarded to SW_4. Similarly, SW_3 examines the second bit of the label. If the second bit is zero, the packet will be sent to the output with label *00*; otherwise, the packet will be sent to the output with label *01*. Thus, the label on an incoming packet determines where the packet will emerge from the switch.

Figure 10.8b shows an 8-input switch composed of three stages: the first stage consists of four 2-input switch elements, and the next two stages are embedded in a pair of 4-input switches. The first stage examines the first bit of the label. If the first bit is 0, the packet is routed to the upper 4-input switch; if the first bit is 1, the packet is routed to the lower 4-input switch. A 4-input switch examines the next two bits of the label to choose among its four outputs. Thus, all outputs from the upper 4-input switch correspond to labels that begin with 0, and all outputs from the lower 4-input switch correspond to labels that begin with 1.

The worst case behavior of a Banyan switch is somewhat surprising. For example, consider what happens in the 8-input switch illustrated in Figure 10.8b if each of the eight inputs receives a packet that has label 000. At the first stage, only one-half of the packets will be forwarded without blocking. Similarly, in the second stage, only one-half of the remaining packets will be forwarded. Finally, in the third stage, only one packet will be forwarded. The point is:

> *The worst case in a Banyan switch occurs when all inputs receive packets with exactly the same label. Only one packet will emerge from the output; all others will be blocked.*

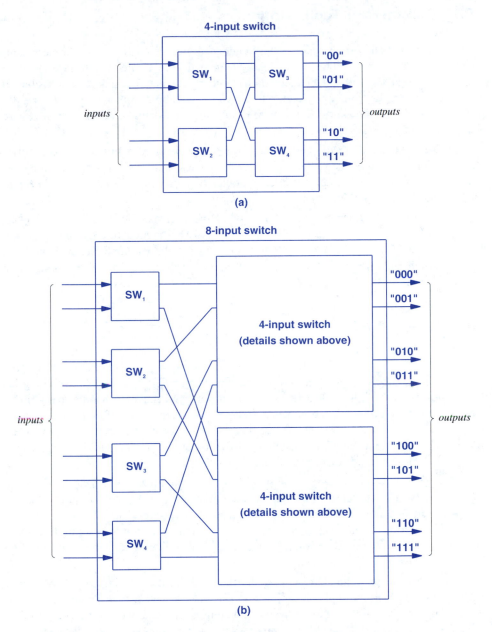

Figure 10.8 (a) Details of a 4-input Banyan switch formed by interconnecting four 2-input switching elements, and (b) an 8-input Banyan switch formed by interconnecting two 4-input switches.

10.16 Commercial Technologies

In 1999, a group of network system vendors formed a consortium to define a standard for switching fabric interconnection. Their goal is to create an interface standard that is both scalable and independent of the underlying details, making it possible to connect a processor from one vendor to a switching fabric from another. Originally known as *CSIX*, the consortium has merged into the *Network Processor Forum*, where work on the standard continues.

While industrial consortia and standards bodies work on defining standards, individual vendors have produced a variety of technologies and products for switching fabrics. Examples of switching fabric technologies include: *HyperTransport*, *InfiniBand*, *PCI-X*, *Packet-Over-SONET*, *RapidIO*, and *Utopia*.

Variations and extensions exist for most of the designs discussed in this chapter. For example, a *knockout switch* extends the basic crossbar architecture by adding packet filters, concentrators, and queues. Modifications to the Banyan architecture have been defined, including: Batcher that uses merge-sort hardware to avoid blocking, and Sunshine, an improvement of Batcher.

10.17 Summary

A switching fabric is a hardware mechanism used inside a network system to provide an interconnection among I/O ports and, possibly, a CPU. The ideal switching fabric scales to handle a high data rate on a given port, and scales to handle many ports. Because practical switching fabrics cannot achieve the ideal, a set of architectures have been created that each represent a tradeoff among performance, scalability, and cost. Synchronous switching fabrics transfer fixed-size blocks at regular intervals; asynchronous switching fabrics allow transfers at arbitrary times.

At one extreme, switching fabric performance is maximized when the fabric has a separate physical data path for each pair of communicating ports. At the other extreme, cost is minimized when the fabric consists of a single data path that is shared among all ports. The former is known as a space-division approach, and is exemplified by a crossbar architecture; the latter is known as a time-division approach, and is exemplified by a shared bus or shared memory architecture.

An intermediate architecture is possible that uses limited sharing to provide better performance than a time-division architecture, but has less cost than a fully connected fabric. Intermediate architectures are known as multistage, and usually are composed of a hierarchy of smaller switches. A Banyan switch is an example of an intermediate architecture.

FOR FURTHER STUDY

McKeown [1997] discusses the need for switched backplanes to achieve high speed. Ahmadi and Denzel [1989] surveys high-performance switching fabric architectures.

EXERCISES

10.1 Read about commercial crossbar switches. What is the bandwidth of a single path through a crossbar switch?

10.2 How large should the input buffer be on a switching fabric? Why?

10.3 What is the maximum delay that a packet at the head of the queue can cause in a switch that uses packet granularity, operates at 2.4 Gbps, and switches IP datagrams?

10.4 What is the maximum delay that a packet at the head of the queue can cause in a switch that operates at 2.4 Gbps and uses block granularity with a block size of 64 octets?

10.5 Compute the aggregate data rate required for a fabric that uses a shared bus architecture if the fabric is used in a gigabit Ethernet switch with 32 ports.

10.6 Survey commercial products that operate at high speed to determine the switching fabric architectures used in practice.

10.7 Read more about DQDB. How is a large packet sent across a DQDB fabric?

10.8 What potential advantage does a shared memory architecture have over a crossbar architecture? (Hint: think of the type of service.)

10.9 Draw a Banyan network for 16 inputs with full details, and label intermediate connections with the label prefix used to reach the connection.

10.10 What block size should a switching fabric use to transfer protocols such as Ethernet, IP, and ATM? Why?

10.11 Derive a formula for the number of 2-input switch elements in a Banyan fabric that has 2^n inputs.

10.12 If a queue is added along each internal interconnection of a Banyan switch, how many queues are needed for a switch with 2^n inputs?

10.13 What is the maximum number of transfers that can occur in an 8-input Banyan switch at any time? Does the answer change if a single packet queue is placed between each stage of the switch?

10.14 Read about commercial architectures and classify each as single stage or multistage, time division or space division, and input-buffered, output-buffered, or both.

Network Processors:
The Technology And
Its Role In The
Implementation Of
Network Systems

Chapter Contents

11

Network Processors: Motivation And Purpose

11.1 Introduction

Previous chapters consider the hardware and software used in early network systems. This chapter describes two additional steps in the evolution of network systems architecture: third generation architectures and network processors. We will see that the two are related, and will understand the motivation for the new technologies. Later chapters continue the discussion of network processors by examining both the hardware details and the associated software that processes packets.

11.2 The CPU In A Second Generation Architecture

Recall from Chapter 9 that a second generation network system extends the first generation architecture by using smart network interfaces that contain hardware to handle many of the packet processing tasks†. Moving protocol processing to interface cards reduces the load on the CPU. Second generation systems improve performance further by introducing the concept of a *fast data path* to allow packets to move directly from one interface to another without using the CPU. Chapter 10 discusses mechanisms used to implement a fast data path: switching fabrics that provide high-speed interconnections among interfaces.

Second generation designs have both strengths and limitations. The chief advantage of a second generation architecture arises from its ability to handle more network connections than a first generation architecture. By offloading processing from the

---

†The first generation architecture is depicted in Figure 8.5 on page 107, and the second generation architecture is depicted in Figure 9.4 on page 129.

CPU, a second generation system allows expansion: network interfaces can be added and the switching fabric can be extended to accommodate additional connections. The disadvantage of a second generation system arises from the dependence on a general-purpose processor for some tasks. Even if the CPU is only used to handle a small percentage of packets, the number of packets passed to the CPU increases linearly with the aggregate packet rate. Thus, if the system has a high aggregate packet rate, the central CPU can become a bottleneck.

11.3 Third Generation Network Systems

To further reduce the load on the CPU, engineers designed a third generation of network processing systems. Third generation systems use specialized hardware to de-centralize protocol processing: a designer chooses hardware appropriate for each protocol processing task, and replicates the hardware on each network interface. Doing so removes protocol processing from the CPU, and allows a network interface to handle exceptions and higher layer protocols. Figure 11.1 illustrates the architecture.

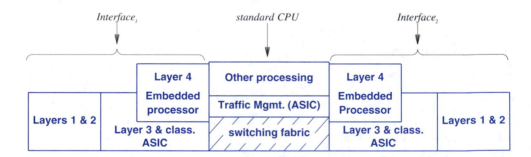

Figure 11.1 Conceptual organization of a third generation network system with an embedded processor plus ASIC† hardware on each interface card. A switching fabric provides the fast data path between interfaces. An interface can handle most of layers 1 through 4, leaving the central CPU free to run applications.

As the figure shows, the third generation architecture adds considerable functionality to each interface which allows the interface to handle protocols up through layer 4. Furthermore, the type of hardware used depends on the function. For example, layers 1 and 2 (physical and framing) are handled with commodity chip sets. ASIC hardware on each interface is used to provide basic layer 3 functionality, packet classification, and forwarding over the switching fabric. In addition, ASIC hardware provides control and traffic management facilities. Finally, a general-purpose CPU handles routing and other tasks that do not lie on the fast data path.

---

†ASIC stands for *Application Specific Integrated Circuit.*

11.4 The Motivation For Embedded Processors

What hardware should be used to handle higher layer protocols? Most third generation architectures choose an *embedded processor* (i.e., a processor located on an interface and dedicated to tasks associated with packet processing). Software to control the processor is stored in ROM, and the processor uses a conventional RAM to hold packet buffers and other data structures.

To understand why an embedded processor is used, we must look at hardware. First, tasks assigned to an embedded processor do not involve the fast path. Consequently, although an embedded processor is not as fast as an ASIC solution, the speed is acceptable. Second, because layer 4 protocols are large and complex, implementing such protocols is difficult. As a result, an implementation is likely to contain bugs. Protocol complexity makes an embedded system attractive because the protocols can be implemented in software. When a problem is discovered, a new version of the software can be built and loaded into ROM; no further hardware changes are required. We can summarize:

> *Third generation systems use an embedded processor to handle layer 4 functionality and exception packets that cannot be forwarded across the fast path. An embedded processor architecture is chosen because ease of implementation and amenability to change are more important than speed.*

11.5 RISC vs. CISC

When selecting a CPU for use in an embedded system, most engineers choose a *RISC* processor (*Reduced Instruction Set Computer*) instead of a *CISC* processor (*Complex Instruction Set Computer*). There are several reasons. Because the large instruction set in a CISC processor is intended for application programs, the extra instructions do not aid in protocol processing. RISC chips have a less complex hardware interface, which makes hardware design easier. The less complex instructions in a RISC design allow the CPU to operate at higher clock rates. RISC processors may also be more attractive for reasons unrelated to programming: they usually cost less and consume less power.

RISC chips have become so pervasive in embedded system designs that many companies use the term *RISC processor* as a synonym for *embedded processor*. In later chapters, we will see that network processor vendors also use the term *RISC processor* to refer to an embedded processor.

11.6 The Need For Custom Silicon

Although an embedded RISC processor dedicated to packet processing can handle a higher aggregate packet rate than a general-purpose processor, an embedded processor can become a bottleneck for sufficiently high data rates. During the 1990s, for example, embedded processors became a bottleneck as network data rates grew from OC-3 to OC-12, OC-48, and beyond. By the mid-1990s, engineers had concluded that the only viable technology capable of handling backbone Internet connections was custom silicon — the idea became widely accepted throughout the industry. By the late 1990s, companies building high-speed network systems routinely employed VLSI designers, who were asked to build ASICs for their products.

Although it offers the advantage of highest speed, custom silicon has several disadvantages:

- High cost
- Long time to market
- Difficult to simulate
- Expensive and time-consuming to change
- Little reuse across products
- Limited reuse across versions
- No consensus on framework or support chips
- Requires expertise

High cost. Silicon design rules and low-level details make any chip design tedious† and expensive. In addition to salary for an ASIC engineer and an ASIC verification engineer, fabrication costs usually exceed a million dollars. Building an ASIC for network systems is especially difficult because most chip designers have little or no experience with protocol processing. Furthermore, because protocol standards are written at a high level of abstraction, the specifications do not map directly into hardware. Thus, most ASIC designers must spend time learning about protocols before they can translate the protocol specifications into silicon.

Long time to market. The development cycle for a typical ASIC ranges from eighteen to twenty months. The process, which is known informally as a *silicon spin* or simply a *spin*, includes time for design, simulation, and testing.

Difficult to simulate. To reduce costs, ASIC designers rely on simulation to debug a design before committing the design to silicon. Simulation does not work well for network protocols. The chief difficulty occurs because simulation is time consuming and requires engineers to focus on small functional units. To thoroughly simulate a network protocol requires large, complex packet sequences. Consequently, extensive simulation of a protocol stack is infeasible.

---

†Most ASIC designs use *Complementary Metal Oxide Semiconductor* (*CMOS*) technology. Although design rules vary among technologies, silicon implementation is always tedious.

Expensive and time-consuming to change. One of the chief drawbacks of custom VLSI designs arises from the high cost of change. In addition to being expensive, a change involves a silicon respin that requires many months. Thus, even correcting a minor problem incurs high overhead and major delay.

Little reuse across products. Because each custom chip is tailored for use in a specific system, a chip cannot easily be used in other systems. For example, an ASIC designed for use in an IP router cannot be used in a layer 2 bridge.

Limited reuse across versions. It may seem that the initial design bears the majority of the cost, and that once a custom chip has been designed, subsequent versions of the product will cost much less. However, successive versions of a product usually involve additional features, and small changes in functionality can require major redesign.

No consensus on framework or support chips. The problem of ASIC design is exacerbated by the lack of a standardized framework for building network systems. Vendors who manufacture chip sets for physical layer protocols each choose the exact hardware interface for their chips. In addition, vendors who manufacture switching fabrics each select a hardware interface for their fabric. There is no consensus about either the general approach or interface details. Hardware heterogeneity means that it is impossible to construct an ASIC chip that can be used in an arbitrary system.

Requires expertise. ASIC design and verification requires a team of highly trained engineers. Designers must have a working knowledge of special hardware design languages such as *VHDL* and *Verilog*.

The disadvantages of ASICs are significant because they impose unreasonable constraints on the design of new hardware. Consequently, designers face a dilemma:

> *Although an embedded processor cannot handle packet rates from the highest-speed networks, ASIC hardware has extremely high cost, is difficult to implement, and requires many months to fabricate a chip after even small changes.*

11.7 Definition Of A Network Processor

What hardware technology can be used to build the next generation of network systems? Many vendors are excited about a new approach that provides an alternative to embedded processors and ASIC hardware. The goal is ambitious: create a technology that has the advantages of custom silicon without the disadvantages. Specifically, vendors are striving to retain the high speed of ASIC hardware, while reducing the time and cost required to design and implement or modify network systems.

Integrated circuits, known by the generic term *network processors*, form the basis of the technology. Because network processors represent an integration of two approaches, the chips need to combine the best features of both. On one hand, to be viable as a replacement for an embedded processor, a network processor must offer the same key benefits:

- Relatively low cost

- Straightforward hardware interface

- Ability to access memory

- Programmability

On the other hand, to be viable as a replacement for custom silicon, a network processor must offer the key benefits of ASIC hardware:

- Ability to scale to high data rates

- Ability to scale to high packet rates

We can summarize:

> *A* network processor *is a special-purpose, programmable hardware device that combines the low cost and flexibility of a RISC processor with the speed and scalability of custom silicon (i.e., ASIC chips). Network processors are building blocks used to construct network systems.*

11.8 A Fundamental Idea: Flexibility Through Programmability

Low overall cost results from *flexibility*: technology that can be changed quickly and adapted to a variety of uses reduces the development cycle and allows reuse. To keep costs low, network processors must be as flexible as a conventional RISC processor. For example, unlike an ASIC coprocessor, a network processor is not limited to a particular protocol or a particular layer of the stack. Instead, a network processor is designed to accommodate an arbitrary protocol. As a result, a network processor can be used at any layer of the stack in applications such as a layer 2 bridge, a layer 3 router, a layer 4 splicer, or a layer 5 load balancer.

The key to flexibility arises from *programmability*†. Unlike the ASIC approach, network processors are designed so they can be used without building a new chip. Instead, a network processor resembles a conventional processor — the hardware remains fixed, and software determines how the network processor handles packets. As a result, a system that uses network processors can be designed and implemented much faster than a system that uses ASICs. Similarly, a network system built around a network processor can be changed or upgraded quickly (i.e., as fast as a system built around an embedded processor).

The ability to upgrade a system without changing the hardware means that network processors result in higher *component reuse* across versions of a given product. Interestingly, programmability also results in higher component reuse across multiple pro-

---

†Although technologies such as *Programmable Gate Arrays* (PGAs) and *Field Programmable Gate Arrays* (*FPGAs*) offer flexibility, their small size, limited computational power, and high cost make them inappropriate for all protocol processing.

ducts because it encourages a company to reapply expertise — if the company uses the same network processor in multiple products, experience gained when building the software components for one product can reduce the development cost of software for other products. We can summarize:

> *A network processor does not have knowledge of specific protocol(s) hardwired into the instruction set. Instead, network processors achieve flexibility by having packet processing specified with software.*

11.9 Instruction Set

Programmability alone is insufficient because a network processor must achieve higher speed than a conventional RISC processor. Therefore, the key to a successful design lies in choosing an instruction set and an overall architecture that can be optimized for protocol processing.

In theory, the choice of an instruction set is straightforward: in addition to instructions for conventional operations, such as arithmetic, additional instructions are needed to perform packet processing functions. In practice, choosing an instruction set is extremely difficult. On one hand, speed usually arises from specialization — the more a designer knows about the problem being solved, the more the hardware can be optimized to solve the problem. On the other hand, adding instructions for specific protocols or specific operations defeats the overall purpose of a general-purpose technology. Thus, to keep network processors as general as possible, instructions do not focus on optimization of a single protocol. Instead, designers attempt to identify abstract operations that are common to many protocols, and produce instructions that can be used to implement the operations efficiently.

Because the problem of choosing an optimal instruction set is complex, no solution is best for all situations. In addition to the criteria discussed above, systems designers must be concerned with issues such as power consumption, heat dissipation, and cost. Thus, many variants have been created that represent tradeoffs among speed, programmability, and other factors.

Later chapters consider network processors in detail. Chapter 12 discusses packet processing functions and the overall complexity, and Chapter 13 examines network processor architectures. Chapter 15 surveys architectures used in commercial products.

11.10 Scalability With Parallelism And Pipelining

Scalability ranks among the most important concerns of network processor vendors. Because underlying silicon technology limits the maximum clock rate of a network processor, no single processor can scale to handle arbitrary packet rates. Thus, network processor architectures rely on two standard techniques for scaling: *parallelism* and *pipelining*.

As with the choice of instruction set, the choice of parallel and pipelined hardware is difficult, and many questions arise. Which functional units should be replicated on each chip? How is the hardware controlled and used? When one network processor is insufficient, how many copies of each chip are needed? How can multiple network processors be interconnected? What is the appropriate combination of parallel and pipeline architectures? Chapter 13 discusses network processor architectures, including the important issues of parallelism and pipelining; Chapter 15 surveys approaches that vendors have adopted.

11.11 The Costs And Benefits Of Network Processors

Much of the excitement over network processors arises from economics. For companies producing network systems, network processor technology can dramatically lower the cost and the time needed to produce new equipment — building with a network processor is much less expensive than using an ASIC design. Just as important, network processors lower long-term costs by making it possible to modify or improve a product without the high cost required to modify custom hardware. Consequently, the industry is using network processors in commercial products; the trend is expected to continue. For chip vendors, network processors help retain customers who might otherwise be forced to build ASIC designs. Furthermore, demand is expected to be high because a typical network system will use multiple network processors. For example, imagine a 64-port gigabit Ethernet switch with one network processor per interface.

How much does a network processor chip cost? Like the price of any new chip, the initial prices of network processors were relatively high. In particular, the unit price for a network processor is higher than the price of a commodity RISC chip†. However, prices are expected to drop once development costs have been met. Ultimately, the cost of a network processor should be approximately the same as for a RISC processor because production costs are equivalent. The important point is that, even with current prices, using a network processor is much less expensive than building custom silicon.

Of course, no technology provides economic benefits without some overhead. In the case of network processors, the lower cost comes at the price of performance — a system implemented with network processors cannot be optimized as much as a system implemented with custom ASICs. Figure 11.2 illustrates how network processors compare to other technologies.

As the figure indicates, network processors occupy a middle ground. Although the resulting systems are not as fast as those built from ASICs, a system using network processors can outperform a system that uses embedded RISC processors. More important, a system that uses network processors costs less than a system that uses ASIC hardware.

Figure 11.2 also indicates the challenge for manufacturers who are building network processors. To compete with ASIC designs, network processors must have higher performance. To compete with software-based systems, network processors must have

---

†At the time of this writing, one vendor sells a network processor for $750; by comparison, RISC chip costs vary from $50 to $300.

lower overall costs. Chapter 13 discusses architectural features aimed at increasing performance. Later chapters discuss one way vendors attempt to lower the cost of using a
network processor: they provide support systems that make it easier to develop and test
network processor code.

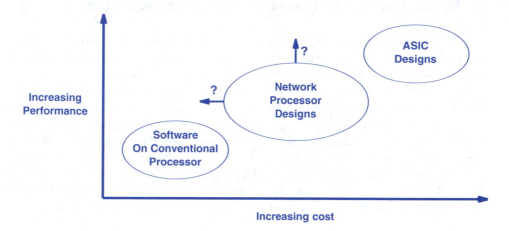

Figure 11.2 An illustration of the performance and overall cost of three main
network technologies. Software-based systems that have low
cost have low performance; ASIC designs that have high performance have high cost for design and change; network processor
designs occupy the middle.

11.12 Network Processors And The Economics Of Success

As discussed above, proponents of network processors argue that an important
motivation for using them arises from the lower cost. Opponents observe, however, that
an irony arises in which the economics of extreme scale favor ASICs over network processors. That is, when volume is sufficiently high, an ASIC costs less than a network
processor. To understand why, consider two facts related to production costs. First, because they are smaller, ASICs have higher yields (i.e., there is a lower probability that a
production flaw will ruin a given chip). Second, because they are less complex, much
less effort is required to test an ASIC. The point is: if one ignores the initial development cost, the cost to fabricate an ASIC chip will always be substantially lower than the
cost to fabricate a network processor.

If the above analysis is correct and the unit production cost of an ASIC is less than
the unit production cost of a network processor, the economic situation is clear: scale
matters. Certainly, the cost to produce a single system favors a network processor
design. If we amortize the initial development cost across all units produced, however,
even a million dollar investment becomes insignificant when sufficient ASIC units have

been sold. So, the irony is that network processors, which can lower initial development costs, appear to occupy an interesting economic niche because they are best suited for products that are produced in moderate quantity.

11.13 The Status And Future Of Network Processors

At the time of this writing, the first generation of network processors is available commercially, and is being used to create network systems. A second generation of chips is emerging. Prices continue to drop, making network processors more attractive as an alternative to embedded processors. Additional work is needed, however, to refine both the hardware and support software.

Like most new technologies, the first generation of network processor chips is somewhat uneven. Although the initial chips include most of the requisite functionality, they are difficult to program and have unexpected performance bottlenecks. Experience with the initial versions has led most vendors to refine their designs and create a second round of network processor chips. Newer versions of the chips are expected to offer much higher performance, making them more competitive with ASIC designs.

11.14 Summary

The first generation of network systems was built on conventional computer systems; the second generation added a fast data path and more power to network interface cards, permitting NICs to handle lower-layer packet processing such as framing. The third generation of network systems extends the second generation architecture by adding an embedded processor to each network interface. The embedded processor implements higher layer protocols and handles packets that cannot be forwarded across the fast path.

Although a third generation architecture suffices for many systems, custom silicon must be used to achieve the highest speed. Because custom silicon is inflexible, the initial implementation and subsequent changes are both expensive and time consuming.

Network processor technology has emerged to serve as the basis for fourth generation network systems. A network processor is a programmable silicon device that is tailored to process packets at high speed. The goal of network processors is ambitions: combine the speed of custom silicon with the flexibility and low development cost of software-based systems. Network processors currently fill an economic middle ground between ASIC and embedded systems designs. Future generations of network processors are expected to have higher performance and lower cost.

FOR FURTHER STUDY

Crowley et. al. [2000] characterizes the workloads that a network processor needs to support. Kennedy and Melnick [1999] and Husak and Gohn [2000] each argues that network processors lower the time-to-market. Husak [2000] defines network processors and compares approaches.

EXERCISES

11.1 To assess the potential market for network processors, obtain an estimate of the number of Ethernet switches sold in a year and assume sixteen network processors will be used in each switch.

11.2 Consult the technical descriptions of commercial network system products and make a list of the embedded RISC processors each uses.

11.3 Find a company that fabrics silicon chips and obtain an estimate of the cost.

11.4 To assess the cost of ASIC engineering, obtain an estimate of the cost for two man-years of an ASIC design engineer and one man-year of an ASIC verification engineer.

11.5 Study FPGA technology. Can all protocol processing tasks be performed using FPGAs? Why or why not?

11.6 Consult network processor vendors' advertising. What is the highest aggregate data rate the advertising claims a network processor can handle?

11.7 Search the web and compare the price and performance of network processor chips to the price and performance of RISC chips. Under what circumstances is it advisable to use each?

11.8 Obtain an estimate of the costs to produce and test an ASIC and a network processor, ignoring initial development costs.

11.9 Extend the previous exercise by amortizing the ASIC development over total units produced to find the volume at which the total cost for a system that uses ASICs is less than the total cost for a system that uses network processors.

Chapter Contents

12

The Complexity Of Network Processor Design

12.1 Introduction

The previous chapter introduces network processors by defining the overall goals and describing the economic motivation for using them. This chapter begins a discussion of network processor internals and functionality by considering general design issues. Network processors are among the most complex processing devices, and the chapter focuses on the complexity of their design. It reviews the support needed for protocol processing tasks, and discusses how network processors fit into the overall network system architecture. The next chapter continues the discussion by examining the internal organization and architecture of network processors.

12.2 Network Processor Functionality

How should a network processor be designed? The answer depends on the operations the network processor will perform and the processor's role in the network system. There are two broad issues. On one hand, a network processor requires functionality sufficient for packet processing. On the other hand, the exact functions needed in a network processor depend on the architecture of the system in which the network processor will be used. Specifically, the functions depend on the way processing is divided between the network processor and other parts of the system.

The general problem to be solved, protocol processing, is well understood. The industry has experience implementing protocols, and specific requirements are well-known for each protocol and each layer of the stack. A network processor is not designed for a specific protocol. In fact, the instruction set on a typical network processor does not include any instructions devoted to a specific protocol†. Instead, the goal is *generality* — a network processor should have functionality sufficient to handle any protocol.

Part of the challenge in designing a network processor arises because designers seek *minimality*, not merely *comprehensiveness*. Comprehensiveness can be met in an obvious way: a designer incorporates an exhaustive set of instructions that each handle one feature of one protocol. Unfortunately, the resulting design is inelegant and makes inefficient use of silicon. In contrast, a minimalistic approach produces a chip that is both elegant and efficient. However, minimality requires considerable effort: a designer must analyze differences among protocols, identify features that are common, and devise a minimum set of instructions sufficient to handle all the features. We can summarize:

> *A network processor is not designed to process a specific protocol or part of a protocol. Instead, designers seek a minimal set of instructions that are sufficient to handle an arbitrary protocol processing task at high speed.*

12.3 Packet Processing Functions

The first step in designing a general-purpose network processor consists of identifying the functions needed across many protocols. Recall from Chapter 6, for example, that packet processing tasks include the following:

- Error detection and correction
- Traffic measurement and policing
- Frame and protocol demultiplexing
- Address lookup and packet forwarding
- Segmentation, fragmentation, and reassembly
- Packet classification
- Traffic shaping
- Timing and scheduling
- Queueing
- Security: authentication and privacy

---

†Although special-purpose network processors exist, we begin with a discussion of general-purpose network processors and consider special-purpose designs later.

Although each of the tasks listed above can be handled with the general-purpose instruction set found on a traditional CPU, designers strive to optimize network processor performance by adding instructions that can perform the tasks faster. For example, consider queueing. Although a network processor handles queues of packets, it does not need to handle other types of queues. Thus, instead of instructions that manipulate an arbitrary queue, a network processor can contain instructions that are optimized for packet queues. Similarly, because most protocols rely on a CRC or checksum for error detection, a network processor can contain instructions that compute such values at high speed.

Several questions arise. First, is the above list sufficient to encompass all protocol processing? Second, which of the above functions are the most important to optimize? Third, how do the above functions map onto hardware units in a typical network system? Fourth, which of the hardware units in a typical network system can be replaced with a network processor? Fifth, what minimal set of instructions is sufficiently general to implement the above functions? None of the questions can be answered easily, but they are all important because they provide the basis for future research and development.

12.4 Ingress And Egress Processing

To help reduce complexity, hardware designers often use a divide-and-conquer approach that divides a complex problem into smaller subproblems and then solves each subproblem separately. The solutions for individual subproblems must then be integrated into a final solution. When applied to the design of network processors, the divide-and-conquer approach leads designers to collect related protocol processing tasks into separate groups and to work on each group separately. Once a group has been identified, a designer can define a set of network processor instructions suitable for the group. To complete the design, the sets of instructions for each group must be integrated into the final instruction set.

An example of divide-and-conquer will help clarify the concept. One of the most common ways to divide packet processing tasks partitions them into two groups. The first group, which is known as *ingress*, focuses on arriving packets, and the second group, which is known as *egress*, focuses on departing packets. The next two sections discuss each group.

12.4.1 Ingress Processing

Ingress processing encompasses all operations performed as packets arrive. For example, ingress processing includes error detection because the receiving computer verifies the CRC or checksum in each incoming packet. Similarly, ingress processing includes demultiplexing or classification† because a system performs such operations to determine how to handle a packet.

---

†Some designs defer classification until egress to reduce the amount of state information that must be propagated from the ingress side to the egress side.

Some ingress processing requires the system to maintain state information. For example, reassembly requires the system to collect fragments. Most traffic policing algorithms require state because the system must keep a history of traffic.

Ingress processing includes support functions such as queueing and scheduling, and requires a forwarding function to control the disposition of packets. Ingress processing also prepares packets for transfer across a switching fabric, which may include dividing the packet into fixed-size blocks. Finally, ingress operations include header modification and transport layer termination. We can summarize the set of operations associated with ingress†:

Ingress Processing

Error detection and security verification
Classification or demultiplexing
Traffic measurement and policing
Address lookup and packet forwarding
Header modification and transport splicing
Reassembly or flow termination
Forwarding, queueing, and scheduling

12.4.2 Egress Processing

Egress processing encompasses operations applied as a packet departs. The egress side extracts each packet from the switching fabric, which may involve collecting pieces from multiple fabric transfers. Egress processing includes error detection because a sending computer must insert a CRC or checksum in each outgoing packet. Egress processing includes segmentation or fragmentation because a packet cannot be divided into small pieces for transmission until the exact details of the output port are known. Traffic shaping and the associated support functions of queueing and scheduling are also performed when packets are ready to be transmitted. Finally, egress processing includes the addition of security features (e.g., packet encryption). We can summarize the set of operations associated with egress:

Egress Processing

Addition of error detection codes
Address lookup and packet forwarding
Segmentation or fragmentation
Traffic shaping
Timing and scheduling
Queueing and buffering
Header modification
Output security processing

†Although the division into ingress and egress suggested here is typical, it is not absolute: some designs use slight variations.

It may seem that the division between ingress and egress is artificial and ambiguous because a single packet passes through both. When does ingress processing end and egress processing begin? The division is easiest to understand from the perspective of the underlying architecture: ingress processing occurs before a packet passes across the switching fabric for the first time, and egress processing occurs after the packet passes across the switching fabric for the last time. In a typical third generation system, a packet crosses the fabric exactly once, which makes the division straightforward†. Figure 12.1 illustrates the concept.

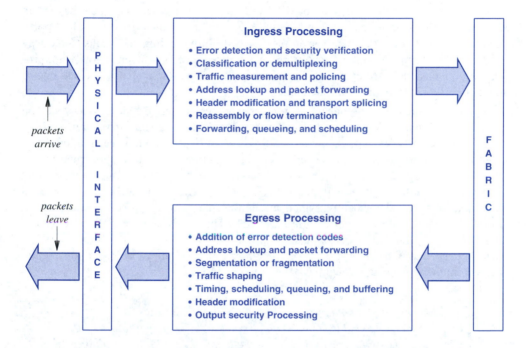

Figure 12.1 Illustration of ingress and egress processing and the data flow through the resulting system. The switching fabric separates ingress from egress.

By clearly separating incoming packets from outgoing packets, the figure helps us imagine the organization of the underlying hardware. Ingress hardware is associated with an input port, and egress hardware is associated with an output port. More important, the figure allows us to understand an alternative to an integrated network processor design that may be needed in cases where an integrated solution proves to be technically or economically infeasible (e.g., too large to fit on a silicon wafer or too expensive). In such cases, divide-and-conquer allows the designer to salvage much of the effort: instead of producing a single, complex device that solves the entire problem, the designer

---

†Although it is possible to design a network system that does not use a switching fabric, the conceptual division of processing into ingress and egress still holds.

can choose to create several special-purpose devices, each optimized for one particular subproblem. Indeed, many of the early commercial hardware devices followed the division outlined above: a vendor built a pair of special-purpose chips, one devoted to ingress processing and the other devoted to egress processing.

12.5 Parallel And Distributed Architecture

If we want to build an integrated network processor that solves the entire packet processing problem, what basic approach should we use? It is tempting to imagine a network processor on the fast data path, handling all packet processing (i.e., the system forwards each incoming packet to the network processor and then on to an output port). Unfortunately, a network processor on the fast path limits scaling analogous to the way a conventional processor limits scaling in a centralized design — even if a network processor contains hardware optimized for protocol processing, the underlying clock rate of the network processor limits throughput.

To avoid creating a bottleneck, engineers who design network processors focus on scalability. There are three general techniques available to enable maximum scaling. First, a typical network processor contains a variety of hardware units, each tailored to a specific function. As a result, packet processing functionality can be performed by the type of hardware best suited to the task. Second, to improve the aggregate processing rate, critical hardware units within a network processor are replicated. The replicated units can operate independently, which means that the network processor can perform multiple operations in *parallel* or in a *pipeline*†. Third, a typical network processor is designed to operate in a *distributed* environment. That is, network processors are designed so that if multiple processors are interconnected, they can work together to achieve higher aggregate throughput. We can summarize:

> *Unlike a conventional processor, scalability is essential for network processors. To achieve maximum scalability, a network processor offers a variety of special-purpose functional units, allows parallel or pipelined execution, and operates in a distributed environment.*

The focus on scalability makes the design of network processors especially difficult. Designers must choose among hardware units that each handle a specialized task, replicated hardware that operates in parallel, and hardware that supports distributed execution. Furthermore, because they have little experience with network protocols, hardware designers have not developed heuristic rules for network processor design. Chapter 13 illustrates that the many possibilities have resulted in a plethora of designs.

---

†Chapter 13 explains the parallel and pipeline approaches in detail.

12.6 The Architectural Roles Of Network Processors

The design of network processors is further complicated because they are not restricted to a single position in the overall architecture. Instead, network processors can be used in several ways, and designers strive for a single device that serves as many uses as possible. To understand the range of possible uses, we will begin by considering a third generation architecture†.

One goal of network processor design is a hardware device that can augment or replace any of the functional units in a network system. To understand why the goal makes network processor design complex, consider the following architectural roles:

- Replacement for a conventional CPU
- Augmentation of a conventional CPU
- On the input path of a network interface card
- Between a network interface card and a switching fabric
- Between the switching fabric and an output interface
- On the output path of a network interface card
- Attached to the switching fabric like other ports

12.7 Consequences For Each Architectural Role

Although the architectural roles listed above involve basic packet and data movement, the specific operations performed at each step vary. A design optimized to fill one niche in the architecture may not work well in another. The following paragraphs discuss each architectural role.

Replacement for a conventional CPU. To replace a conventional CPU, a network processor must have all the usual capabilities plus special facilities to optimize packet processing. That is, the instruction set needs both conventional and special instructions. Conventional instructions include the arithmetic and data manipulation operations needed for protocol processing. For example, a network processor must be able to access packets in memory, parse packet headers, and use linked data structures with pointers. A network processor may need floating point hardware if implementations of queueing disciplines and traffic shaping use floating point computation‡. Finally, to distinguish it from a conventional CPU, a network processor needs special instructions to manipulate packets.

Augmentation of a conventional CPU. If a network processor is attached to a conventional CPU, the CPU performs most packet processing and only uses the network processor to handle specific tasks. There are two architectural approaches: preprocess-

---

†An illustration of third generation architecture appears in Figure 11.1 on page 154.

‡The highest speed implementations of queueing and shaping do not use floating point.

ing or coprocessing. As the name implies, a preprocessor acts as an in-line filter to handle incoming packets before they arrive at the CPU. Typically, a preprocessor retrieves a packet from a hardware port and performs ingress operations such as classification. The coprocessor approach is more general than preprocessing because a CPU can choose to use a network processor for any operation that the network processor can perform faster. Thus, the coprocessor approach is more powerful because it can handle either ingress or egress operations.

The chief advantage of using a network processor to augment a CPU, instead of replacing the CPU, arises from lower design complexity: network processor hardware is easier to design and implement because the designer concentrates on packet processing functionality without considering conventional instructions. The chief disadvantage of augmentation arises from the extra hardware required to interface the CPU and network processor: a mechanism is needed that allows the CPU to invoke the network processor efficiently.

On the input path of a network interface card. As we have seen, each generation of network systems moves additional packet processing to the network interface. A network processor on the input path must be able to retrieve packets from an input port and perform ingress operations. The chief advantage of using a network processor in place of other hardware arises from its flexibility — ingress processing can be changed easily†.

Between a network interface card and the switching fabric. Recall that a fabric such as a crossbar provides switched paths, which means that a path must be established before the fabric can be used. A network processor can act as the intermediary between a network interface card and the switching fabric; the network processor interacts with the fabric controller to establish a path, transfer data, and relinquish the path.

Between the switching fabric and an output interface. Some switching fabrics use a distributed control mechanism in which each output port controls its own access. When an input port is ready to use the fabric, the input port notifies the output port, usually with a separate mechanism such as an independent bus. The output port schedules requests and notifies each potential sender when the fabric is ready for the transfer. A network processor can coordinate access of the output port.

On the output path of a network interface card. A network processor in the output path handles egress operations analogous to the way a network processor on the input path handles ingress operations. The network processor must be able to accept packets from the switching fabric, manage queues, implement traffic shaping, and send packets to the output port.

Attached to the switching fabric like other ports. A network processor can be attached to the switching fabric like any other port. Because packets can be sent from an input port across the fabric to the network processor and from the network processor across the fabric to an output port, the network processor can serve as an intermediate station. More important, because the fabric allows scaling, the set of intermediate net-

---

†At least one vendor's network processor (Motorola's C-Port) also handles lower-layer functions such as packet delineation, auto-negotiation, and CDMA backoff.

work processors can be expanded easily. To permit maximum parallelism, the system can arrange to distribute incoming packets among the entire set of network processors.

12.8 Macroscopic Data Pipelining And Heterogeneity

The ability to connect a network processor to the switching fabric introduces an interesting new possibility: a macroscopic data pipeline†. We can imagine a pipeline in which each stage is implemented with a network processor. The network processors are each attached to the switching fabric which provides the interconnection among stages — the processor that implements stage i transfers packets across the switching fabric to the processor that implements stage $i+1$.

A pipeline interconnected with a switching fabric allows two interesting optimizations. First, the architecture supports heterogeneous network processors. Because the stages are independent, the network processor used to implement one stage can differ from the network processor used to implement another stage. Thus, instead of using general-purpose network processors that attempt to solve all packet processing problems, a designer can choose among special-purpose network processors that are optimized for a specific task. Second, the use of a switching fabric allows stages to be skipped. Suppose, for example, that stage k handles IP reassembly. If the previous stage finds a complete datagram, the reassembly stage can be skipped (i.e., stage $k-1$ can transfer the packet directly to stage $k+1$). Thus, a switching fabric overcomes one of the major drawbacks of a pipeline by allowing optimized forwarding. The point is:

> *In addition to replacing elements of a traditional third generation architecture, network processors can be attached directly to a switching fabric and used to implement stages of a macroscopic data pipeline. The fabric allows forwarding among stages to be optimized.*

12.9 Network Processor Design And Software Emulation

We have argued that building a general-purpose network processor is complex. To master complexity, hardware designers usually rely on software emulation. Before constructing a chip, the designer builds a software emulator, and uses the emulator to assess the performance and correctness of the design. The designer obtains a set of applications and benchmarks, compiles the software into code for the new chip, and uses the emulator to measure the resulting performance.

Unlike a conventional processor, however, traditional software benchmarking does not work well for network processor design. Because a network processor includes many low-level hardware details arranged in an internal architecture that differs from other network processors, applications and benchmarks cannot easily be shared among all network processors. Instead, the software must be rewritten to match the architec-

---

†The concept of a pipeline is illustrated in Figure 8.6 on page 110.

ture. More important, when software is ported from one architecture to another, the software may need to be reorganized completely, which makes performance comparisons difficult. Consequently, designers face a chicken-and-egg problem. Once a hardware architecture has been created, programmers can build software that makes optimal use of the design, and once software has been created, hardware designers can choose an architecture that matches the software design. In the case of an emerging field like network processors, where designers are experimenting with a wide range of possible architectures, design of hardware and software must be closely integrated. The point is:

> *Because a network processor includes many low-level hardware details that require specialized software, the hardware and software designs are codependent; software for a network processor must be created along with the hardware.*

12.10 Summary

The goal of network processor designers is a single, general-purpose, optimized hardware device that can serve at an arbitrary place in the overall system architecture and handle arbitrary protocol processing. The goal makes the design complicated because it includes conventional processing such as arithmetic and data manipulation operations as well as specialized packet processing.

To help identify fundamental operations, designers partition packet processing tasks into related groups. One of the most popular divisions consists of two groups, one for ingress operations and the other for egress operations. The boundary between ingress and egress occurs when a packet passes across the switching fabric.

To achieve high performance, network processors use three general optimization techniques. Individual hardware units are optimized for a specific task, critical hardware is replicated to support parallel execution, and a distributed paradigm is used to allow multiple, interconnected network processors to work together. Tradeoffs among the three optimizations further complicate the design process.

Because network processor hardware and software are closely related, neither can be defined first. Instead, the software and hardware must be designed together.

FOR FURTHER STUDY

Menzilcioglu and Schlick [1991] considers the design of a network processor. Several network processor vendors have issued white papers that describe the inherent complexity. For example, Agere systems [1999] discusses challenges related to network processor design. EZchip Technologies [1999] presents the issues from another vendor's point of view. More current examples of vendors' white papers can be found by searching the web.

EXERCISES

12.1   Use the list of protocol processing tasks on page 166 to categorize the tasks necessary to implement the following protocols: ARP, IP, UDP, TCP, and HTTP.

12.2   Define a set of hardware primitives for traffic policing and a set for classification. Compare the two.

12.3   Define a set of hardware primitives for transport layer splicing.

12.4   Is floating point computation required for traffic shaping? Why or why not?

12.5   Examine the third generation architecture illustrated on page 154. Does the architecture map easily into the ingress / egress model presented in this chapter? Why or why not?

12.6   Consider building software to run on a network processor at the same time the architecture is being developed. What tools can you propose to speed the development process?

12.7   If a set of N identical network processors are attached directly to a switching fabric and incoming packets are distributed to the set round-robin, which of the packet processing functions on page 166 do not work well in such a parallel architecture? Why?

Chapter Contents

13

Network Processor Architectures

13.1 Introduction

The previous chapters introduce network processors, and explain both the economics and inherent complexity. This chapter focuses on the internal organization of a network processor. It lists characteristics, and describes broad architectural approaches. The next chapters continue the discussion. Chapter 14 discusses scaling, and Chapter 15 uses a set of commercial chips to show how the architectural approaches relate to actual products.

13.2 Architectural Variety

The economic advantages of network processors have provided vendors a compelling motivation for their development — potential profits are high. As a result, many commercial chips have been created. The inherent complexity has made a wide range of architectures possible, and the lack of an installed customer base has given vendors considerable freedom in experimenting with new designs. As a result, many architectural variations exist.

Although vendors share the broad concept of a network processor, the specifics vary considerably. No industry consensus exists regarding the functions needed for protocol processing or on how to map the functions into special-purpose hardware. In fact, designers remain uncertain about the optimal role of network processors in the overall system architecture. There is no agreement about which hardware building blocks to include in a network processor, exactly what hardware functions to replicate, or how to organize the components on a network processor chip. Finally, designers do not agree on how to build distributed interconnections among network processors that are efficient and scalable.

13.3 Primary Architectural Characteristics

The inherent complexity of network processors and variety of designs make architecture difficult to understand. More important, because each network processor represents a complex combination of conventional processing, special-purpose hardware, and replicated units, no obvious taxonomy exists. Thus, instead of attempting to classify architectures, we will characterize them. The list of primary characteristics includes:

- Processor hierarchy
- Memory hierarchy
- Internal transfer mechanisms
- External interface and communication mechanisms
- Special-purpose hardware
- Polling and notification mechanisms
- Concurrent execution support
- Programming model and paradigm
- Hardware and software dispatch mechanisms
- Implicit or explicit parallelism

The next sections each describe one characteristic and explain how the characteristic applies to network processor architecture.

13.3.1 Processor Hierarchy

The term *processor hierarchy* refers to hardware units that perform various aspects of packet processing, and includes both programmable and fixed processors. The processor hierarchy for a network system extends from the lowest levels to the highest, and encompasses special-purpose hardware dedicated to a single task as well as general-purpose CPUs. Figure 13.1 provides an example of the processors that comprise an eight-level hierarchy.

As the figure indicates, the complete processor hierarchy may not reside on a network processor. Instead, a network processor chip contains hardware sufficient to handle some levels, and relies on external hardware to handle other levels. For example, some network processors contain special-purpose framer and transmission hardware to implement low-level I/O details such as CRC computation, signaling, and other aspects of frame transmission; other network processors require such functions to be provided by external chips. Similarly, many network systems include a conventional CPU that handles supervisory functions such as monitoring system performance, running routing protocols, and providing an interface a system administrator can use for configuration.

Level	Processor Type	Programmable?	On Chip?
8	General purpose CPU	yes	possibly
7	Embedded processor	yes	typically
6	I/O processor	yes	typically
5	Coprocessor	no	typically
4	Fabric interface	no	typically
3	Data transfer unit	no	typically
2	Framer	no	possibly
1	Physical transmitter	no	possibly

Figure 13.1 The processor hierarchy used in a typical network system. As the last column of the figure shows, many levels of the hierarchy are located onboard the network processor chip.

The processor hierarchy is among the most interesting aspects of network processors because a single network processor includes many physical processors that must work together. A network processor can provide: one or more embedded RISC processors used to handle higher layers of protocols and provide overall control, one or more specialized coprocessors that are each optimized for a particular packet processing task, multiple I/O processors† that can perform ingress or egress processing at wire speed, one or more fabric interfaces that handle interaction with the switching fabric, and one or more data transfer units that handle moving packets between I/O devices and memory. Section 13.6 discusses the relationship of the processor hierarchy to data flow and scaling.

13.3.2 Memory Hierarchy

Computer designers use a *memory hierarchy* to achieve high performance with low cost. Because high-speed memory is expensive‡, a hierarchy is arranged with a small amount of memory that operates at the highest speed, a larger amount of memory that operates at a slower speed, and so on. As a result, the largest amount of memory in the system operates at the lowest speed. To maintain high performance with a hierarchical memory, a programmer places data that is accessed most frequently in the highest-speed memory, and relegates bulk data that is accessed infrequently to lower-speed (and lower cost) memory. Because data can be moved from one memory to another, the choice of which items to place in highest-speed memory can be dynamic.

---

†We have chosen a generic term because no uniform terminology exists. Various vendors use terms such as *packet engine*, *microengine* and *picoengine* for their particular I/O processor.

‡High speed refers to memory with low *latency* and high throughout. Each memory technology represents a tradeoff among latency, throughput, and cost; Chapter 14 lists examples.

A memory hierarchy is an essential complement to a network processor because the main goal of using a network processor is to lower the overall system cost. A network processor chip does not usually contain a large amount of memory, nor does the hardware dictate the exact use of the memory hierarchy. Instead, the processor contains interface hardware that provides access to various levels of an external memory hierarchy; the programmer chooses which data to place in each memory. For example, consider using a network processor to build an IP router. If the programmer expects to spend more time accessing the routing table than processing the payload of a packet, the programmer can place the routing table in higher-speed memory. Similarly, if a programmer expects that a system will spend significantly more time processing headers than payloads, the programmer can choose to place the packet header in a higher-speed memory than the packet payload.

Of course, the memory associated with a network processor is not "slow" compared to the memory on a conventional computer system — even the slowest memory must be fast enough to send and receive packets at the aggregate data rate handled by the processor. The highest-speed memory must operate much faster than typical memory because the network processor must be able to execute hundreds or thousands of instructions per packet. Figure 13.2 provides an example of the size and relative latency of a typical memory hierarchy.

Memory Type	Rel. Speed	Approx. Size	On Chip?
Control store	100	10^3	yes
G.P. Registers†	90	10^2	yes
Onboard Cache	40	10^3	yes
Onboard RAM	10	10^3	yes
Static RAM	5	10^7	no
Dynamic RAM	1	10^8	no

Figure 13.2 An example of a memory hierarchy used with a network processor. The number of levels in the hierarchy as well as the exact memory size and performance depend on the network processor.

The figure lists memory access rates relative to the speed of *Dynamic Random Access Memory* (*DRAM*)‡. For example, the figure shows that *Static Random Access Memory* (*SRAM*) operates approximately twice as fast as DRAM.

We can summarize the motivation and use of a memory hierarchy:

> *A memory hierarchy allows a network processor to achieve high performance at reasonable cost. Although typical network processor hardware includes support for a multilevel memory hierarchy, the choice of which memory to use for each data item must be made by a programmer.*

---

†G.P. registers are *general-purpose* registers.

‡Because the figure only lists approximate rates, we do not distinguish among types of memory. For example, some vendors use *Synchronized Dynamic Random Access Memory* (*SDRAM*).

13.3.3 Internal Transfer Mechanisms

The term *internal transfer mechanism* refers to any mechanism on a network processor chip that provides a data path between functional units. In most cases, packets reside in memory, and internal transfer mechanisms are used to send metadata such as a pointer to a packet or information extracted from the packet header. In some architectures, however, an entire packet is passed among functional units within the chip. Finally, in addition to packet data, internal transfer mechanisms are used to exchange auxiliary data such as an IP routing table or a list of addresses culled from the incoming packets.

Because a network processor chip contains multiple, independent processors, internal communication is crucial for performance — if the internal data path is slow, overall performance can suffer. The problem of performance is complicated because programmers are free to choose how the processor and memory hierarchies will be used. Thus, a chip designer cannot know exactly how an internal transfer mechanism will be used. To ensure that the transfer bandwidth is sufficient for all possible uses, most network processors include multiple transfer mechanisms. Examples include:

- Internal bus
- Hardware FIFO
- Transfer registers
- Onboard shared memory

Internal Bus. One of the most prevalent internal transfer mechanisms is known as an internal bus. Like a conventional computer bus, an internal bus provides a data path to which multiple units attach. Although it is possible to use a distributed access mechanism, many internal buses include separate controller hardware that arbitrates access and ensures only one unit attempts to transfer across the bus at a given time.

Hardware FIFO. As an alternative to a bus, some network processors provide transfer hardware in the form of a FIFO (First In First Out)†. A FIFO provides for buffered transfers that allow a sender and receiver to operate asynchronously. A FIFO contains a fixed number of *slots* that each can hold a fixed amount of data (e.g., a slot can hold a block of 64 bytes). Initially, all N slots in a FIFO are empty. As long as the FIFO is not full, a sender can deposit an item in the next available slot; as long as the FIFO is not empty, a receiver can extract the next item. Thus, the sender can deposit up to N items in the FIFO before the receiver extracts any of them. A FIFO can absorb a packet burst that results either from packets arriving quickly or from one stage of a pipeline handling packets more quickly than the next stage.

Transfer Registers. A third alternative for an internal transfer mechanism consists of a set of hardware transfer registers. Like a hardware FIFO, transfer registers provide buffered transfer — a sender can deposit an item in an empty transfer register, and a receiver can extract an item from a transfer register that contains an item. Unlike a FIFO, a transfer register mechanism does not impose a sequential access paradigm. Instead,

---

†Programmers use the term *queue* to refer to the general concept; hardware engineers use the term *FIFO*.

the hardware allows *random access*, which means that the registers can be written or read in any order.

Onboard Shared Memory. As a fourth alternative, a network processor can contain onboard memory used to transfer items. A sender places an item in the shared memory from which the receiver extracts the item. Although shared memory provides more flexibility, it is less popular than other mechanisms because it requires more silicon real estate† and entails additional interface hardware to achieve high performance.

13.3.4 External Interface And Communication Mechanisms

Although designers attempt to squeeze as much processing power as possible onto a single chip, the network processor must connect to other hardware in the network system. External connections include:

- Standard and specialized bus interfaces
- Memory interfaces
- Direct I/O interfaces
- Switching fabric interface

Standard And Specialized Bus Interfaces. A network processor needs to connect to one or more external buses (i.e., buses that connect devices in the network system). A bus may be a standard in the computer industry such as a PCI bus, or may be designed specifically for network processors such as an *LA-2* bus specified by the *Network Processor Forum* (*NPF*). In either case, most network processors contain bus interface hardware that handles the details of electrical connections and providing bus access to processors on the chip.

Memory Interfaces. A network processor needs access to external memories. In most cases, the memory connects through a bus. However, a network processor can contain additional hardware to optimize memory interaction (e.g., an onboard cache). Optimizations may result in *weak ordering* in which the hardware issues *read* or *write* operations in a different order than the programmer specifies. In such cases, the memory interface must provide primitives that allow the programmer to control situations where ordering is critical.

Direct I/O Interfaces. Network processors can connect to high-speed I/O devices over a bus. For example, the connection between a network processor and an Ethernet port can occur over a bus. However, it is also possible for a network processor to have a direct connection to a device or to have a connection to intermediate hardware which then connects to a specific device. In either case, interface hardware on the network processor chip allows processors on the chip to access the external I/O device. For example, a network processor can contain hardware that follows the *System Packet Interface Level 3 or 4* (*SPI-3* or *SPI-4*) standard or the *SerDes Framer Interface* (*SFI*) standard‡. Direct connections are also used for extremely low-speed I/O (e.g., a serial line used for device management).

---

†The term *silicon real estate* refers to the physical area on a chip.
‡The *Optical Internetworking Forum* (*OIF*) controls the SPI and SFI standards.

Switching Fabric Interface. Some network processors are designed to connect to a specific type of switching fabric. In such cases, the network processor contains hardware that handles the interface details. As an alternative, the *Network Processor Forum* (*NPF*) has adopted the *CSIX* standard for switching fabric interfaces. Their goal is to allow network processors to follow an interface standard that is independent of the underlying fabric.

13.3.5 Special-Purpose Hardware

In addition to coprocessors, which are part of the processor hierarchy, network processors can contain at least two types of special-purpose hardware. First, a network processor can contain one or more units that provide control, synchronization, or coordination among internal processors contending for access to shared resources. Second, a network processor can have one or more configurable hardware units that are used to manage or control I/O devices or other hardware units.

We have already mentioned that a shared internal bus can have additional control hardware that coordinates access among all units that share the bus. Each shared resource, including each external memory and bus connection, requires a special-purpose coordination mechanism. Some network processors generalize the idea of coordination by introducing more powerful control units that each synchronize access to a set of resources.

The second form of special-purpose hardware strikes a compromise between a special-purpose coprocessor and a fully programmable processor. Like a coprocessor, the unit must be invoked — a processor on the chip uses the unit to perform a task. Unlike a coprocessor, however, the functionality is not fixed. Instead, the hardware is configurable — configuration parameters are set, and then the unit is invoked repeatedly. The advantage of configurable hardware arises from speed: after configuration has been performed, the unit operates faster than a programmable processor.

13.3.6 Polling And Notification Mechanisms

A network processor must handle asynchronous events such as the arrival of a packet on an Ethernet port, a protocol timer expiration, or the completion of a transfer across the switching fabric. Two possible hardware mechanisms exist to handle asynchrony: *polling* and *notification*. A network processor may employ either, or may provide both and allow the programmer to choose between them.

A polling mechanism requires an active element (e.g., a processor) to repeatedly test hardware associated with the event. For example, an I/O interface device can be configured to set a bit whenever a packet arrives. A processor clears the bit, starts the I/O device, and then repeatedly tests the bit. When it finds the bit set, the processor retrieves and processes a packet.

An alternative to polling uses a notification mechanism; notification can be implemented with a hardware or software *interrupt*. A processor specifies that notification is needed, initiates an operation, and then proceeds with other tasks. When the notification occurs, the processor is diverted from its current activity to handle the event. For example, an I/O interface device that uses an interrupt mechanism can be configured to interrupt a processor when a packet arrives. The interrupt causes the processor to suspend processing temporarily and execute the code that handles the incoming packet. High-speed systems tend to use polling to avoid the overhead of interrupts.

13.3.7 Concurrent Execution Support

The term *concurrent execution*† refers to a well-known programming paradigm used to maximize performance. Concurrency is used in cases where a computation blocks to wait for an external event such as a packet arrival. To optimize overall throughput, a concurrent system allows a set of independent *processes* or *threads of execution* to remain ready to execute at all times. When one thread blocks (e.g., to wait for I/O), the processor switches to another thread and continues execution.

Typical network processors provide support for concurrent threads at multiple levels. In an embedded RISC processor, concurrency is often supported by an operating system. In low-level I/O processors, which have no operating system, the hardware must provide support. That is, a programmer creates multiple threads of execution, informs the hardware about each, and then allows the hardware to switch among threads automatically. Two broad questions arise:

- Does thread execution span multiple processors?
- Are threads preemptable?

The first question relates concurrent execution to parallel hardware. An architecture that supports a *global* implementation of threads allows a thread to migrate from one processor to another; an architecture that supports a *local* implementation of threads associates each thread with a processor and does not allow the thread to execute on any other processor. In a local system, a processor can only switch among the threads that have been assigned to it. Global thread support provides more flexibility, but incurs interprocessor overhead.

The second question relates thread execution to external events. An architecture that supports *preemption* allows an external event (e.g., the arrival of a packet) to force a processor to switch from one thread to another. The alternative to preemption allows a running thread to determine when to relinquish the processor and switch to another thread. Preemption has the advantage of making programming easier because it automates switching among threads. A system that does not use preemption gives the programmer more control over processing.

---

†The alternative to concurrent execution is known as *sequential processing*.

13.3.8 Hardware Support For Programming

Although each network processor contains hardware support for a programming paradigm, there is no universal agreement on the fundamental approach†. The two most prevalent forms of hardware support for programming can be characterized as:

- Asynchronous event handlers
- Communicating threads

Asynchronous Event Handlers. A style of programming in which a programmer creates a set of handlers and associates each with a specific event. When the event occurs, the system invokes the corresponding event handler. Events can arise from the hardware (e.g., a packet arrives at a physical port) or from the software (e.g., a low-level handler determines that a frame contains an IP datagram, and passes the frame to an IP handler).

Communicating Threads. A conventional sequential programming model in which one or more threads execute independently. If more than one thread exists, the threads use an interprocess communication mechanism to pass data from one to another (e.g., a low-level thread determines that a frame contains an IP datagram, and sends the frame to the thread that handles IP). Thus, in the communicating threads model, a thread typically executes an infinite loop such as:

```
do forever  {
        wait for next input packet, P;
        process P;
        send P on to next thread;
}
```

When interprocess communication extends from a thread running on one processor to a thread running on another, the hardware's internal transfer mechanism is used for communication.

13.3.9 Hardware And Software Dispatch Mechanisms

The term *dispatch* refers to the overall control of parallel or concurrent tasks. When work becomes available, a dispatcher assigns the work to a specific processor or thread. Some network processors provide hardware support for dispatching; others allow software to control dispatching. In general, software dispatching is used on a processor that has an operating system, and hardware dispatching is used by low-level I/O processors that do not have an operating system.

---

†Section 13.5 discusses software architecture and programming paradigms.

13.3.10 Implicit Or Explicit Parallelism

Two broad styles of parallelism are used in network processors; the chief difference arises in the way software is structured. A hardware architecture that uses *explicit parallelism* exposes parallelism to the programmer, and requires that the software be constructed to exploit the parallel hardware. That is, a programmer must choose how and when to use each copy of a functional unit, and must write code to coordinate among multiple copies. In most cases, the exact number of copies of each functional unit is encoded in the software.

A hardware architecture that uses *implicit parallelism* completely hides parallel copies of functional units. That is, a programmer creates software as if a single copy will be executing. The hardware handles parallelism automatically by replicating the program as needed.

Explicit parallelism has the advantage of giving a programmer more control over execution, but the disadvantage of requiring a programmer to build code that understands the underlying hardware — a program must be rewritten before it can be used on a network processor that has more or fewer copies of a functional unit. Implicit parallelism has the advantages of reducing programming complexity and keeping software independent of the exact number of copies of a functional unit. Because it handles allocation among parallel hardware units automatically, implicit parallelism allows a programmer to create a program using the familiar paradigm of single-thread execution.

13.4 Architecture, Packet Flow, And Clock Rates

Although each network processor includes many details as outlined above, a design tends to emphasize one aspect over another. We can use the main emphasis of a design to define five broad categories of network processor architectures:

- Embedded processor plus fixed coprocessors
- Embedded processor plus programmable I/O processors
- Parallel (number of processors scales to handle load)
- Pipelined processors
- Dataflow

One of the most important differences in the network processor architectures centers on the way traffic flows through the hardware. To understand the difference consider how traffic is handled. For example, Figure 13.3 illustrates a single, embedded processor that performs three operations per packet. All traffic flows through the processor, which performs the set of operations on each packet.

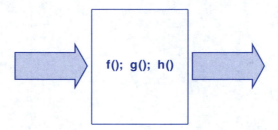

Figure 13.3 Illustration of packet flow through an architecture that uses an embedded processor. The label indicates that the processor performs operations *f, g,* and *h* sequentially.

Figure 13.4 illustrates the packet flow in a parallel architecture in which incoming traffic is divided among a set of processors. Each processor performs the full set of operations on each packet it receives†.

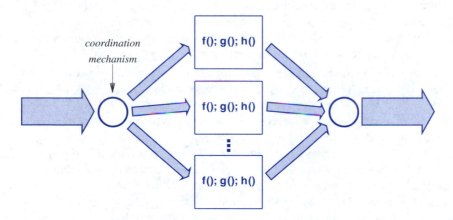

Figure 13.4 Illustration of packet flow through a parallel architecture. If the architecture has N processors, each processor handles approximately 1/N of the traffic.

In a pipeline architecture, each processor performs one operation. Figure 13.5 illustrates the packet flow.

---

†The architecture is known as a *run-to-completion* model because all operations on a packet are completed before the packet is forwarded.

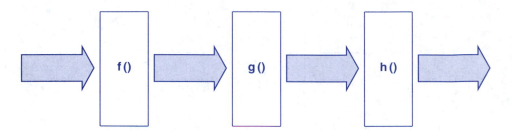

Figure 13.5 Illustration of packet flow through a pipeline architecture. Each
processor performs one operation as packets flow through the
pipeline.

A crucial difference among the architectures arises from the clock rates needed to
process data. To understand the difference, assume that data arrives at a constant rate.
To perform three operations on data, the clock rate in a single processor must exceed
the rate of the arriving data. In the parallel case, where each processor receives 1/N of
the data, the clock rate of a processor needs to be approximately 1/N of the rate of a
single processor (of course, the coordination mechanism must run at the rate of arriving
data). Finally, because a pipeline processor only needs to perform one operation, the
processor's clock rate is approximately equal to the rate of the arriving data.

A *dataflow* architecture represents a departure from conventional approaches. In
essence, a dataflow processor consists of a large memory, into which items can be
placed, and selector hardware that dispatches processing. Each item in memory includes a *tag* that specifies the processing needed. When a functional unit becomes
available, the selector chooses an item for the unit to handle. As an example, consider
an incoming frame. The frame is deposited in memory with a tag that specifies classification. When a classifier unit becomes available, the selector extracts the frame from
memory and passes the frame to the classifier. If it finds an IP datagram in the frame,
the classifier places the frame back in memory with a tag that specifies IP processing.
When an IP processor becomes available, the selector extracts the frame from memory
and passes it to the IP processor.

To increase performance, a dataflow architecture can have multiple functional units
that operate in parallel (e.g., multiple classifier units). Parallelism has the advantage of
reducing the load on a given functional unit, which means that the clock rate of the unit
can also be reduced. However, the selector and memory must operate faster than the arriving data rate.

Of course, the most sophisticated network processors do not fit easily into a single
category because they combine features. For example, a network processor can include
both fixed coprocessors and programmable I/O processors. Thus, the above categories
are neither rigid nor exact — they provide a qualitative assessment of emphasis; many
network processors are hybrids.

13.5 Software Architecture

Although network processor architecture refers primarily to hardware, a design may impose a specific software architecture. Many network processor vendors offer a reference system that illustrates how the vendor envisions software being built; customers often modify the reference software instead of starting from scratch. Thus, a network processor vendor can influence the software architecture. Most software architectures follow one of the following patterns:

- Central program that invokes coprocessors like subroutines
- Central program that interacts with code on intelligent,
    programmable I/O processors
- Communicating threads
- Event-driven program
- RPC-style (program partitioned among processors)
- Pipeline (even if hardware does not use pipeline)
- Combinations of the above

It should be apparent that some of the software architectures match the underlying hardware. For example, a chip that includes hardware dispatch for asynchronous events lends itself to an event-driven software architecture. Similarly, a chip that offers support for threads and data transfer lends itself to a communicating threads architecture.

An RPC-style architecture uses the *Remote Procedure Call* concept — instead of constructing independent programs, the programmer builds a single program which has components running on multiple processors. RPC-style is an especially useful way to span the processor hierarchy. For example, a single program can be built in which the main component runs on an embedded RISC processor and subcomponents run on I/O processors. The main component handles computation, and invokes the subcomponents to handle ingress and egress operations.

A *pipeline* architecture is interesting because it is possible to create a software pipeline even if the underlying hardware does not use a pipeline. For example, consider a pipeline where each stage is implemented by a thread. A packet passes through the pipeline by moving from one thread to another. The threads can execute on a set of parallel processors that are not configured in a pipeline. In fact, a software pipeline can be implemented by creating multiple threads on a single processor†.

13.6 Assigning Functionality To The Processor Hierarchy

A software architecture that makes optimal use of the underlying hardware must be designed to match the processor hierarchy. In particular, high performance requires that each processor be used to handle tasks appropriate to the processor's capability. Figure 13.6 lists example uses of programmable processors.

---

†A pipeline implemented in software, without hardware support, can incur significant overhead.

General purpose CPU
    Highest level functionality
    Administrative interface
    System control
    Overall management functions
    Routing protocols

Embedded processor
    Intermediate functionality
    Higher-layer protocols
    Control of I/O processors
    Exception and error handling
    High-level ingress (e.g., reassembly)
    High-level egress (e.g., traffic shaping)

I/O processor
    Basic packet processing
    Classification
    Forwarding
    Low-level ingress operations
    Low-level egress operations

Figure 13.6 Example uses of the programmable processors on a network processor chip. Programmable I/O processors handle many of the basic packet processing tasks.

Low levels of the processor hierarchy operate at the highest speed. For example, the physical transmitter and framing levels define the system's wire speed (i.e. the maximum rate at which data can enter and leave the overall system). To avoid a bottleneck, data transfer, fabric interface, and coprocessor hardware is designed to operate at wire speed. The hardware allows packets to flow to the I/O processor level at full speed.

Because the instruction set on an I/O processor contains microcode instructions that operate at a lower level than instructions on an embedded processor, an I/O processor can run at a faster clock rate. Consequently, to maximize performance, work should be performed on an I/O processor whenever possible. The same principle holds for the division of work between an embedded processor and a general-purpose CPU: work should be performed on an embedded processor whenever possible. Thus, we can summarize:

> *To maximize performance, packet processing tasks should be assigned to the lowest-level processor capable of performing the task.*

The assignment of tasks can be understood best if we consider the data flow through the system. As many packets as possible are handled by lower level processors, which are the fastest. Figure 13.7 illustrates the concept.

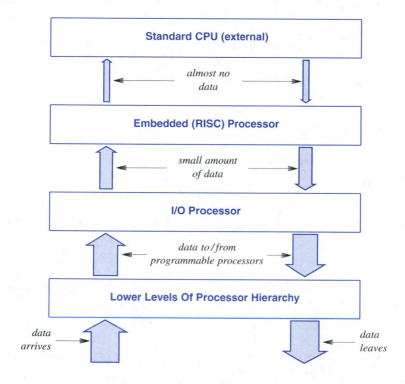

Figure 13.7 Illustration of packet flow through the processor hierarchy. Performance is maximized when lower levels handle packets locally without passing them up the hierarchy.

13.7 Summary

Vendors are experimenting with a variety of network processor architectures. The architectures can be characterized by the processor and memory hierarchies, internal and external communication, polling and notification, support for concurrent and parallel execution, programming and software architectures, and dispatch mechanisms. A network processor architecture may emphasize an overall style such as: sequential, parallel, pipeline, or dataflow, or may represent a complex hybrid.

Implementation of the processor hierarchy is especially important. Performance is maximized by assigning a task to the lowest-level processor that can handle the task.

FOR FURTHER STUDY

Amdahl et. al. [1964] discusses the architecture of a mainframe computer with programmable I/O devices. Further discussion can be found at:

http://www.cisco.com/warp/public/537/1.html

Bux et. al. [2001] analyzes requirements for high-speed packet forwarding. Crowley, Fiuczynski, and Baer [2000] consider the performance of multithreaded network processor architectures. Various vendors produce white papers that describe the reason for their architectural choices.

EXERCISES

13.1   Read about network processor architectures. What additional characteristics do vendors tout?

13.2   Does the list of processors in Figure 13.1 form a true hierarchy? Explain why or why not.

13.3   Read about network processors, and estimate the relative speed of processors in the processor hierarchy.

13.4   Compare the memory hierarchy used with network processors to the memory used with a traditional computer system. Explain the similarities and differences.

13.5   Read about *Content Addressable Memory* (*CAM*). How can CAM be used to speed performance of a network processor?

13.6   Should a network processor expose parallel hardware to the programmer? Why or why not?

13.7   Which is easier to program: a network processor that uses interrupts or a network processor that requires polling? Which is faster? Why?

13.8   Where is the bottleneck on a sequential, parallel, and pipeline architecture? Explain.

13.9   Estimate the clock rate needed for a RISC processor that forwards layer 3 packets (IP datagrams) from an OC-192 line.

13.10 Some vendors use a software architecture composed of a classifier plus a set of functions. The classifier is configured so that each function corresponds to a classification — when a classification succeeds, the function is invoked. Does such a scheme fit into the software architecture categories defined in the chapter? Why or why not?

13.11 Assign network processing tasks to the example hierarchy in Figure 13.7, and estimate the percentage of incoming packets that reach each level of the hierarchy.

Chapter Contents

14

Issues In Scaling A Network Processor

14.1 Introduction

The previous chapter describes network processor architecture, and introduces the concepts of processor and memory hierarchies. This chapter extends the discussion by focusing on the fundamental issue of scaling. The chapter considers the relationship between scaling and the conceptual hierarchies as well as the technological details that impose limits on scale. The next chapter shows how the architectural concepts apply to commercial network processors.

14.2 The Processing Hierarchy And Scaling

Recall from the previous chapter that processors are arranged in a conceptual hierarchy, and that performance is optimized when each layer of the hierarchy handles most of the data it receives without passing packets up to higher layers†. The flow of data helps us understand the relationship between the processor hierarchy and processor scaling. Because they handle more data, lower levels of the hierarchy need more capacity than higher levels. There are two main possibilities: increased clock rate or increased parallelism.

As an example, consider the case of physical network interfaces. To increase capacity, the data rate of an interface can be increased or the number of interfaces can be increased. In either case, a corresponding increase is needed in low-level hardware that connects the interface to the rest of the system. If the data rate of an interface is in-

---

†Figure 13.7 on page 191 illustrates data flow through a processor hierarchy.

creased, the corresponding bandwidth of the data transfer hardware must also be increased. If the number of interfaces is increased, additional internal data transfer paths must be added.

14.3 Scaling By Making Processors Faster

Increasing the processing rate of a single processor does indeed allow some scaling. However, two problems arise. First, inherent limits on underlying technology limit the rate at which a given processor can operate. Second, and more important, a processor may block waiting for an external event (e.g., waiting for a packet to arrive, a coprocessor to finish an operation, or a memory access). Once external delays dominate the overall processing time, further increases in processor speed will not help scale.

We have already discussed one way to achieve higher throughput when external delays dominate: multiple threads of execution. If multiple threads remain ready to execute, a processor can switch to a new thread whenever the current thread blocks. Thus, as long as at least one thread remains ready to run, the processor does not block. Conceptually, using threads changes the model of blocking by associating the delay with a thread rather than with the processor. As a result, threads allow a processor to handle increased traffic without an increase in processor speed†. We can summarize:

> *As an alternative to increased processor speed, a designer can add support for multiple threads of execution. Either technique permits a processor to scale.*

14.4 Scaling By Increasing The Number of Processors

An alternative to making a processor faster consists of adding more copies of the processor and arranging for them to work in parallel. How many copies should be added? Because lower levels of the processor hierarchy handle more data flow than higher levels, less processing power is required for each successively higher level. A single, general-purpose CPU can manage a system that includes many network processors that each contain an embedded processor. Similarly, a single embedded processor can handle traffic from multiple I/O processors. Finally, an I/O processor can handle traffic from multiple network interfaces. Thus, lower levels of the hierarchy benefit the most from parallelism. Engineers use the term *fan out* to capture the notion that parallelism increases down the hierarchy. Figure 14.1 illustrates the concept.

It may seem that adding additional processors to one or more levels of the hierarchy solves the problem of scale. However, two potential bottlenecks exist that limit scalability. First, because multiple processors need a mechanism to coordinate, the coordination mechanism may become a bottleneck. Second, because additional processors generate more traffic, internal data paths and memory may become a bottleneck. We will consider memory later.

---

†The number of useful threads is limited by the ratio of I/O access time to computation time — once the CPU is saturated, adding more threads does not increase throughput.

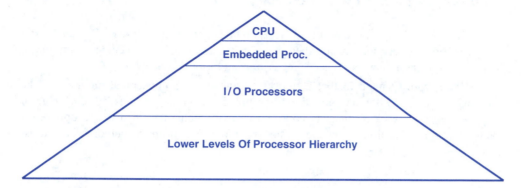

Figure 14.1 An illustration of fan out in a processor hierarchy. Lower levels must have the most parallelism because each higher level handles fewer packets than the previous level.

A processor coordination mechanism is needed whenever parallel processors are available to act on data. For example, consider a frame that arrives in a system that has multiple I/O processors. A coordination mechanism must exist that allows exactly one processor to access the frame. Once the capacity of the coordination mechanism has been met or exceeded, adding additional processors will not increase the system capacity. Instead, processors will remain blocked waiting for the coordination mechanism. Thus, to avoid a bottleneck, the coordination mechanism must be extended as processors are added. One approach incorporates coordination into the hierarchy by replicating the coordination mechanism and restricting a given coordination mechanism to a small set of inputs.

14.5 Scaling By Increasing Processor Types

As an alternative to increasing the number of processors, it is possible to add new processor types. There are three possibilities: additional levels can be inserted in the processor hierarchy, new types of coprocessors can be arranged in a heterogeneous pipeline, or new types of coprocessors can be added to offload computation from an embedded processor or I/O processor.

In principle, special-purpose coprocessors that work under control of a conventional processor can contribute to scale because they speed some operations (e.g., a coprocessor can perform route table lookup much faster than a conventional processor). In practice, however, the conventional processor often remains a bottleneck. The mechanism used to pass data and results to a coprocessor can also become a bottleneck. Thus, a pipelined set of coprocessors can often operate faster than coprocessors under central control because each coprocessor in a pipeline performs its assigned task without relying on detailed coordination.

14.6 Scaling A Memory Hierarchy

All processor scaling requires a corresponding scaling of memory. Without faster memory for both instructions and data, memory accesses quickly become a bottleneck. Thus, without faster memory, faster processors can become useless.

Recall from Chapter 13 that memory is arranged in a conceptual hierarchy. The memory hierarchy is not tied directly to the processor hierarchy. Instead, the range of memory types allows a designer to choose a memory technology that is appropriate for each situation. The choices involve a tradeoff among four primary memory characteristics:

- Size
- Latency and cycle time
- Specific use
- Cost

Memory size. The size of memory may be determined a priori or may be related to the scale of the system. As an example of a memory size that can be determined a priori, consider an IP forwarding table. The amount of memory needed to store the table depends on the number of routes, not on the speed or number of networks to which the system connects. A core router provides an upper bound on forwarding table size because it contains the largest possible forwarding table. Currently, a core router contains fewer than 200,000 unique entries.

As examples of memory size that depend on the system, consider a table that stores next-hop information† and the memory devoted to packet buffers. The size of a next-hop table depends on the number of routers that can be reached directly; the amount of memory needed for packet buffers depends on the data rate of attached networks and the number of such networks. More memory is needed for each as the system scales.

Memory latency and cycle time. We can use *access latency*, the time required for a basic operation, as a first approximation of memory speed. Figure 14.2 lists the latency of two basic memory technologies.

Memory Technology	Abbreviation	Typical Latency
Static RAM	SRAM	1.5-10 ns
Dynamic RAM	DRAM	50-70 ns

Figure 14.2 Two basic memory technologies and the latency of each.

As the figure shows, DRAM has an access latency of approximately 60 nanoseconds, which means that a DRAM memory chip can respond to a request within 60 nanoseconds. The connection between a processor and memory usually consists of a

---

†A next-hop table is used to avoid replicating the next hop information in a forwarding table.

bus; the processor sends requests over the bus to the memory, and the memory uses the bus to send responses back to the processor. To avoid increasing the memory latency, the bus interface must be designed to avoid introducing delay.

In the case of a network processor, the latency along a path to memory can be significant. To understand why, observe that memory can be *external* to the network processor (i.e., not on the chip). The connection to external memory requires a *memory controller*. When an onboard processor makes a memory request, the request passes to the controller. The controller translates the request into a format suitable for the external bus, and sends the request over the bus to the external memory. Similarly, when it receives a reply over the bus, the memory controller translates the reply to internal form, and forwards the reply to the processor. Although a memory controller is optimized to provide fast access, longer wires, the need for stronger electrical signals, and narrow data paths make external access approximately an order of magnitude slower. To summarize:

> *External memory takes approximately an order of magnitude longer to access than memory located on a network processor chip.*

Although it is important, latency alone does not suffice as a measure of memory speed. Because packet processing often involves storing a large block of data (i.e. a packet), the overall performance of memory depends on the rate at which the memory can handle a sequence of individual operations. We define the *memory cycle time* to be the minimum interval required between two consecutive requests. For example, the time required for a *Read Cycle* (*tRC*) determines how quickly a memory can respond to a series of read requests, and the time required for a *Write Cycle* (*tWC*) determines how quickly a memory can respond to a series of write requests. The point is:

> *Because packet processing involves large data items, memory cycle time can be as important as latency.*

Specific use. In addition to latency, the intended use of memory affects the design. For example, searching a hash table requires random access — the location selected for a given probe is not likely to be near the location selected for the previous probe. Thus, the memory used for hashing should be optimized for random probes. Because a packet transfer references a set of adjacent bytes, memory used for packet storage should be optimized for sequential access. For example, sequential access can be optimized by arranging a controller to *prefetch* data — when a byte is requested, the controller starts to retrieve successive bytes.

Memory Cost. Cost is a primary consideration in a memory hierarchy — a designer chooses the minimum cost memory that satisfies a given use. In particular, memory with slower access times usually costs less. Thus, although it is faster than DRAM, SRAM costs more. Consequently, to reduce costs, designers choose DRAM over SRAM if slower access latency is sufficient.

14.7 Scaling By Increasing Memory Size

Because a given memory is not restricted to one type of processor, the memory hierarchy is not directly linked to a processor hierarchy. Therefore, the size of memory at a given level of the hierarchy does not correspond to the number of processors. Instead, the size of memory tends to be inversely proportional to cost, with the largest amount of memory having lowest cost. Figure 14.3 illustrates the relationship of memory size to the memory hierarchy.

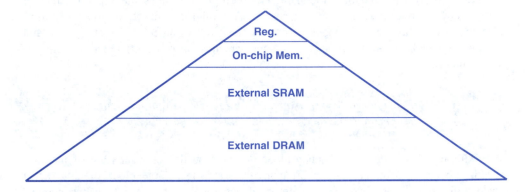

Figure 14.3 An illustration of memory size in a memory hierarchy. To keep costs low, the largest memory is the least expensive.

14.8 Scaling By Increasing Memory Bandwidth

We said that memory speed is measured with latency and cycle times. It may seem that memory bandwidth is equally important. For example, consider the transfer of a packet from a physical interface into memory. Suppose the transfer requires K nanoseconds into a memory that has an access latency of N nanoseconds on a data path that is 32 bits wide. Because the data path is much smaller than a packet size, many memory operations are required, which means that N will be many times larger than K. If the data path is doubled from 32 bits to 64 bits, however, the total time required for the transfer is reduced from K to approximately $K/2$ (i.e., increasing the bandwidth makes the transfer "faster").

If either lower latency or greater bandwidth can speed transfer, should we consider bandwidth when reporting memory speed? As a general principle, the two concepts are treated separately because they arise from different constraints. Latency is an inherent limit; bandwidth is not. A system designer can choose to increase memory bandwidth merely by constructing a parallel data path; the designer cannot decrease the latency of an underlying chip. Although increasing memory bandwidth improves the throughput for large transfers, increased bandwidth has three drawbacks. First, increased bandwidth does not reduce the overall time required for small transfers. Thus, increasing bandwidth will not improve performance in all cases. Second, larger memory bandwidth increases parallelism of the data path, which requires more physical space on the chip and more external connections. As a later section discusses, both space and external connections are limited. Third, although increasing the memory bandwidth increases the access granularity, the size must be chosen to accommodate the packets that are expected. For example, if the average packet size is N bytes, a transfer bandwidth of $N-1$ bytes means that two memory cycles are required to store a packet. As a result, the memory subsystem must operate twice as fast as the data stream even though the second memory cycle is largely unused. The point is:

Although increasing memory bandwidth reduces the time required for a large data transfer, larger bandwidth introduces problems of granularity and space, and does not improve performance for small transfers.

14.9 Scaling By Increasing Types Of Memory

By only considering two broad categories of memory, we glossed over an important consideration: many variations exist. In particular, memory technologies have been devised that are optimized for a specific use. Figure 14.4 lists examples.

Memory Technology	Abbreviation	Purpose
Synchronized DRAM	SDRAM	Synchronized with CPU for lower latency
Quad Data Rate SRAM	QDR-SRAM	Optimized for low latency and multiple access
Zero Bus Turnaround SRAM	ZBT-SRAM	Optimized for low latency with random access
Fast Cycle RAM	FCRAM	Low cycle time optimized for block transfer
Double Data Rate DRAM	DDR-DRAM	Optimized for low latency
Reduced Latency DRAM	RLDRAM	Low cycle time and low power requirements

Figure 14.4 Examples of memory technologies that are optimized for specific purposes. A network processor can use a variety of memories with each memory devoted to one task.

As an example of memory especially suited to network processing, consider, *Zero Bus Turnaround SRAM* (*ZBT-SRAM*). ZBT-SRAM has low latency, and is optimized for random access. Unlike most other memory technologies, ZBT-SRAM does not introduce idle bus cycles during a series of random accesses. Thus, ZBT-SRAM works well for operations such as hash table lookup.

If a network system expects to store large packets (e.g., maximum-size IP datagrams), a memory with low cycle times increases performance. For example, *Fast Cycle RAM* (*FCRAM*), which is optimized for block access, works well as a memory to hold large packet buffers.

In addition to choosing technologies that are optimized for a specific situation, it is possible to introduce additional levels in the memory hierarchy. An exercise considers expanding the memory hierarchy.

14.10 Scaling By Adding Memory Caches

Caching is a well-known technique used to reduce memory latency. A cache, which operates at higher speed than memory, is placed between a processor and memory to hold copies of values that have been accessed recently. A cache lowers the average access time because subsequent lookups for an item retrieve an answer from the (faster) cache instead of from memory†.

Can caching be used with network processors? Yes. In principle, caching has potential for significant improvement. Because it avoids the high delay associated with an external memory interface, a cache onboard a network processor can reduce latency dramatically. The lower effective latency can allow the network processor to scale to handle more data. In particular, once a packet header has been loaded into an onboard cache, header fields can be examined without incurring an external memory reference.

Despite its potential advantages, caching does not solve the general problem of scale. There are two reasons: low temporal locality and the need for large cache size.

Low Temporal Locality. Because it only optimizes subsequent lookups, the effectiveness of a cache depends on repetition. If a processor references the same value repeatedly, we say that the processor exhibits a high *temporal locality of reference*. Ironically, packet processing tasks do not have high locality of reference over time — instead of keeping a packet and accessing its contents repeatedly, a network system tends to examine a packet once and then forward it. More important, repetition occurs the least in core routers that experience the traffic from many sites. When traffic is highest, even tasks such as IP route lookup exhibit lower locality of reference. Thus, although it can help optimize tasks such as the examination of fields in a single packet header, a cache is least effective for the task that is most critical: handling a stream of packets at high speed.

Large cache size. Two main optimizations exist that allow a cache to compensate for low temporal locality of reference. Either the cache can have more entries, or the cache can use a larger granularity of reference. Additional entries allow a cache to re-

---

†A hardware mechanism, known as a *post write buffer*, is complementary to a cache: a cache optimizes fetch operations, and a post write buffer optimizes store operations.

tain values longer. For example, if a packet travels to the same destination as a previous packet, a cache can retain route data, making the second lookup faster. Additional entries in the cache allow the cache to retain the route data even if the packets are separated further in the input stream. Similarly, a large granularity of reference means that the cache fetches data in large blocks (e.g., sixteen bytes at a time). Thus, when a program references a byte, the cache loads the entire block, which speeds access to subsequent bytes. For example, if packet headers are stored in contiguous memory and the cache granularity is large enough to include two headers, a reference to one header preloads the next header into the cache. Unfortunately, additional entries and larger granularity result in larger physical cache size, which means the cache occupies more space on the chip and, depending on the technology, may require longer to search. We can summarize:

> *Although it can improve performance, caching usually does not allow a network processor to scale arbitrarily because caching is least effective on a large sequence of packets that exhibit low temporal locality of reference.*

14.11 Scaling With Content Addressable Memory

Content Addressable Memory (CAM) is a memory mechanism that supports rapid (i.e., parallel) searching as well as data storage. CAM is primarily used to improve the performance of table lookup operations. Some network processors require CAM to achieve wire speed processing.

To understand how high-speed lookup operates, one must know that CAM, unlike most other memories, is not merely an array of bytes. Instead, CAM is arranged as a two-dimensional array with fixed-size slots as Figure 14.5 illustrates.

When designing a system, a hardware engineer chooses a CAM slot size appropriate for the intended use†, and then engineers the CAM hardware accordingly. For example, a CAM designed to store IP addresses requires four octets per slot. A CAM designed to store TCP endpoint addresses requires twelve octets per slot (i.e., enough for a pair of IP addresses and a pair of protocol port numbers). We will see that the latter example is especially appropriate for CAM used with a network processor.

---

†Typical values for the width of a CAM slot are between 100 and 200 bits.

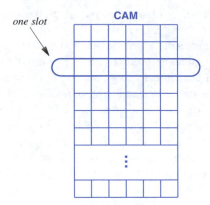

Figure 14.5 Illustration of content addressable memory organized into a two-dimensional array. Each row in the array corresponds to a *slot* of the memory.

The lookup operation offered by CAM consists of parallel matching: a processor supplies a *search key*, and the CAM returns the set of slots in which items match the key, typically in under 100 ns. The exact details of how a CAM reports matching entries depend on the type of CAM and the interface hardware. Some CAM implementations produce a list of matches. That is, whenever it performs a match, the CAM generates a list of the slot numbers that match the key. Other implementations return a *bit vector* to indicate matches. That is, if it contains N slots, the CAM returns a vector of N bits. A bit in the vector is set to 1 if the search key matched the corresponding slot, and 0 otherwise. The processor must then scan the bit vector to determine which slots matched.

The basic CAM described above is known as a *binary CAM* because each slot contains a binary value. To make lookup as flexible as possible, designers use a variation known as a *ternary CAM (TCAM)* that does not require a key to match all the data within a slot. More important, a ternary CAM does not specify the locations of each match a priori. In essence, instead of two possible values for each bit, a ternary CAM allows three: *zero*, *one*, or *don't care*. When a match is performed, only bits with values zero or one are checked; bits marked don't care are ignored.

How is a ternary CAM implemented? In one implementation, the hardware stores a binary value plus a *mask* in each entry. The mask is exactly the same length as a slot, and bits in the mask specify which bits in a slot should be compared to corresponding bits in the key during a search. That is, when it performs a fetch operation, a ternary CAM returns the entire slot. When it performs a comparison of a key with a slot, however, a ternary CAM only compares bits specified in the mask. Although a CAM operates on all slots in parallel, it is easiest to think of the computation as a set of tests executed sequentially:

```
for each slot, i, do the following  {
        if ( ( mask[i] & key ) == ( mask[i] & slot[i] ) )  {
                declare that slot  i  matches key;
        else
                declare that slot i does not match key;
        }
}
```

14.12 Using CAM for Packet Classification

A ternary CAM is especially helpful in producing a high-speed classification mechanism. To understand how, recall from Chapter 9 that parallel hardware classification uses a two-step process in which values are first extracted from fields of packet headers and then tested to determine if they correspond to a specific type. A ternary CAM can be used to perform the second step in parallel. Furthermore, when a match occurs, a CAM can bind the packet to a specific classification ID.

An example will clarify the concept and show how a CAM aids in classification. Assume that we need to classify Web traffic and UDP DNS traffic, and that the classification rules test the 2-octet Ethernet frame type field, 1-octet IP header length field, 1-octet IP protocol field, and 2-octet protocol port number. Further assume that each slot in the CAM consists of eight octets, with a key in the first six octets and a classification code in the other two. To use the CAM, a classifier extracts the fields and forms a 6-octet value. The value is padded with two octets of zeroes (to make it the same size as a slot), and then passed to the CAM as a search key. The mask used with each entry in the CAM specifies that only the first six octets are to be matched; others are marked as *don't care*. The CAM uses the key and mask to select a slot as Figure 14.6 illustrates.

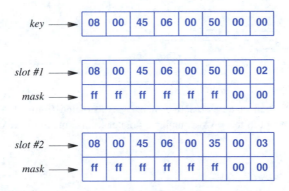

Figure 14.6 An illustration of using a CAM for classification with binary values shown in hexadecimal. Only the bits covered by the mask are checked.

In the figure, the CAM reports that the key matches slot number 1 because each bit of the key that corresponds to a mask bit of 1 matches the corresponding bit of slot 1. Once the CAM lookup completes, the processor that supplied the key extracts the value from slot 1. The slot includes two additional octets that specify a classification ID of:

00.02

In practice, the concept of using a CAM to hold additional information can be generalized to provide an *associative store*. Instead of placing additional information in each slot, an associative store places additional information in a separate RAM. Thus, each slot in the CAM contains two values: a search key and a pointer to the additional information in RAM. Indirection, through a pointer, allows a programmer to change the binding between a search key and additional information without changing the hardware. Figure 14.7 illustrates the organization.

As the figure shows, each CAM slot can point to an arbitrary address. The ability to use an arbitrary pointer permits flexibility because it allows a designer to choose the degree of independence — multiple slots can point to a given location in RAM or each slot can point to a unique location.

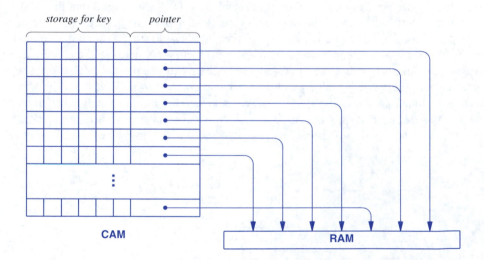

Figure 14.7 Illustration of an associative memory constructed from a CAM. Each slot in the CAM contains a pointer to information in RAM.

14.13 Other Limitations On Scale

Although the processors and memory described above form the basis for scaling, several other factors impose constraints.

Physical space limits. As designers realize, the limited physical space on a network processor chip places an important constraint on scale. All functional units occupy space, including programmable processors, fixed coprocessors, memory, and internal interconnections. Finite space bounds the amount of parallelism and memory. A designer cannot add an arbitrary number of processors to a chip, nor can a designer add arbitrary amounts of memory. Although less obvious, the space available on a chip also limits choices for items such as internal interconnections. In particular, the bandwidth of an internal data path (e.g., an internal bus) usually depends on the number of parallel wires. As a consequence, increasing the bandwidth of a data path increases the space needed†.

Clock Skew And Propagation Limits. As a signal propagates along a long physical path on a chip, physical properties such as resistance and capacitance cause the signal to deteriorate. Skew is especially critical for a clock signal that is used to control and synchronize components on the chip. The chip must be designed to prevent a clock signal from becoming so *skewed*, that functional units on one part of the chip do not synchronize with functional units on another part. Propagation delay and clock skew limit the size of a chip and the lengths of data paths.

Pin limits. The term *pin* refers to a physical connection on a chip that is used to connect the chip to the rest of the system; the term *pinout* refers to assignment of functionality to the pins. The limited number of pins on a chip restricts scalability. For example, consider a bus used to connect a network processor to an external memory. To provide addressing for the largest amount of memory and to achieve the highest possible throughput, the bus must be as wide as possible. However, because each bus line requires a pin, a bus cannot be arbitrarily wide. More important, if a separate pin cannot be devoted to each bus line, the hardware must use a time-division approach in which data is multiplexed across fewer pins one piece at a time. Because multiplexing across fewer pins introduces additional delay, throughput is lower, which limits scalability.

Of course, limits on pins can be overcome with a design that uses two or more chips. However, multiple chips occupy more physical space, and often impose additional constraints on the architecture. In particular, multiple chips are best suited to pipeline architectures. Thus, increasing the scale of a design may not be feasible with multiple chips because the use of multiple chips may force a change in the architecture.

Internal and external communication limits. Recall from earlier chapters that many packet processing tasks are I/O-bound, which means that the speed with which data can be transferred can impose a limit on scale. Once the transfer capacity has been reached, adding additional memory or processors will not improve the overall processing speed.

---

†Chip manufacturers argue that as long as Moore's law holds, space is less important than other constraints. As a practical matter, however, designers must contend with space limits.

There are two types of communication mechanisms: internal mechanisms provide communication onboard, and external mechanisms provide communication among network processors or between a network processor and other devices. Internal mechanisms include buses; external mechanisms include both external buses and switching fabrics.

Power consumption and heat dissipation. Another issue in scaling arises from basic electrical and thermodynamic properties: power consumption and the consequent heat production. Scaling a network processor by adding processors or memory increases the amount of power used. Unfortunately, the additional power consumption generates heat, which must be dissipated to prevent thermal failure. Furthermore, when designers choose components for a network system, they consider how each component adds to the overall power consumption. Thus, in addition to other factors, scale is limited by power and heat considerations.

14.14 Software Scalability

Another issue of scale arises from a surprising source: the software used on a network processor. It may seem that software is the least important aspect of scale because software can be changed easily. One might imagine, for example, that accommodating software scale is trivial — a programmer merely needs to change a few constants and recompile the software.

Unfortunately, network processor software does not always scale easily. On many network processors, a programmer writes code in a low-level language (i.e., macro assembly language), and embeds explicit knowledge of the underlying hardware. For example, in some systems, a programmer must understand the exact number of processors at each level of the hierarchy, and must be aware of the latency and throughput characteristics of each memory. The programmer carefully optimizes the code by hand.

Software scaling can be equally challenging in a pipeline architecture because each processor in the pipeline has limited speed and memory. The size of the instruction memory can limit the number of new features that can be added. The CPU speed can limit the amount of time spent processing a given packet. Thus, if software is spread across a pipeline, scaling can be difficult.

In general, software scaling is never trivial. Because small changes can result in timing differences that affect the overall execution speed, each change must be validated carefully. A programmer may need to run extensive simulations or use tools that aid in timing analysis. We can summarize:

> *Although an ideal network processor would make it possible to create software that is independent of the number of processors, many network processors require a programmer to tailor the code to the hardware. Moving the software to a larger scale system requires making substantial changes manually.*

14.15 Bottlenecks And Scale

Although many options exist for scaling individual components of a network processor, a single, overriding question always remains: what is the bottleneck? Increasing the speed of memory will not improve the overall performance unless memory is a bottleneck. Similarly, adding additional parallel processors will not improve the overall performance unless processing is a bottleneck.

The bottleneck in a network processor may not be easy to discover because it can arise from an unexpected combination of hardware and software components. More important, removing one bottleneck may reveal another. In theory, increasing the number of processors will scale a parallel architecture because each processor only needs to handle $1/N$ of the traffic. Thus, as the number of processors increases, the total traffic can increase. In practice, however, as the number of processors increases, other bottlenecks appear (e.g., the mechanism used to dispatch work among processors or the bandwidth of internal data paths). Similarly, it may seem that scaling a pipeline architecture means upgrading the slowest processor in the pipeline. Once the bottleneck has been identified and eliminated, however, the next slowest processing point will become the new bottleneck; the overall difference in performance can be negligible.

14.16 Summary

Scaling is a complex issue, and no single approach provides arbitrary scale. The processor hierarchy allows a fan out in which a processor at one level can support multiple processors at the next lower level. Although processors can be replicated and the speed of a processor can be increased, each scaling strategy has limits.

The memory hierarchy follows a pattern in which a small amount of memory at each level is sufficient to support more memory at a lower level. Multiple memory technologies exist; a designer can choose a technology that is appropriate for each purpose. Content addressable memory that provides high-speed lookup is especially useful for operations such as classification. Techniques like caching, while important, cannot provide arbitrary scaling.

In addition to primary considerations such as processors and memories, all hardware scaling is constrained by physical, electrical, and optical details. The physical space on a chip limits the number of items that can be added, the number of pins available limits the number of external connections, and the heat produced limits the power that can be consumed.

Software is an important aspect of scaling because the software for many network processors is built for a specific hardware configuration. As a result, scaling the hardware requires a programmer to modify and optimize the software manually.

FOR FURTHER STUDY

Chiueh and Pradhan [1999] considers the design of memory for network processors. Bux et. al. [2001] discusses scaling for high speed. Nie et. al. [1999] also considers scaling issues.

EXERCISES

14.1 Suppose a designer determines that the processors at level i in the processor hierarchy form a bottleneck. Will adding another level in the hierarchy help? Why or why not?

14.2 Consult network processor vendors' documentation to find the clock rates of embedded processors found on network processor chips, and compare them to the clock rates of stand-alone RISC processors. What can you conclude about the potential for increasing clock rates of embedded RISC processors?

14.3 Argue for or against the following proposition: expanding the memory hierarchy by adding an additional level can help a network processor scale.

14.4 What is the chief advantage of a network processor design in which parallelism is hidden from the programmer? Of a design in which the programmer must explicitly allocate and use parallel hardware?

14.5 Investigate the price of CAM to determine how expensive it would be to use commercially available CAM to construct a table that contains 5,000 slots, each of which contains a 20-octet key and a 4-octet pointer.

Chapter Contents

15

Examples Of Commercial Network Processors

15.1 Introduction

Previous chapters introduce network processors. They describe both the economic benefits that make network processors enticing to vendors and the inherent complexity that makes network processors difficult to design.

The previous chapter defines a set of characteristics, and covers the fundamental concepts that underlie network processor architectures. This chapter shows how the concepts apply to a set of products from commercial vendors.

15.2 An Explosion Of Commercial Products

Between the late 1990s and early 2000s, network processors transformed from an interesting curiosity to a mainstream product. Once the benefits were known, demand increased rapidly; network processors became the technology of choice for system builders who needed to reduce both overall costs and the time to market. Chip vendors responded by introducing many products. By 2002, over 30 vendors offered network processor products.

As earlier chapters point out, commercial products cover a wide range of architectures. On one hand, vendors experimented with a variety of features: some chips contain many special-purpose coprocessors, and other chips contain general-purpose, programmable processors. On the other hand, each vendor chose a particular combination of price and performance, with some producing less sophisticated (and less expensive) chips that offer moderate performance, and others producing more sophisticated chips that have high performance.

15.3 A Selection of Products

The next sections contain examples that illustrate the concepts in Chapter 13†. Each section describes a commercially available network processor, and lists its architectural characteristics. The examples have been chosen to illustrate the wide range of possible architectures; the selection is neither meant to be exhaustive nor to imply that these vendors or products are in any way better than others. The amount of information in the descriptions varies because some vendors release more technical details than others.

15.4 Multi-Chip Pipeline (Agere)

Agere Systems Incorporated (formerly the microelectronics division of Lucent Technologies) offers network processors under the name *PayloadPlus*. The Agere system is interesting for three reasons: a multiple chip architecture, use of a programmable classifier, and emphasis on ingress processing.

Architecture. Agere's system consists of three physically separate chips that are designed to work together‡. Figure 15.1 shows the interconnections among chips, and illustrates the flow of packets through the resulting pipeline.

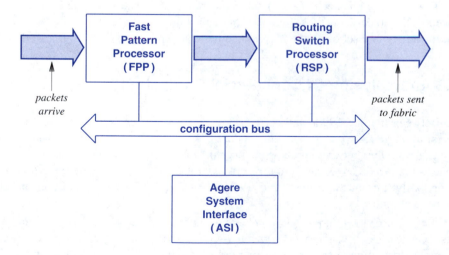

Figure 15.1 Illustration of Agere's network processor architecture; three separate chips are interconnected to form a pipeline.

---

†In addition to the examples here, later chapters discuss the Intel architecture.

‡A second generation, the 10G, which is scheduled to be available shortly after publication of this text, integrates the functionality onto a single chip.

As the figure shows, the Agere system works well for ingress — the *Fast Pattern Processor* (*FPP*) and *Routing Switch Processor* (*RSP*) form the basic pipeline that handles data on the fast path. Arriving packets are sent to the FPP, which forwards a packet plus a set of instructions for processing to the RSP. Packets that leave the RSP travel across the switching fabric. The third chip, the *Agere System Interface* (*ASI*), is a coprocessor that supplies important functionality to help improve performance. The ASI collects statistics about packets that are used for traffic management. In addition, the ASI provides an interface to a separate microprocessor (not shown) which manages the overall system and handles packets that are exceptions to normal processing.

The system contains additional connections that are not shown in the diagram. For example, a connection extends from the configuration bus to the physical interface hardware to allow the ASI chip to coordinate the flow of data between the interface and the FPP chip. An additional connection extends from the ASI to the FPP chip to allow the ASI to communicate with the FPP.

Figure 15.2 illustrates the internal architecture of an FPP chip.

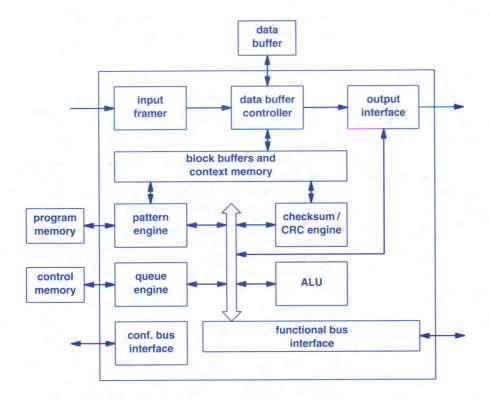

Figure 15.2 The internal architecture of Agere's FPP chip. Packets arrive at the input framer, and leave via the output interface.

Processors And Functional Units. Each chip in the Agere system contains multiple processors and functional units. Figure 15.3 lists example functional units on the FPP chip.

Processor Or Unit	Purpose
Pattern processing engine	Perform pattern matching on each packet
Queue engine	Control packet queueing
Checksum/CRC engine	Compute checksum or CRC for a packet
ALU	Conventional operations
Input interface and framer	Divide incoming packet into 64-octet blocks
Data buffer controller	Control access to external data buffer
Configuration bus interface	Connect to external configuration bus
Functional bus interface	Connect to external functional bus
Output interface	Connect to external RSP chip

Figure 15.3 Examples of functional units and processors on the Agere FPP chip. The internal bus allows processors to coordinate.

The *Functional Bus Interface* (*FBI*) is interesting because it implements a form of *Remote Procedure Call* (*RPC*). That is, code running on an FPP chip can use the FBI to invoke a function on an external coprocessor. The facility makes it possible to add ASIC hardware that extends the functionality of the FPP — each ASIC implements a function that is invoked via the FBI.

In addition to processors, the FPP contains interface hardware for each external connection. For example, the *pattern processing engine* needs to access an external *program memory*, and the *queue engine* needs to access an external *control memory*. To handle packet transfer, the FPP contains an *input interface and framer* that divides an incoming packet into 64-octet blocks, and an *output interface* that passes outgoing packets to the RSP chip. The FPP also contains hardware that provides an external interface for the *configuration bus*. Finally, the central transfer mechanism on the chip consists of a *functional bus* to which the onboard processors attach; the FPP includes an external interface for the functional bus, which allows the ASI chip to control processing.

Figure 15.4 illustrates the internal structure of an RSP chip.

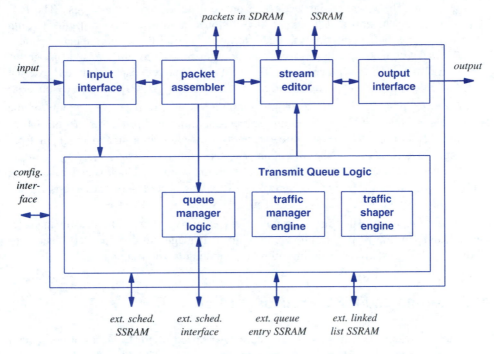

Figure 15.4 The internal architecture of Agere's RSP chip. Packets arrive from the FPP chip after they have been classified.

The RSP chip contains a set of processors and functional units as Figure 15.5 lists. The three engines on an RSP chip, the *stream editor*, *traffic manager*, and *traffic shaper*, are implemented with *Very Long Instruction Word* (*VLIW*) processors.

Processor Or Unit	Purpose
Stream editor engine	Perform modifications on packet
Traffic manager engine	Police traffic and keep statistics
Traffic shaper engine	Ensure QoS parameters
Input interface	Accept packet from FPP
Packet† assembler	Store incoming packet in memory
Queue manager logic	Interface to external traffic scheduler
Output interface	External connection for outgoing packets
Configuration bus interface	Connect to external configuration bus

Figure 15.5 Examples of the functional units and processors on the Agere RSP chip. The units are interconnected.

---

†Some vendors use the term *Protocol Data Unit* (*PDU*) instead of *packet*.

Memory. The Agere design uses both onboard and external memories. The FPP chip divides packets into data blocks, which it stores in an external *data buffer* (a *data buffer controller* on the chip provides the interface). The FPP uses an onboard memory for the blocks currently being processed; external memories are used to hold programs and instructions for the processors. The RSP chip stores packets in an external SDRAM, and uses higher-speed *Synchronous Static RAM* (*SSRAM*) for priority queues.

Programming Support. Ease of programming is among the strong points of the Agere design. Internally, the FPP is a pipelined, multithreaded processor that has 64 independent contexts. However, Agere's network processor hides the parallelism from the programmer, and allows the programmer to use high-level languages. Agere offers a classification language†, *FPL* (*Functional Programming Language*), and a scripting language, *ASL* (*Agere Scripting Language*). FPL is translated into instructions for the pattern processing engine, which can perform classification at wire speed.

Other Features. The Agere design offers extensive support for traffic management. Logic on the RSP chip allows the chip to manage multiple packet queues, including applying external scheduling rules and handling traffic shaping.

15.5 Augmented RISC Processor (Alchemy)

Alchemy Semiconductor Inc. (acquired by Advanced Micro Devices) offers several versions of a network processor that run at various speeds. The Alchemy chip provides an example of a RISC processor that is augmented with packet processing instructions.

Architecture. The Alchemy architecture consists of an embedded RISC processor plus coprocessors. The heart of an Alchemy chip is a MIPS-32 CPU that has been enhanced for packet processing. The CPU includes a five-stage instruction pipeline, pipelined register file access, and zero penalty branching that increase performance. Several instructions have been added to the instruction set. A *multiply and accumulate* instruction has been added to optimize computation of a CRC or checksum. Instructions have also been added to count leading 1s or 0s, to prefetch memory, and to conditionally move values. Figure 15.6 illustrates the organization of an Alchemy chip, and shows how the processor connects to other units.

Processors And Functional Units. As the figure shows, the embedded RISC processor can access a variety of I/O controllers and functional units. The chip also contains a real-time clock unit.

Memory. The Alchemy chip contains two onboard caches: a 16KB instruction cache and a 16KB data cache. In addition, the chip has external connections to both an SDRAM and an SSRAM. The external SSRAM connects over a bus that also provides access to flash memory, ROM, and PCMCIA devices.

Programming Support. Because it uses an enhanced MIPS processor, the Alchemy chip can be programmed in C. The vendor provides software development tools, operating systems software for the embedded processor (e.g., Linux, VxWorks, or Windows CE), and other support software.

---

†See Chapter 16 for a discussion of classification languages and examples.

Other Features. According to the vendor, power dissipation is low (e.g., less than 0.25 watts for the 400 MHz version of an Au1000 chip).

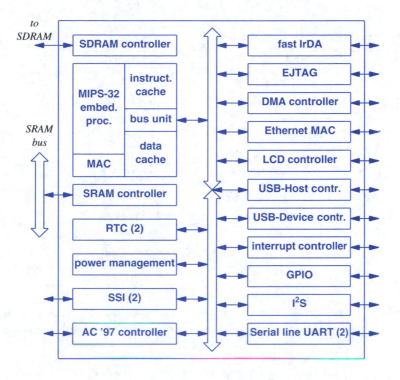

Figure 15.6 The internal architecture of Alchemy's Au1000 chip. Two internal buses provide interconnections: a system bus (the top bus) and a peripheral bus (the bottom bus).

15.6 Embedded Processor Plus Coprocessors (AMCC)

Applied Micro Circuits Corporation (*AMCC*)† offers a series of network processors that operate at various speeds. The product names begin with *nP* followed by four digits. AMCC's design illustrates how parallelism can be used to handle higher aggregate data rates.

Architecture. The AMCC architecture can be characterized as an embedded RISC system plus a set of coprocessors. Versions of the AMCC chip that are designed to handle higher data rates offer parallel embedded RISC processors. Figure 15.7 illustrates the architecture of an AMCC chip.

Processors And Functional Units. As the figure shows, the 7510 version of an AMCC chip contains six embedded processors (called *nP cores*) that function in parallel. In addition, the chip contains coprocessors (i.e., a *packet transform engine*, *policy*

---

†The network processor subsidiary of AMCC was formerly known as MMC Networks.

engine, and metering engine), and various other functional units that provide an external interface. An external coprocessor handles longest prefix match searches.

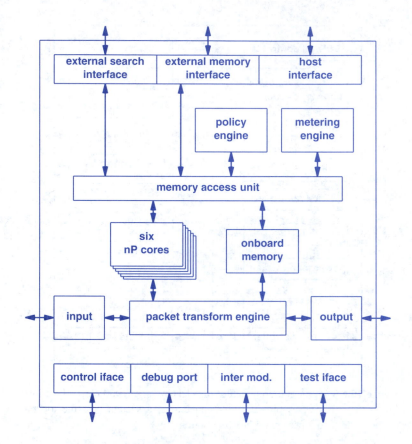

Figure 15.7 The internal architecture of AMCC's nP7510 chip. The chip contains additional interconnections among functional units that are not shown.

Memory. Like most other network processors, AMCC's nP series offers both on-board and external memory. From a processor's point of view, only one type of memory access is required because a single memory access unit on the chip provides access to both the internal and external memories.

Programming Support. Programming is straightforward. Core processors are programmed in C or C++, and AMCC offers support software consisting of a compiler, assembler, and debugger. Interestingly, the AMCC design allows a programmer to write code without understanding or planning for explicit parallelism. Instead, a program is written as if it will execute on a single processor; the hardware arranges to handle parallelism automatically.

Other Features. The *metering engine* on the chip allows the hardware to collect statistics needed for SNMP's *RMON* (*Remote Monitoring*), and the *policy engine* provides high-speed lookup and table management.

15.7 Pipeline Of Homogeneous Processors (Cisco)

Cisco Systems, Inc. has developed a network processor under the name *Parallel eXpress Forwarding* (*PXF*). The Cisco network processor provides an example of a special-purpose chip that is designed for use in Cisco routers.

Architecture. The PXF uses parallel processors arranged in a pipeline architecture. A single chip contains thirty-two embedded processors that can be divided into four parallel pipelines. Figure 15.8 illustrates one possible arrangement.

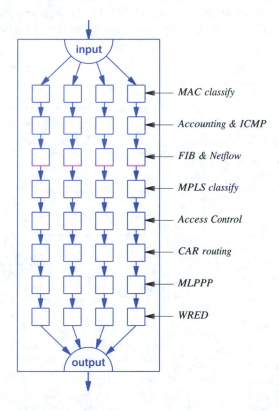

Figure 15.8 An illustration of how Cisco's PXF network processor can be used. Thirty-two embedded processors are partitioned into four separate pipelines.

Other Features. Because it is designed for internal use rather than as a general-purpose product, Cisco's network processor is optimized to work with Cisco routers. For example, the network processor interfaces with Cisco's IOS software. In addition, the Cisco design allows a separate *Route Processor* to provide control functions such as route propagation protocols and network management (via SNMP).

15.8 Configurable Instruction Set Processors (Cognigine)

The network processor produced by Cognigine Corporation provides an example of an unusual facility: *reconfigurable logic* in which onboard processors do not have a fixed instruction set.

Architecture. The Cognigine architecture is a hybrid of up to sixteen parallel processors that can be interconnected to form a pipeline. Each processor is called a *Reconfigurable Communications Unit* (*RCU*); RCUs are interconnected by a *Routing Switch Fabric* (*RSF*). Figure 15.9 illustrates the internal structure of an RCU.

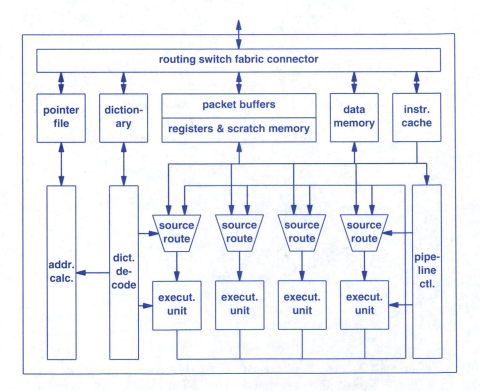

Figure 15.9 The internal structure of a Cognigine network processor (RCU). The *pipeline controller* can reconfigure data paths.

Processors And Functional Units. Each RCU contains four parallel onboard execution units that are dynamically reconfigurable. Each execution unit uses Cognigine's *Variable Instruction Set Communications* (*VISC*) code. Like a conventional processor, a VISC instruction performs one basic operation. Each VISC instruction includes operand size, operand routing, and predicates. Unlike a conventional processor, however, the exact details of the instruction set are not fixed a priori. Instead, the chip contains a dictionary that specifies the interpretation of each instruction. More important, the dictionary is configurable — values can be loaded into the dictionary or changed dynamically. Thus, a programmer can define a set of instructions, load interpretations for the instructions into the dictionary, and then build a program that uses the instructions. For example, a programmer can define an instruction set that is optimized to handle a specific set of network processing tasks or a particular protocol.

Besides reconfigurable processors, the Cognigine chip provides reconfigurable onboard interconnections. For example, the chip includes four 64-bit reconfigurable data paths per RCU. In addition, the chip provides four 32-bit address paths per RCU. The reconfigurable paths make it possible to interconnect a set of RCUs in a pipeline.

Memory. An RCU has access to several forms of memory. For example, the chip offers access to both internal Synchronous Static RAM (SSRAM) and external Double Data Rate Synchronous Dynamic RAM (DDR-SDRAM). The VISC dictionary is kept in a separate memory. The memories form a hierarchy where the onboard registers and scratch memory are the fastest, the onboard instruction cache and data memory are next fastest, and the external memory used for packet buffers is the slowest.

Other Features. To permit maximal parallelism, the RCU has hardware support for multiple threads of execution. The Cognigine chip offers onboard interface hardware for external bus connections, including a PCI bus connection. Finally, in addition to a C compiler and assembler, Cognigine offers software support for a classification language.

15.9 Pipeline Of Heterogeneous Processors (EZchip)

EZchip Corporation's *NP-1* network processor provides an example of a chip that uses special-purpose, heterogeneous processors. Each processor type is designed to handle a specific function; a set of heterogeneous processors is arranged in a pipeline.

Architecture. The NP-1 network processor consists of a pipeline of parallel processors that are known as *Task Optimized Processors* (*TOPs*). A chip contains multiple types of TOPs; each type has an internal instruction set and data paths optimized for a particular protocol processing task. Figure 15.10 illustrates the architecture.

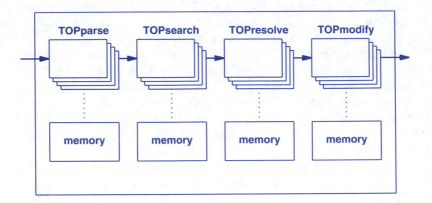

Figure 15.10 Internal architecture of an EZchip NP-1 network processor.
Each of the four banks of processors is optimized to perform a
specific task.

Processors And Functional Units. The EZchip design contains four types of processors; Figure 15.11 lists the purpose of each.

Processor Type	Optimized For
TOPparse	Header field extraction and classification
TOPsearch	Table lookup
TOPresolve	Queue management and forwarding
TOPmodify	Packet header and content modification

Figure 15.11 The four types of processors available on the EZchip network
processor and the tasks for which each is optimized.

Other Features. The EZchip architecture contains high-speed onboard SRAM that can be used for packet buffers and table lookup. In addition, the design contains an interface to external DRAM (no external SRAM or CAM is needed). Although not shown in the diagram, the chip contains an interface that allows an external processor to control operations.

15.10 Extensive And Diverse Processors (IBM)

The Microelectronics division of IBM Corporation produces a set of network processors under the name *PowerNP†*. Among the most sophisticated and powerful network processors, IBM's PowerNP provides an example of an architecture that includes a wide range of embedded processors, coprocessors and other functional units.

Architecture. The IBM network processor contains programmable protocol processors plus a set of coprocessors that handle searching, frame forwarding, filtering, and frame modification. The architecture consists of a central set of embedded processors surrounded by support units. Figure 15.12 illustrates the overall architecture.

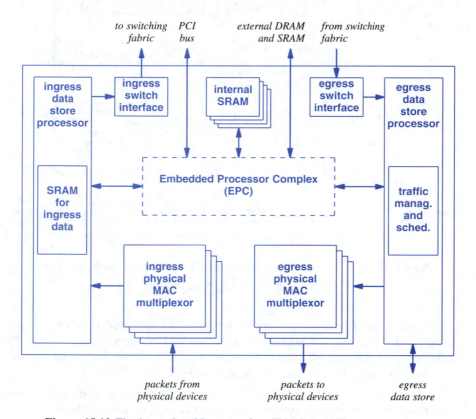

Figure 15.12 The internal architecture of an IBM PowerNP network processor. The high-level diagram hides details such as the structure of the area labeled *Embedded Processor Complex* and additional external connections.

Figure 15.13 expands the level of detail in the architectural diagram by showing the contents of the *Embedded Processor Area (EPC)* on an IBM chip.

---

†IBM offers multiple products; one model is named *NP4GS3*.

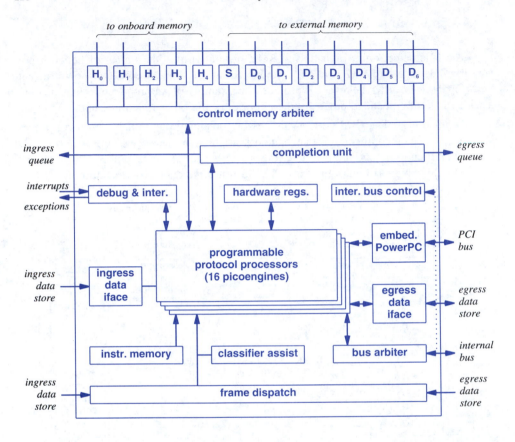

Figure 15.13 Illustration of some of the detail inside the Embedded Processor
Complex area on an IBM network processor.

Processors And Functional Units. As the figures imply, the IBM chip contains
many types of processors. In addition to an embedded PowerPC processor, the EPC
contains sixteen programmable protocol processors called *picoengines*†. Each picoengine is multithreaded, which further increases performance.

To achieve high speed, frames are preprocessed before being passed to the protocol
processors in the *Embedded Processor Complex*. The *ingress physical MAC multiplex-
or* accepts an incoming frame from a physical interface, verifies the CRC, and then
passes the frame to the *ingress data store*. Only the first part of the frame, which contains headers, is passed to the protocol processors; the remainder of the frame is stored
in memory. After a frame has been processed, the *ingress switch interface* handles the
details of forwarding the frame across the switching fabric to the correct output processor.

----

†IBM sometimes uses the more formal term *Core Language Processor* in place of *picoengine*.

Hardware outside the embedded processor complex also handles output. The *egress switch interface* accepts frames that arrive over the switching fabric, and places them in the *egress data store*. The *egress physical MAC multiplexor* controls frame transmission by extracting the frame from the *egress data store* and transferring it to the physical interface.

In addition to programmable picoengines, the IBM chip contains many special-purpose coprocessors. Figure 15.14 lists examples.

Coprocessor	Purpose
Data Store	Provides frame buffer DMA
Checksum	Calculates or verifies header checksums
Enqueue	Passes outgoing frames to switch or target queues
Interface	Provides access to internal registers and memory
String Copy	Transfers internal bulk data at high speed
Counter	Updates counters used in protocol processing
Policy	Manages traffic
Semaphore	Coordinates and synchronizes threads

Figure 15.14 Eight coprocessors found on an IBM network processor and the function of each.

Memory. As well as providing access for external memory such as DDR-SDRAM, the PowerNP contains various onboard memories and a *control memory arbiter* to coordinate access. An onboard SRAM provides high-speed local access that can be used as a staging area for incoming packets. In addition, the chip contains onboard instruction storage for programmable processors (e.g., picoengines have access to a private 128KB instruction store).

Programming Support. IBM provides extensive programming support. In addition to the usual tools such as compilers and assemblers, IBM offers a simulation package that allows a programmer to develop and debug software. The IBM simulation package is available for a wide variety of platforms such as Solaris, Linux, and Windows.

Other Features. The onboard coprocessor that handles traffic management works at wire speed. Thus, the IBM chip is able to check each packet to verify that traffic adheres to pre-established parameters.

15.11 Flexible RISC Plus Coprocessors (Motorola)

Motorola Corporation sells network processors under the *C-Port* brand. The *C-5*, *C-5e*, and *C-3* models offer a choice of speed and power dissipation. Motorola's network processor is interesting because it provides an example of a single chip where the onboard processors can be arranged to work in a dedicated, parallel, or pipeline configuration. The ability to choose a configuration for each processor makes the C-Port design flexible.

Architecture. A Motorola C-Port network processor is intended to handle both ingress and egress. Figure 15.15 illustrates the intended use — the figure shows how C-Port chips can connect multiple physical interfaces to a switching fabric.

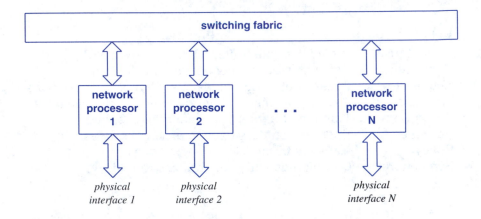

Figure 15.15 Conceptual organization of a packet processing system that uses Motorola's C-Port network processors. Each network processor can handle both ingress and egress.

Processors And Functional Units. A C-Port chip contains sixteen processor blocks, called *Channel Processors* (*CPs*), that handle packet processing tasks. A CP can be configured to operate in one of three ways:

- In a dedicated configuration
- In a parallel cluster
- In a pipeline

The most straightforward approach uses a *dedicated configuration* that establishes a 1-to-1 relationship between a CP and a physical interface. In a dedicated configuration, one CP handles the I/O for an interface (i.e., the CP handles both incoming and outgoing packets). A dedicated configuration is appropriate for a low-speed or medium-speed interface (e.g., 100Base-T Ethernet or OC3) because a single CP has sufficient power to process the packets that arrive.

To handle higher-speed interfaces, a set of CPs can be configured to operate in a *parallel cluster*. When a packet arrives on the interface, any CP in the cluster that is currently idle can handle the packet. Because the exact number of CPs in a cluster can be configured, a designer can choose a cluster size appropriate for the interface speed and the amount of processing performed on a packet.

The C-Port architecture also allows CPs to be configured in a *pipeline*. Packets that arrive over an interface associated with a pipeline are each sent to the first CP in the pipeline. After it finishes performing operations on the packet, the first CP forwards the packet to the second CP in the pipeline. Similarly, each processor in the pipeline performs a set of operations and forwards the packet to the next processor. The final processor in the pipeline forwards the packet off the chip (i.e., either sends the packet to the switching fabric or to a physical interface).

Figure 15.16 illustrates the internal architecture of a C-Port C-5 chip†, and shows the CPs configured into parallel clusters.

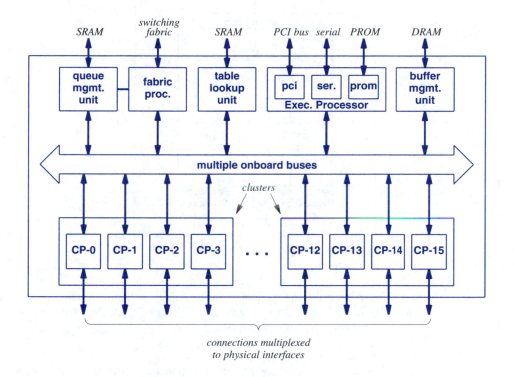

Figure 15.16 The internal architecture of Motorola's C-Port chip. The diagram shows the sixteen channel processors (labeled CP-0 through CP-15) configured in parallel clusters of four channel processors per cluster.

In addition to CPs, the C-Port chip contains several coprocessors. The *Executive Processor* provides overall chip configuration and management. The Executive Processor communicates with a host computer over a PCI bus or a serial line. The *fabric pro-*

---

†The diagram also applies to the C-5e model, which differs from the C-5 because it allows an external queue controller with 2^{16} queues (the C-5 has 512 onboard queues).

cessor provides a high-speed interconnection between onboard buses and an external switching fabric. The *table lookup unit* implements high-speed table searches. The *buffer management* and *queue management* units manage and control packet buffers and packet queues.

The name *Channel Processor* is somewhat misleading because a CP is not a single processor. Instead, each CP is a complex mechanism that contains a RISC processor plus several functional units that help handle packets at high speed. Figure 15.17 illustrates the components of a CP and their interconnection.

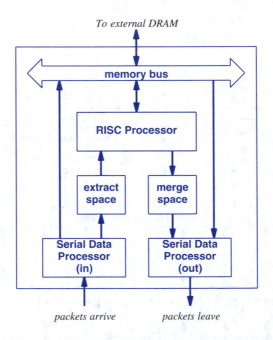

Figure 15.17 The internal architecture of a single CP with a RISC core plus functional units to handle ingress and egress. Each C-Port chip contains a total of sixteen CPs.

As the figure shows, the CP contains parallel components for ingress and egress. On ingress, a programmable *Serial Data Processor*† (*SDP*) handles tasks such as checksum or CRC verification, decoding, header parsing, and field extraction. On egress, a separate SDP handles frame alteration, checksum or CRC calculation, framing, and encoding. The RISC processor performs classification and traffic management, including policy enforcement and traffic shaping.

Programming Support. The C-Port network processor is programmed using C or C++. The vendor supplies a compiler, simulator, an API, and libraries of reference software for tasks such as physical interface access, table lookup, buffer manipulation, and queue management.

---

†The name *Serial Data Processor* is misleading because an SDP consists of five microsequencers and other hardware that work together.

15.12 Summary

Many commercial vendors offer network processor products. This chapter considers a small set of commercial examples that illustrate the range of possible architectural styles and features. The examples show the wide variety of designs used in commercial products.

We discussed examples of multi-chip and single-chip processors, an embedded RISC processor, an embedded RISC processor plus coprocessors, a pipeline of homogeneous processors, a pipeline of heterogeneous processors, configurable instruction sets, extensive heterogeneous processors, and processors that can be reconfigured to act individually, in parallel, or in a pipeline.

FOR FURTHER STUDY

Williams [2001] considers network processor architectures. Additional information is available on the web. For example, each commercial vendor offers a data sheet or product brief that lists the details of each product. Many vendors also provide white papers that describe the motivation for design choices.

EXERCISES

15.1   Conduct a survey to determine which vendors offer commercial network processors, and make a list of products.

15.2   Characterize the network processors offered by the vendors listed in Exercise 15.1 according to the basic architecture.

15.3   Read the vendors' literature and make a list of the maximum data rate that each vendor claims for their network processor.

15.4   Read the vendors' literature and obtain an estimate of the total memory size and bandwidth available on each network processor.

15.5   Investigate commercial support and programming systems used to create network processor software. What languages are used?

Chapter Contents

16

Languages Used For Classification

16.1 Introduction

Earlier chapters describe classification, and explain why it plays a fundamental role in high-speed packet processing. Chapter 13 discusses network processor architectures, and Chapter 15 illustrates how various designs use programmable processors to handle ingress operations, including classification.

This chapter continues the discussion by examining languages that programmers use to implement classification. The chapter considers the role and properties of special-purpose classification languages, describes the relationship to hardware, and shows example languages.

16.2 Optimized Classification

Because it can avoid processing protocol layers sequentially, classification has the potential to operate much faster than traditional demultiplexing. More important, a programmable network processor offers the advantage of high-speed classification without the need for custom hardware. To realize the potential, however, a network processor implementation of classification must supply two features. First, the network processor hardware needs sufficient processing power to perform classification at wire speed. Second, the programming support facilities must offer a way for programmers to create classification code that is optimized for the underlying hardware.

16.3 Imperative And Declarative Paradigms

How should classification rules be specified? There are three broad approaches available from which to choose:

- Declarative paradigm
- Imperative paradigm with implicit parallelism
- Imperative paradigm with explicit parallelism

A *declarative paradigm*, which is also known as a *nonprocedural paradigm*, arranges for a programmer to specify classification rules without giving an algorithm or implementation details. In particular, declarative systems do not permit a programmer to specify the order of individual comparisons or the sequence of operations. In essence, a declarative paradigm allows a programmer to specify *what* should be done without specifying *how*.

An *imperative paradigm*, which is also known as a *procedural paradigm*, requires a programmer to specify an exact sequence of steps to be performed when classifying a packet. That is, the programmer specifies in detail *how* to perform classification. Imperative specification allows the programmer to control all aspects of classification, including the extraction of fields from headers, the maintenance and access of state information, and the order in which comparisons are performed.

Implicit and explicit parallelism refer to whether the language requires a programmer to control a mapping of the program to parallel hardware. A language that offers implicit parallelism hides details of the underlying hardware, and allows a programmer to write code as if a single processor will execute the program. The compiler and/or run-time system choose how to map the program onto multiple processors. A language that offers explicit parallelism requires the programmer to define the code that each processor will execute and to control interactions among the processors.

The choice among paradigms depends on several factors:

- Underlying hardware architecture
- Network data rates and packet rates
- Software support availability

From a programmer's point of view, the availability of support software often dominates the decision. A network processor vendor chooses a paradigm, and provides support software for its customers to use when implementing classification. Instead of creating their own support software, most customers adopt whatever the vendor supplies. Thus, most customers implicitly follow the paradigm that the chip vendor selects.

16.4 A Programming Language For Classification

To ensure that the classification rules are stated in a precise and unambiguous form, the specifications follow a formal set of standards known as a *classification language* (i.e., a special-purpose programming language designed for classification). A classification language can follow an imperative or declarative paradigm. In either case, the language determines both the syntactic and semantic interpretation of programs. That is, the language specifies exactly how a programmer represents a program as well as the computations that the program performs.

16.5 Automated Translation

The overall goal of building a classification language is automation — once a program has been written in the language, a compiler can translate the program into code for a network processor. If the system is designed well, the language and compiler can offer four potential advantages over coding classification by hand. First, separating the classification rules from other aspects of system design helps programmers spot inconsistencies and errors, which improves correctness. Second, focusing on classification rather than general-purpose computing allows a language designer to create a language that is easier to use, which improves programmer productivity. Third, isolating classification processing from the rest of the code helps reduce the cost of reusing classifications in related products. Fourth, a compiler that understands and exploits the nuances of the underlying hardware can produce highly optimized code, which improves the performance of the resulting system.

The key to achieving the above advantages lies in careful design of a classification language and compiler. Should classification languages follow an imperative or declarative paradigm? Vendors disagree. Although few defend the use of assembly language, some vendors assert that programmers prefer a conventional, imperative language (e.g., C) that allows the programmer to control the order of operations. Other vendors assert that a compiler can produce better optimizations than an average programmer and that a special-purpose declarative language can be optimized the most. As we will see, there is no easy answer because the choice depends on many factors, including the underlying hardware. Customers face an important issue that is orthogonal to the paradigm debate: incompatibilities among languages from multiple vendors. Customers point out that even if one language has benefits over another, the lack of a de facto standard means that programmers spend time learning a new language before they can write or modify specifications for a new network processor.

16.6 Language Features That Aid Programming

From the point of view of programming convenience, the following characteristics are desirable in a classification language:

- *High-level.* Although network hardware operates at a low level (e.g., provides bit manipulation), classification languages should allow programmers to specify operations in a language that focuses on protocols instead of hardware.

- *Declarative.* Although they do not permit a programmer to express the exact steps the hardware executes, declarative languages help hide the details of the underlying hardware, and accommodate a wider range of hardware architectures.

- *Data oriented.* Because classification focuses on high-speed data processing, a classification language should include data specification facilities that are sufficient to define the contents and layout of protocol headers that use arbitrary levels of encapsulation.

- *Efficient.* Because a network system must continue to operate at wire speed, a classification language must produce code that can handle events such as the creation of dynamic classification without delay.

- *General or extensible.* Either a classification language must be sufficiently general to handle arbitrarily complex packet formats, or it must include an extensibility mechanism that allows a program to invoke an external processor.

- *Explicit links to actions.* A network system performs classification as a prelude to further packet processing (e.g., forwarding). Because the system uses the result of classification to choose an appropriate action, a classification language can improve correctness by providing an explicit link between classifications and semantic actions.

16.7 The Relationship Between Language And Hardware

Although programmer convenience is important, the underlying hardware can constrain the language, the compiler, or the run-time support system. The next paragraphs consider example architectures and the consequences of each.

•RISC processor dedicated to classification. If an embedded RISC processor is dedicated to classification, a conventional, imperative language like C can work well. Programmers find the language familiar, and compilers are readily available to translate

programs into code for RISC hardware. More important, many commercial compilers contain code optimization facilities to generate code that makes maximal use of the underlying hardware.

•*RISC processor shared with other tasks.* If an embedded RISC processor supports tasks other than classification, the run-time system must contain facilities for task synchronization and coordination. The language can hide facilities or allow programmers explicit access. Declarative languages tend to hide; imperative languages usually provide explicit access. For example, if the run-time system uses *semaphores* to provide mutual exclusion, an imperative language allows a task to use *signal* and *wait* functions to access semaphores.

•*Multiple, parallel RISC processors.* If the underlying hardware offers multiple processors that can execute in parallel, a language that hides parallelism can work better than a language that exposes parallelism to the programmer. To understand why, consider program execution. On one hand, a language with explicit parallelism relies on the programmer to specify how activities map to parallel hardware. On the other hand, a declarative language or an imperative language with implicit parallelism allows a compiler to map activities onto parallel hardware. More important, an imperative language with explicit parallelism constrains the possible optimizations from which the compiler can choose. As a result, implicit parallelism allows a compiler to introduce more optimizations.

•*RISC processor plus special-purpose coprocessor(s).* Consider hardware in which a RISC processor invokes a special-purpose coprocessor to perform classification. The language used depends on the relative power and architecture of the coprocessor. For example, if the RISC processor handles most of the effort and only relies on the coprocessor for basic tasks such as comparisons, the language can be tailored to the RISC processor. If the coprocessor handles all classification, the language can be tailored to the coprocessor architecture.

•*State Machine.* Some vendors offer classification hardware that does not follow a conventional vertical code structure. For example, it is possible to build a programmable classifier that uses a state machine such as a *Field Programmable Gate Array* (*FPGA*). In such cases, a declarative language can be appropriate because no direct mapping exists from an imperative language to the underlying hardware.

16.8 Efficiency And Execution Speed

One of the central issues surrounding classification languages concerns the execution speed of the resulting code. Several questions arise. Can a high-level language allow a network processor to operate at wire speed? Should a high-level language merely generate an overall structure and allow a programmer to supply optimized code for individual functions? Alternatively, can a compiler optimize code better than a programmer?

The underlying hardware can determine some of the answers. A state machine such as an FPGA is more difficult to understand and program manually than a conventional processor. Thus, a compiler may be able to produce faster code for a state machine than a programmer. Other exotic hardware can also be amenable to compiler optimizations. For example, instruction sets used in programmable network processors often have timing restrictions — the execution of successive instructions can overlap as long as the instructions do not access the same functional unit. A compiler that is programmed to understand the intricacies of the hardware may be able to determine an instruction ordering that is faster than the ordering specified by a programmer.

16.9 Commercial Classification Languages

Examples of classification languages will help clarify the concepts. We will consider two: Intel's *Network Classification Language* (*NCL*) and Agere's *Functional Programming Language* (*FPL*). Although the details differ, each illustrates how classification can be specified without using a conventional imperative language.

16.10 Intel's Network Classification Language (NCL)

Like most classification languages, NCL mixes declarative and imperative paradigms. Although a basic program contains declarations that do not specify an exact sequence of steps, NCL does allow a programmer to associate an action with each classification rule. Furthermore, the programmer thinks of an action as a function to be invoked. Thus, an NCL program can be viewed as a set of declarative classification rules that invoke an imperative action when a rule matches a packet.

NCL declarations are optimized for protocols in which the fields occupy fixed positions and have fixed lengths. Like structure declarations in C, NCL declarations express each field position as a multiple of octets (i.e., the starting position of each field must lie on a byte† boundary). Unlike C structure declarations, however, NCL declarations do not correspond to sequential fields in memory. Instead, the location and size of each item is specified using *position : length* pairs, enclosed in brackets. For example, the notation:

$$X\,[\,12:4\,]$$

specifies a four-octet field (i.e., thirty-two bits) that lies twelve octets from the beginning of the item named X.

In addition to specifying fields that lie on octet boundaries, NCL allows a programmer to specify fields on a bit boundary. To do so, the programmer uses NCL's *bit*

---
†We assume 8-bit bytes throughout the text.

range operator, which consists of an integer value enclosed in less-than and greater-than signs. For example, the notation:

$$Y [<4>:<2>]$$

declares a two-bit field that lies four bits from the beginning of the item named *Y*.

16.11 An Example Of NCL Code

NCL uses the keyword *protocol* to begin a series of declarations that correspond to a particular protocol header. The body of the protocol declaration, which is enclosed in braces, specifies a set of names that can be referenced for the protocol. Usually, each name in the set corresponds to a distinct field in the packet header. We will see, however, that names can correspond to multiple fields or to computed values. Figure 16.1 contains an NCL declaration of an IP datagram header that includes twelve names.

```
protocol ip {                    /* declaration of datagram header */
      vershl   { ip[0:1] }
      vers     { ( vershl & 0xf0 ) >> 4 }
      tmphl    { ( vershl & 0x0f ) }
      hlen     { tmphl << 2 }
      totlen   { ip[2:2] }
      ident    { ip[4:2] }
      frags    { ip[6:2] }
      ttl      { ip[8:1] }
      proto    { ip[9:1] }
      cksum    { ip[10:2] }
      source   { ip[12:4] }
      dest     { ip[16:4] }

      demux  {
      ( proto == 6 )          { tcp at hlen }
      ( proto == 17 )         { udp at hlen }
      ( default )             { ipunknown at hlen }

      // note: other protocol types can be added here

      }
}                               // end of datagram header declaration
```

Figure 16.1 An example NCL declaration for fields in an IP datagram header with keywords shown in italic. Names that are used, but not declared here, must be declared elsewhere.

The code in the figure illustrates several features of NCL. First, NCL allows a choice of C or C++ style comments. As in C++, text following // is treated as a comment that the compiler ignores; as in C, text between /* and */ is ignored. Thus, each of the following is a comment:

/* declaration of datagram header */

// note: other protocol types can be added here

The declaration provides a name for each item in the protocol that will be referenced in the program. In NCL, each name must be declared before it can be used. For example, the programmer has chosen the name *cksum* to refer to the IP checksum field. As the declaration shows, the IP checksum field begins ten octets from the start of the IP header and has a length of two octets. Similarly, the programmer has chosen the name *source* for the IP source address field, and the name *dest* for the IP destination address field.

Once a declaration is given, fields within a protocol header can be referenced by naming the protocol and a field within the protocol. Each reference to a named item consists of a protocol name and a field name separated by a dot. Thus, once protocol *ip* has been declared, the program can use *ip.dest* to reference the IP destination address in an IP header.

The code in the figure illustrates an important aspect of NCL: an alternative way to declare a bit field that does not lie on a byte boundary. Recall that in an IP datagram, the first two fields (i.e., the version field and the header length field) each occupy four bits. The example NCL code begins by declaring *vershl* to be a one-octet field that starts at location zero. In other words, the name *vershl* corresponds to a one-octet field that contains both the IP version number and the header length. The name *vers* is then declared by specifying a C-like expression that extracts the high-order four bits of the *vershl* field:

(vershl & 0xf0) >> 4

The expression specifies using a *logical and* with hex constant *0xf0* to extract the high-order four bits and then a *right shift* to place them in the low-order four bits of the result.

The specification for the header length value, *hlen*, illustrates another mechanism in NCL: the use of a temporary name. Recall that the *header length* field in a datagram specifies the size of the IP header measured in thirty-two bit multiples. Thus, to compute the size of the header in octets, the value must be multiplied by four. Although NCL does not include operators for multiplication, division, or modulo arithmetic, multiplication or division by a power of two can be achieved with logical bit operators. For example, the code in Figure 16.1 uses the expression:

$$(\text{vershl} \ \& \ \text{0x0f})$$

to declare *tmphl* equal to the length bits from the datagram (the low-order four bits of the first octet). In a separate declaration, *hlen* is defined by the expression:

$$\text{tmphl} << 2$$

which specifies shifting the value left by two bits (i.e., multiplying the value by four).

The example in Figure 16.1 also illustrates how an NCL program references encapsulated headers. Ironically, although it is designed for classification, NCL uses the keyword *demux* to specify encapsulation. The example code contains specifications for the encapsulation of TCP and UDP.

A list of items, enclosed in braces, follows the *demux* keyword. Each item consists of a pair: a Boolean expression and an encapsulation. NCL interprets the declaration to mean that the encapsulation is defined whenever the Boolean expression evaluates to true. The encapsulation specifies a protocol name and an offset (measured in octets from the beginning of the header); the keyword *at* separates the name and offset. To accommodate variable-size headers, the offset can refer to fields of the encapsulating header. In Figure 16.1, for example, encapsulation declarations use the IP header length as an offset for the encapsulated protocol. The declaration is:

$$\{ \ \text{tcp} \ \textit{at} \ \text{hlen} \ \}$$

NCL interprets the declaration to mean that the *tcp* protocol header occurs *hlen* octets beyond the beginning of the IP header (recall that *hlen* gives the IP header size measured in octets). Thus, NCL positions the TCP segment *hlen* octets from the start of the IP datagram, which corresponds to the IP payload area.

The Boolean expression in a demux item specifies a condition that must be true for the encapsulation to hold. As we have seen, a typical protocol header contains a *type* field that specifies the format of the payload. To accommodate such encapsulations, NCL allows a Boolean expression to reference the value of header fields. For example, the line:

$$(\ \text{proto} == 6 \ ) \ \ \{ \ \text{tcp} \ \textit{at} \ \text{hlen} \ \}$$

specifies that if field *proto* of the IP header contains the value 6, the *tcp* protocol can be found at location *hlen*.

In addition to a list of Boolean functions, NCL allows a demux statement to contain a *default*. If any of the explicit Boolean expressions evaluates to *true*, NCL selects the corresponding encapsulation; if none of the Boolean expressions succeeds, NCL selects the default encapsulation. In the example code, the default corresponds to an encapsulation named *ipunknown*.

NCL does not contain built-in definitions of standard protocol headers. For example, NCL does not define protocol names like *ip* or *tcp*. Thus, the code in Figure 16.1 is incomplete — a declaration for *tcp* must be included in the NCL program, or an error will result.

We said that although it is declarative, NCL allows a programmer to specify an action to be taken when a classification is recognized. As an example, consider a network system designed to record all the IP source addresses from packets that contain web traffic. Web traffic is defined to consist of an IP datagram that contains a TCP segment in which the destination port is 80. An NCL program uses a *rule* construct to specify the appropriate condition and an action to be invoked. Figure 16.2 contains an example NCL rule for web traffic.

rule web_filter { ip && tcp.dport == 80 } { web_proc(ip.source) }

Figure 16.2 An example of an NCL rule that gives a classification and action for web traffic.

As the figure shows, the statement begins with the *rule* keyword. The programmer has chosen rule name *web_filter*, and has specified that *web_proc* is the action to be taken (i.e., the procedure to be invoked) when the classification succeeds. Although NCL must be able to find all the procedures that comprise a program, each procedure can be placed in a separate file. For example, before the code in Figure 16.2 can be used, a programmer must create a file that contains the code for *web_proc*.

In the example code, the rule statement specifies that the IP source address field, *ip.source*, is passed to procedure *web_proc* as an argument. Procedure *web_proc* can perform arbitrary computation, including accessing or modifying state information.

16.12 NCL Intrinsic Functions

NCL predefines a pair of *intrinsic* functions that handle checksum verification or computation: *chksumvalid* and *genchksum*. Intrinsic functions are limited to protocols that use a 16-bit one's complement checksum (i.e., protocols in the TCP/IP stack).

A programmer can use the keyword *intrinsic* in a protocol declaration to associate an intrinsic function with the protocol. Each of the TCP/IP protocol declarations supplied by Intel includes an intrinsic function, making it possible to reference the function by giving the protocol name. Figure 16.3 lists the predefined intrinsic functions.

Function Name	Purpose
ip.chksumvalid	Verifies validity of IP checksum
ip.genchksum	Generates an IP checksum
tcp.chksumvalid	Verifies validity of TCP checksum
tcp.genchksum	Generates a TCP checksum
udp.chksumvalid	Verifies validity of UDP checksum
udp.genchksum	Generates a UDP checksum

Figure 16.3 The intrinsic functions predefined in NCL. When applied to a fragment, an intrinsic function produces partial results (e.g., a partial checksum).

16.13 Predicates

In addition to predefined intrinsic functions, NCL offers a facility that allows programmers to define *named predicates* that can be used in the conditional part of a rule. The predicate definition consists of a name followed by a Boolean expression enclosed in braces. Figure 16.4 defines a predicate that evaluates to *true* if and only if an IP datagram can be fragmented.

predicate ip.fragmentable { ! ((ip.frags >> 14) & 0x01) }

Figure 16.4 An example NCL predicate declaration. The predicate tests the *DO NOT FRAGMENT* bit.

As the figure shows, the predicate is named by specifying a protocol and the name of a predicate for the protocol. The example uses the name *ip.fragmentable*. The Boolean expression references fields that are defined by the protocol (e.g., *ip.frags*). In the example declaration, the Boolean expression extracts the *DO NOT FRAGMENT* bit from the *frags* field, and inverts the value. Thus, if the bit is zero, the predicate returns *true* to indicate the datagram is fragmentable, and if the bit is one, the predicate returns *false*.

16.14 Conditional Rule Execution

Although the goal of classification is high speed, some classification rules contain dependencies. For example, a classification of an IP datagram cannot proceed unless the checksum is valid. Similarly, port numbers in a TCP segment cannot be used unless the TCP checksum is valid. NCL allows a programmer to specify such conditions by using a *with* statement to enclose a set of rules and conditionals. Figure 16.5 contains an example *with* statement that encloses a *predicate* statement and a *rule* statement.

```
predicate TCPvalid { tcp && tcp.cksumvalid }
with { ( TCPvalid ) {
    predicate SynFound { (tcp.flags & 0x02) }
    rule NewConnection { SynFound } { start_conn(tcp_dport) }
}
```

Figure 16.5 Illustration of a *with* statement used for conditional execution. The enclosed statements are executed only if the condition holds.

In the example, the *with* statement restricts execution unless condition *TCPvalid* holds (i.e., the TCP checksum is valid). If the checksum is valid, NCL examines the TCP *flags* field to determine whether the segment is a SYN segment. If the segment is a SYN, NCL calls procedure *start_conn*.

16.15 Incremental Protocol Definition

An NCL program allows an existing protocol definition to be expanded. To do so, the programmer gives an additional declaration that names a new field:

```
field protocol_name.field_name { definition }
```

For example, suppose a program contains a declaration of the IP protocol as Figure 16.1 shows. The programmer can use the following statement to declare a three-bit flags field that is located six octets beyond the IP header:

```
field ip.flags { ip[6 : <3>] }
```

Incremental additions to a protocol are especially useful because they permit a programmer to build a single, generic declaration for a protocol and add fields for a particular program without altering the underlying declaration.

16.16 NCL Set Facility

Recall that a *stateful* classification scheme uses the previous history of packets when making a classification decision. For example, instead of merely saving a list of IP source addresses, a stateful classifier might use the list to ensure that all subsequent packets from a given source address receive the same classification. NCL includes two features that support stateful classification. First, NCL allows classification rules to invoke procedures as part of conditions. Second, NCL includes a *set* mechanism that provides optimized storage and searching.

NCL's set mechanism is used to store state information in a table. Each entry in the table can have one or more *key values* that are used to search the table. To define a set, the programmer chooses three items:

- A name for the set.
- The number of keys for each entry. Up to seven keys can be specified; each key is a binary value of up to four octets.
- An estimated set size. The estimated size must be a power of two, and is a hint used for optimization; the set can grow larger than the estimate.

NCL uses the keyword *set* to begin the declaration and the keyword *size_hint* to define the estimated size of the set. Keys in an entry are positional — the declaration specifies the number of keys, but does not give a name to each. The example declaration in Figure 16.6 illustrates the syntax by declaring a set in which each entry holds one key.

```
set my_addrs              /* define a set of IP addresses */

    < 1 > {               /* number of keys in each entry */

    size_hint { 256 }

}
```

Figure 16.6 Illustration of an NCL set declaration. Each entry contains one key, and the programmer estimates the set will contain two hundred fifty-six items.

Once a set has been declared, a programmer can specify one or more *named searches* that can be referenced in the program. The declaration specifies a qualified name that consists of a set name, a dot, and a search name. Figure 16.7 contains an example search declaration to be used with the set declared in Figure 16.6.

search my_addrs.ip_src_lookup

(ip.source)   /* search key is IP source addr. */

Figure 16.7 An illustration of an NCL named search declaration. The declaration specifies using field *source* of an IP datagram as a key to search table *my_addrs*.

In the figure, the programmer has defined a named search to look up an IP source address in a set; the search is named *ip_src_lookup*. The parenthesized list in a named search specifies values to be used as keys. In the case of set *my_addrs*, the set holds only one key, so only one value is needed.

To use a named search, a programmer must reference the name in an expression. For example, referencing *my_addrs.ip_src_lookup* causes the program to extract the IP source address field from the current packet (i.e., *ip.source*), and search set *my_addrs*. If the value is present, the search returns *true*; otherwise, the search returns *false*. Thus, a named search can be used any place in the code where a Boolean expression can be used.

Note that although a search declaration depends on a specific protocol, the underlying set does not. That is, a set such as *my_addrs* uses positional keys, and does not declare the type of a key. The set can be used with a key that has been extracted from an arbitrary header or a key that has been computed (presumably, the programmer will be careful to ensure that all values stored in a set have the same type). Each search declaration mentions a specific protocol name that must be previously declared with a *protocol* declaration. Thus, a programmer can only use a search with a specific header. In the example, an *ip_src_lookup* search can only be used with a packet that matches the *ip* declaration.

16.17 Other NCL Features

As expected, NCL contains other facilities that make programming easier. For example, NCL uses a C-style of *symbolic constants* to make constants easier to recognize and change. The following line defines *TABLESIZ* to be a symbolic constant with the value 256.

#define TABLESIZ 256

Following the definition, a symbolic constant can be used any place in a program that a constant can appear.

NCL also offers a *source include* facility and conditional preprocessor directives that each follow the C preprocessor style. For example, the lines:

```
#ifndef IP-PROTO
#include progfile
#endif
```

cause NCL to conditionally include a file named *progfile*. The directive *ifndef* abbreviates *if not defined*. NCL tests symbolic constant *IP-PROTO*. If the constant has not been defined, NCL proceeds to replace the three lines with a copy of the file named *progfile*. As in C, a programmer can use *ifndef* to ensure that a declaration is included exactly once.

16.18 Agere's Functional Programming Language (FPL)

Like NCL, FPL offers a mixture of declarative and imperative paradigms. However, FPL is unusual. Unlike most declarative languages, FPL does not use structured data declarations to describe the positions of header fields. Unlike most imperative languages, FPL does not require the programmer to specify detailed steps to be taken to extract or manipulate data. Instead, FPL centers on pattern matching — the language is oriented around a pattern matching paradigm, and each action is connected to a pattern match.

FPL is also unusual because the pattern matching facilities are specifically designed for networking. Thus, FPL differs from pattern matching languages such as awk or SNOBOL4 in which the pattern matching facilities are designed to handle syntactic patterns.

Finally, FPL is unusual because the language is intended for fast data path data processing and is optimized for use with the Agere network processor. Each language construct maps into an efficient operation on the underlying hardware. In particular, the pattern matching facilities in the language map well onto the capabilities of Agere's pattern processing engine.

16.19 Two Pass Processing

An FPL program implements a *two-pass paradigm*. In essence, the program contains two distinct parts that are referred to as passes. The *first pass* collects blocks of data that comprise a packet, and verifies that all blocks arrive without error. Once a complete packet has been collected and stored in memory, the *second pass* classifies and forwards the packet.

The motivation for two passes arises from the underlying hardware. When it transfers a packet from a network interface to the pattern processing engine, the hardware divides the packet into small, fixed-size blocks. Agere's 2.5G hardware uses a block size of 64 octets; the 10G hardware uses a block size of 80 octets. If an incoming packet is smaller than the transfer block size (e.g., an ATM cell), the hardware places the packet in a single block. If an incoming packet is larger than the block size, the hardware divides the packet into multiple blocks. The hardware delivers status information along with each block to specify the port from which the block was received, whether it is the initial or final block of a packet, and whether the network interface detected any errors. The FPL program uses the status information to determine where each packet begins and ends; there is no ambiguity about packet boundaries.

The first pass of an FPL program collects the blocks that comprise a single packet, and verifies that they arrive without error. Because multiple network interfaces operate independently, a block can arrive from any interface at any time; the hardware port number is used to associate an incoming block with a queue that holds the blocks for a given interface. Once the last block of a packet has arrived, the first pass informs the queue manager, which makes the packet available to the second pass.

The second pass performs operations such as classification, and then sends the packet on to the routing engine. Figure 16.8 illustrates the overall flow of data through an FPL program.

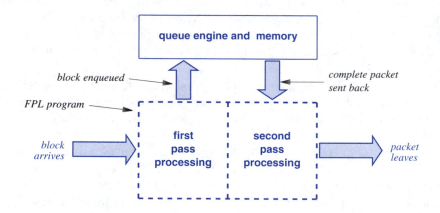

Figure 16.8 Illustration of the conceptual flow of data through an FPL program. The first pass is invoked once for each block; the second pass is invoked once for a packet.

FPL does not poll the network interface to determine when a packet arrives. Instead the hardware invokes FPL automatically. When a block arrives from the interface hardware, the pattern processing engine invokes the first pass of the FPL program; when a complete packet has been received, the pattern processing engine invokes the second pass of the FPL program.

A small amount of status information travels through the system along with each data block. Some of the status information originates in the hardware (e.g., the hardware reports the port over which the packet was received and whether the block is the initial or final block of the packet). Other status information originates in software. In particular, each pass of the FPL program computes a small status value, and forwards the value along with a packet. The value passed from the first pass to the second pass is known as a *tag*, and is referenced in the second pass using the variable name *$tag*. On a system in which ports connect to heterogeneous networks (e.g., ATM and Ethernet), the first pass generates a tag that specifies the hardware type over which the packet arrived. The second pass also generates and forwards status information. In particular, the second pass computes classification or routing information for the packet, and forwards the information to the routing engine.

16.20 Designating The First And Second Pass

FPL uses *SETUP directives* to identify the starting points that correspond to the first and second pass. A *ROOT* directive identifies the start of the first pass, and a *REPLAYROOT* directive identifies the start of the second pass. For example, the code:

> // Directives to define first and second passes
> SETUP ROOT(HandleBlock)
> SETUP REPLAYROOT(HandleFrame)

specifies that the first pass of the program should begin processing at the label *HandleBlock*, and the second pass of the program should begin at the label *HandleFrame*. The example also illustrates that FPL follows the C++ comment convention: any text that occurs after two slashes is a comment that the compiler ignores. Thus, the first line in the example above is a comment.

16.21 Using Patterns For Conditionals

A few examples will help clarify how a language can focus on pattern matching as a primary paradigm. For example, consider the first pass of a program that accepts blocks of an incoming Ethernet frame. When a block becomes available, the hardware invokes the first pass of the FPL program, which enqueues the block for second-pass processing. To enqueue a block, the program invokes one of two built-in procedures: *fQueue* or *fQueueEof*. The only difference is that procedure *fQueueEof* is used for the final block of the packet. Each of the calls causes the program to terminate and wait to be invoked again.

The decision about whether a block is the last block of a packet is trivial because the answer is given by a 1-bit variable, *$framerEOF*, which the hardware sets. To choose between *fQueue()* and *fQueueEof()*, the first pass merely needs to test variable *$framerEOF*. A conventional, imperative programming language uses a conditional statement to perform a test and choose a procedure to execute:

> if ($framerEOF) then fQueueEof(); else fQueue();

In FPL, however, a conditional test is performed by pattern matching — the programmer specifies the test by creating a pattern for each possible outcome and matching the variable to the patterns. Figure 16.9 contains example code that illustrates the concept.

```
#include "fpp.fpl"

// Code for the first pass of a program that handles Ethernet packets

SETUP   ROOT(HandleBlock);

// Pass 1

HandleBlock:  EtherBlock($framerEOF:1);

EtherBlock:   0b0  fQueue(0:2, $portNumber:16, $offset:6, 0:1, 0:2);
EtherBlock:   0b1  fQueueEof(0:2, $portNumber:16, $offset:6, 0:1, 0:2, 0:24);
```

Figure 16.9 Example FPL code for the first pass of a program that processes Ethernet frames. The code is invoked once for each block, and conditionally calls built-in procedure fQueue() or fQueueEof() to enqueue the block.

In the figure, the programmer includes a file that provides definitions for Agere's FPP†, and uses the *ROOT* directive to declare label *HandleBlock* as the point at which first-pass processing begins. Thus, the hardware will invoke *HandleBlock* for each block of the frame. The code at *HandleBlock* appears to contain a procedure call to a procedure named *EtherBlock()* with an argument of the form:

$$\$framerEOF : 1$$

The colon notation, which is used throughout FPL, denotes a binary value, where the item to the left of the colon specifies the value, and the number to the right of the colon specifies the number of bits. Thus, the ''argument'' passed to *EtherBlock* consists of exactly one bit.

Despite appearances, *EtherBlock* is not a procedure in the imperative language sense. Instead, it is a label in FPL that corresponds to a set of pattern match statements, each of which has the form:

label: pattern action

The argument to *EtherBlock* is a value against which pattern matching is performed. In the example code, the programmer has specified two possible pattern matches for *Ether-Block*. The first consists of a pattern with the value zero (written as a 1-bit binary item

---

†Recall from Chapter 15 that the Fast Pattern Processor (FPP) is part of the Agere hardware.

using the notation *0b0*†), and specifies an action named *fQueue()*. The second pattern consists of the value one (also written as a 1-bit string), and specifies an action named *fQueueEof()*.

When multiple patterns correspond to a given label, FPL applies the patterns to the object and follows the pattern that matches the data. In Figure 16.9, for example, FPL compares the argument to *EtherBlock* with the two patterns 0b0 and 0b1. If the argument matches 0b0, FPL calls built-in procedure *fQueue*; if the value matches 0b1, FPL calls built-in procedure *fQueueEof*. Thus, a programmer can use pattern matching to implement conditional execution.

16.22 Symbolic Constants

Like other languages, FPL allows a programmer to declare *symbolic constants* that make the code easier to understand. FPL follows the C programming language syntax for definition of symbolic constants by using a *#define* statement. Instead of using explicit constants 0b0 and 0b1 for the code in Figure 16.9, a programmer could define meaningful names to make the program more readable. For example, the programmer might choose names that give the purpose of each constant:

```
#define   NORMBLOCK      0b0        // not the last block of the frame
#define   LASTBLOCK      0b1        // the last block of the frame
```

16.23 Example FPL Code For Second Pass Processing

As an example of second-pass processing, consider a classification problem. Suppose a program is being built to classify Ethernet frames into one of three possible categories. Further suppose that each of the three categories has been assigned a classification number that is passed along when the frame is sent to the routing processor:

Assigned Number	Meaning
1	Frame carrying an ARP message
2	Frame carrying an IP message
3	Frame other than the above

Figure 16.10 shows an example of the FPL code to perform the classification and assign a value to each frame.

---

†A constant that begins with *0b* consists of a bit string.

```
// Code for the second pass of a program that classifies Ethernet frames

// Symbolic constants used for classifications

#define   FRAMETYPEA     1        // ARP frames
#define   FRAMETYPEI     2        // IP frames
#define   FRAMETYPEO     3        // Other frames (not the above)


SETUP   REPLAYROOT(HandleFrame);

// Pass 2

HandleFrame:
            fSkip(96)                       // skip past dest & src addresses
            cl = CLASS                      // compute class from frame type
            fSkipToEnd()
            fTransmit(cl:21, 0:16, 0:5, 0:6);

CLASS:  0x0806:16                   fReturn(FRAMETYPEA);
CLASS:  0x0800:16                   fReturn(FRAMETYPEI);
CLASS:  BITS:16                     fReturn(FRAMETYPEO);
```

Figure 16.10 Example FPL code for the second pass of a program that classifies each Ethernet frame into one of three categories.

The code begins with the definition of three symbolic constants that give readable names for each of the three classification values. The program uses directive *SETUP REPLAYROOT* to specify that second-pass processing starts with label *HandleFrame*.

16.24 Sequential Pattern Matching Paradigm

The interesting code in Figure 16.10 begins at label *HandleFrame*. When the second pass is invoked, an Ethernet frame is ready, and pattern matching begins at the first bit of the frame. The code performs four steps. First, it invokes the built-in function *fSkip()* to skip past the first ninety-six bits of the frame (i.e., destination and source address fields of the Ethernet header). Second, the program invokes a pattern named *CLASS*, and assigns the result of the invocation to variable *cl*. Third, the program calls built-in function *fSkipToEnd()* to read remaining bits of the frame from memory (required by FPL). Fourth, the program uses built-in function *fTransmit()* to finish the pass by sending the frame on to the next processor (usually a routing processor).

The easiest way to understand FPL pattern matching is to imagine a packet being processed sequentially. Pattern matching proceeds by moving forward through the packet; each field in the packet must be matched as it is reached. Thus, an FPL program cannot check protocol header fields in arbitrary order — the programmer must specify how to handle each bit of the packet. In particular, at each step, the program must specify the exact size of the object to be matched, and give the semantics associated with the match. For example, the call to built-in function *fSkip(96)* moves forward across ninety-six bits, leaving the internal pointer at the start of the sixteen-bit frame *type* field. A pattern that matches the frame type must be exactly sixteen bits long, and will leave the internal pointer at the start of the frame data area.

FPL optimizes pattern matching by folding common initial sequences into a single match. For example, consider the two code segments in Figure 16.11.

```
IP:      0x4  0x5  fSkip(152)        fReturn(IPOPTIONS0);
IP:      0x4  0x6  fSkip(160)        fReturn(IPOPTIONS1);
IP:      0x4  0x7  fSkip(168)        fReturn(IPOPTIONS2);
IP:      0x4  BITS:4                 fReturn(IPUNKNOWN);
```

(a)

```
IP:      0x4  IPHDR;
IPHDR:   0x5  fSkip(152)             fReturn(IPOPTIONS0);
IPHDR:   0x6  fSkip(160)             fReturn(IPOPTIONS1);
IPHDR:   0x7  fSkip(168)             fReturn(IPOPTIONS2);
IPHDR:   BITS:4                      fReturn(IPUNKNOWN);
```

(b)

Figure 16.11 (a) An example FPL program in which a set of patterns shares a common initial sequence, and (b) an equivalent program with the common sequence folded. A compiler performs the folding automatically.

The code in part (a) of the figure consists of a function for IP with four patterns. Each pattern begins with the same initial sequence, a match of the four-bit IP version number. When presented with the code, the FPL compiler folds the initial pattern sequence into a separate control function. Part (b) of the figure illustrates the concept by showing code that only has a single copy of the shared pattern. In essence, *IP* has been converted to a pattern that first matches constant *0x4*, and a new label, *IPHDR*, has been introduced to handle the remainder of the pattern.

Eliminating common initial sequences in a pattern is analogous to eliminating common prefixes in an IP routing table. Thus, the same general approach applies to each. In fact, an Agere pattern matching chip uses an internal representation of patterns that is similar to the trie data structure used to hold IP routing tables†.

---

†An explanation of the trie structure can be found on page 58.

16.25 Tree Functions And The BITS Default

FPL uses the term *control function* to refer to a series of pattern matches that specify a single sequence of steps, and *tree function* to refer to code that specifies multiple, mutually exclusive possibilities. A tree function is declared by using the same label on multiple pattern matching statements. For example, label *CLASS* in Figure 16.10 corresponds to a tree function because the label appears on three pattern matching statements.

The three patterns that comprise the tree for *CLASS* consist of 0x0806:16 (for ARP), 0x0800:16 (for IP), and BITS:16. *BITS* is an FPL pattern that matches any bit string of the specified length. For example, *BITS:48* will match any Ethernet address because it matches an arbitrary string of forty-eight bits. *BITS* has special meaning in a tree function because it provides a *default match* — if none of the explicit patterns matches, FPL follows the BITS pattern. In Figure 16.10, for example, if the frame type field does not match 0x0806 (ARP) or 0x0800 (IP), FPL follows the BITS match.

16.26 Return Values

Recall from our discussion of first-pass processing that a pattern statement can have an action following the pattern. When the pattern matches, FPL executes the associated action. We saw earlier that the action associated with pattern matching can be used to provide conditional execution among a set of procedures. The example in Figure 16.10 illustrates another possible use: the assignment of a value.

To understand assignment, look at the three statements in Figure 16.10 that begin with the label *CLASS*. The action on each statement consists of a call to the built-in function *fReturn()*. Function *fReturn* takes an argument, which it returns as the value of the pattern invocation. When it encounters a frame carrying ARP, *CLASS* matches 0x0806, and FPL executes action *fReturn(FRAMETYPEA)*. Similarly, *CLASS* returns *FRAMETYPEI* for a frame carrying IP, and *FRAMETYPEO* as the default.

The value from *fReturn()* is passed back to the statement that invoked *CLASS*. In the example code, the value is assigned to variable *cl*, making it available for use later in the program.

16.27 Passing Information To The Routing Engine

As the final step of processing a packet, the second pass must call *fTransmit()* to send the packet on to the next processing engine. The first argument to *fTransmit()* consists of a binary value twenty-one bits long. FPL uses the argument to pass status information along with an outgoing frame. In the example code, the outgoing status information consists of the value of variable *cl*, which was assigned during the *CLASS* match. Thus, the routing engine will receive the classification along with the packet.

As a special case, the Agere routing engine interprets a status value of zero to mean *discard*. If an FPL program finds an error in a packet or needs to discard the packet for another reason, the second pass merely invokes *fTransmit()* with the first argument set to zero. As an example, the classifier in Figure 16.10 can be transformed into a packet filter by redefining constant *FRAMETYPE0* to have the value zero. After the change, only packets of type ARP or IP will be processed; all others will be discarded.

16.28 Access To Built-in And External Functions

FPL provides a program with access to many functions. In addition to the built-in functions described above, FPL includes built-in functions for operations such as CRC and checksum computation. Thus, an FPL program can validate the CRC on an Ethernet frame or the checksum used by IP, TCP, or UDP.

External functions allow a program to perform computation on hardware other than in the FPP. In particular, the *Agere System Interface* (*ASI*) in the Agere network processor provides many computational functions that an FPL program can use. For example, the ASI functions allow a program to perform Boolean operations (*and*, *or*, and *not*), store and retrieve values from memory, and access packet policing functions.

In addition to predefined functions, ASI hardware includes programmable compute engines that allow a programmer to build external functions for use with an FPL program. The functions are written in *Agere Scripting Language* (*ASL*). Unlike FPL, ASL is an imperative language — the syntax and semantics follow the C language. Thus, ASL allows a programmer to augment the pattern-oriented processing in FPL with arbitrary computation.

16.29 Other FPL Features

FPL includes many features and details not discussed in this overview. The following sections provide examples.

16.29.1 FPL Constant Syntax

FPL offers a variety of ways to represent constants. As we have seen, a programmer can specify a value in decimal (e.g., 18), hexadecimal (e.g., 0x12), or binary such as 0b10010. In addition, FPL includes two forms that make it easy to denote network addresses. *Dashed hex* constants are often used to represent an Ethernet address, and *dotted decimal* constants are often used to represent IP addresses.

A dashed hex constant represents each octet of the value in hexadecimal, with a minus sign separating octets. For example, the 48-bit Ethernet broadcast address can be written in dashed hex notation as:

ff-ff-ff-ff-ff-ff

TCP/IP protocol standards use dotted decimal notation to express Internet addresses. FPL allows dotted decimal constants, and extends the notation to include patterns that match IP addresses. For example, consider the tree function in Figure 16.12.

ipAddrMatch:	*.*.*.*	fReturn(0);
ipAddrMatch:	10.*.*.*	fReturn(1);
ipAddrMatch:	128.10.*.*	fReturn(2);
ipAddrMatch:	128.211.*.*	fReturn(2);
ipAddrMatch:	128.210.*.*	fReturn(3);

Figure 16.12 Illustration of FPL's extended dotted decimal notation used in a pattern. The example is a tree function for IP addresses.

The code in the figure consists of a tree function for some of the IP addresses in use at Purdue University, and assigns each a return value. For example, any IP address between 10.0.0.0 and 10.255.255.255 is assigned the return code one; any IP address between 128.210.0.0 and 128.210.255.255 is assigned return code three. The first entry in the figure gives a default value — any address not specified by the other patterns is assigned the return code zero. The order of entries in the tree function is unimportant because FPL uses a longest-prefix rule to select a match. Thus, although it appears first in the figure, the default entry is only used if none of the other patterns match.

16.29.2 FPL Variables

FPL provides several predefined variables. Figure 16.13 lists examples.

Variable	Pass	Meaning
$framerSOF	1	Is the current block the first of a frame?
$ferr	1	Did the hardware framer detect an error?
$portNumber	1	Port number from which block arrived
$framerEOF	1	Is the current block the last of a frame?
$offset	1 or 2	Offset of data within a buffer
$currOffset	1 or 2	Current byte position being matched
$currLength	1 or 2	Length of item being processed
$pass	1 or 2	Pass being executed
$tag	1 or 2	Status value sent from pass 1 to pass 2

Figure 16.13 Examples of predefined FPL variables along with the pass in which they are available.

16.29.3 FPL Support For Dynamic Classification

In addition to the statically-defined tree functions illustrated in this chapter, FPL provides facilities that support dynamic classification. That is, the language permits a tree function to be created and modified as the program runs. Thus, it is possible to use values in the stream of incoming packets to determine the set of classes.

16.30 Summary

Because classification plays a fundamental role in packet processing, vendors have developed special programming languages to express classification rules. Classification languages can be declarative or imperative, and imperative languages use explicit or implicit parallelism. To ease programming, a classification language should be declarative, high-level, data oriented, and linked to actions. The underlying hardware can determine the type of language as well as whether a compiler or human programmer produces more highly optimized code.

We examined two classification languages that are available commercially: Intel's NCL and Agere's FPL. Both examples take a declarative approach, and have features that connect classification rules to actions. FPL is unusual because pattern matching forms the central paradigm.

FOR FURTHER STUDY

Intel's SDK Reference Manual [Intel 2001a] describes NCL and its use. Agere's Functional Programming Language User's and Reference Guide [Agere 2002] defines FPL and contains examples. In addition, a white paper entitled *The Case For A Classification Language* can be found on the Agere web site at:

    www.agere.com/enterprise_metro_access/docs/classification_new.pdf

EXERCISES

16.1   Survey network processor vendors to determine which languages they use for classification.

16.2   Extend the previous exercise to correlate classification languages with the underlying hardware architecture.

16.3   Write an NCL declaration for a TCP segment, and define predicates for each of the *FLAGS* bits.

16.4   Write an NCL declaration for ICMP, and be sure to include multiple ICMP message types.

16.5   Is it possible to write an NCL declaration that handles IP options? Why or why not?

16.6   Is it possible to write an NCL declaration that handles the TCP window scaling option? Why or why not?

16.7   Write second-pass code for an FPL program that parses fields of an IP header.

16.8   Write second-pass code for an FPL program that classifies packets into four categories: broadcast frames, multicast frames, unicast frames that carry IP, and other. Be careful to avoid all ambiguity.

16.9   Write an FPL tree function that handles IP datagrams that contain arbitrary numbers of IP options.

16.10   Write an FPL program that acts as an Ethernet bridge between two network segments that each contain four computers. (Hint: assume the MAC addresses of the computers are known.)

16.11   If you have access to hardware facilities, compare the performance of a classifier built using a classification language to a classifier built manually.

Chapter Contents

17

Design Tradeoffs And Consequences

17.1 Introduction

Previous chapters discuss network processor technologies, including the motivation, architecture, and scaling. This chapter discusses a set of engineering tradeoffs inherent in creating and using network processors. The chapter is intended to raise issues, not to settle disputes. It lists possibilities and some of the consequences; it poses questions, presents alternative solutions, and discusses tradeoffs without attempting to resolve the discussion.

17.2 Low Development Cost Vs. Performance

Chapter 11 considers the fundamental tradeoff of network processor technology: a system that uses a network processor will cost less to design than a system that uses custom ASIC hardware, but will have lower performance. Because the definitions of cost and performance are vague, several questions arise. For example, can we quantify the cost difference between a network processor and custom hardware? Can we quantify the performance difference?

Economic costs are especially difficult to quantify because they include both short-term and long-term aspects: the costs of initial development and the cost of upgrades. The value of a shorter development cycle depends on the market, which changes over time. The requirements or underlying technologies can change between the time a design is conceived and the time a product is delivered to customers. Thus, a quantitative assessment of benefits of using network processors is elusive. Fortunately, the cost of developing a custom ASIC is so high that a precise economic analysis is unnecessary — except in unusual circumstances, a system built using network processors will cost less to develop than the same system built using a custom chip.

17.3 Programmability Vs. Processing Speed

We can ignore the economic costs and consider the engineering tradeoff between programmability and speed. Programmable devices, which offer flexibility and adaptability, are especially suited in a field such as networking where the products keep evolving. However, custom hardware offers the highest speed. Under what circumstances is speed more important than flexibility?

A conventional CPU with a general-purpose instruction set only suffices for a low data rate. Thus, a system designer can only use general-purpose CPUs in low-end systems. A few years ago, the choice between programmability and speed was fairly obvious. The advent of specialized network processors changes the decision focus. Instead of requiring a system designer to choose between a general-purpose CPU and custom silicon, the onus rests on the network processor designer, who must choose an architecture and instruction set. In making a choice, the designer strikes a balance between programmability and processor speed.

17.4 Performance: Packet Rate, Data Rate, And Bursts

It may seem that understanding performance is straightforward; the computer industry has invented ways to measure conventional processors. Previous chapters suggest that two broad measures of performance suffice: the maximum data rate and the maximum packet rate. Unfortunately, precise performance assessment of network processors is as elusive as precise economic assessment. First, benchmarking and quantitative performance measurement requires us to measure a processor as it performs a specific set of tasks. Unfortunately, because network processors are used in a wide variety of systems, no small set of tasks can characterize the work a network processor will perform. Second, quantitative measurement requires us to measure a network processor under load. That is, we must choose the network traffic that a system will receive.

Network traffic is especially troublesome to model because it requires us to agree on traffic patterns. To see why, recall that packets tend to arrive in bursts. Thus, a steady stream of packets, which is often used as a first-order approximation, does not provide a realistic test of performance in the field — the system may run out of buffers when presented with a burst of packets. Thus, accurate assessment requires a bursty distribution; we must choose properties such as the average burst size and the average spacing between bursts. Unfortunately, there is little agreement on the type of traffic that comprises a typical workload. As a result, it is extremely difficult to obtain quantitative assessments of the capability or performance of a network processor.

17.5 Speed Vs. Functionality

Yet another way to recast the performance debate focuses on the tradeoff between speed and functionality. The instruction set on a network processor is optimized to handle specific tasks. As the set of tasks is expanded, more instructions must be added to the instruction set. An enhanced network processor offers more functionality, but incurs a cost: because instructions do not all require the same amount of time to execute, the chip must contain complex scheduling and synchronization mechanisms. The result is increased overhead. If enough instructions are added, the instruction set becomes completely general, and the network processor becomes a general-purpose CPU.

17.6 Per-Interface Rate Vs. Aggregate Data Rate

One of the tradeoffs that can be made in the design of a network system focuses on the data rate that the system will accommodate. If the mechanisms associated with an individual interface form the system bottleneck, performance will be limited by the per-interface data rate. If the central switching fabric forms the bottleneck, performance will be limited by the aggregate data rate. In most designs that use network processors, a network processor is assigned to an individual physical interface or a small set of physical interfaces. Thus, the designer must balance the maximum data rate of a network processor with the aggregate data rate of the switching fabric.

17.7 Network Processor Speed Vs. Bandwidth

Vendors are quick to point out that network processors have become powerful rapidly. Early network processors handled OC-12 data rates. Within a year, many handled OC-48. At the time of this writing, a few vendors claim to handle OC-192. During the same period, the bandwidth of backbone Internet connections has also increased. Therefore, an interesting question arises about the long-term: will network processor capabilities or the bandwidth of network connections increase more rapidly?

Do more transistors make a difference? The processing power of a network processor generally follows Moore's Law† — as the number of transistors on a chip increases, chip designers can increase the processing power. Because VLSI chips provide the electronic interfaces for high-speed optical networks, Moore's law indirectly affects bandwidth. However, increases in bandwidth also depend on advances in optical components such as lasers and fiber. As a result, it is not clear whether the power of network processors or bandwidth is increasing faster.

---

†Moore's law, attributed to Gordon Moore, is the observation that the density of silicon circuits, measured in the number of transistors per square inch, will double every eighteen months. When originally stated, the law referred to doubling each year; in the 1970s, the rate slowed to eighteen months.

17.8 Coprocessor Design: Lookaside Vs. Flow-Through

Coprocessor hardware comes in two varieties: *lookaside* and *flow-through*. A lookaside system operates like a procedure call — the main processor invokes a coprocessor when needed. Flow-through coprocessors handle data in a pipeline fashion by making modifications as data passes through. Which style works best for network processors? Flow-through coprocessors have two disadvantages: to avoid becoming a bottleneck, they must work at wire speed, and they are more closely integrated into the design, which makes them difficult to change. Lookaside coprocessors have the advantage of modularity because a design can be extended to accommodate additional coprocessors without major changes to the architecture. However, lookaside coprocessors have the disadvantage of requiring the main processor to transfer all the information that the coprocessor needs for computation.

17.9 Pipelining: Uniform Vs. Synchronized

A pipeline can operate two ways. In a *uniform pipeline*, the functional units along the pipeline each take the same time to process a packet. In a *nonuniform pipeline*, the function performed by a unit determines the amount of time taken. The chief advantage of a nonuniform pipeline arises from its ability to handle arbitrary protocols: the processing time for a unit is determined by the functionality required. To accommodate differing speeds among stages, a buffer is required between each stage of the pipeline and the hardware must synchronize timing and forwarding among stages. More important, the slowest stage in a nonuniform pipeline can become a bottleneck. The chief advantage of uniformity arises from cost savings: no buffering or synchronization is required. However, a uniform pipeline has the disadvantage of requiring each stage to finish in the same amount of time. Usually, enforced uniformity means that faster stages must wait for the slowest stage.

17.10 Explicit Parallelism Vs. Cost And Programmability

Several chapters, including Chapter 14, discuss the use of parallelism as a technique that can increase speed and overall scalability. We said that one of the fundamental tradeoffs involves the choice between explicit and implicit parallelism. The issue can also be cast as a choice between speed and programmability. Explicit parallelism requires less sophisticated hardware, but can make a chip difficult to program. Implicit parallelism requires additional hardware to hide parallel activities from the programmer. The extra hardware adds cost and can reduce performance slightly, but makes a chip easier to program.

17.11 Parallelism: Scale Vs. Packet Ordering

An interesting problem arises from the use of parallelism: *packet reodering*. To adhere to the protocol specification, a system such as a bridge or an ATM switch must ensure that packets remain in their original order. Even protocols that tolerate packet reordering (e.g., TCP running over IP) perform significantly better when packets arrive in order. Thus, architectures that use parallelism to achieve large scale usually include mechanisms to preserve packet order.

The tradeoff involved in packet ordering arises because relaxing the constraint on ordering can increase overall throughput of a given system. The synchronization mechanism in a parallel architecture must run at the rate of arriving data, which is approximately N times faster than the rate of a single processor (where N is the number of parallel processors). Furthermore, if ordering must be preserved, output must wait for a packet. Thus, relaxing the requirement for ordering helps in two ways. First, because it does not need to perform complex packet synchronization tasks, coordination hardware can operate faster. Second, because a packet can be sent without delay, the system does not stall a processor or leave an output port idle.

17.12 Parallelism: Speed Vs. Stateful Classification

To ensure noninterference, parallel processors must synchronize access to shared state information. Sharing causes a potential reduction in speed because only one processor can update the shared information at any time. Thus, increased sharing reduces the overall speed. The tradeoff between speed and shared state is especially important for network systems that update the state frequently. Packet classification illustrates the tradeoff well because the type of classification determines the speed. A static classification (i.e. one in which header values are compared to constants) can achieve a speed of N when run on N parallel processors. However, a dynamic classification (i.e., one in which the set of classes is determined from values in the stream of packets) has lower performance because state information must be kept. The tradeoff is not limited to conventional classification: a NAT box that must store an inverse mapping in a table is subject to lower performance than a NAT box in which entries do not change.

17.13 Memory: Speed Vs. Programmability

Memory is often divided into separate banks that allow simultaneous access. In most cases, however, maximum access speed can only be achieved by placing data carefully into banks to avoid access contention. The tradeoff is programmability: because a programmer must be aware of memory banks, programming is more difficult.

17.14 I/O Performance Vs. Pin Count

The width of a bus limits the total throughput — a wider bus allows greater throughput. As noted in Chapter 14, a tradeoff arises for external bus access because a wider bus uses more pins. Pin count imposes a practical constraint: fewer pins reduce package cost, which can be important because packaging costs for high-speed devices often dominate the chip cost.

17.15 Programming Languages: A Three-Way Tradeoff

Programming languages exhibit an interesting three-way tradeoff among ease of programming, functionality, and the speed of the resulting code. It is only possible to maximize two of the three properties.

Ease Of Programming Vs. Functionality. If one demands high speed, the tradeoff reduces to a choice between ease of programming and functionality. A programming language that contains a small set of high-level constructs tailored for a specific task is the easiest language to use. However, such a language lacks the functionality required for arbitrary tasks. A programming language that includes features sufficient for many disparate tasks is difficult to use because a programmer faces several ways to perform each task. Thus, designers must choose between a language that makes it easier to program and one that handles increased functionality.

Ease Of Programming Vs. Speed. If one demands functionality, the tradeoff reduces to a choice between ease of programming and speed. Although they are easiest to use, high-level programming languages do not map as efficiently to low-level hardware. Thus, the code that results from using a high-level language may not perform as well as the code produced by a low-level language. In particular, many network processors require a programmer to use assembly language to achieve maximal throughput.

Speed Vs. Functionality. If one demands ease of programming, the tradeoff reduces to a choice between speed and functionality. If a language is restricted to a specific application, a compiler can generate highly optimized code. As more functionality is added to the language, however, it becomes more difficult to generate optimized code. Thus, the language designer must tradeoff decreased functionality for faster code.

17.16 Multithreading: Throughput Vs. Programmability

The chief reason network processors support multithreading is higher throughput: by allowing a programmer to specify multiple computations, the processor can continue to execute even if a thread blocks to wait for I/O or a coprocessor. The chief disadvantage of multithreading is increased programming complexity: a programmer must coordinate the activities of threads. Even in cases where the hardware handles preemption and switching among threads automatically, a programmer needs to ensure that threads coordinate the use of shared resources. Thus, the tradeoff occurs between higher throughput and ease of programming.

17.17 Traffic Management Vs. Blind Forwarding At Low Cost

ISPs and other organizations that charge for service demand network systems that can manage traffic by giving priority service to traffic that yields the highest profit. From an architectural point of view, the question becomes a tradeoff between traffic management, speed, and cost. At low speeds, an embedded RISC processor can perform traffic management along with other functions. At high speeds, however, traffic management requires special-purpose hardware, which increases the overall cost. So the questions become: at what bandwidth is it necessary to build special-purpose hardware for traffic management? Is it possible to architect a network processor in which traffic management operates at wire speed when needed, and is unintrusive when not needed? Can the cost of adding traffic management hardware be minimized?

17.18 Generality Vs. Specific Architectural Role

Section 12.6 lists a set of architectural roles in which a network processor can be used. Instead of looking at how a network processor can be used to replace pieces of a generic system architecture, we can consider its role in a broader sense.

Overall Purpose Of A Network System. A network system can be: part of the *access* mechanism, part of the *metro* interconnect, part of the *edge*, or part of the *core*. Each use implies a set of facilities that are needed. The tradeoff is between having a single, general-purpose network processor that can be used in any system and a set of special-purpose processors that are each designed for one purpose.

Protocols To Be Supported. Connection-oriented protocols such as ATM, MLPPP†, and MPLS‡ require more hardware support than connectionless protocols such as conventional IP or Ethernet. The tradeoff centers on the choice between a set of protocol-specific network processors and a single, general-purpose architecture.

17.19 Memory Type: Special-Purpose Vs. General-Purpose

Previous chapters discuss some of the tradeoffs in the choice of memory. For example, network processors often use a combination of SRAM and DRAM because each has advantages (access times, interface hardware, and cost). Furthermore, specific memory technologies offer performance characteristics such as low cycle times.

---

†*MultiLink Point-to-Point Protocol*, a technology used with ISDN to double the throughput.

‡*Multi-Protocol Label Switching*, a technology used to transfer IP datagrams over a connection-oriented infrastructure.

One particular memory tradeoff stands out as especially important: the choice between Content Addressable Memory (CAM) and SRAM or DRAM. The disadvantages of CAMs include greater expense and higher power dissipation than SRAM or DRAM. However, CAM has several advantages. CAM provides more functionality per I/O pin because a single CAM lookup replaces several SRAM/DRAM accesses. A single CAM memory can replace several SRAM or DRAM memories. CAM can eliminate lookup coprocessors.

Because it has high cost, CAM is usually restricted to high-end processors, where higher cost can be justified to achieve high performance. Despite the advantages, designers often avoid CAM to lower cost. Furthermore, CAMs are most attractive when rapid lookup is required in a database that consists of a small number of large records. As the number of entries in the database grows, CAM becomes less attractive.

17.20 Backward Compatibility Vs. Architectural Advances

Underlying technologies continue to change rapidly for two reasons. First, increases in chip density allow designs to contain more processing power and memory. Second, designers continue to experiment with new, special-purpose support chips and new internal architectures. For example, consider memory: although a wide variety of memory technologies exist, memory vendors continue to invent new types (e.g., QDR-DRAM emerged after DDR-DRAM).

An interesting tradeoff occurs whenever a network processor vendor builds a next generation because the vendor must choose between changing the architecture to incorporate new technologies and maintaining *backward compatibility*. The potential advantages of new technology include higher speed and improved functionality. From a customer's point of view, however, a backward compatible design is also desirable because using the same architecture entails little or no additional cost (changes in architecture can impose significant costs because the customer's software must be rewritten and retested).

17.21 Parallelism Vs. Pipelining

Many designers argue that there are only two basic approaches to building network processors — a parallel approach or a pipeline approach — which means that a fundamental tradeoff occurs between the two. In practice, however, few designs follow either approach exclusively. Instead, each design contains a mixture of pipelines and parallelism. In particular, parallelism can be used to build a pipeline in which the amount of processing varies among stages. That is, a given stage can contain parallel processors. The tradeoff is difficult because the network processor designer does not know exactly how the chip will be used. Thus, the designer can only estimate the amount of processing needed at each stage.

17.22 Summary

Because network processors are complex devices used for a variety of purposes, many design tradeoffs exist. Often, tradeoffs represent a choice among greater functionality, higher performance, and lower cost.

EXERCISES

17.1 Search the Web to find commercial network system products that are implemented with network processors. What is the highest data rate advertised?

17.2 Research the changes in bandwidth and general-purpose CPU speeds over the past ten years. Assume network processors will follow the same trend as general-purpose processors, and predict whether bandwidth or the speed of network processors will increase more rapidly.

17.3 Examine network processor architectures to determine which commercial vendors use lookaside coprocessors and which use flow-through.

17.4 Compare the lookup times and cost of DRAM and CAM.

17.5 Compare the expressive power and ease of programming offered by a classification language such as FPL or NCL to the expressive power and ease of programming offered by a conventional language such as C. Approximately how many lines of code does a layer 2 bridge occupy in each language?

17.6 A network processor vendor often reports the performance of its chip when executing *reference code* (i.e., code the vendor has built for a common task such as layer 2 forwarding). Find out whether the reference code is compiled from a high-level classification language or a low-level language. What can you conclude about the tradeoff between convenience and performance?

17.7 The IBM network processor uses parallelism to achieve high speed. How does the architecture solve the problem of packet reordering?

17.8 The text cites dynamic classification and NAT as examples of systems that require shared state information. Find further examples.

17.9 Choose a tradeoff discussed in this chapter, and quantify the costs.

17.10 Compile a description of the tradeoffs not mentioned in this chapter. Hints: internal buses: number vs. width, caches: data vs. instruction cache, instruction memories: multiple vs shared, and switching fabric design.

An Example
Network Processor And
Associated Technologies:
Intel's IXA

Chapter Contents

18

Overview Of The Intel Network Processor

18.1 Introduction

Chapters in the previous section of the text provide a general discussion of network processors. This section begins an in-depth examination of a specific network processor that provides a concrete illustration of the general concepts. The example we have chosen is a network processor by Intel†. Chapters in the section discuss the hardware, describe a commercially-available testbed environment for the Intel chip, and present detailed programming examples.

This chapter begins by presenting an overview of the Intel architecture. It considers characteristics of the chip, describes the basic organization, and defines terminology. Because the Intel processor is complex, we begin with a conceptual, high-level view of the architecture. Later chapters in the section expand the descriptions further, and provide more detail about each unit.

18.2 Intel Terminology

Like most vendors, Intel has defined a plethora of names and terms related to its network processor technology. Some of the terms apply broadly to the general architecture, and others are restricted to a specific chip or to a specific functional unit on the chip. As one might expect, the terminology is further complicated because the technology evolves. For example, changes occur in terminology between releases of the software and as the reference platform changes. We will attempt to define and use ter-

---

†The author gratefully acknowledges Intel's support of his lab and this project with donations of hardware, software, and documentation.

minology consistently; readers are warned, however, that some of the vendor's documents (especially older documents) may use variations of the terminology.

18.3 IXA: Internet Exchange Architecture

The term *Internet Exchange Architecture* (*IXA*) refers broadly to the Intel network processor architecture. We will see that although it focuses primarily on network processor hardware, IXA includes software architecture as well because programmable hardware cannot be defined without envisioning the software that uses the facilities.

IXA encompasses both control plane and data plane processing (i.e., both *slow path* and *fast path* processing). IXA defines hardware abstractions, application program interfaces (APIs), and interconnection mechanisms, but does not give details. Instead, IXA defines the conceptual organization. A later section considers IXA in more detail.

18.4 IXP: Internet Exchange Processor

The term *Internet Exchange Processor* (*IXP*) refers to a network processor chip that implements the IXA architecture. Although an IXP design must adhere to the IXA architecture, each IXP model can define details such as the number and type of onboard functional units, the degree of processor parallelism, the maximum size of memories, and the internal data bandwidths.

Intel currently offers four models of IXP network processor chips that follow the architecture. The chief differences among the four lies in the packaging (432 or 520 pins), power consumption, and miscellaneous features such as hardware support for CRC or ECC computation. Figure 18.1 lists the models and characteristics†.

The distinction among the four models is often blurred in the vendor's literature because the term *IXP1200* is also used as a broad reference to any of the four chips. We will follow the convention throughout this chapter, and use IXP1200 to mean any of the four models.

Model Number	Pin Count	Support For CRC	Support For ECC	Possible Clock Rates (in MHz)
IXP1200	432	no	no	166, 200, or 232
IXP1240	432	yes	no	166, 200, or 232
IXP1250	520	yes	yes	166, 200, or 232
IXP1250‡	520	yes	yes	166 only

Figure 18.1 Specific Intel network processors that follow Intel's Internet Exchange Architecture.

---

†Chapter 27 describes Intel's second generation chips, which are expected to be available in 2003.
‡A version of the 1250 that tolerates an extended temperature range.

18.5 Basic IXP1200 Features

Although Intel sells a variety of bus interface chips and other hardware that can be used to interface with their network processor, an IXP network processor consists of a single chip. The chip contains a complex set of programmable and non-programmable processors and functional units. As one measure of complexity, an IXP chip contains 1536 individual hardware registers that provide a programming interface to the underlying hardware. Figure 18.2 summarizes the principle components.

- One embedded RISC processor

- Six programmable packet processors

- Multiple, independent onboard buses

- Processor synchronization mechanisms

- Small amount of onboard memory

- One low-speed serial line interface

- Multiple interfaces for external memories

- Multiple interfaces for external I/O buses

- A coprocessor for hash computation

- Other functional units

Figure 18.2 A list of the major facilities found on Intel's IXP1200 network processor chip. In addition to the hardware facilities on the chip, the vendor offers a software development environment.

Successive sections of this chapter consider each of the features and describe their purpose; later chapters expand the descriptions and give more detail.

18.6 External Connections

The diagram in Figure 18.3 illustrates the major external connections that an IXP1200 supports. In addition to the connections shown, a chip contains connections for a clock, power, and other low-level signals.

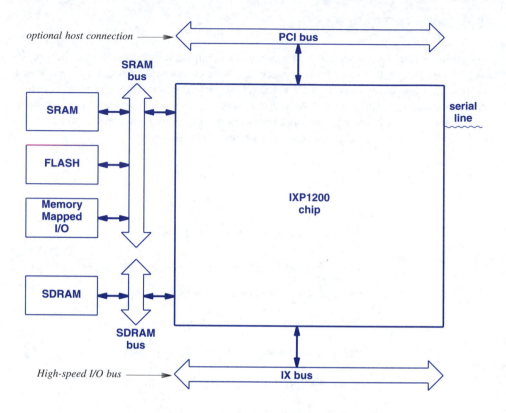

Figure 18.3 Illustration of the external connections for an Intel IXP1200 network processor.

As the figure shows, the IXP1200 has three types of external connections: a serial line interface, two interfaces for external I/O buses, and two interfaces for external memory buses. Figure 18.4 lists the speed of each connection.

Type	Bus Width	Clock Rate	Data Rate
Serial line	(NA)	(NA)	38.4 Kbps
PCI bus	32 bits	33-66 MHz	2.2 Gbps
IX bus	64 bits	66-104 MHz	4.4 Gbps
SDRAM bus	64 bits	≤ 232 MHz	928.0 MBps†
SRAM bus	16 or 32 bits	≤ 232 MHz	464.0 MBps

Figure 18.4 The speed and data width of external I/O connections from Intel's IXP1200 network processor. Unlike I/O devices, memory rates are measured in megabytes per second.

†MBps abbreviates *Mega Bytes per second.*

18.6.1 Serial Line Interface

The IXP1200 contains *Universal Asynchronous Transmitter and Receiver* (*UART*) hardware that provides an interface to a conventional serial line. We will see that the serial line connects to the embedded RISC processor. Because it is intended for control and management functions, the serial line does not operate as fast as the other I/O interfaces. Thus, although a programmer can choose to send data across it, the serial interface is not suitable for use in the fast path.

18.6.2 PCI Bus

An IXP1200 has a PCI† bus that provides two main functions. First, it allows the IXP1200 to connect to I/O devices such as disks. Second, it enables a designer to use a conventional CPU as a general-purpose control processor. Because PCI technology is popular, a variety of I/O devices follow the standard. In addition, the popularity means that many support chips are available that provide the connection between a processor and a PCI bus.

18.6.3 IX Bus

Although PCI technology is popular, the overall throughput is limited to approximately 2.2 Gbps. Thus, to handle higher data rates, Intel invented a new bus technology known as an *Intel Exchange bus* (*IX bus*). The IX bus has two main purposes. First, the IX bus forms the fast data path over which data is transferred between the IXP1200 and high-speed network interfaces (e.g., Gigabit Ethernet interfaces). Second, the IX bus provides a communication mechanism to which multiple IXP1200s can connect. Thus, the IX bus makes it possible to build a network processor architecture in which multiple IXP1200 chips work together.

18.6.4 SDRAM Bus

The SDRAM bus is dedicated to a single task: it provides access to external SDRAM memory. In the IXP, SDRAM provides low cost, high bandwidth memory that is used as the primary storage for bulk data such as complete frames or packets. In addition to sixty-four data lines, the SDRAM bus has lines used to pass addresses, lines used to control fetch or store operations, and a line that passes the clock signal. The memory uses the clock signal to synchronize fetch and store operations with the IXP1200 clock.

---

†PCI stands for *Peripheral Component Interconnect*, a bus standard that is popular on PCs.

18.6.5 SRAM Bus

The interface used to access SRAM is completely separate from the interface used to access SDRAM. Although we use the term *SRAM bus* to describe the external mechanism, the term is somewhat misleading because the mechanism is more general than a typical memory bus. Unlike the SDRAM bus, for example, the SRAM bus is shared — the bus provides access to several external hardware units. In addition to high-speed Static RAM that is used during packet processing, the SRAM bus provides access to memory such as *ROM* or *FlashROM* that can be used during bootstrap. The SRAM bus also provides access to a memory-mapped device interface. We will see that the device interface on the SRAM bus is used for control rather than for data transfer.

18.7 Internal Components

The internal architecture of an IXP1200 is complex because the chip contains buses, memory, processors, interfaces, and other functional units. Figure 18.5 lists the primary functional units.

Quantity	Component	Purpose
1	Embedded RISC processor	Control, higher layer protocols, and exceptions
6	Packet processing engines	I/O and basic packet processing
1	SRAM access unit	Coordinate access to the external SRAM bus
1	SDRAM access unit	Coordinate access to the external SDRAM bus
1	IX bus access unit	Coordinate access to the external IX bus
1	PCI bus access unit	Coordinate access to the external PCI bus
several	Onboard buses	Internal control and data transfer

Figure 18.5 A list of the major internal components of Intel's IXP1200 network processor.

We begin by considering how the internal components connect to external buses; later sections consider each of the components in more detail. Figure 18.6 gives a high-level architectural view of the IXP1200 that shows the interconnections between internal and external units.

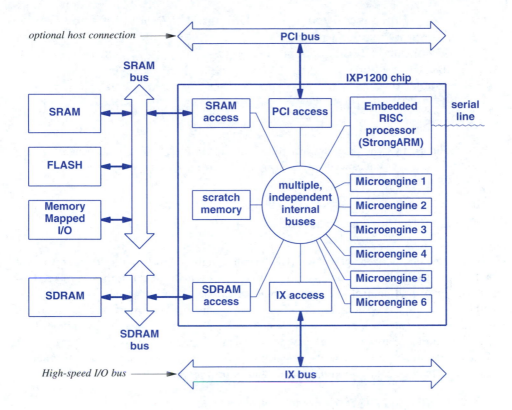

Figure 18.6 Conceptual organization of Intel's IXP1200 showing the logical connection between major components on the chip and external buses.

18.8 IXP1200 Processor Hierarchy

The IXP1200 uses a five-level processor hierarchy, with three levels of the hierarchy present on the chip and the other two levels provided by external hardware. Figure 18.7 lists the processor types and the properties of each.

Processor Type	Onboard?	Programmable?
General-Purpose Processor	no	yes
Embedded RISC Processor	yes	yes
I/O Processors	yes	yes
Coprocessors	yes	no
Physical Interfaces	no	no

Figure 18.7 The processor hierarchy used with an Intel IXP1200. Although onboard coprocessors are not programmable, they may be configurable.

18.8.1 General-Purpose Processor

The general-purpose processor (GPP) at the highest level of the hierarchy is not part of the IXP1200 chip. In many systems, an external general-purpose processor is needed for overall control and management functions; the GPP is not part of the fast path. For example, consider a system that employs one network processor per interface. In such cases, a network processor does not need to be involved in global routing decisions. Such decisions can be assigned to a general-purpose processor that interacts with all network processors. The general-purpose processor can gather routing information from all networks, choose optimal routes, and inform individual network processors.

18.8.2 Embedded RISC Processor (StrongARM)

Intel uses the term *core processor* to refer to the embedded RISC processor. The RISC processor on the IXP1200 is a *StrongARM*, a specific model of processor that uses the *ARM* architecture†. The StrongARM core, which runs a conventional operating system such as Linux, acts as a control point that manages the microengines and provides an interface through which the chip can be downloaded and configured. In addition, the StrongARM handles higher layers of the protocol stack as well as any packet that raises an exception. Thus, the embedded processor is not intended to handle regular fast path processing.

18.8.3 I/O Processors (Microengines)

Intel uses the term *microengine* for a packet processor; the IXP1200 contains six microengines. In contrast to the embedded RISC processor, a microengine is a low-level device that only offers a few basic instructions. Microengines, which form the basis of fast path processing, are intended to handle low-level transfer among I/O devices and memory as well as basic packet processing tasks such as frame demultiplexing. Unlike the embedded RISC processor, a microengine does not run an operating system.

---

†The ARM architecture takes its name from the company that designed it, ARM Limited, which was previously named *Advanced RISC Machines*.

18.8.4 Coprocessors And Other Functional Units

The IXP1200 contains several additional coprocessors and functional units, some of which form part of the fast path. For example, the chip contains a *hash unit* that can be used to compute a forty-eight bit or sixty-four bit adaptive polynomial hash function at high speed. The IXP1200 also contains four *timers* that work with a *real-time clock*, support for an external JTAG connection, and four General-Purpose I/O (*GPIO*) pins. A later section describes one of the most important functional units: the IX bus controller, which is part of the *FBI*† unit.

18.8.5 Physical Interface Processors

Physical interface hardware is not part of the IXP1200. Thus, additional chips are required to implement layer 1 and layer 2 processing. Intel offers interface chips that handle POS/PHY (Packet Over SONET PHYsical layer interface) as well as conventional Ethernet framing. High-speed physical interfaces use the IX bus to communicate with the IXP1200, which means that the network interface hardware must also be able to use the IX bus interface.

18.9 IXP1200 Memory Hierarchy

The IXP1200 memory hierarchy consists of multiple memories. Figure 18.8 lists items in the memory hierarchy along with the size and purpose of each.

Memory Type	Maximum Size	On Chip?	Typical Use
GP Registers	128 regs.	yes	Intermediate computation
Inst. Cache	16 Kbytes	yes	Recently used instructions
Data Cache	8 Kbytes	yes	Recently used data
Mini Cache	512 bytes	yes	Data that is reused once
Write buffer	unspecified	yes	Write operation buffer
Scratchpad	4 Kbytes	yes	IPC and synchronization
Inst. Store	64 Kbytes	yes	Microengine instructions
FlashROM	8 Mbytes	no	Bootstrap
SRAM	8 Mbytes	no	Tables or packet headers
SDRAM	256 Mbytes	no	Packet storage

Figure 18.8 Some of the elements in the memory hierarchy on Intel's IXP1200 available to the StrongARM processor. Larger memories are external to the chip.

†Intel reports that the exact origin of FBI is unknown; the acronym may have meant *FIFO Bus Interface*.

Programmers need to focus on some elements of the memory hierarchy, but can essentially ignore others. For example, although they provide performance improvements, most caches remain *transparent* to a programmer (i.e., the programmer does not need to allocate space in the cache). A programmer focuses on three primary memories: SRAM, SDRAM, and Scratch (also known as *Scratchpad*). The programmer must decide exactly how to use each. That is, the programmer chooses which of the three memories will be used to hold each data item.

Figure 18.8 gives one of the criteria used to choose a memory: the maximum size. In addition, each memory has other characteristics that Figure 18.9 lists.

Memory Type	Addressable Data Unit (bytes)	Relative Access Time	Special Features
Scratch	4	12-14	synchronization via test-and-set and other bit manipulation, atomic increment
SRAM	4	16-20	stack manipulation, bit manipulation, read/write locks
SDRAM	8	32-40	direct transfer path to I/O devices

Figure 18.9 Characteristics of the three primary memory types used with the Intel IXP1200. Relative access times are given in basic clock cycles.

As the figure shows, each type of memory has properties that make it appropriate for some tasks. Although it is small, Scratch memory offers the fastest access times and bit manipulation facilities such as *test-and-set*. Thus, Scratch memory works well for synchronization among parallel processors (e.g., among microengines). SRAM has longer access times than scratch memory, but is faster than SDRAM. In addition, SRAM has facilities that allow the manipulation of stacks. Thus, SRAM works well to hold packet headers or lists of packets. Finally, because it has a direct transfer path to I/O devices, is large, and has higher bandwidth, SDRAM works well to hold incoming or outgoing packets.

Programmers, who must decide which data items to store in each type of memory, are sometimes surprised to learn that memory access times are much larger than instruction execution times. For example, Figure 18.9 reports that an SDRAM access takes between thirty-two and forty clock cycles. One clock cycle is the time required to execute a microengine instruction, which means that a microengine can execute more than thirty instructions during the time it takes to fetch one value from SDRAM. Chapter 20 discusses the disparity between memory access and instruction execution times, and considers consequences for programmers.

18.10 Word And Longword Addressing

In addition to access times and special features that make each memory type suited to certain tasks, programmers must be aware of each memory's *addressable data unit*. Figure 18.9 reports the addressable data units for each of the three primary memory types. A two-byte unit (i.e., sixteen bits) is known as a *word*†, a four-byte unit (i.e., thirty-two bits) is known as a *longword*‡, and an eight-byte unit (i.e., sixty-four bits) is known as a *quadword*.

To understand the consequences of addressable data units that are larger than bytes, consider Scratch memory which is organized into longwords. The underlying mechanism does not provide access to individual bytes. Instead, every memory reference loads or stores four bytes. More important, addressing refers to longwords rather than individual bytes. Thus, address zero corresponds to the first word which is composed of bytes zero through three. Address one corresponds to the next word, which is composed of bytes four through seven. Address two corresponds to bytes eight through eleven, and so on.

The organization of memory into words or longwords means a programmer must plan data layouts carefully. For example, suppose a programmer defines a pair of items that each occupies sixteen bits, and places the items in adjacent memory locations. If they are allocated within a single word, both items can be retrieved with a single memory reference. If the items span a word boundary, however, two separate memory references will be required to retrieve them (i.e., it will take twice as long to access the two items). We can summarize:

> *Memory is organized into addressable data units of words or longwords. To achieve optimal performance, programmers must understand the memory organization and allocate items to minimize access times.*

18.11 An Example Of Underlying Complexity

The architecture diagram in Figure 18.6 (page 279) presents a high-level conceptual view that hides many details. In fact, each box in the figure corresponds to a complex set of subparts, and each interconnection corresponds to a complex set of paths. Although a full understanding of all the hardware details is beyond the level of the text, it is helpful to have an idea of the underlying complexity. As an example, consider the

---

†Chapter 19 discusses a variation of the terminology used with the embedded RISC processor.
‡The term longword is often abbreviated *long*.

units that provide access to an external bus. Although Figure 18.6 presents them as
fundamental components, each access unit contains multiple subparts and has many
connections to other hardware on the chip. Figure 18.10 shows some of the detail in
the *SRAM access* unit.

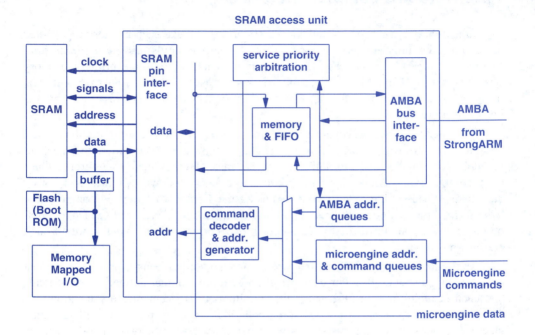

Figure 18.10 Some of the detail in the SRAM access unit found on Intel's
IXP1200 network processor.

As the figure indicates, the access unit contains separate physical paths for addresses, data, and control information. Thus, instead of a single connection between the
microengines and the SRAM access unit, there are two. Commands and addresses are
sent from the microengines to a subpiece that manages command queues. When a command is ready, the subpiece forwards the command and address information to a command decoder subpiece, which places an address on the SRAM pin interface hardware.
Meanwhile, data from the microengines is sent to the SRAM pin interface across a
separate bus.

Figure 18.10 also reveals that the chip contains several separate data paths that are
hidden in Figure 18.6. For example, when it communicates with the SRAM interface
unit, the StrongARM uses an internal bus that follows the *Advanced Microprocessor
Bus Architecture* (*AMBA*). Microengines do not use the AMBA bus. Instead, they have
a separate connection and a separate queue of requests. A priority mechanism arbitrates
between the two queues so that only one request passes to the SRAM pin interface at
any time.

Do architectural details like those in Figure 18.10 matter to a programmer? Unfortunately, some of them do. Although they do not need to know that separate wires carry addresses and data, programmers must understand contention, synchronization, and timing. Thus, programmers concentrate on understanding the interconnections of components, the resources that are shared, and the consequences of issuing instructions in a particular order.

18.12 Other Hardware Facilities

The IXP1200 contains many other facilities not covered in this overview. Later chapters consider facilities that are pertinent to programming, including the *READY bus*, *hardware contexts*, and *transfer registers (FIFOs)*.

18.13 Summary

This chapter begins a discussion of the Intel network processor, a commercially-available network processor that provides a concrete example of the concepts in previous chapters. Intel uses the term IXA to refer to the hardware and software architecture of their network processor, and the term IXP to refer to specific network processor chips. In particular, we examined the IXP1200.

The IXP1200 consists of a single chip that contains three members of the processor hierarchy (an embedded RISC processor, six microengines, and several coprocessors). In addition to instruction store and cache memories, the chip contains a small amount of Scratch memory. Finally, the chip contains interface hardware that supports several external interfaces, including a memory hierarchy and two I/O buses.

Our high-level overview of the hardware abstracts away many details; the chip is more complex. Each of the functional units on the chip has an intricate substructure that is not shown in the high-level architectural diagrams. As an example of the underlying complexity, an SRAM interface unit contains many subpieces interconnected by multiple physical paths.

FOR FURTHER STUDY

Further information on the hardware architecture can be found in the vendor's Hardware Reference Manual [Intel 2001c].

EXERCISES

18.1   Read Intel's documentation to learn more about the hardware organization of the IXP1200. Which functional units are grouped into the FBI?

18.2   Read Intel's documentation for the IXP1200, and compare the complexity of the SRAM interface described here to the complexity of the SDRAM interface. How do they differ?

18.3   What is the primary reason a network processor uses separate interfaces for SRAM and SDRAM?

18.4   Consult a computer architecture text to learn more about memory hardware. What is the advantage to a network processor of a memory in which the addressable unit consists of words instead of bytes?

18.5   Consider the IXP1200 architecture. Why is atomic increment a useful feature in an on-board memory?

Chapter Contents

19

Embedded RISC Processor
(StrongARM Core)

19.1 Introduction

The previous chapter provides an architectural overview of Intel's IXP1200 network processor. This chapter begins a discussion of individual components on the chip. The chapter covers the embedded RISC processor, which Intel refers to as the *StrongARM core†*. Instead of presenting all hardware details, the chapter focuses on understanding the role of the embedded processor and the facilities that software can use. Later chapters discuss other components of the IXP1200 chip, and illustrate how software uses the mechanisms.

19.2 Purpose Of An Embedded Processor

As the previous chapter indicates, Intel's IXP1200 contains a single embedded RISC processor. To understand the purpose of the embedded processor, we must consider how the IXP1200 chip fits into a network system. In a system with a few low-speed network interfaces, for example, a single IXP1200 can handle multiple interfaces; in a network system with higher-speed interfaces, an IXP1200 must be dedicated to each interface. The overall system architecture determines the role of the embedded processor because a system that contains multiple IXP1200s usually includes a general-purpose processor that performs active control and coordination among them. Figure 19.1 illustrates the two basic approaches.

---

†Engineers often use the term *core* to refer to a programmable processor that is part of a network processor.

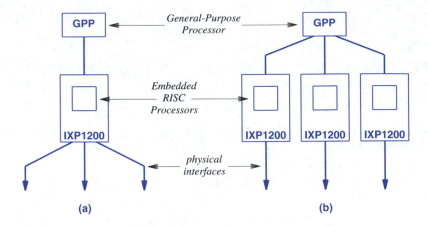

Figure 19.1 Illustration of two possible systems designs: (a) a single IXP1200 that handles multiple network interfaces, and (b) multiple IXP1200s each dedicated to a single network interface. The tasks assigned to the embedded RISC processor depend on the design.

In a design that uses a single IXP1200 chip to process packets from all physical interfaces, the onboard RISC processor handles administrative tasks for the entire system. In a system that includes a general-purpose processor, tasks related to the entire system are handled by the general-purpose processor; the embedded processor on a given chip only handles tasks related to the chip. Thus, the embedded RISC processor may be assigned some or all of the following tasks:

- Bootstrapping
- Exception handling
- Higher-layer protocol processing
- Interactive debugging
- Diagnostics and logging
- Memory allocation
- Application programs (if needed)
- User interface and/or interface to the GPP
- Control of packet processors
- Other administrative functions

Most of the tasks are self-explanatory. Administrative and control functions include: starting and stopping packet processing, creating or modifying the data structures used by the packet engines, and specifying configuration details such as the address of each network interface. Bootstrapping involves initialization of both memory and processors on the chip. At system startup, for example, the embedded RISC processor boots first. Once it is running, the processor loads code into the microengine instruction store and starts the microengines†.

If a system includes multiple IXP1200s, the general-purpose processor handles administrative tasks for the entire system. To do so, the general-purpose processor must communicate with the embedded RISC processor on each IXP1200. For example, in a multi-chip system, the general-purpose processor runs routing protocol software. Once it computes a global routing table, the general-purpose processor passes the information to the embedded processor on each IXP1200. Each embedded RISC processor accepts routing information from the GPP, and modifies the local forwarding table accordingly. Forwarding tables reside in memory that is shared between the embedded processor and the packet engines. The embedded processor maintains the table; the packet engines use the table to look up the next hop for each packet.

Although it is not intended to be used in the fast data path, the embedded RISC processor does handle some data packets. First, it handles *exceptions* such as packets that do not match any classification rule or packets that generate an error (e.g., an IP datagram for which the destination is unreachable). Thus, the embedded RISC processor is usually assigned the task of generating ICMP error messages. Second, the embedded RISC processor can handle packets destined for the local system. In a small system, for example, the embedded processor implements higher-layer protocols such as TCP; in a larger system, the embedded processor forwards TCP packets to the general-purpose processor.

19.3 StrongARM Architecture

The embedded RISC processor on the IXP1200 consists of a *StrongARM* processor; the name arises because a StrongARM implements a variation of the *ARM V4* architecture. The main characteristics of the StrongARM include:

- Reduced Instruction Set Computer (RISC)
- Thirty-two bit arithmetic with configurable endianness
- Vector floating point provided via a coprocessor
- Byte addressable memory
- Virtual memory support
- Built-in serial port
- Facilities for a kernelized operating system

19.4 RISC Instruction Set And Registers

Following the RISC paradigm, the StrongARM instruction set contains a relatively small set of instructions. Furthermore, to ensure that the processor can complete one in-

---

†Chapter 21 discusses a testbed, and describes the boot process in more detail.

struction on each clock cycle, the instructions are designed to execute quickly. Thus, the StrongARM does not offer instructions in which execution time depends on the size of the operands. In particular, there are no instructions such as string copy or string compare that operate on a block of memory.

Like most RISC processors, the StrongARM depends on registers to achieve high speed. To execute an instruction rapidly, operands must be present in registers before the execution begins. That is, in a typical instruction, the processor extracts operands from two registers, performs an operation, and leaves the result in a third register. If operands are available, the processor is designed to complete one instruction on each clock cycle.

19.5 StrongARM Memory Architecture

The StrongARM is classified as a thirty-two bit processor because registers store thirty-two bit values and operations such as *add* or *shift* produce thirty-two bit quantities. Moreover, the processor contains *load* or *store* operations that transfer thirty-two bit values from or to memory†.

The ARM architecture takes an interesting approach to the question of whether arithmetic is big or little endian: the choice is not predetermined. Instead, the mode can be configured when the processor boots. The bootstrap code that Intel supplies with the IXP1200 configures the StrongARM to be big-endian. That is, the most significant byte of an integer is stored in a memory location that has the lowest address. The next-most significant byte of the integer is stored in the second byte, and so on.

The StrongARM presents a running program with a *byte-addressable* view of memory. That is, a program can define individual data items that occupy adjacent byte locations in memory, and can fetch or store each byte of a structure. As with many computers, however, an integer transfer requires the item to be *aligned*. Thus programmers and compilers align integer data values on boundaries that are exact multiples of thirty-two bits.

Recall from Chapter 18 that the IXP1200 provides facilities for both SRAM and SDRAM memory. Further recall that the minimum addressable units used with SRAM and SDRAM differ (four or eight bytes). How can the StrongARM provide byte-addressability if the underlying memory systems use longword or quadword addressability? The answer lies in interface hardware: separate *instruction* and *data caches* that fit between the processor and memory. When it fetches or stores values, a cache uses addressing appropriate to the underlying memory. When it communicates with the processor, the cache uses byte addressing. Thus, if a program on the StrongARM loads a single byte from SDRAM, the data cache must fetch eight bytes (the minimum addressable unit of SDRAM). The cache then extracts the referenced byte, and passes it to the processor. Similarly, when a program stores a single byte into SDRAM, the data cache must fetch the appropriate eight-byte unit, modify the byte that has been stored, and then write the entire eight-byte unit back into SDRAM.

---

†The ARM Reference Manual and some of the Intel literature use the term *word* to refer to a thirty-two bit value. Unfortunately, the terminology conflicts with other parts of the Intel literature, which define a *word* to be a sixteen-bit value.

19.6 StrongARM Memory Map

Like most systems, the StrongARM defines a linear *address space* into which all external memories are mapped. The address space, which contains 2^{32} bytes, includes: SRAM, SDRAM, Scratchpad memory, the PCI bus, special registers used to transfer data to or from microengines, and other memory-mapped I/O devices. Figure 19.2 shows how external memories and hardware devices are mapped into the address space.

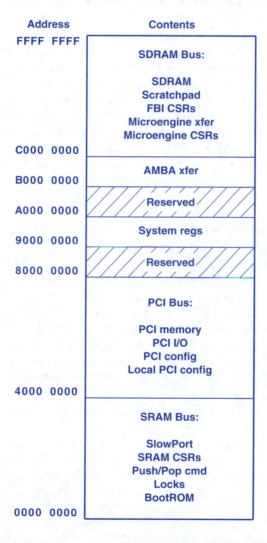

Figure 19.2 Illustration of the thirty-two bit (i.e., 2^{32} byte) physical address space used with the StrongARM processor. The address space includes memory-mapped I/O devices as well as memories such as SRAM and SDRAM.

As the figure shows, one quarter of the address space starting at location zero maps to the SRAM bus. Similarly, the highest quarter of the address space maps to the SDRAM bus. The choice of mapping is especially important for bootstrap because it allows the bootstrap ROM code to occupy low memory addresses, which are used during startup.

19.7 Virtual Address Space And Memory Management

The StrongARM hardware includes a memory management unit used to provide *virtual memory*. The memory management unit allows a program to a run in a *virtual address space*; the hardware maps parts of the virtual space onto physical addresses. That is, the system can be configured so a running program can access part or all of the physical address space. Furthermore, the memory mangement unit makes it possible to use *demand paging*, a facility in which the size of the virtual space exceeds the physical memory and pages of memory are stored on external secondary storage when not needed. Although demand paging is too slow for fast-path processing, it can be useful for debugging or diagnostics. Chapter 23 describes how StrongARM software uses virtual memory.

19.8 Shared Memory And Address Translation

In later chapters, we will see that the StrongARM and packet processors are closely integrated and that they each perform some aspects of packet processing. Shared memory forms one of the most important mechanisms that the processors use to make interchange efficient. To see how shared memory can be used, consider a network management function that requires a system to generate a formatted summary of packet arrival statistics. The StrongARM is the most appropriate processor on which to run formatting and external interface software, and packet processors are most appropriate to gather statistics. A shared memory allows packet processors to increment counters as packets arrive or depart, and allows the StrongARM to extract and format the values at any time. Similarly, the StrongARM can use shared memory to create and maintain the tables that packet processors consult when forwarding packets.

Unfortunately, as the next chapter shows, packet processors do not follow the same memory architecture as the StrongARM. First, the StrongARM uses byte addressability; packet processors do not. Second, although the StrongARM maps all memory into a single, large address space, packet processors do not. That is, addresses used by the packet processors differ from those used by the StrongARM. The consequence is:

> *Because the StrongARM and packet processors do not use the same memory architecture, linked lists and other data structures that contain pointers do not make sense in both address spaces.*

Whenever a pointer is passed between the StrongARM and a packet processor, the pointer must be translated from one address space to another. As a general rule, the StrongARM handles all address translation. Thus, when it creates a forwarding table, the StrongARM translates all pointers into addresses that a packet processor can understand. Similarly, when it receives a pointer from a microengine, the StrongARM translates from the microengine's native addressing into an equivalent value in the StrongARM address space.

19.9 Internal Peripheral Units

The IXP1200 contains four mechanisms that can only be accessed by the StrongARM processor (i.e., they cannot be accessed by microengines):

- One UART
- Four 24-bit countdown timers
- Four General-Purpose I/O (GPIO) pins
- One Real-Time Clock (RTC)

The mechanisms are classified as *internal peripheral devices* because they are internal to the IXP1200, but appear to the StrongARM as peripheral devices.

19.9.1 Serial Connection Through UART Hardware

The IXP1200 includes *Universal Asynchronous Receiver and Transmitter* (*UART*) hardware that provides a *serial line* according to EIA standard RS-232C. Only the StrongARM can access the serial line, which serves as a *console device*. More important, the UART hardware can be configured to generate an interrupt for the StrongARM when either the transmit side is ready for a new character or the receive side has received a character. Thus, the StrongARM does not need to poll the device.

19.9.2 Countdown Timers

The IXP1200 contains four *countdown timers* that can be configured to interrupt the StrongARM when they reach zero. The countdown rate is also configurable: a timer can run at the StrongARM clock rate, the StrongARM clock rate divided by sixteen, or the StrongARM clock rate divided by two hundred fifty-six. Only the StrongARM can use the timers, which means that the StrongARM must handle all protocol processing tasks that involve timeout.

19.9.3 General-Purpose I/O Pins

The StrongARM has access to four *General-Purpose I/O* (*GPIO*) pins through the
FBI interface. The four pins provide an external connection that can be connected to
additional hardware or can be used for debugging. The GPIO pins can be configured in
one of several possible modes. In one configuration, the StrongARM has complete control of all four pins (i.e., the pins can operate external hardware under direct control of
the StrongARM). In other configurations, some or all of the pins are given special
meaning by the FBI unit (i.e., the pins implement a standard hardware signaling protocol).

19.9.4 Real-Time Clock

The IXP1200 includes a *Real-Time Clock* (*RTC*) that counts up with a granularity
of one tick per second. The StrongARM can use the RTC for long-term timing (e.g.,
aging a route or running an application every thirty seconds). The RTC can also be
used as an alarm — the mechanism can be configured to interrupt the StrongARM
when the count reaches a predetermined number. Thus, the RTC handles large-
granularity timing, and the four countdown timers handle small-granularity timing.

19.10 Other I/O

As Figure 19.2 shows, other I/O devices appear in the StrongARM's physical address space. Thus, device driver software running on the StrongARM can access
memory mapped devices on external buses. In particular, both the SRAM bus and PCI
bus appear in the address space. Thus, the StrongARM can use either the PCI bus or
SRAM bus to access device *Control and Status Registers* (*CSRs*) and the data transfer
facilities.

19.11 User And Kernel Mode Operation

Like many processors, the StrongARM provides multiple modes of operation that
offer levels of protection. In particular, the processor provides hardware support for a
kernelized operating system. The operating system kernel runs at highest privilege, has
access to the entire address space, and can control all I/O.

Application programs running under the operating system each execute as a *user-
level process*. Applications do not have privilege, cannot directly control I/O devices,
and cannot access the entire address space. Instead, the application runs in a protected
virtual address space that cannot be accessed by other applications. The kernel supplies
all services. When it needs to perform I/O, for example, an application program must
request the kernel to perform the operation and return the result.

19.12 Coprocessor 15

The Intel chip contains a coprocessor facility that allows the StrongARM to configure and control several hardware facilities on the IXP1200. Known as *coprocessor 15*,
the mechanism is *local* to the StrongARM, which means that the coprocessor cannot be
accessed from the microengines. The StrongARM invokes coprocessor 15 to configure
the MMU†, the read and write buffers, clocking functions, and the cache. In addition,
coprocessor 15 can be used to set *breakpoints* in the code for testing.

19.13 Summary

The IXP1200 contains a single embedded processor, a StrongARM core. In a
small network system that contains a single IXP1200, the StrongARM handles all exceptions and administrative details. In a large network system that includes multiple
IXP1200s, a general-purpose processor (GPP) handles system control and administra-
tion; the StrongARM on each IXP1200 receives commands from the GPP and applies
them locally.

The physical address space on the StrongARM encompasses the SDRAM bus,
SRAM bus, PCI bus, and various other I/O devices. A memory management unit on
the StrongARM can provide a protected virtual address space for each application program.

The StrongARM has exclusive access to internal peripheral devices such as a serial
line, countdown timers, GPIO pins, and a real-time clock. Because timer access is restricted to the StrongARM, the StrongARM must participate in all protocol processing
tasks that involve use of the timers.

The StrongARM provides hardware support for protection modes that allow it to
run a kernelized operating system. The operating system kernel, which executes with
privilege, can access I/O devices and the complete physical address space. An application program running under the operating system requests the operating system to perform I/O on its behalf.

FOR FURTHER STUDY

Seal [2000] describes the ARM architecture in general, including the instruction
set, interrupts and exceptions, and condition codes. Intel [2001c] provides details about
the StrongARM implementation used on the IXP1200 and the internal peripherals to
which it attaches.

---

†The Memory Management Unit (MMU) handles the mapping between virtual and physical address
spaces.

EXERCISES

19.1   Read about instruction timing. Which set of ARM instructions incurs the most clock cycles?

19.2   At what point in the bootstrap sequence does the StrongARM access the bootstrap ROM?

19.3   What is the largest virtual address space that the StrongARM's memory management unit can provide? How does it compare with the size of the physical address space?

19.4   What are the exception types used in the StrongARM?

19.5   The ARM instruction set dedicates several bits of each instruction to condition codes. Why are condition code bits present, and how are they used?

19.6   What types of hardware or software interrupts are available on the StrongARM? What are their priorities?

19.7   How does a fast interrupt request differ from an ordinary interrupt request?

19.8   What is the Real-Time Clock divisor, and why is it used?

19.9   Read about the SRAM bus address space. How are bit test and clear operations useful? Why are read and write locks included?

19.10 Read about SDRAM prefetch and non-prefetch memory. When is each used?

Chapter Contents

20

Packet Processor Hardware (Microengines And FBI)

20.1 Introduction

Previous chapters provide an overview of the Intel IXP1200 network processor and the StrongARM embedded processor. This chapter considers the programmable packet processors on the IXP1200 that Intel refers to as *microengines*. In addition to discussing hardware, the chapter reviews the concept of instruction stalls. Later chapters discuss the programming model, the interaction between software running on a microengine and software running on the StrongARM, and program optimizations that avoid stalls.

20.2 The Purpose Of Microengines

In terms of the processor hierarchy on the IXP1200, microengines comprise the lowest level of the hierarchy that is programmable. As a consequence, using microengines to handle protocol processing results in higher throughput than using higher levels of the processor hierarchy to handle the same tasks. In particular, microengines are intended for processing on the *fast data path*.

As a further optimization to increase fast path processing, the IXP1200 contains six microengines that operate in parallel. Although parallelism can allow microengines to achieve substantially higher aggregate throughput than is possible using the StrongARM processor, high speed can be difficult to achieve in practice because microengines must be allocated to specific tasks.

Microengines are intended to handle both ingress and egress protocol processing tasks. Typically, microengines are responsible for:

- Packet ingress from physical layer hardware
- Checksum verification
- Header processing and classification
- Packet buffering in memory
- Table lookup and forwarding
- Header modification
- Checksum computation
- Packet egress to physical layer hardware

As we will see in the next sections, however, microengines do not perform operations directly; they rely on a variety of auxiliary functional units.

20.3 Microengine Architecture

A microengine has the following general characteristics:

- Programmable microcontroller
- RISC design
- One hundred twenty-eight general-purpose registers
- One hundred twenty-eight transfer registers
- Hardware support for four threads and context switching
- Five-stage execution pipeline
- Control of an Arithmetic Logic Unit (ALU)
- Direct access to various functional units

20.4 The Concept Of Microsequencing

As the above list of characteristics indicates, a microengine is not a conventional CPU. Instead, a microengine is a low-level device that functions as a *microsequencer*. That is, the microengine does not contain native instructions for each possible operation — most of the instructions merely invoke other functional units on the chip.

Two examples will clarify the concept. First, consider arithmetic operations such as addition or subtraction. On a conventional CPU, each arithmetic operation is given a unique *opcode*; a program specifies the opcode for the desired instruction. For example, a program on a conventional CPU might contain an instruction *Add R2, R3* that specifies the integer value in register three should be added to the value in register two.

On a microengine, however, arithmetic operations are combined into a single op-code that references the microengine's *Arithmetic Logic Unit* (*ALU*). To add two integer values, for example, a program running on a microengine invokes the *alu* operation and specifies *add* as one of the operands.

In fact, the microengine contains only three instructions related to arithmetic computation, bit rotation, and bit shifting. The *ALU* instruction invokes the ALU. The *ALU_SHF* instruction invokes the ALU, which performs the specified arithmetic operation and then applies bit shifting to the result. Finally, the *DBL_SHIFT* instruction concatenates two longwords, applies bit shifting to the value, and saves the result in a longword.

As a second example of microengine instructions, consider memory references. On a conventional CPU, the hardware associates an *addressing mode* with each operand. The addressing mode specifies whether the operand is a constant (known as an *immediate* value) or a reference to a value in memory. Thus, a program might contain an instruction *Load R3, X* to copy the current value of an integer in memory location *X* into register three.

In contrast to a conventional CPU such as the StrongARM, a microengine does not provide any addressing modes that refer to memory, nor does the microengine have a native *load* instruction. Instead, a programmer must issue an instruction that specifies: a memory interface, an address in memory, and an operation (i.e., fetch or store). For a fetch operation, the microengine must wait for the memory interface hardware to finish the operation before the value can be moved into a register for use by the program. The point is:

> *Because it functions as a microsequencer, a microengine does not provide native hardware instructions for arithmetic operations, nor does it provide addressing modes for direct memory access. Instead, a program running on a microengine controls and uses functional units on the chip to access memory and perform operations.*

20.5 Microengine Instruction Set

The entire microengine instruction set consists of thirty-two basic opcodes. Figure 20.1 summarizes the instruction set and states the purpose of each instruction.

Instruction	Description
Arithmetic, Rotate, And Shift Instructions	
ALU	Perform an arithmetic operation
ALU_SHF	Perform an arithmetic operation and shift
DBL_SHIFT	Concatenate and shift two longwords
Branch and Jump Instructions	
BR, BR=0, BR!=0, BR>0, BR>=0, BR<0, BR<=0, BR=count, BR!=count	Branch or branch conditional
BR_BSET, BR_BCLR	Branch if bit set or clear
BR=BYTE, BR!=BYTE	Branch if byte equal or not equal
BR=CTX, BR!=CTX	Branch on current context
BR_INP_STATE	Branch on event state
BR_!SIGNAL	Branch if signal deasserted
JUMP	Jump to label
RTN	Return from branch or jump
Reference Instructions	
CSR	CSR reference
FAST_WR	Write immediate data to thd_done CSRs
LOCAL_CSR_RD, LOCAL_CSR_WR	Read and write CSRs
R_FIFO_RD	Read the receive FIFO
PCI_DMA	Issue a request on the PCI bus
SCRATCH	Scratchpad memory request
SDRAM	SDRAM reference
SRAM	SRAM reference
T_FIFO_WR	Write to transmit FIFO
Local Register Instructions	
FIND_BST, FIND_BSET_WITH_MASK	Find first 1 bit in a value
IMMED	Load immediate value and sign extend
IMMED_B0, IMMED_B1, IMMED_B2, IMMED_B3	Load immediate byte to a field
IMMED_W0, IMMED_W1	Load immediate word to a field
LD_FIELD, LD_FIELD_W_CLR	Load byte(s) into specified field(s)
LOAD_ADDR	Load instruction address
LOAD_BSET_RESULT1, LOAD_BSET_RESULT2	Load the result of find_bset
Miscellaneous Instructions	
CTX_ARB	Perform context swap and wake on event
NOP	Skip to next instruction
HASH1_48, HASH2_48, HASH3_48	Perform 48-bit hash function 1, 2, or 3
HASH1_64, HASH2_64, HASH3_64	Perform 64-bit hash function 1, 2, or 3

Figure 20.1 The instruction set of a microengine on the Intel IXP1200.

20.6 Separate Memory Address Spaces

The microengine architecture differs from the StrongARM in another way: microengine hardware does not map memory or I/O devices into a linear address space. Thus, unlike the StrongARM, a microengine does not view memory as a seamless, uniform repository. Instead, a program running on a microengine must specify the exact memory for which a transfer is required.

Figure 20.1 illustrates how the concept of separate address spaces affects the architecture: the instruction set must include a separate instruction for each type of memory and each type of I/O device. For example, the *SDRAM* instruction can access a location in SDRAM, but not in SRAM. Similarly, the *SCRATCH* instruction can access the Scratchpad memory, but not SRAM or SDRAM.

The separation has a significant consequence for programmers: it requires early binding of data items to specific memories. That is, when writing a program, the programmer must choose the memory into which each data item will be placed. We can summarize:

> *Because the microengine architecture uses a separate address space for each type of memory, a programmer must use an early binding scheme in which each data item is permanently allocated to a specific type of memory.*

20.7 Execution Pipeline

We said that both the StrongARM and microengines use a RISC architecture, and that a RISC processor is designed to execute one instruction on each clock cycle. In fact, the hardware cannot perform an entire instruction in one cycle. Instead, the hardware uses a form of parallelism to achieve high speed: the processor divides the execution of an instruction into *stages*, and overlaps the execution of multiple instructions by executing multiple stages from several instructions at the same time. Architects use the term *execution pipeline* to refer to hardware that overlaps execution of stages†. Most RISC processors use a pipeline to achieve high speed.

To understand how pipelining speeds processing, imagine an idealized processor. Each time it handles one instruction, our idealized processor performs two actions. First, it *fetches* the next instruction from memory, and then it *executes* the instruction. For purposes of our discussion, assume that the idealized processor take one clock cycle for each action. It should be clear that the processor takes two clock cycles for each instruction.

Now consider adding pipeline execution. That is, suppose we extend the idealized processor by giving it two parallel hardware units: one that can *fetch* an instruction and one that can *execute* an instruction. If the two hardware units are arranged correctly, the idealized processor will be able to fetch the next instruction while it executes the

---

†The reader should not confuse the pipeline used inside a processor (which handles instructions) with the pipeline architecture used by a network processor (which handles packets).

current instruction. As a result, as soon as it finishes executing instruction *N*, the execution unit can begin executing instruction *N+1*. Thus, the processor will be able to execute one instruction on each clock cycle, effectively doubling the speed.

In practice, execution is much more complex than our idealized example. For example, each microengine on the IXP1200 uses a five-stage execution pipeline that allows the microengine hardware to work on five separate instructions simultaneously. While it executes stage *k* of an instruction, the hardware executes stage *k-1* of the next instruction. Figure 20.2 illustrates sequential instructions executing on a microengine.

	clock	stage 1	stage 2	stage 3	stage 4	stage 5
	1	inst. 1	-	-	-	-
Time	2	inst. 2	inst. 1	-	-	-
	3	inst. 3	inst. 2	inst. 1	-	-
	4	inst. 4	inst. 3	inst. 2	inst. 1	-
	5	inst. 5	inst. 4	inst. 3	inst. 2	inst. 1
	6	inst. 6	inst. 5	inst. 4	inst. 3	inst. 2
	7	inst. 7	inst. 6	inst. 5	inst. 4	inst. 3
	8	inst. 8	inst. 7	inst. 6	inst. 5	inst. 4

Figure 20.2 Illustration of a five-stage execution pipeline used by a microengine on the IXP1200. Once the pipeline is full, the microengine completes one instruction on each clock cycle.

As the figure illustrates, no results are produced during the first four clock cycles after the microengine starts because the first instruction has not been through the last stage. Once the first instruction completes stage five, however, the pipeline is full, and an instruction can complete on each successive clock cycle.

How does the microengine hardware divide instruction execution into five stages? Figure 20.3 lists the stages, and describes the task performed during each.

Stage	Description
1	**Fetch the next instruction**
2	**Decode the instruction and get register address(es)**
3	**Extract the operands from registers**
4	**Perform ALU, shift, or compare operations and set the condition codes**
5	**Write the results to the destination register**

Figure 20.3 The five execution stages uses in a microengine on the IXP1200.

20.8 The Concept Of Instruction Stalls

The continuous flow of instructions through a pipeline is a crucial part of high-speed execution — an instruction can complete on each clock cycle only if the pipeline remains full. Unfortunately, the ideal pattern illustrated in Figure 20.2 does not always occur in practice. Consider, for example, the sequence of two instructions shown below when executed on a processor that uses an execution pipeline.

K: ALU operation to add the contents of R1 to R2
K+1:   ALU operation to add the contents of R2 to R3

The sequence causes a problem because both instructions reference register R2. In terms of the pipeline operations listed in Figure 20.3, instruction K will not write a value into register R2 until stage five. However, instruction $K+1$ needs to extract operands from registers in stage three. How can stage three of the pipeline extract a value for use with the second instruction before the value has been assigned by the first instruction? It cannot. Instead, the processor hardware *stalls*. That is, processing for instruction $K+1$ waits until the needed value is in place. Figure 20.4 illustrates how the stall affects pipeline execution.

	clock	stage 1	stage 2	stage 3	stage 4	stage 5
Time	1	inst. K	inst. K-1	inst. K-2	inst. K-3	inst. K-4
	2	inst. K+1	inst. K	inst. K-1	inst. K-2	inst. K-3
	3	inst. K+2	inst. K+1	inst. K	inst. K-1	inst. K-2
	4	inst. K+3	inst. K+2	inst. K+1	inst. K	inst. K-1
	5	inst. K+3	inst. K+2	inst. K+1	-	inst. K
	6	inst. K+3	inst. K+2	inst. K+1	-	-
	7	inst. K+4	inst. K+3	inst. K+2	inst. K+1	-
	8	inst. K+5	inst. K+4	inst. K+3	inst. K+2	inst. K+1

Figure 20.4 An example pipeline in which instruction K+1 stalls at stage three to await the result from instruction K.

In the figure, instructions K and $K+1$ use the same register. During the fourth clock cycle, instruction $K+1$ reaches stage three of the pipeline — the stage at which operands are extracted from the register. However, instruction K will not place a value in the register until stage five (time 5). Thus, instruction $K+1$ stalls at stage three to await the value. Once the value is available, at time 6 in the figure, pipeline processing continues.

The figure shows that execution does not appear to stop when a stage stalls. Instead, output of the pipeline continues, and the delay does not become apparent for several clock cycles. In the figure, for example, the stall first occurs at time 4 (when instruction $K+1$ reaches stage 3). However, execution continues until time 6, when the stall prevents an instruction from reaching stage 5. We say that a *bubble* passes along the pipeline and eventually reaches the last stage.

The concept of instruction stall is especially important for low-level processors such as microengines that handle the fast data path. The code must be optimized to achieve maximum throughput. The point is:

> *Understanding the execution pipeline is important for programmers because dependencies among instructions can cause the processor to stall, which lowers performance.*

20.9 Conditional Branching And Pipeline Abort

A program seldom executes long sequences of straight-line code. Instead, the program contains *conditional flow* in which the computation performed depends on the data. For example, microengine code might use a checksum value to determine whether to accept or reject a packet. In terms of machine instructions, a test is encoded using a *conditional branch* instruction.

A conditional branch can also cause a stall in the execution pipeline because the hardware, which is prefetching values, cannot follow both possible paths. In the usual case, microengine hardware proceeds to feed successive instructions into the pipeline as if no branch will occur. If a branch does occurs, the hardware must *abort* early stages of the pipeline and begin processing at the branch location.

Microengines include many hardware details that can help optimize branches. For example, if a programmer expects the branch to be taken frequently, the programmer can specify that the microengine pipeline should prefetch from the "branch taken" location rather than from the "branch not taken" path. Because the option is specified by a token named *guess_branch*, the technique is referred to as the *guess branch* technique.

20.10 Memory Access Delay

Although a bubble in a processor's execution pipeline can delay processing, the delay is small (i.e., a few cycles). Other delays, however, can be substantial. In particular, because a microengine operates much faster than external memory, a single memory access delays execution for many cycles. Programmers who are accustomed to working on a conventional system are often surprised to learn about the disparity between processor and memory speeds. Figure 20.5 summarizes the approximate number of microengine cycles required to access each of the principle memory types that an IXP1200 uses.

Type Of Memory	Approximate Access Time (in clock cycles)
Scratchpad	12 - 14
SRAM	16 - 20
SDRAM	32 - 40

Figure 20.5 The delay that occurs when a microengine accesses memory. Delay is measured in clock cycles, which is equivalent to the number of instructions that can be executed.

As the figure shows, delays range up to forty cycles. When running at full speed, a microengine can complete one instruction per cycle, which means that a single memory access can require as much time as executing forty instructions.

Even if a cache is used, memory access is significantly slower than computation; a microengine can execute between twelve and forty instructions in the same time it takes to perform one memory access.

20.11 Hardware Threads And Context Switching

How can we overcome the delay caused by memory access? The microengine hardware offers a mechanism to improve performance: hardware support for multiple *threads of execution* or *contexts*. Each of the six microengines has four threads. More important, because the hardware maintains separate state information for each thread (e.g., a program counter and a set of signal events), the hardware can switch rapidly between threads without requiring software support. Hence, unlike a conventional CPU, a microengine context switch requires zero or one extra cycle.

The hardware on each microengine supports four threads, and can switch from one thread to another in at most one cycle†.

Conceptually, microengine threads operate like threads in a conventional operating system — multiple threads remain ready to execute so that a new thread can run as soon as the current thread blocks or voluntarily gives up the processor. In particular, each memory access causes a thread to block; while one thread waits for the access to complete, the microengine executes another thread. Figure 20.6 illustrates the concept by showing an example.

---

†Although the Intel literature uses the terms *zero-overhead context switch* and *low-overhead context switch* to refer to context switches that require zero or one extra cycle, a microengine context switch can require up to three cycles to flush and reload the pipeline.

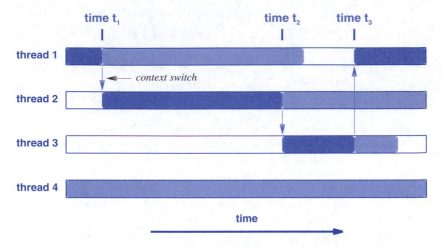

Figure 20.6 An illustration of thread execution among four threads. A white area indicates a thread that is currently idle but ready to run, a dark blue area indicates a thread being executed by a microengine, and a light blue area indicates a thread that is blocked (e.g., waiting for a memory access or I/O).

The figure shows the state of four separate threads over the same period of time. The diagram begins on the left, with the microengine executing thread 1 and thread 4 blocked (e.g., waiting for I/O). At time t_1, the microengine encounters an operation that causes thread 1 to block (e.g., a request to read a value from SDRAM). A *context switch* occurs in which the processor moves from the blocked thread to a thread that is currently ready. In the example, the processor moves from thread 1 to thread 2.

Thread 2 executes until time t_2, when the processor encounters an operation that blocks thread 2. A second context switch occurs. At time t_2, only thread 3 remains ready to execute (threads 1 and 4 remain blocked waiting for memory access and I/O to complete). The processor switches to thread 3, which executes until it blocks at time t_3. Because thread 1 is ready (i.e., its blocking operation is complete), the microengine can switch back to thread 1.

The advantage of threads should be clear: instead of stalling to wait for memory accesses or I/O, a microengine can continue to perform useful work. In terms of packet processing, for example, each hardware thread can be assigned to handle a packet. When the thread handling packet 1 blocks to read from memory (e.g., to extract a field from the packet header), the thread handling packet 2 can proceed to execute. Thus, although it only has a single CPU, a microengine can process four packets concurrently without long idle times — when progress on one packet is temporarily blocked, the hardware switches to another. The point is:

> *Hardware threads increase overall throughput by allowing a microengine to handle up to four packets concurrently; with threads, computation can proceed without waiting for memory access.*

What happens if all four threads associated with a microengine block? For example, suppose that four threads are each handing a packet, and that the next instruction to be executed in each requires a memory access (e.g., each thread is about to access or modify a field in a packet). The microengine will switch among the four threads in rapid succession, and each thread will block. The entire sequence will take less time than one memory access. After the fourth thread blocks, the microengine cannot execute a thread because no thread will be ready. In such cases, the microengine hardware pauses and waits until a thread becomes ready again (i.e., the blocking operation finishes).

20.12 Microengine Instruction Store

We use the term *instructions* to refer to the object code that has been compiled for a specific processor, and *instruction store* to refer to the memory in which the code resides during execution. Which memory should be used as an instruction store for microengine programs? We have already seen that SRAM and SDRAM cannot serve as an instruction store because they operate too slowly. To reduce memory contention and improve performance, the IXP1200, like most network processors, provides a separate memory system dedicated to the task of holding microengine instructions.

An instruction store can be organized in one of two ways: a single instruction store can be shared by all packet engines, or each packet engine can have a private instruction store. The chief advantage of using a single instruction store lies in the ability to share: one copy of the code can be placed in the memory, and all packet engines can use the copy. The chief disadvantage of a single, shared instruction store arises from a high rate of contention — because all packet engines need to access the share instruction store, they must contend for use.

Giving each packet engine a private instruction store avoids contention and increases performance. However, replicating the instruction store requires more space on a chip. As a result, vendors often choose a compromise — separate instruction stores are used to provide high speed, but the size of each instruction store is kept small to save space on the chip.

Intel's IXP1200 provides an example of the compromise. On one hand, each microengine has a private instruction store. Thus, the microengines run at rated speed because they do not contend with one another. On the other hand, each instruction store is limited to two thousand forty-eight instructions†.

---

†Before it starts a microengine running, the StrongARM must ensure that the instruction store has been loaded with the code the microengine will execute.

20.13 Microengine Hardware Registers

To function as a microcontroller, a microengine must interact with many hardware devices. Much of the interaction occurs through a set of *hardware registers*. Some of the hardware registers function like the registers found on a conventional processor — the register serves a high-speed storage area that can be used to hold intermediate results during a computation. Other hardware registers are dedicated to special purposes, and do not store values at all. Instead, accessing one of the special-purpose registers causes the underlying hardware to perform an operation.

20.14 General-Purpose Registers

Each microengine has a total of one hundred twenty-eight *general-purpose registers* (*GPRs*) that each hold a thirty-two bit value. Like GPRs on a conventional CPU, GPRs on a microengine are used for arithmetic computation.

20.14.1 Context-Relative Vs. Absolute Registers

General-purpose registers can be used in two ways. The entire set of registers can be shared among all four contexts, or the registers can be divided among the four contexts. In the former case, the programmer must handle mutual exclusion — if two contexts both attempt to use the same register for two distinct purposes, the results are unpredictable. In the latter case, the hardware guarantees that each of the four contexts has control over thirty-two of the GPRs; no mutual exclusion is needed because a given context cannot change the values in registers owned by another context.

To accommodate the two styles of using GPRs, microengine hardware includes two forms of register addressing. An *absolute register address* consists of an integer that uniquely specifies one of the registers. A *relative register address* consists of a small integer that specifies one of the registers devoted to the current hardware thread (i.e., current *context*). Thus, an absolute register address always refers to the same register; the register denoted by a relative register address depends on the hardware thread that is executing when the address is encountered.

20.14.2 Register Banks

It may seem that absolute addressing should merely number registers from zero through one hundred twenty-seven, and that relative register addressing should use values from zero through thirty-one. In practice, however, microengine hardware, like most RISC processors, follows the practice of partitioning GPRs into separate *register banks*. Thus, both absolute and relative register addresses must specify a bank as well as a register within the bank. The division into banks is important because it allows the hardware to be optimized: parallel data paths leading to the banks allow the hardware to access one register in each bank simultaneously.

A microengine divides general-purpose registers into two banks, which Intel calls the *A bank* and the *B bank*. To optimize performance, data values must be arranged in the banks carefully — maximum speed is obtained when each instruction can reference one register from the A bank and one register from the B bank. To aid in optimization, the relative addressing mode partitions registers so that each hardware thread has an equal number of registers from the A and B banks. Figure 20.7 illustrates how the microengine hardware numbers the registers in absolute and relative addressing modes†.

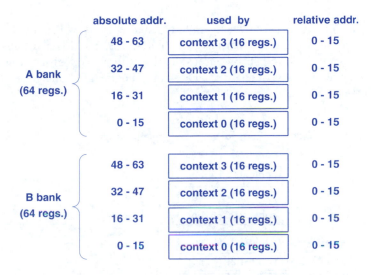

Figure 20.7 Absolute and relative addresses used for the general-purpose registers on an Intel microengine. In relative addressing mode, half of the registers assigned to a context are taken from each bank.

The notions of register addressing and register banks are each important to programmers. A programmer can choose to use absolute addressing, relative addressing, or a combination of the two. We can summarize:

The general-purpose registers available on a microengine can be addressed using absolute or relative addressing; the registers are divided into banks to permit simultaneous access.

---

†In practice, the microengine assembler uses a *register coloring* algorithm to assign data to register banks automatically.

20.15 Transfer Registers

Because it operates much faster than memory and other external devices, a microengine includes interface hardware that buffers external data transfers. The interface consists of *transfer registers* through which all access occurs. For example, to read a value from memory and place it in a general-purpose register, a program first specifies that the value be copied from an address in memory into one of the transfer registers. The program then specifies that the value be moved from the transfer register into a general-purpose register. Similarly, to write a value into memory, the value must first be placed in one of the transfer registers; the value can then be moved from the transfer register into memory.

Each microengine has one hundred twenty-eight transfer registers, which are divided into four types according to the external bus (i.e., SDRAM or SRAM) and transfer direction (i.e., read or write). Like general-purpose registers, transfer registers can be addressed using absolute or context relative addressing. Figure 20.8 illustrates the transfer register types and addresses.

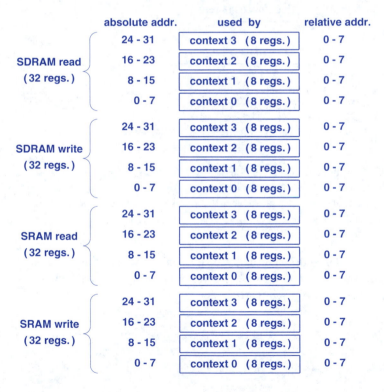

Figure 20.8 Absolute and relative addresses used for the transfer registers on an Intel microengine. All external data transfers go through the transfer registers.

Although they appear to be associated with external memory, transfer registers handle all external transfers. Thus, the labels *SRAM* and *SDRAM* refer to external buses. In particular, the SRAM bus provides an interface to memory mapped I/O and Flash memory†.

20.16 Local Control And Status Registers (CSRs)

Recall from the previous chapter that device *Control and Status Registers* (*CSRs*) are mapped into the address space on the StrongARM. A subset of the CSRs are *local* — instead of corresponding to an external device, the local CSRs are used to control the IXP1200. The StrongARM uses local CSRs to load and control microengines; each microengine can access its own local CSRs, but cannot access the CSRs of other microengines. Figure 20.9 lists local CSRs and their meaning.

Local CSR	Purpose
USTORE_ADDRESS	Load the microengine control store
USTORE_DATA	Load a value into the control store
ALU_OUTPUT	Debugging: allows StrongARM to read GPRs and transfer registers
ACTIVE_CTX_STS	Determine context status
ENABLE_SRAM_JOURNALING	Debugging: place journal in SRAM
CTX_ARB_CTL	Context arbiter control
CTX_ENABLE	Debugging: enable a context
CC_ENABLE	Enable condition codes
CTX_*n*_STS	Determine context status‡
CTX_*n*_SIG_EVENTS	Determine signal status
CTX_*n*_WAKEUP_EVENTS	Determine which wakeup events are currently enabled

Figure 20.9 Local CSRs used on the Intel IXP1200 and their purpose. The StrongARM uses the first two local CSRs when it loads code into a microengine control store.

20.17 Inter-Processor Communication

Although local CSRs provide a way for the StrongARM to control the microengines, it is also necessary for code running on a microengine to interact with the StrongARM. For example, a microengine may need to inform the StrongARM that a packet needs processing. The hardware provides several possibilities for communication:

---

†For more information on external connections, refer to Figure 18.3 on page 276.

‡The notation in the figure is an abbreviation; the hardware contains a separate CSR for each of the four contexts.

- Thread-to-StrongARM communication.
- Thread-to-thread communication within one IXP1200.
- Thread-to-thread communication across multiple IXP1200s.

Thread-to-StrongARM communication can be accomplished through two mechanisms: *interrupts* or *shared memory*. A microengine can raise an interrupt on the StrongARM, or shared memory can be used with polling. Two threads within a single IXP1200 can communicate through a *signal event* mechanism that uses an internal bus known as the *command bus*. Finally, in a system that contains multiple IXP1200s, a thread running on one IXP1200 uses the *Ready bus* to communicate with a thread running on another IXP1200.

20.18 FBI Unit

The *FBI unit* forms an integral part of the interface between the programmable processors and high-speed I/O or other functional units. The StrongARM and microengines can both access the FBI. From a processor's point of view, the FBI has complete control of:

- Scratchpad memory
- Hash unit
- FBI Control and Status Registers
- Control and operation of the Ready bus
- Control and operation of the IX bus
- Data buffers that hold data arriving from the IX bus
- Data buffers that hold data sent to the IX bus

More important, the FBI unit operates like a DMA controller for the FIFOs — a microengine requests a transfer by issuing a command to the FBI unit. The FBI unit handles commands independently, and informs the microengine when a command completes. Because the microengine does not actively participate in a transfer, the microengine can proceed with other computations (e.g., can switch to another hardware context).

The *Ready bus* is an eight-bit bus used to control a network interface device (which is sometimes called a MAC device). A microengine can use the Ready bus to poll the status of an interface (e.g., to determine whether a packet has arrived on the interface) or to assert flow control. In addition, the Ready bus can be used as a communication channel that connects to another IXP1200.

The IX bus is the primary bus used for high-speed I/O, including packet transmission and reception. The FBI unit is used to interrogate status of the IX bus or to control operations such as packet transmission and reception.

20.19 Transmit And Receive FIFOs

All I/O across the IX bus uses a set of hardware buffers known as *FIFOs*. The IXP1200 partitions FIFOs into two sets, with one set used for each direction of transfer. The set of *Receive FIFOs* (*RFIFOs*) handles incoming data (usually packets), and the set of *Transmit FIFOs* (*TFIFOs*) handles outgoing data.

The FIFOs form the only path between an external device and a microengine. To receive a packet, for example, a microengine must instruct the physical interface to move the packet into one of the Receive FIFOs. Once the packet has been placed in a Receive FIFO, the microengine instructs the FBI to move the packet from the Receive FIFO into memory. Similarly, to transmit a packet, a microengine instructs the FBI to move the packet from memory to a Transmit FIFO, and then instructs the physical interface to extract the packet from the Transmit FIFO and send it†.

The term *FIFO* is somewhat misleading because the RFIFO units function as randomly-accessed storage rather than as a strict queue. Each FIFO contains sixteen slots, each of which consists of ten quadwords, which means a slot contains eighty bytes. A microengine can select any slot or slots for a transfer; they do not need to be accessed in order. A small packet (e.g., an ATM cell or a minimum-size Ethernet frame) fits in a single slot. Larger packets must be divided into pieces, with each piece no larger than a single slot. The MAC hardware divides each incoming packet into pieces of no more than sixty-four bytes; software running on the microengines must divide each outgoing packet into pieces.

20.20 FBI Architecture And Push/Pull Engines

To understand how programs use the FBI, it is important to realize that the FBI contains active components that handle data transfers. Intel uses the terms *Push Engine* and *Pull Engine* for the two active components, which operate independently and in parallel. The Push Engine moves data into one of the processors (e.g., from a Receive FIFO to a microengine transfer register), and the Pull Engine moves data away from a processor (e.g., from a microengine transfer register to a Transmit FIFO).

The Push Engine and the Pull Engine in the FBI do not function like coprocessors. Instead, each engine accepts a series of commands that arrive over the microengine *command bus*. The engine stores each incoming command in a *command queue* for later execution. There are three separate queues: a *pull queue* for commands that move data from microengine transfer registers, a *push queue* for commands that move data to microengine transfer registers, and a queue for commands that invoke the hash unit. When an engine becomes idle, an arbiter chooses a queue, extracts the next command, and sends the command to the engine. Figure 20.10 illustrates the conceptual architecture.

---

†It is also possible for a microengine to transfer data to or from the FIFOs without going to memory.

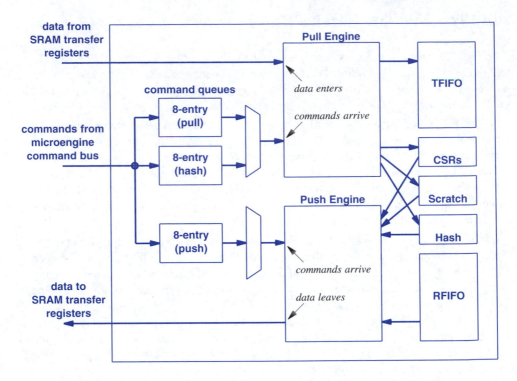

Figure 20.10 A simplified illustration of the FBI architecture on Intel's
IXP1200. The Push Engine and Pull Engine operate in paral-
lel.

The figure omits many details. For example, in addition to the external connections shown, the FBI unit has inputs for commands that arrive over an *AMBA* bus from
the StrongARM. The FBI also includes a *fast path* that is not shown. The fast path by-
passes the engines to allow a command to access CSRs without waiting for the command to be enqueued or for the Pull or Push Engine to act on the command.

20.21 Scratchpad Memory

The FBI unit controls access to the onboard *Scratchpad memory*, which contains
four Kbytes of memory organized into 1K words of four bytes each. In addition to
serving as a local data store, Scratchpad memory offers two operations that microengine
threads can use to coordinate. First, Scratchpad memory includes an atomic bit manipulation mechanism for mutual exclusion that is known as *test-and-set*. Second,
Scratchpad memory includes an autoincrement facility.

Test and set allows multiple processors to attempt to set a bit in memory. The hardware guarantees that only one microengine will succeed in setting the bit; others receive notification that the bit was already set. Autoincrement allows a microengine to increment a value in memory without moving the value across the normal data path into a general-purpose register. Because the normal data path between the Scratchpad memory and general-purpose registers requires going through the SRAM transfer registers, using autoincrement reduces latency considerably.

20.22 Hash Unit

The ALU in a microengine does not include instructions for multiplication or division. However, multiplication and division are used in protocol processing. In particular, high-speed table lookup often involves *hashing*, a technique that uses both multiplication and division. To enable microengine programs to perform lookup and other tasks that require multiplication or division, the IXP1200 includes a configurable coprocessor known as the *hash unit*. To use the hash unit, a microengine specifies the operation, and then requests a hash to be performed. All access is handled by the FBI.

Unlike a conventional coprocessor, the hash unit does not operate synchronously. Instead, the hash unit has two input buffers, and a microengine can issue from one to three hash requests with a single instruction. The FBI passes the requests to the hash unit sequentially.

To initiate a hash operation, a microengine first places one to three data values in a contiguous set of SRAM transfer registers (two contiguous SRAM transfer registers are used for each data value). The microengine then uses the FBI to invoke the hash unit.

The hash function can be summarized as computing a quotient, $Q(x)$, and a remainder $R(x)$:

$$A(x) * M(x) / G(x) \rightarrow Q(x) + R(x)$$

$A(x)$ denotes the input value, $M(x)$ denotes the hash multiplier (which is stored in the CSRs of the FBI unit), and $G(x)$ is one of two built-in values that depends only on the length of the hash being computed. The multiplier, $M(x)$ is the only configurable item — a program must choose a multiplier when using the hash unit.

Mathematically, we think of the hash computation as a fixed polynomial algorithm. Given a binary input value, we view the bits as coefficients of a polynomial. For example, the value:

$$20401_{16}$$

can be represented as a polynomial over the field [0,1]†:

$$x^{17} + x^{10} + 1$$

---

†Multiplication corresponds to a *logical and* operation, and addition or subtraction corresponds to an *exclusive or* operation.

Two values of G are available; one value is used when computing a forty-eight bit hash (i.e., to hash an Ethernet address), and the other is used for a sixty-four bit hash. The hexadecimal value:

$$G(x) \;=\; 1001002000401_{16}$$

is used to compute a forty-eight bit hash. It is equivalent to the polynomial:

$$G(x) \;=\; x^{48} + x^{36} + x^{25} + x^{10} + 1 \qquad \text{(48 bit)}$$

The value

$$10040000800020001_{16}$$

(used to compute a sixty-four bit hash) is equivalent to the polynomial:

$$G(x) = x^{64} + x^{54} + x^{35} + x^{17} + 1 \qquad \text{(64 bit)}$$

An example may help clarify the mathematics. Consider a forty-eight bit hash using the following values:

$$A = 800000000001_{16} \qquad (\text{represented as } x^{47} + 1)$$
$$G = 1001002000401_{16} \qquad (\text{represented as } x^{48} + x^{36} + x^{25} + x^{10} + 1)$$
$$M = 20D_{16} \qquad (\text{represented as } x^{9} + x^{3} + x^{2} + 1)$$

The hash unit computes R, the remainder of A times M divided by G†:

$$H(A) \;=\; R \;=\; A * M \;\%\; G$$

We see that

$$A(x) * M(x) \;=\; x^{56} + x^{50} + x^{49} + x^{47} + x^{9} + x^{3} + x^{2} + 1$$

Furthermore,

$$A * M \;=\; Q * G + R$$

where:

$$Q(x) \;=\; x^{8} + x^{2} + x^{1}$$

(i.e., Q is 106_{16}), and R is:

$$R(x) \;=\; x^{47} + x^{44} + x^{38} + x^{37} + x^{33} + x^{27} + x^{26} + x^{18} + x^{12} + x^{11} + x^{9} + x^{8} + x^{3} + x^{1} + 1$$

Thus, H(A) = R, so

$$H(A) \;=\; 90620C041B0B_{16}$$

---

†We use the % operator from the C programming language to denote a remainder.

20.23 Configuration, Control, and Status Registers

As we have seen, the FBI unit contains many functional units (e.g., FIFOs and the hash unit), and connects to many buses, including the microengine command bus, the Ready bus, and the IX bus. Each functional unit is controlled through a set of registers. For example, the IX bus provides registers that can be used to configure and control operation of both the bus itself (e.g., whether the bus operates in 64-bit mode or 32-bit mode) as well the devices attached to the bus (e.g., whether a MAC device or the IXP handles control signals). In addition, control and status registers are available that can be used to find such details as the status of threads running on the microengines. The list of registers is extensive. The point is:

> *In addition to basic functional units, the IXP contains hundreds of registers that allow software to configure, control, or interrogate the status of functional units, buses, and attached devices.*

20.24 Summary

Each Intel IXP1200 contains six programmable packet processors known as microengines that are intended to handle low-level tasks such as: packet ingress, header processing, table lookup and forwarding, and packet egress. Like most RISC architectures, a microengine has transfer registers, general-purpose registers, and uses an execution pipeline. External access causes the pipeline to stall. Each microengine supports four hardware threads, and the microengine switches context when a thread blocks.

The IXP1200 contains an FBI unit that both the microengines and the StrongARM processor can access. The FBI manages a hash unit, Scratchpad memory, and the IX bus. The FBI, which contains two active engines that can move data, operates independently and in parallel with the microengines.

FOR FURTHER STUDY

Chapter 4 of the Intel Hardware Reference Manual (Intel [2001a]) provides further details about microengine hardware, the FBI, the hash unit, and the registers used to control various buses.

EXERCISES

20.1   Choose a microengine program, and identify instruction stalls.

20.2   Extend the illustration of the FBI architecture to include the AMBA connection with the StrongARM.

20.3   How does a microengine know when all Pull command slots in the FBI are full?

20.4   How many minimum-size Ethernet packets can be present in the Transmit FIFO at one time?

20.5   How many maximum-size Ethernet packets can be present in the Transmit FIFO at one time?

20.6   Does the FBI give priority to the StrongARM or to the microengines? Why?

Chapter Contents

21

Reference System And Software Development Kit (Bridal Veil, SDK)

21.1 Introduction

Previous chapters describe the architecture and hardware available on Intel's IXP1200 network processor. This chapter describes a commercially available testbed system for the IXP1200 and the associated development software that programmers use to create and download code. Later chapters discuss the programming model, and describe the construction of software that can be downloaded.

21.2 Reference Systems

Before they adopt a specific network processor for use in a network system, engineers need a way to evaluate the network processors available from specific companies. Evaluation means that an engineer must be able to create and run software on each vendor's network processor. To aid in the evaluation process, most network processor vendors offer a *reference system*, which is also called a *reference platform* or an *evaluation testbed*. A reference system typically includes five basic items:

- A hardware testbed
- Development software
- Simulator or emulator
- Download and bootstrap software
- Reference implementations

A hardware testbed usually provides a small, but realistic system that includes a network processor, memory, and I/O facilities. Development software includes compilers, assemblers, and libraries that programmers use to create software for the network processor. A simulator or emulator allows a programmer to test and debug software before downloading it onto a testbed. Downloading and bootstrapping facilities handle the task of copying software onto the hardware testbed and starting the network processor. Finally, reference implementations consist of software that the vendor provides to demonstrate their network processor's capability and to serve as an example. Typical reference implementations include functionality such as a layer 2 bridge or code to perform IP forwarding. Because it allows customers to modify and enhance existing code rather than start from scratch, reference code speeds the development cycle.

21.3 The Intel Reference System

Like other vendors, Intel Corporation provides a reference system for their network processors. The Intel system is divided into two major pieces: a hardware testbed and a *Software Development Kit*.

21.3.1 Intel's Hardware Testbed

Interestingly, Intel's hardware testbed is not manufactured as a stand-alone system. Instead, the testbed consists of a board that plugs into the PCI bus on a standard PC. The PC, which runs a conventional operating system, provides a development environment on which a programmer can work to write and test code for the network processor. The programmer uses conventional tools (e.g., editors and compilers) to prepare software. Once the code has been compiled, the programmer invokes tools that copy the compiled code over the PCI bus to the testbed and start the network processor.

The testbed board, which is sometimes referred to by Intel's internal code name *Bridal Veil*, contains sufficient facilities to allow a programmer to test all aspects of a system†. That is, the board combines a network processor, memory, and I/O interfaces into a working system. Figure 21.1 lists the major features of the Bridal Veil board.

Ethernet connections on the board allow a programmer to separate test traffic from production traffic. To test network processor software, the programmer can connect the four Ethernet ports to various sources of traffic while the PC remains connected to a production network. Thus, the board can be tested under extreme load or with illegal packets without affecting the PC.

---

†The Bridal Veil board is manufactured by Radisys Corporation.

Quantity or Size	Item
1	IXP1200 network processor (232MHz)
8	Mbytes of SRAM memory
256	Mbytes of SDRAM memory
8	Mbytes of Flash ROM memory
4	10/100 Ethernet ports
1	Serial interface (console)
1	PCI bus interface
1	PMC expansion site

Figure 21.1 Hardware facilities on Intel's testbed system. The board is designed to allow engineers to evaluate a network processor.

21.3.2 Intel's Software Development Kit

Intel uses the name *Software Development Kit* (*SDK*) to refer to all support software for their reference platform. Much of the SDK consists of cross-development tools that run on a conventional PC to allow a programmer to prepare, download, and test software for the network processor. Figure 21.2 lists the software components included in Intel's SDK.

Software	Purpose
C compiler	Compile C programs for the StrongARM
NCL compiler	Compile NCL programs for the StrongARM
MicroC compiler	Compile C programs for the microengines
Assembler	Assemble programs for the microengines
Simulator	Simulate an IXP1200 to debug code
Downloader	Load software into the network processor
Monitor	Communicate with the network processor and interact with running software
Bootstrap	Start the network processor running
Reference Code	Example programs for the IXP1200 that show how to implement basic functions

Figure 21.2 Major items included in Intel's Software Development Kit. The software allows programmers to use a conventional PC to build and download programs.

As the figure shows, Intel's SDK includes both compilers and assemblers that programmers use to create code for the IXP1200. A conventional C or C++ compiler or an assembler allows programmers to create software that runs on the StrongARM. An

NCL compiler is available that produces code for the StrongARM. Either a MicroC compiler or an assembler can produce code that runs on the microengines. The assembler is an essential tool because performance is maximized when microengine code is highly optimized. Assembly language allows a programmer to specify all details of a program, including the exact instruction ordering. Thus, to avoid stalls, programmers often write assembly code.

21.4 Host Operating System Choices

We said that the cross-development tools from the SDK run on a PC that has a conventional operating system. In fact, two host operating systems may be needed because some software for the StrongARM must be compiled under *Linux* and code for the microengines must be assembled under *Windows NT*.

Does a programmer need two separate PCs? Although the use of two PCs is possible, most programmers prefer to use a single operating system. Consequently, it is possible to choose a primary operating system and rely on emulation or remote access to invoke the other system when needed. In the lab at Purdue University, for example, Linux is the primary operating system. Consequently, each PC in the lab runs Linux, with a Windows emulator, named *Wine*, used to run the microengine assembler†. Wine runs as a user process under Linux, and provides facilities that run WindowsNT binaries. Wine provides the same *Application Program Interface (API)* as WindowsNT. Thus, although it is designed to run under Windows, the microengine assembler can run under Linux without needing a separate PC or a copy of Windows NT.

As an alternative, it is possible to choose the opposite approach in which *WindowsNT* is the primary system. In such cases, a Linux emulator must be used to run the compiler that produces StrongARM code. Emulators, such as *Cygwin*, are available to fill the role.

21.5 Operating System Used On The StrongARM

The StrongARM processor on the IXP1200 is powerful enough to run a conventional operating system. An operating system makes programming easier by providing support for basic functions such as memory management, concurrent processes, and I/O. An operating system also helps provide isolation among application programs because each program can run in an isolated address space.

Intel's SDK allows a programmer to choose between two operating systems for the StrongARM: *Embedded Linux* or *VxWorks*. The choice must be made when compiling code to be loaded into the IXP1200. The operating system is loaded, along with other code, during system bootstrap.

Both operating systems provide services such as memory management, processes, and context switching that are needed for concurrent execution of application programs.

---

†Another approach uses *VMware* to allow multiple systems to co-exist on the same physical computer.

Furthermore, both operating systems are designed to be used with an embedded processor. Because Embedded Linux offers the same general API as other versions of Linux, programmers can port applications to it easily. VxWorks† requires fewer system resources (i.e., less memory and lower overhead) and provides real-time operation, but it does not offer a widely-known API.

21.6 External File Access And Storage

How can the StrongARM run an operating system such as Linux that relies on secondary storage when neither the IXP1200 nor the Bridal Veil board includes a disk? The answer lies in a combination of two well-known techniques:

> RAM disk   A simulated disk stored in memory
>
> Remote Files   Files stored on a remote file server

RAM disks were invented to optimize file system performance on a conventional computer. In essence, a RAM disk reserves an area of memory, which is then used to emulate a disk device. Like a real disk, a RAM disk requires a device driver. The driver presents a conventional API to the operating system that allows the system to fetch or store blocks. Unlike a conventional driver, however, the RAM disk driver merely performs a memory copy between the reserved area and the operating system buffer. Thus, when the driver fetches a block from the RAM disk, software converts the block number into an address in the reserved region, and copies the block as requested. Additional optimization is possible: a RAM disk driver can use pointers or address translation hardware to avoid copying altogether.

Because RAM is volatile, a RAM disk is not permanent — the RAM disk is created each time the system boots; files stored in a RAM disk do not persist. Thus, conventional computers use RAM disks for temporary files (e.g., intermediate files during a compilation), but not for permanent storage. The StrongARM operating system uses a RAM disk.

> *Embedded Linux creates a RAM disk for the root file system when the StrongARM boots. Because the RAM disk is volatile, however, files stored on the RAM disk do not survive a reboot.*

To provide access to permanent files, Embedded Linux uses the *Network File System* (*NFS*) to mount a file system from a remote server. Thus, from the viewpoint of applications running on the StrongARM, the testbed system has access to external files. More important, mounting is performed early in the bootstrap process, which means that software to be loaded into the network processor can be obtained from files on the remote server.

---

†VxWorks is derived from the Xinu operating system, which was created by the author.

In the lab at Purdue, where network processors are shared among many students, we have extended the NFS facility to mount two remote file systems instead of one. One file system, which contains system images and software to be downloaded, is mounted with *read-only* access permission. A second file system that provides external storage while the network processor runs is mounted with *read-write* access permission. Furthermore, the read-write file system can be cleared whenever one student finishes work and another begins. The separation of file systems ensures that no one will accidentally erase or overwrite system files that are needed for downloading.

21.7 PCI Ethernet Emulation

How does the testbed system communicate with the host computer? Physically, the testbed board plugs into the host's PCI bus, and communication occurs across the bus. Logically, however, the communication uses *Ethernet emulation*. That is, the host runs a device driver, D, that transfers Ethernet frames across the PCI bus. When an application sends information to the testbed, the application opens a socket as if the intended recipient is located across an Ethernet. Code in the host operating system passes each outgoing frame to driver D, which forwards the frame over the PCI bus to the testbed. Similarly, driver D accepts frames that arrive from the testbed over the PCI bus, and passes them through the socket to the application. The use of Ethernet frames is a historical artifact — an earlier version of the testbed hardware used a dedicated Ethernet connection instead of a PCI connection.

21.8 Bootstrapping The Reference Hardware

To use the testbed, a programmer must first boot the hardware, and can then download and run programs. The hardware bootstrap process involves five steps as Figure 21.3 illustrates.

1. Power on the host, which causes the network processor board to power on and run a boot monitor from Flash memory.

2. A device driver on the host communicates across the PCI bus with the boot monitor to load an operating system (e.g., Embedded Linux) and an initial RAM disk configuration into the network processor's memory.

3. The host signals the boot monitor to start the StrongARM.

4. When it finishes booting, the operating system runs a login process on the serial line and starts a telnet server.

5. Both the host operating system and the operating system on the StrongARM configure the PCI bus to act as an Ethernet emulator; the StrongARM uses NFS to mount two file systems, R and W, from a server running on the host.

Figure 21.3 The five steps required to boot the Intel network processor testbed. A loadable device driver on the host allows the PCI bus to emulate an Ethernet.

21.9 Running Software

After the five steps in Figure 21.3 have been followed, the StrongARM is running and ready to control the remaining facilities on the IXP1200. To run software, a user follows the six steps that Figure 21.4 lists.

1. Compile code for the StrongARM and microengines, and place the resulting files in a directory, D†. The Intel SDK uses the terms *ACE files* and *microblock group files* (.uof files) for the compiled code.

2. Create a system configuration file named *ixsys.config* and place in directory D.

3. Copy the entire contents of directory D to the read-write public download directory, W, that has been mounted by the testbed. (This step is not necessary if only one programmer has access to the testbed.)

4. Run a telnet client program on the host that forms a connection to the testbed system, and log onto the StrongARM.

5. On the StrongARM, change to NSF-mounted directory R, and run shell script *ixstart* with file *ixsys.config* as an argument.

6. To stop the IXP1200, run the *ixstop* script.

Figure 21.4 The six steps required to load and run software on the testbed after the StrongARM has been booted.

---

†Note: in practice, it is usually preferable to generate the code before booting the testbed.

21.10 System Reboot

Because the testbed board is designed to allow programmers to create, modify, and test code, programming errors are expected. In some cases, a program can leave the underlying hardware in an ambiguous or undesirable state. To prevent such conditions from affecting subsequent use of the testbed, it must be completely rebooted.

The version of Linux that comes with the SDK includes a *reboot* command that a user can issue while logged in (e.g., over the telnet connection). Once the user reboots the hardware, the IXP1200 reinitializes itself; the hardware is left in the same state as if the board had just received power. Consequently, the user must follow the steps in Figure 21.3 to reload the StrongARM†.

21.11 Alternative Cross-Development Software

In addition to the Intel SDK, several groups have developed various pieces of software for the Bridal Veil testbed. Researchers at Princeton University created a variant known as *Vera*. Researchers at Columbia have created a more dynamic version of software known as *Netbind*. Commercial vendors such as *Teja* or *Consystant* offer programming environments that claim to speed the software development process.

Under the SDK, most microengine code is written in assembly language. As section 21.3.2 points out, Intel offers a MicroC compiler that accepts a subset of C and produces code for the microengines.

21.12 Summary

Most network processor vendors offer customers a reference system that allows customers to experiment with the vendor's network processor. Intel's reference system consists of two pieces: a single-board testbed and a Software Development Kit. The board, which plugs into a PCI bus, contains a network processor, memory, and I/O interfaces; the Software Development Kit contains facilities used to download and boot the testbed, software used to prepare programs for the StrongARM and microengines, a simulator that can be used to test code, and example code for common functions.

The StrongARM component of the IXP1200 runs an operating system such as Embedded Linux. To permit file access, the operating system creates a RAM disk and uses NFS to provide external file access.

---

†At Purdue University, additional software has been created that automatically reloads the StrongARM when a user reboots the network processor.

FOR FURTHER STUDY

The SDK that is available from Intel includes a Reference Manual, Intel [2001a], and a Developer's Guide, Intel [2001b]. The manuals describe each of the cross-development tools and give further details about the downloading process. Information about the commercial testbed hardware can be found at:

http://www.radisys.com/oem_products/networkprocessors.cfm

Information on the Netbind software can be found at:

http://comet.ctr.columbia.edu/genesis/netbind/

The Vera software is documented in Karlin and Peterson [April 2002] and on the web site:

http://www.cs.princeton.edu/nsg/vera/

Information about the Teja programming environment can be found at:

http://www.teja.com/

Information about the Consystant development environment can be found at:

http://www.consystant.com/

EXERCISES

21.1   Most development environments contain example code. Compare and contrast the functionality, size, and modifiability of layer 3 forwarding code available for each of the following development environments: IXA SDK Microcode, MicroC, Netbind, Vera, Teja, and Consystant.

21.2   Install Intel's SDK, and configure the environment to create code for an IXP1200.

21.3   The Bridal Veil board contains a PMC expansion site. Find a network system that requires an expansion site (i.e., a system that is impossible to design and test without an expansion site).

21.4   In addition to storing the bootstrap code, how can Flash memory on the Bridal Veil board be used?

21.5   There is an apparent circularity in the use of NFS to store configuration information: the testbed board uses the network to access NFS files, but the NFS files contain configuration information for the network. How does the Intel SDk overcome the circularity?

Chapter Contents

22

Programming Model (ACE)

22.1 Introduction

Earlier chapters in this section focus on Intel's IXP1200 network processor, including the hardware architecture and constituent components. The previous chapter describes the hardware and software that comprise Intel's reference system. This chapter begins a discussion of programming. It covers basic program abstractions, explains how software is related to processors on the chip, and shows how multiple pieces of software interact. Later chapters continue the discussion by providing additional details and examples.

22.2 The ACE Abstraction

Intel uses the term *Active Computing Element* (*ACE*) to denote the basic programming abstraction used with the IXP1200†. An ACE can be characterized as follows:

- Fundamental software building block
- Used to construct packet processing systems
- Runs on StrongARM, microengine, or host
- Handles control plane and fast or slow data path processing
- Coordinates and synchronizes with other ACEs
- Can have multiple outputs
- Can serve as part of a pipeline

---

†Some Intel literature expands the acronym to *Action/Classification Engine*

22.3 ACE Definitions And Terminology

Intel defines terminology that helps describe and characterize ACEs. The following are three basic terms:

- *Library ACE.* An ACE that has been built by Intel and made available as part of the reference software in the Intel Software Development Kit. For example, the Intel reference software includes a Layer 2 bridge ACE.

- *Conventional ACE.* An ACE that is built by Intel customers. For example, an engineer who is using the Intel network processor in a product will build a Conventional ACE to perform the processing needed for the product. Conventional ACEs can incorporate items from *Action Service Libraries* that are supplied by Intel. The term *Standard ACE* is a synonym for *Conventional ACE.*

- *MicroACE.* An ACE that contains two components: a *core component* that runs on the StrongARM and a *microblock component* that runs on a microengine.

Intel further defines terms that characterize the overall role of a microblock with respect to the microengine on which it runs. A *source microblock* acts as the initial point by receiving packets that originate outside the microengine (i.e., packets that arrive from a MAC interface device). A *transform microblock* acts as an intermediate point in a pipeline by accepting and forwarding packets to other microblocks on the same microengine. Finally, a *sink microblock* acts as the last point in a microengine that sends packets to a destination outside the microengine (e.g., a MAC device). The terminology will become clear when we explain microblock groups.

22.4 Four Conceptual Parts Of An ACE

An ACE can contain four conceptual parts†. The four parts are associated with the following functionality:

- *Initialization.* The initialization code is invoked once, before any other code is executed to build data structures and initialize variables that the ACE uses.

- *Classification.* When a packet arrives, the ACE classifies the packet. The scheme includes a *default classification* that is selected if no other classification succeeds.

- *Actions.* An ACE contains one action for each possible classification, including the default classification. An action is invoked whenever a packet satisfies the corresponding classification.

- *Message and event management.* An ACE can generate or handle messages and asynchronous events that provide communication with another ACE or with the underlying hardware.

---

†This chapter presents a high-level view of ACEs; the next chapter provides more information on ACE implementation.

22.5 Output Targets And Late Binding

To keep ACEs flexible, the exact disposition of outgoing packets is not specified in the source code. Instead, indirection is used to allow the output of an ACE to be changed after the ACE has been compiled. A programmer creates a set of *target names*, and uses a name to specify each output. After an ACE has been combined with other ACEs to form a working system, target names can be bound to specific destinations. For example, the output of one ACE can be bound to the input of another.

Intel software does not actually bind target names until ACEs have been loaded into the network processor. In fact, bindings can be made or changed dynamically using functions *ix_res_bind* and *ix_res_unbind*. Furthermore, leaving a target unbound does not cause a problem; unbound targets implement a silent discard. That is, directing a packet to an unbound target merely causes the packet to be dropped. We can summarize:

> *Intel software uses a late-binding system in which ACE outputs are specified as named targets and bound at run-time. A target can be left unbound to implement packet discard.*

22.6 An Example Of ACE Interconnection

We think of an ACE as an asynchronous unit of computation. Thus, instead of building a single monolithic ACE, software can be divided into several smaller ACEs that operate asynchronously. A typical network system contains at least three ACEs connected in a pipeline: one devoted to input (i.e., move packets from an input port to a queue in memory), one devoted to packet processing, and one devoted to output. Figure 22.1 illustrates an example interconnection.

Figure 22.1 Conceptual interconnection of three ACEs in a pipeline with arrows showing the direction of packet flow. Connections between ACEs are formed at run time by binding the output target of one ACE to the input of another.

As the figure shows, the ingress ACE performs a source function by obtaining packets from the input ports and passing them to the processing ACE. The processing ACE performs a transform function by accepting packets from the ingress ACE and sending packets to the egress ACE. Finally, the egress ACE performs a sink function by sending packets to the output ports. Most systems include at least three ACEs.

22.7 Division Of An ACE Into Core And Microblock

Figure 22.1 hides many details. In particular, the figure does not specify whether code in the ACE runs on the StrongARM or on one of the microengines. In fact, most ACEs contain code for both — a core component of the ACE runs on the StrongARM, and a microblock runs on one of the microengines. The Intel software provides a mechanism that allows the two components of an ACE to pass packets in either direction between them.

As an example, consider a system that performs IP forwarding. In addition to transient traffic, some datagrams will be destined for the local system (i.e., the StrongARM). Thus, we can imagine four conceptual ACEs that perform the needed functionality: ingress, egress, IP forwarding, and an interface to the local IP protocol stack. Figure 22.2 illustrates how the ACEs might be partitioned into core and microblock components, and uses arrows to show the possible interactions among the components.

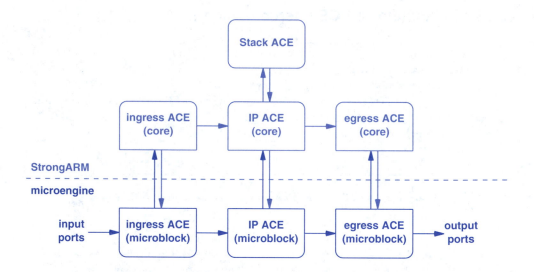

Figure 22.2 Illustration of a system in which three ACEs contain both a core component and a microblock component. The Stack ACE does not contain a microblock component.

The division of work between microengines and the StrongARM is crucial to attain high throughput. In general, microengines, which comprise the fast data path, only handle common cases; they rely on the StrongARM for all exceptions. Thus, when it encounters a packet that does not fit the expected conditions, a microblock does not attempt to handle the problem. Instead, the microengine passes the packet to the core component for processing. In the figure, for example, the ingress microblock examines the frame type and status reported by the MAC hardware (e.g., the CRC). If a frame contains IP and the hardware does not report an error, the ingress microblock forwards the frame to the IP microblock. Otherwise, the ingress microblock forwards the frame to its core component for processing†. Similarly, if the IP microblock finds a datagram destined for the local machine, the IP microblock forwards the packet to its core component, which further forwards the packet to the Stack ACE.

Although arrows in Figure 22.2 show several potential communication paths, packets do not follow all the paths. In particular, although core components of both the ingress and IP ACEs can communicate with their corresponding microblock, neither sends packets. The two paths are only used when the StrongARM needs to manage or control operations (e.g., to instruct the ingress microblock to stop accepting packets from a particular physical interface). If the StrongARM generates an outgoing packet, the packet passes down the stack, through the Stack ACE, through the core component of the IP ACE, and over to the core component of the egress ACE. The core component of the egress ACE forwards the packet to the egress microblock for transmission.

22.8 Microblock Groups

One of the challenges of using the ACE model arises from the parallelism in the underlying hardware. On one hand, a programmer uses ACEs to divide processing into logical units such that each unit solves one part of the problem. On the other hand, ACEs must be mapped to specific microengines. There are several possible approaches: a microengine can be dedicated to run the microblock of exactly one ACE, a microengine can run the microblocks of several ACEs in a pipeline, or multiple microengines can run copies of a pipeline. Each approach has advantages and disadvantages. Using a separate microengine for each microblock means the run-time structure matches the conceptual division of the problem and allows microengines to operate in a pipeline. However, passing a packet between two microengines incurs more overhead than passing a packet among microblocks on the same microengine because inter-engine communication requires the packet to be placed in a queue. Furthermore, one microblock per microengine can lead to inefficient resource utilization: unless each ACE spends the same amount of time processing a packet, one microengine will sit idle waiting for another to finish processing a packet. Finally, allowing a microengine to run code for multiple ACEs reduces idle time and lowers the overhead for packet forwarding, but introduces contention and requires a larger instruction store.

Intel uses the term *microblock group* to denote a set of microblocks that run on a single microengine; the programmer specifies microblock groups in a configuration file. Figure 22.3 illustrates one possible way to organize the microblocks from Figure 22.2 into groups.

---

†The ingress ACE that Intel supplies with their reference code differs from our example because the Intel ingress ACE does not pass packets to the core component.

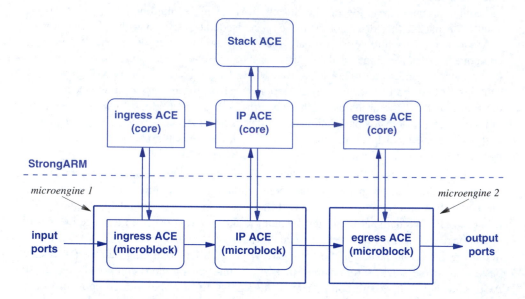

Figure 22.3 Illustration of microblocks collected together into microblock groups. Each group corresponds to the code that executes on a microengine.

22.9 Replicated Microblock Groups

We said that it is possible to increase parallelism by replicating a microblock group onto multiple microengines. Doing so introduces additional complexity for three reasons. First, the core component is not replicated, which means that a single core component must communicate with multiple microblock groups. Second, the replicated microblock groups contend for input. For example, when a packet becomes available, only one of the replicated microblock groups can handle the packet. Third, each replicated microblock group can generate output, which much be passed on to another ACE. Thus, the next ACE along the pipeline must be prepared to accept input from all replicated copies of the predecessor. Figure 22.4 shows input and output for a replicated microblock group.

22.10 Microblock Structure

A microblock is composed of two parts: an *initialization macro* that is invoked to initialize data structures and a *processing macro* that is invoked to handle a packet. Initialization is unusual because no memory allocation is possible. Instead, data structures must be allocated by the core component on the StrongARM; initialization merely places values in the data structures.

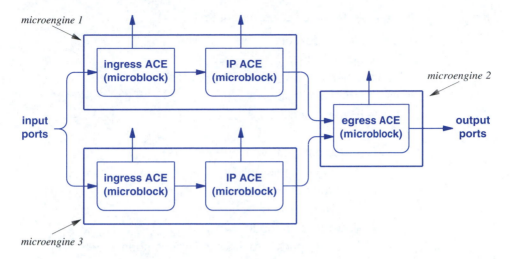

Figure 22.4 Illustration of a microblock group replicated on microengines 1 and 3. Both copies of a microACE connect to the same core component, and both copies share access to input devices.

22.11 The Dispatch Loop

A general mechanism is needed to control packet flow among microblocks because packets do not all follow the same path. In fact, a given packet may not be processed by all the microblocks that are present on a microengine. To understand why, consider Figure 22.4, which shows two microblocks executing on microengine 1. If it receives a non-IP packet (e.g., an ARP request), the ingress microblock must forward the packet up to the core component. If it receives a packet carrying IP, the ingress microblock must pass the packet to the IP microblock (which executes on the same microengine).

Intel uses the term *dispatch loop* to refer to a small piece of code that controls packet flow among microblocks within a microblock group. In essence, a dispatch loop functions like a main program that consists of an infinite loop. Each hardware thread executes the dispatch loop; the loop invokes microblocks similar to the way subroutines are invoked in a conventional program. When a microblock finishes processing, control returns to the dispatch loop, which uses the returned value to determine what to do next. In Figure 22.4, for example, the dispatch loop for microengine 1 first invokes the ingress microblock. When it finishes with a packet, the ingress microblock chooses a *return code* and returns control to the dispatch loop. The return code specifies the packet disposition (e.g., whether the packet should be sent to the IP ACE microblock that is running on the same microengine, sent to the core component on the StrongARM, or discarded). Similarly, the IP microblock must return a code that specifies whether the packet should be sent to the egress ACE microblock, sent to the IP core component on the StrongARM, or discarded. Thus, we can imagine a dispatch loop that follows the general structure illustrated in Figure 22.5†.

---

†Actual code contains many low-level details that have been omitted. In particular, the dispatch loop must check for error conditions such as the Ethernet hardware reporting that a frame contains an invalid CRC.

```
/* Example Dispatch Loop Algorithm */
Allocate global registers;
Initialize dispatch loop;
Initialize Ethernet devices;
Initialize ingress microblock;
Initialize IP microblock;
while (1) {
        Get next packet from input device(s);
        Invoke ingress microblock;
        if ( return code == 0 ) {
                Drop the packet;
        } else if ( return code == 1 ) {
                Send packet to ingress core component;
        } else {  /* IP packet */
                Invoke IP microblock;
                if ( return code == 0 ) {
                        Drop packet;
                } else if ( return code == 1 ) {
                        Send packet to IP core component;
                } else {
                        Send packet to egress microblock;
                }
        }
}
```

Figure 22.5 A dispatch loop algorithm for the microblock group on microengine 1 in Figure 22.4. Return code zero indicates that the packet should be dropped.

22.12 Dispatch Loop Calling Conventions

When it invokes a processing macro, the dispatch loop supplies three implicit arguments (i.e., arguments passed in registers):

- A *buffer handle* for a frame that contains a packet.
- A set of state registers that contain information about the frame (which the microblock can modify).
- A variable (always named *dl_next_block*) in which to store a return code.

The stored state information can include items generated by software (e.g., a classification) for the frame. In addition, items can be modified as the packet is processed (e.g., the length of the packet can change if a network system modifies options in the IP header).

How are return values assigned? The programmer, who writes both the microblock code and the dispatch loop code, can determine the possible values and the meaning assigned to each. As a convention, a return value of zero is used to indicate that the packet should be dropped; a programmer can assign a meaning to successive integers starting at one. If microblocks are arranged in a strict pipeline, programmers can use the return value one to mean that the packet should be sent to the ''next'' microblock in the pipeline. In such cases, the dispatch loop must be programmed to know the exact sequence of microblocks that forms the pipeline. The algorithm above suggests another variation: a return code of one indicates that the packet should be sent to the core component of the ACE.

22.13 Packet Queues

Because a dispatch loop uses the return code to decide how a packet should be processed, the exact set of microblocks that process a given packet depends on the contents of the packet. Consequently, the time taken to process a packet depends on the packet contents. The variance in processing times is especially important when a packet moves from code running on one processor to code running on another.

To ensure highest speed, each ACE must be allowed to execute independently, without waiting for the succeeding ACE to accept a packet. Intel software uses *communication queues* to allow processors to proceed independently. When it is ready to forward a packet to an ACE on another processor, an ACE places the packet in a communication queue. When a packet reaches its input queue, an ACE extracts and processes the packet. Thus, a queue allows the ACE on a processor to continue execution without waiting for the ACE on the succeeding processor.

Each communication queue is unidirectional. When bidirectional communication is needed, a pair of queues must be defined. For example, Figure 22.6 illustrates how communication queues relate to the conceptual interconnections in Figure 22.3.

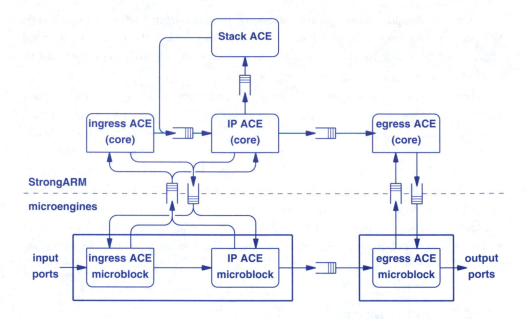

Figure 22.6 Illustration of communication queues used with ACEs. Queues
permit processors to execute in parallel.

As the figure shows, communication queues are not restricted to inter-processor
communication — they are also used among core components on the StrongARM.
Thus, to send a packet to the egress ACE, the core component of the IP ACE places the
packet in the communication queue between the two. The core component of the egress
ACE will extract the packet from the queue.

22.14 Exceptions

Intel uses the term *exception* to refer to packets passed from a microblock component of an ACE to the corresponding core component on the StrongARM. As we
have seen, a microblock uses the return code mechanism to specify a disposition to the
dispatch loop. Intel defines symbolic constant *IX_EXCEPTION* that can be used to
specify a packet should be sent to the StrongARM.

To forward a packet to the core component, the dispatch loop places the packet in
the communication queue that leads to the core. In fact, all replications of a microblock
group share a single queue. There is never any ambiguity about which core component
should receive a packet because a queue contains additional information that specifies
the packet's destination.

How are components identified? Every ACE is assigned a unique identification known as an *ACE tag*. The value is assigned when the ACE is started, and is known to both the core and microblock components. The dispatch loop uses the ACE tag to associate an exception with the correct core component. Furthermore, the buffer used to transfer the packet contains an *exception code* that the sender supplies to designate details about the exception. Thus, a microblock specifies an exception type that informs the core component about the exact reason for the exception.

The core component of an ACE must include an *exception handler* that accepts and processes exception packets from the corresponding microblock. The handler uses the exception code to determine how the packet should be processed. Possible actions include:

- Consume the packet and free the buffer.

- Modify the packet before sending it on.

- Send the packet back to the microblock group for further processing†.

- Forward the packet to another ACE on the StrongARM.

22.15 Crosscalls

We have seen that ACEs include a queue mechanism used to transfer packets from one ACE to another. Intel provides another mechanism for all non-packet communication. Known as a *crosscall*, the mechanism is related to *remote procedure call* (*RPC*) technology‡. Crosscalls make it possible for an ACE to invoke a function in another ACE or in an application program.

Using a crosscall requires the programmer to plan ahead: both the caller and callee must be programmed to use the crosscall mechanism. As with conventional RPC, a crosscall is specified by declaring the procedure that can be called and the arguments the procedure expects. The Intel software uses the *Interface Definition Language* (*IDL*) for the specification. An IDL compiler reads the specification, and generates *stubs* that handle the details of marshaling arguments and making the call.

Intel defines three types of crosscalls:

- Deferred — The caller does not block; return notification is asynchronous.

- Oneway — The caller does not block; no value is returned.

- Twoway — The caller blocks, and the callee returns a value.

---

†Sending a packet back to a microblock group is unusual, and a programmer must be careful to avoid an infinite loop.

‡Object-oriented languages use the term *Remote Method Invocation* (*RMI*) for the concept.

A *twoway* crosscall corresponds to traditional RPC. The caller blocks until the called procedure returns; the call returns a value. Although an ACE can receive a two-way call, an ACE is prohibited from making a twoway crosscall because an ACE may not block. Therefore, ACEs can only make deferred or oneway crosscalls. As the name implies, a oneway crosscall only provides a notification because the called procedure cannot return a value. Deferred crosscalls provide a middle ground — although the called procedure returns a value, the calling program continues to execute. Later, when the called procedure finishes, the return notification occurs asynchronously.

The crosscall mechanism uses early binding. That is, the type of a crosscall is determined by the programmer, and is fixed when the IDL specification is compiled. Changing the type requires the programmer to recompile the source and download a new image to the IXP1200.

22.16 Application Programs Outside The ACE Model

The ACE model encompasses software that runs on the StrongARM and the microengines to handle packets. Additional software is sometimes needed for management or control plane processing. For example, it might be necessary to run a routing protocol or an application that provides a user interface for the manager. Applications outside the ACE model can also use the crosscall mechanism to communicate. Either an external application or an ACE can initiate the crosscall (i.e., become a caller), and either side can receive a crosscall (i.e., become a callee).

22.17 Summary

Intel defines an Active Computing Element (ACE) to be the fundamental unit of code that runs on an Intel network processor. In addition to the core component that executes on the StrongARM, an ACE can contain a microblock component that executes on a microengine.

Microblocks are collected into groups; a microblock group can be replicated on one or more microengines. Two mechanisms are used to communicate among ACEs. Packets are passed between ACEs in queues; non-packet communication among ACEs uses a crosscall mechanism. An application program outside the ACE model can also use the crosscall mechanism to communicate with an ACE.

FOR FURTHER STUDY

Intel's SDK Developer's Guide [Intel 2001b] provides details about the creation of MicroACEs; the SDK Reference Manual [Intel 2001a] describes ACEs supplied by Intel.

EXERCISES

22.1   Consider an ACE that performs the forwarding function for an IP router. How should the code be divided between a microengine component and a core component? Why?

22.2   Why are microblocks from multiple ACEs organized into microblock groups? (Hint: consider the size of the control store on the microengines.)

22.3   Study some of the example ACEs provided in the IXA SDK. Explain the design trade-offs, including how the functionality is divided between the StrongARM and microengines.

22.4   Intel's SDK uses a late binding scheme in which the target of an ACE is bound at run time. Does late binding make the code more or less efficient? Explain.

22.5   Devise an ACE for a traffic policer that monitors up to one hundred separate TCP connections and discards packets on any connection that consumes more than twelve percent of the bandwidth. What parts of the ACE must run on the StrongARM? Explain.

Chapter Contents

23

ACE Run-Time Structure And StrongARM Facilities

23.1 Introduction

Earlier chapters in this section describe the Intel network processor hardware. The previous chapter focuses on software by describing the ACE programming model used in the Intel SDK. This chapter continues the discussion by examining the facilities and mechanisms used to implement ACEs. It considers ACE creation, initialization, termination, and binding as well as the run-time structures used to support ACE execution. The next chapters extend the discussion to include details of the microblock components that run on the microengines.

23.2 StrongARM Responsibilities

As noted in the previous chapter, Intel's SDK defines the fundamental unit of programming to be an ACE (i.e., the primary code programmers create follows the ACE model). In practice, an IXA application consists of a set of ACEs that are designed to function together. That is, when they are loaded into an IXP1200, the ACEs that comprise an application must be bound together and combined with additional software that provides the necessary run-time support.

In addition to cross-development facilities that allow a programmer to create ACEs, Intel's SDK includes an integrated support system that supplies the functionality needed at run-time. Figure 23.1 lists items for which the Intel system includes support.

- Loading ACE software onto the network processor
- Creating and initializing each ACE
- Resolving names
- Managing the operation of ACEs
- Allocating and reclaiming resources such as memory
- Controlling microengine operation
- Providing communication among ACE core components
- Providing an interface to non-ACE applications
- Providing an interface to operating system facilities
- Forwarding packets between the core component of an ACE
  and the microblock(s)

Figure 23.1 Functionality for which the Intel SDK provides support.

23.3 Principle Run-Time Components

Figure 23.2 illustrates the principle run-time components of the Intel system, and lists the mechanisms used to implement the components on the StrongARM. As the figure shows, the run-time support consists of four main pieces: a *Resource Manager*, *Object Management System* (*OMS*), an *Operating System Specific Library* (*OSSL*), and an *Action Services Library* (*ASL*). The next sections describe the purpose of each piece and explain how the piece is implemented; later sections show how the pieces are used when ACEs are loaded and run.

23.4 Core Components Of ACEs

From a programmer's point of view, the StrongARM's primary responsibility consists of running the core components of ACEs. Each core component is implemented as an independent, user-level process. We will see, however, that Intel uses an asynchronous programming model that affects how a core component is structured. In principle, for example, a core component has access to all the usual operating system facilities. In practice, the asynchronous model constrains the actions that are allowed. In particular, we will see that functions in a core component are prohibited from directly executing functions that block the calling process. Thus, code in a core component may not directly call a system function such as *read* that can block.

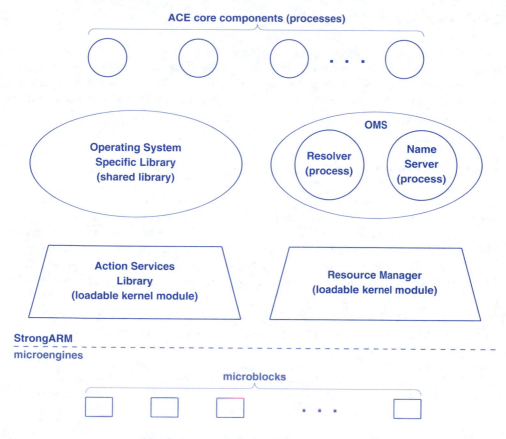

Figure 23.2 Principle components in Intel's run-time system that support ACE execution, and the implementation used for each.

23.5 Object Management System (OMS)

Intel uses the term *Object Management System* (*OMS*) to refer to software that binds names into underlying objects. The OMS software consists of two subsystems: a *Resolver* and a *Name Server*. In addition to providing bindings, the two subsystems modify and store global state information.

23.5.1 Resolver

Intel's *Resolver* is implemented as a user-level process on the StrongARM. The Resolver plays an especially important role in inter-ACE communication because the Resolver binds the named targets in an ACE to specific destinations (e.g., to the input of another ACE). Thus, calls to the Resolver are used to establish the data flow among ACEs.

23.5.2 Name Server

The *Name Server*, which is also implemented as a user-level process on the StrongARM, provides one level of indirection for named objects. For example, each ACE has both a name and a unique numeric tag assigned. The Name Server allows a programmer to use names for ACEs in programs and delay binding the names to numeric values until run-time.

23.6 Resource Manager

Intel's *Resource Manager*, which runs on the StrongARM as a loadable kernel module, provides access to facilities in the operating system, and handles communication with the microengines. The Resource Manager is especially important for memory management because the StrongARM and microengines do not use the same addressing scheme. The Resource Manager accesses address translation tables to convert between the virtual address space used on the StrongARM and the physical address spaces used on microengines.

The Resource Manager provides a set of *system calls* for managing microengines, physical ports, and memory. Most important, the Resource Manager provides the path from ACE code that runs on the StrongARM to microblocks that run on the microengines. During startup, the Resource Manager loads software into each microengine; during execution, the Resource Manager handles the queues of packets sent between the core component of an ACE and the corresponding microblocks.

23.7 Operating System Specific Library (OSSL)

As the name implies, Intel's *Operating System Specific Library* (*OSSL*) software is implemented as a shared library†. The role of the OSSL is portability: it allows IXA programs to be written without referencing facilities in a specific operating system. Instead, each program is written to call functions in the OSSL. For example, instead of calling Linux semaphore functions to coordinate two processes, the code is written to call OSSL functions. OSSL must translate each call into an equivalent set of calls in the underlying operating system.

The chief advantage of OSSL emerges when we consider using an alternative operating system on the StrongARM. For example, Intel allows the StrongARM to run VxWorks or Embedded Linux. Because the ACE code is written to call OSSL routines, only OSSL needs to be changed to use the alternative operating system; the original ACE code can run unchanged.

---

†OSSL is mentioned in some of the vendor's documents, but is not documented in the SDK Reference Manual.

23.8 Action Services Library

The *Action Services Library* (*ASL*) consists of a loadable kernel module that provides run-time support for core components, including an event processing loop and network libraries (e.g., buffer management and TCP/IP support).

23.9 Automated Microengine Assignment

Intel's SDK software does much more than load and run ACE code that the programmer creates. The SDK handles a major decision: it automatically assigns microblock groups to microengines. In fact, the SDK selects both the number of parallel copies of a microblock group and the specific microengines on which the copies will execute.

How can the SDK determine which microengines should run on a given microblock? First, interface hardware is classified according to its speed (e.g., a 10/100 Ethernet port is low speed, and a gigabit Ethernet port is classified as high speed). Second, the programmer creates a configuration file that specifies which microblocks handle ingress and egress for various speed interfaces. A program in the SDK uses the information to choose microengine assignments for each microblock. Figure 23.3 lists the configuration values.

Numeric Value	Meaning
0	Slow ingress file
1	Slow egress file
2	Fast ingress file for Port 1
3	Fast ingress file for Port 2
4	Fast egress file

Figure 23.3 Numeric values used in the configuration file. Intel's SDK uses the values when choosing how to assign microblocks to microengines.

When it starts, the Resource Manager uses the number and type of physical interfaces to determine how many copies of ingress and egress microblocks are needed. The configuration file is used to determine the exact microblock that handles each type of ingress or egress. We can summarize:

Intel's SDK completely automates microengine assignment. SDK software chooses the number of replications of each microblock, and assigns each copy to a specific microengine.

23.10 ACE Program Structure

Although the core component of an ACE runs as a Linux process, a programmer does not write a conventional Linux process that starts with a *main* program. Instead, the programmer creates independent program pieces such as data declarations, an initialization function, a termination function, and a set of functions to handle specific events. The pieces are then integrated into a working program by the SDK. Figure 23.4 lists the pieces of ACE code that a programmer supplies.

- An *initialization function* that is called when the ACE begins.

- An *exception handler* to receive packets sent by the microblock component and (optionally) an NCL program.

- A set of *action functions* that each correspond to one possible packet classification.

- A set of *crosscalls* the ACE is willing to accept.

- A set of *timer functions* used to handle timed events.

- A set of *callback functions* used to handle returned values.

- A *termination function* that is called when the ACE terminates.

Figure 23.4 Pieces of code a programmer creates when using the Intel SDK to build an ACE. Some items, such as the initialization and termination functions, are required; others are optional.

23.11 ACE Main Program And Event Loop

After the pieces specified in Figure 23.4 have been created, software in Intel's SDK is used to integrate the pieces into a cohesive program. That is, the SDK supplies a main program, and adds other functions to provide an overall program structure and the necessary run-time support. The entire process is automated, and the generated code is hidden — a programmer does not write or modify code for the main program.

To ensure that the code generated by Intel's SDK can be integrated with functions supplied by a programmer, function calls in the generated code must use the same function names as the programmer. Intel uses two mechanisms to achieve agreement: fixed names and name binding. Fixed names are used for required functions. For example, the SDK mandates that each ACE contain an initialization function named *ix_init*. Similarly, the SDK mandates that each ACE contain a termination function named *ix_fini*. Thus, when creating an ACE, a programmer must supply an *ix_init* and an *ix_fini* function.

Although the details of the generated code remain hidden from a programmer, the easiest way to understand how an ACE works is to imagine that the main program in each ACE operates as follows. After it starts and performs internal initialization, the main program calls the programmer's *ix_init* function to complete initialization. The main program then enters an *event loop*. Once the event loop terminates, the code calls the programmer's *ix_fini* function to release resources. Finally, the main program performs internal cleanup and exits. Figure 23.5 illustrates the sequence of steps.

```
main( )                     /* Core component of an ACE      */
{
      Intel_init( );         /* Perform internal initialization     */
      ix_init( );            /* Call user's initialization function   */
      Intel_event_loop( ):   /* Perform internal event loop        */
      ix_fini( );            /* Call user's termination function    */
      Intel_fini( );         /* Perform internal cleanup          */
      exit( );               /* Terminate the Linux process       */
}
```

Figure 23.5 Conceptual structure of the main program in an ACE core component. The SDK provides the code automatically; the exact details are hidden from the programmer.

23.12 ACE Event Loop And Blocking

The event loop forms the central part of the core component. During the loop, the main program waits for an event to occur (usually from the OMS), and then calls the appropriate function to handle the event. For example, if a packet arrives from the microblock component, the event loop calls the *ExceptionHandler* function. Conceptually, the event loop operates as in Figure 23.6.

From a programmer's point of view, the event loop is completely hidden — an ACE appears to contain a set of functions that are called asynchronously. As the above description implies, the underlying implementation uses a single thread of control for all functions in the core component. Implementing the core component as a single thread has an important consequence for programmers: if any handler blocks, the entire core component will cease to handle other events. We can now understand the restriction against the use of blocking system calls that was described earlier:

Because each core component executes as a single thread of control, a handler function is not permitted to block because doing so will block the entire core component.

```
Intel_event_loop( )
{
      do forever  {
            E = getnextevent( );
            if (E is termination event)  {
                  return to caller;
            }  else if (E is exception event)  {
                  call exception handler function;
            }  else if (E is timer event)  {
                  call timer handler function;
            /* Note: additional event tests can be added here   */
            }
      }
}
```

Figure 23.6 The basic structure of the event loop in an ACE core component. The code must contain a call for each possible event.

23.13 Asynchronous Programming Paradigm And Callbacks

Because it cannot block, the core component of an ACE cannot follow a conventional *synchronous programming paradigm*†. Instead, all operations must be recast in an *asynchronous* paradigm. In particular, because no function can block, a programmer must convert blocking function calls into a pair of asynchronous notifications: one to request that a function be performed, and another to inform the original caller when the function is complete. For example, consider the sequence of synchronous code that Figure 23.7a shows.

To recast the code in an asynchronous model, the programmer must rewrite functions f and g to use an asynchronous approach, and must create two additional functions that can receive asynchronous completion notifications. Intel uses the term *callback* to describe an asynchronous notification of completion; functions used to receive such notifications are known as *callback functions*. Figure 23.7b shows how the example code is structured in an asynchronous version.

Programming in an asynchronous paradigm is difficult for three reasons. First, because it is not intuitive, low-level asynchrony leads to errors in the code. Second, because results depend on timing, asynchronous programs are difficult to test. Third, because asynchronous functions operate on shared values, asynchronous programs tend to have large amounts of global state information, making it difficult to control access.

In the figure, h represents a function that uses synchronous calls; $h1$ is the equivalent asynchronous version. Similarly, function $f1$ is the asynchronous version of function f, and $g1$ is the asynchronous version of function g. As in the synchronous

---

†Some authors use the term *synchronous programming model*.

version, the asynchronous version assigns variables y and z the results from functions $f1$ and $g1$, and increments q by z.

```
h {                      /* Synchronous version            */
        y = f(x);        /* Call f (potentially blocking)   */
        z = g(y);        /* Use the result from f to call g */
        q += z;          /* Use the value of z to update q  */
        return;
}
```

(a)

```
h1 {                     /* Asynchronous version           */
        allocate global variables y, z, and q;
        establish cbf1 as the callback function for f1;
        establish cbg1 as the callback function for g1;
        Start f1(x) with a nonblocking call;
        return;
}

function cbf1(retval) {   /* Callback function for f1        */
        y = retval;
        start g1(y) with a nonblocking call;
        return;
}

function cbg1(retval) {   /* Callback function for g1        */
        z = retval;
        q += z;
        return;
}
```

(b)

Figure 23.7 (a) An example of synchronous code, and (b) the structure of asynchronous code for the same computation. Asynchrony adds complexity for the programmer.

As the code in the figure shows, it is possible to build an asynchronous program that performs operations in strict sequence (e.g., $h1$ invokes $f1$, and the callback function for $f1$ invokes $g1$ only after $f1$ completes). Although it can reproduce the synchronous semantics, strict sequencing is seldom optimal. To optimize performance, a programmer must allow operations to be performed concurrently. That is, the program starts two or more operations, and allows the underlying system to choose the order in which they are performed.

Unfortunately, concurrent asynchrony is difficult to understand. To see why, consider code that calls two functions, *q* and *r*, and adds the results. Even if each of *q* and *r* can block, the synchronous version of the code is trivial and unambiguous:

$$w = q(a) + r(b);$$

To allow concurrent asynchronous execution, a programmer creates an asynchronous version of *q* and *r* (i.e. *q1* and *r1*), specifies a callback function for each, and starts both *q1* and *r1* executing. The order of completion is not fixed — either *q1* or *r1* can complete first. To coordinate asynchronous completion, the programmer must create a data structure that the two callback functions share. When a callback occurs, the callback function checks a variable in the shared data structure to determine whether the other callback occurred previously. If the other callback has already occurred, the final result, *w*, can be computed, and notification can be sent that the result has been computed. If the other callback is still pending, the return value is stored in the shared data structure, and the state variable is set to indicate that only one of the two callbacks has occurred.

As the example shows, synchronous code translates into larger and more complex asynchronous code — even a single line of synchronous code can require multiple asynchronous functions, callbacks, and shared variables to hold state information and intermediate results. The point is:

> *Because it uses the asynchronous paradigm, the core component of an ACE is usually significantly more complex and difficult to understand than a synchronous program that solves the same problem.*

23.14 Asynchronous Execution And Mutual Exclusion

In most programming systems, asynchronous programs execute concurrently, which introduces the possibility of errors in which two functions attempt to access or modify global data at the same time. Such systems usually provide a *mutual exclusion* mechanism that allows independent functions to coordinate their access to shared data. For example, an operating system can provide a *semaphore mechanism* that allows independent processes to coordinate.

Although the Intel runtime system allows asynchronous execution of functions within an ACE, no mutual exclusion is required. To understand why, recall that a single thread of control executes the event loop in the ACE. Thus, although they execute asynchronously, functions within an ACE are not concurrent — only one function executes at any time. Thus, the system guarantees that no changes or accesses to global data will occur while a function is running.

23.15 Memory Allocation

From a hardware point of view, both microengines and the StrongARM have access to all memories. Thus, it is possible for the core and microblock components of an ACE to share memory — either component can store values or retrieve values. Before sharing can occur, however, both components must agree on the exact location and size of the shared block.

Shared memory is complicated for two reasons. First, because they operate as independent processes, ACEs must cooperate to ensure that they do not allocate overlapping blocks of memory. Second, the StrongARM and microengines do not use the same memory addressing scheme. To understand the second issue, recall that the StrongARM maps all memories into a single, uniform virtual address space and uses byte addressing. However, the microengines maintain a separate address space for each memory, and use word addressing where the word size depends on the underlying memory. Thus, a core component and a microblock component cannot use the same address for a given memory location.

Intel software arranges for all memory management to occur on the StrongARM. If a microblock needs memory, the core component of the ACE must allocate the memory and pass the address of the allocated area to the microblock. Intel software assigns the StrongARM responsibility for all address translation. Thus, before sending an address to a microblock, the core component maps the address to an equivalent physical address used by the microengine. Similarly, when it receives an address from a microengine, the core component translates the physical address to an equivalent virtual address. Responsibility for address translation also applies to linked structures that are shared — each pointer in the linked structure is specified as a physical address that the microengine can use; when it examines a shared structure, the core component must translate each pointer into an equivalent virtual address.

Because memory management hardware hides physical addresses from user-level processes, a core component cannot easily map between virtual and physical addresses. Intel software uses the Resource Manager to provide the needed support — when memory allocation is needed, a core component calls the *RmMalloc* function of the Resource Manager. When address translation is needed, a core component calls *RmGetPhysOffset*. Because it runs as a kernel module, the Resource Manager is shared among all ACEs, and has direct access to the physical address space. Thus, in addition to understanding physical memory, the Resource Manager guarantees that requests are serialized.

When it makes an allocation request, a core component must be able to request a block from a specific memory. Thus, the first argument of *RmMalloc* specifies the type of memory being requested (i.e., SRAM, SDRAM, or Scratchpad), and the second argument specifies a handle in which the address of the block is returned. Furthermore, because the request refers to a physical memory, the amount of memory being requested is given in units appropriate for the memory type. Thus, the third argument of *RmMalloc* specifies the number of words of memory needed, where the size of a word depends on the underlying memory. We can summarize:

Intel software arranges for all memory management and address translation to be performed by the StrongARM. To allocate memory, the core component of an ACE invokes the RmMalloc function of the Resource Manager; arguments refer to physical memory.

23.16 Loading And Starting An ACE (ixstart)

As Chapter 21 explains, Intel provides software that automates many of the steps required to download and run ACE software on the testbed board. Specifically, Figure 21.4† lists the basic steps required. First, the programmer compiles source code to obtain object files for both the core and microblock components. Second, the programmer creates a configuration file named *ixsys.config* that specifies the set of files to use. Third, the programmer boots the testbed, and mounts the directory containing the ACE software to be loaded. Fourth, the programmer logs into the StrongARM and runs a script named *ixstart*, passing the *ixsys.config* file as an argument. Figure 23.8 lists the sequence of steps that occur when *ixstart* runs.

1. Load and start the ASL kernel module, Name Server, and Resolver.

2. Load and start device drivers for the network interfaces.

3. Load and initialize the Resource Manager which determines how many copies of each ingress and egress microblock group to run.

4. Parse the configuration file, *ixsys.config*, and check for errors.

5. Start the core components of each ACE, which causes the ACE to call its *ix_init* function.

6. Turn on interfaces, assign microblock groups to specific microengines, and resolve external references (known as *patching*).

7. Bind the ACE targets and physical interfaces.

8. Start the microengines running.

Figure 23.8 The steps that occur when Intel's *ixstart* program is used to start a set of ACEs running.

---

†Figure 21.4 can be found on page 331.

As the figure indicates, *ixstart* does much more than merely download a single file. The script begins with multiple binary files that represent the compiled code for the core and microblock components. External symbols in the files must be replaced by binary values before the files can be executed. Thus, *ixstart* resolves references to external names, and replaces each with the equivalent binary value. Intel refers to the replacement as *patching*. Delaying external symbol resolution has a consequence for programmers: the validity of an external reference may not be checked until *ixstart* runs.

23.17 ACE Data Allocation And Initialization

Usually, the *ix_init* function in each ACE allocates all the memory that the ACE's core and microblock components need. In addition to memory for data structures, *ix_init* is required to allocate a block of data that the Intel software uses to hold information about the ACE. Known as an *ix_ace* structure, the required data block can be embedded in a larger block that includes space for variables that the programmer needs. Figure 23.9 shows how a programmer can declare a structure that contains the required *ix_ace* data block plus an additional integer used as a counter.

```
#include <ix/asl.h>          /* Include Intel's library declarations   */
struct   myace  {            /* Programmer's control block             */
         struct   ix_ace ace;   /* Intel's ace embedded as first item    */
         int      mycount;      /* Counter used by programmer's code    */
         /* Programmer can insert additional data items here...        */
}
```

Figure 23.9 An example ACE data declaration that contains an *ix_ace* structure plus one variable defined by the programmer. Additional variables can be added.

As part of the required initialization, the *ix_init* procedure in an ACE must perform three steps related to the ACE data block: allocate memory for the block, assign the address to a pointer that the SDK software supplies, and pass the address of the block to the SDK function *ix_ace_init*. The pointer to be set is passed as an argument to *ix_init*. Figure 23.10 illustrates how data block initialization proceeds.

```
ix_init ( ... , ix_ace **app , ... )
{
        struct myace *ap;     /* Ptr to programmer's control block     */

        ap = malloc ( sizeof ( struct myace ) );
        *app = & ap->ace ;
        ix_ace_init ( & ap->ace );

        /* Other initialization code goes here... */
}
```

Figure 23.10 Illustration of how the *ix_init* function allocates an ACE data
block as required by the SDK. The SDK supplies additional
arguments to *ix_init* that are not shown.

23.18 Crosscalls

Recall from Chapter 22 that the SDK supports a *crosscall* mechanism that provides remote procedure calls among applications and the core components of ACEs. Also recall that there are three types of calls: *oneway* (no reply is given), *deferred* (the reply occurs asynchronously), and *twoway* (the caller blocks to wait for the reply). The *Object Management System* (*OMS*) implements crosscalls among ACEs and non-ACE applications. Figure 23.11 lists the possible call combinations.

Caller	Called Procedure	Block?
ACE core component	ACE core component	no
ACE core component	non-ACE application	no
non-ACE application	ACE core component	no
non-ACE application	non-ACE application	yes

Figure 23.11 The possible ways a call can occur using the crosscall mechanism in Intel's SDK.

As the figure shows, an ACE can either act as a caller or a callee. That is, the ACE can function as a client that makes calls or as a server that receives calls. However, an ACE cannot block. Therefore, an ACE cannot make a twoway call because the call can block.

23.19 Crosscall Declaration Using IDL

To use the crosscall mechanism, a programmer must create a file that contains an *Interface Definition Language* (*IDL*) declaration for the data types and the functions that operate on the data. For example Figure 23.12 contains an IDL declaration for a packet counter that stores a record of the total number of packets and broadcast packets received.

The IDL code in the figure specifies an interface, *PacketCounter*. The code declares data type, *packetinfo*, to be a structure with two integer fields: one that records the number of packets and another that records the number of broadcast packets. The file also contains declarations for three functions that provide the interface to the packet counter. The functions are used to increment the total packet count, reset the total packet count, and reset both the total packet count and broadcast count.

In the example, function *incTcount* takes an integer argument (*addedpackets*) that gives a value by which the total packet count should be incremented. Because it does not return a value, *incTcount* has been declared to be oneway. Function *resetTcount* takes an integer argument (*newnumpkts*) that specifies a value to replace the packet count. The function uses a deferred call to return the value the counter had before being reset. Finally, the argument to function *resetPinfo* consists of a *packetinfo* structure that specifies new values for both the number of packets and number of broadcasts. The function uses a twoway call to return the value that the packet counter had before being reset.

```
interface PacketCounter
{
        struct packetinfo {
          int  numpackets;      /* Count of total packets     */
          int  numbcasts;       /* Count of broadcast packets*/
        };

        oneway void incTcount ( in  int  addedpackets );
        deferred int resetTcount ( in  int  newnumpkts );
        twoway int resetPinfo ( in  struct  packetinfo );
};
```

Figure 23.12 An example IDL file that declares a data type and three functions that operate on the data. The keyword *in* is used to specify that an argument is sent from the caller to the called program.

In the figure, keyword *twoway* is optional. If no type is specified for a given function, the IDL compiler assumes the call is twoway.

23.20 Communication Access Process (CAP)

To make crosscalls, a program must have two facilities: a thread similar to the event loop in a core component and an access point for communication. The thread repeatedly contacts the OMS, obtains the next event, and calls the function that handles the event. Communication between the thread and the OMS occurs over a *Communication Access Process* (*CAP*), an abstraction provided by the software.

How is a CAP instantiated? For an ACE core component, CAP instantiation occurs when the core component calls *ix_ace_init*†. For non-ACE applications, the application must contain an explicit call that creates the CAP. Furthermore, the programmer must ensure that the application contains an explicit event loop that repeatedly uses the CAP to obtain events.

23.21 Timer Management

Intel's OMS software supports a *timed event* subsystem that allows software running on the StrongARM to manage a set of timers. Timers follow the same asynchronous programming paradigm as other events. Figure 23.13 lists the steps that an ACE takes to use a timer.

1. Initialize H, a handle for an ix_event.

2. Associate handle H with a callback function, CB.

3. Calculate T, a time for the event to occur.

4. Schedule event H at time T.

5. Note: at any time prior to T, event H can be cancelled.

6. At time T, function CB will be called if the event has not been cancelled.

Figure 23.13 The steps needed to create a timed event. When the timer expires, software invokes the specified callback function.

As an example, suppose a timer is needed to perform an action ten seconds in the future. To keep the example short, we will use a trivial action: assign the value 0x090949 to variable x. We will assume that the event occurs once, which means that the handler should free resources (e.g., memory that was allocated when the event was created) and the data associated with the event handle. Figure 23.14 contains the declaration of an event handler function, f.

---

†Recall that the ACE is required to call *ix_ace_init* during initialization.

```
struct farg                              /* Structure passed as argument to f     */
{
    ix_event    e;                       /* Handle for the event                  */
    int         *xp;                     /* Pointer to variable x                 */
};


ix_error f ( ix_event *ep )              /* Function to handle the timer event    */
{
    struct farg *fcp = ( struct farg * ) ep ;  /* Convert argument type           */

    *fcp->xp  =  0x090949 ;              /* Assign x the new value                */

    ix_event_fini ( &fcp->e ) ;          /* Free the dynamic event data and       */
                                         /*    release the event handle           */
    free ( fcp ) ;                       /* Free the farg structure               */
    return 0 ;                           /* Return indicating success             */
}
```

Figure 23.14 Example declaration of an event handler and the structure
passed as an argument. The handler receives an argument that
was specified when the event was created.

The argument passed to function f consists of a pointer to the *farg* structure that
was allocated when the event was created. The structure contains two items: a handle
for the event and a pointer to variable x. The pointer to x allows the event handler to
assign a value without using a global variable name. The handle for the event is needed
because the handler is required to *finish* the event. To do so, the event handler calls
ix_event_fini, which releases resources associated with the event (e.g., memory used to
hold the event). In addition, the event handler frees the *farg* structure.

Figure 23.15 contains an example of the steps needed to create an event. The code
establishes function f as a handler, and schedules the event ten seconds in the future.

```
/* Example code to initiate an event */

/* Data structure */
struct farg *fcp;                  /* Address to be passed to handler        */
int x = 0;                         /* Variable to be changed in ten seconds  */
ix_time now, then;                 /* Variables to hold times                */

fcp = malloc ( sizeof ( *fcp ) );  /* Allocate the farg structure            */
fcp->xp  =  &x ;                   /* Set pointer to the address of x        */

ix_event_init ( & fcp->e )         /* Initialize the event handle            */
ix_event_call ( & fcp->e, f );     /* Set f to be the event handler          */
ix_time_curr ( & now );            /* Get the current time                   */
ix_time_add_sec ( & then, & now, 10 );   /* Add ten seconds to current time  */
ix_event_schedule ( & fcp->e, & then );  /* Schedule event in ten seconds    */
```

Figure 23.15 Example of code to schedule an event ten seconds in the future. The event handler will receive the address of structure farg as an argument.

The code is straightforward. After using *ix_event_init* to initialize the event handle, the code calls *ix_event_call* to specify the handler (i.e., *f*) and the argument to be passed to the handler (i.e., the address of structure *farg*). The code then obtains the current time, adds ten seconds, and places the result in variable *then*. The code uses *then* as the time argument when it calls *ix_event_schedule* to schedule the event.

A timed event occurs only once; the Intel API does not provide a function that can schedule a periodic timed event. If a programmer needs an event to occur repeatedly (e.g., every second), the programmer must arrange to schedule each occurrence of the event. Typically, a programmer arranges for the event handler to reschedule the event each time. That is, as the last step before returning, the callback function computes a new delay and calls *ix_event_schedule* to force the event to reoccur.

23.22 NCL Classification, Actions, And Default

How does Intel's *Network Classification Language* (*NCL*) fit into the ACE model? NCL is used in an ACE core component to handle all packets that are forwarded from another ACE. That is, NCL is not part of the fast path code used on microengines. In fact, the use of NCL is optional — if a programmer does not supply an NCL program for an ACE, each packet that arrives from another ACE is passed to a default function, *ix_action_default*.

When NCL is used, each arriving packet is classified. A programmer can choose to create the classification code from scratch or use some of the NCL specifications that Intel provides for common protocols such as IP. In any case, as Chapter 16 describes, an NCL program associates an *action* with each classification. The code for an action is implemented as a separate function — when a packet matches an NCL classification, the software invokes the action function and passes the packet as an argument. Thus, a programmer must supply a function for each action. In cases where a rule does not contain an explicit action, NCL invokes a *default action* by calling function *ix_action_default*†.

An action function operates like any other asynchronous function in the ACE. In particular, the action function is not permitted to block, and must be written to avoid consuming arbitrary amounts of resources such as memory. The return value from an action function specifies the disposition of the packet. Intel supplies symbolic constants for two predefined dispositions as listed below.

RULE_DONE   Packet processing complete; the packet has been
                   sent to a target or stored

RULE_CONT   Packet processing must continue in current ACE;
                   send the packet back for further classification

Note that the *RULE_CONT* value means that the action function has examined the packet, but has not specified a next target. That is, the packet is being sent back for further classification.

23.23 Summary

Intel software uses the StrongARM to run support software such as the Resource Manager, Object Management System (OMS), and the ACE core components. Intel software uses an asynchronous programming model: the programmer provides a set of functions that are invoked as needed.

The implementation of asynchrony relies on a single thread of control per ACE. The thread executes an event loop that waits for an event from the OMS, and calls the appropriate function to handle the event. The chief consequence of the implementation arises from the need to keep the event loop executing: no function may block. To prevent blocking, callback functions are used.

All memory allocation and address translation is performed on the StrongARM. Because the microengines use separate address spaces and physical memory addresses, the work must be performed by the Resource Manager, which runs inside the StrongARM operating system.

Intel supplies a timer mechanism that allows timed events and a crosscall mechanism that operates like RPC to allow procedure calls between ACEs and between an

---

†Function *ix_action_default* serves two purposes — in addition to providing a default action in an NCL program, it provides a default to which all packets from another ACE are sent, if no NCL program is provided.

ACE and a non-ACE program. Because an ACE cannot block, both mechanisms have nonblocking forms.

FOR FURTHER STUDY

The SDK documentation Intel [2001a] contains further details about the Intel support software and the Action Service Libraries. The SDK Developer's Guide [Intel 2001b] specifies crosscalls.

EXERCISES

23.1   Examine the code for *ix_ace_init*. What underlying facilities does it use?

23.2   Is it possible to devise a new system of software for the IXP1200 that allows programs on the StrongARM to use a synchronous model? Why or why not?

23.3   Estimate the number of functions in the Intel SDK that are related to writing software for the StrongARM.

23.4   Build and test an event timer that increments a variable every five seconds.

23.5   Implement and test an NCL program that classifies packets. What happens if the program does not specify an action for a classification?

23.6   An ACE core component is not permitted to call a function that will block arbitrarily long. What functions other than twoway crosscalls are prohibited?

Chapter Contents

24

Microengine Programming I

24.1 Introduction

The previous chapter describes ACE implementation, and explains the structure of the core component. This chapter and the next focus on the ACE microblock components. We consider features of the microengine assembler, and illustrate common programming tasks. The chapters supplement the vendor's literature by providing a conceptual overview; the vendor's manuals contain further details.

24.2 Intel's Microengine Assembler

By definition, assembly language is designed to match the underlying hardware — each assembly language statement corresponds directly to a machine instruction. For example, Intel's *microengine assembly language* contains a statement for each of the microengine instructions†. Unfortunately, because microengines are low-level devices, the instruction set is designed to be convenient for hardware designers, not to be convenient for programmers. As a result, programming in assembly language can be tedious, and is prone to errors.

How can assembly language simultaneously make it easier to write programs and still allow a programmer to specify the low-level details required for the optimization of microcode? Many RISC assemblers incorporate features that raise the level of the language: the assembly language is augmented with high-level statements that each expand into a sequence of microengine instructions. Although a programmer can use high-level statements for most programming, low-level statements are available when needed.

---

†A list of microengine instructions can be found in Figure 20.1 on page 304.

The high-level mechanisms included in Intel's *microengine assembler* (also known as a *microassembler*) fall into four categories:

- Assembler directives that permit a programmer to control assembler processing.

- A mechanism that allows programmers to use symbolic register names and an automated register allocation facility.

- A macro preprocessor that runs before the assembler and generates code that is then assembled. The preprocessor allows a programmer to create assembly language macros.

- A set of pre-defined macros for common control structures that provide a structured programming environment.

24.3 Microengine Assembly Language Syntax

All assembly language instructions follow the same syntactic form. Each statement starts on a new line, and contains four basic parts:

label: operator   operands   token

where both the *label* and *token* are optional. The *label* denotes a symbolic name that can be referenced as the target of a branch or jump statement, and the *operator* either denotes a single microengine instruction or a high-level command that expands into a sequence of instructions. The number and type of *operands* and the interpretation of the *token* depend on the operation. For example, the statement:

```
Mylabel:    JUMP        Strtloop
```

specifies a *JUMP* instruction that has an operand (i.e., target) *Strtloop*, a label *Mylabel*, and no token. The label *Strtloop* must be defined elsewhere in the program.

As in most languages, statements can be annotated with *comments*. Intel's microengine assembler recognizes three forms:

- C style comments that begin with /* and continue until the next occurrence of */

- C++ style comments that begin with // and extend to the end of the line

- Traditional assembly language comments that begin with ; and extend to the end of the line

The difference between the last two forms arises in the way the assembler disposes of them. The assembler removes C++ style comments early in the first pass, before parsing the remainder of the line. In contrast, the assembler leaves traditional comments in the program through the initial steps of assembly. Thus, if a programmer needs to examine intermediate steps of the assembler as part of debugging, traditional comments can be used to relate the intermediate code to the original program.

In addition to regular statements, Intel's microengine assembler accepts *assembler directives* and *macro preprocessor statements*. Each statement appears on a line by itself. To distinguish assembler directives, the first token of a directive starts with a dot (i.e., a period). For example, the line:

```
.areg          myname              5
```

is a directive that instructs the assembler to associate the symbolic name *myname* with general-purpose register 5 from the A bank. The assembler knows that the line contains a directive because the token *.areg* begins with a dot. Similarly, each preprocessor statement starts on a new line, and is distinguished by the presence of a pound sign (#) at the beginning of the first token. Thus, there is no ambiguity about the type of an assembly statement.

24.4 Example Operand Syntax

The operator in a statement determines the number of operands and the meaning of each. For example, the *alu* instruction which invokes an ALU operation has the general form:

$$\text{alu} [\ dst, \ src_1, \ op, \ src_2 \ ]$$

The *dst* operand specifies a destination for the result, which is usually a register. Operands src_1 and src_2 specify the values to be used in the operation, and *op* specifies the operation to perform. Each operand has specific limitations. For example, the *dst* operand cannot specify a read-only register (e.g., cannot specify a read transfer register). The hardware offers an interesting alternative in which *dst* can specify no destination, which means that a result is computed, but not stored. To do so, a programmer codes two minus signs, $--$, as the destination. We will learn in a Section 24.14 that an ALU operation with no destination allows an important optimization.

In the *alu* instruction, a source can specify the contents of a general-purpose register or encode a constant into the instruction itself. The latter is known as an *immediate value*. The ALU offers two *unary instructions* (i.e., instructions that take one operand). For a unary instruction, two minus signs are used to denote the unused operand, src_1.

Figure 24.1 lists the major ALU operators along with an explanation of each. Note that the ALU does not provide multiply or divide operations.

Operator	Meaning
+	Result is src_1 + src_2
-	Result is src_1 - src_2
B-A	Result is src_2 - src_1
B	Result is src_2
~B	Result is the bitwise inversion of src_2
AND	Result is bitwise *and* of src_1 and src_2
OR	Result is bitwise *or* of src_1 and src_2
XOR	Result is bitwise *exclusive or* of src_1 and src_2
+carry	Result is src_1 + src_2 + carry from previous operation
~AND	Result is bitwise (*not* src_1) and src_2
AND~	Result is bitwise (src_1 *and* (*not* src_2)
+IFsign	If the operation two instructions prior to the current operation caused the sign condition then the result is $src_1 + src_2$; otherwise the result is src_2
+4	Result is $src_1 + src_2$ with the first 28 bits set to zero
+8	Result is $src_1 + src_2$ with the first 24 bits set to zero
+16	Result is $src_1 + src_2$ with the first 16 bits set to zero

Figure 24.1 Major ALU operators available on Intel's microengine. The *alu* instruction specifies which operation to perform.

In addition to the basic *alu* operations described above, the hardware supports an *alu_shf* operation that provides the same functionality as *alu* and also shifts (or rotates) the result. The general form of the ALU plus shift operation is:

$$alu\_shf\ [\ dst,\ src_1,\ op,\ src_2,\ shift\ ]$$

where *shift* can specify a bit rotation or a right or left bit shift. For example, $<<3$ denotes a left shift by three bits, $>>12$ denotes a right shift by twelve bits, and $>>rot3$ denotes a right rotation by three bits.

As another example of operand syntax, consider the memory access instructions, which have the form:

$$sram\ [\ direction,\ xfer\_reg,\ addr_1,\ addr_2,\ count\ ],\ optional\_token$$
$$sdram\ [\ direction,\ xfer\_reg,\ addr_1,\ addr_2,\ count\ ],\ optional\_token$$
$$scratch\ [\ direction,\ xfer\_reg,\ addr_1,\ addr_2,\ count\ ],\ optional\_token$$

Operand *direction* can specify *read* (to extract a value from memory) or *write* (to store a value into memory)†. Operand *count* specifies the number of data units to transfer; a count is always measured in units of the underlying memory (e.g., sdram assumes the count specifies eight-byte units). Although a transfer can exceed the size of a

---

†The *direction* can also specify operations such as *r_fifo_rd* and *bit_wr*.

single transfer register, operand *xfer_reg* only specifies an initial transfer register. If additional registers are needed for the transfer, the hardware automatically uses contiguous registers.

The hardware adds addresses $addr_1$ and $addr_2$ to form the memory address to use in the transfer. Having two separate address fields offers two advantages. First, two fields allow a programmer to use a *base plus offset* approach. For example, a programmer can place the address of a packet in a register. The register is specified as $addr_1$, and an offset within the packet is specified as $addr_2$. Second, the use of two addresses permits scaling because it allows the address space to exceed the size of a single register.

As a final example, consider the operands used with the *immed* operator (short for *immediate*), which allows a programmer to load a constant into a register. The general form is:

immed [*dst, ival, rot*]

where *dst* denotes a destination register, and *ival* denotes an immediate value (i.e., a constant) to be loaded. Although an *ival* is thirty-two bits long, the upper sixteen bits must either contain all ones or all zeroes. Operand *rot* specifies a bit rotation that is applied to *ival* before the result is stored in *dst*; operand *rot* must use one of the following forms:

0	No rotation
<<0	No rotation (same as 0)
<<8	Rotate to the left by eight bits
<<16	Rotate to the left by sixteen bits

For example, the instruction:

immed [somereg, 0xFFFF0DEC, <<8]

shifts 0xFFFF0DEC left eight bits to produce 0xFF0DEC00, and stores the result in register *somereg*.

In addition to the basic *immed* instruction, microengine hardware offers a set of immediate instructions that load part of a register without changing other parts:

immed_b0	Load byte zero (low-order byte) only
immed_b1	Load byte one only
immed_b2	Load byte two only
immed_b3	Load byte three only
immed_w0	Load word zero (low-order 16 bits) only
immed_w1	Load word one only

24.5 Symbolic Register Names And Allocation

Because microengines follow a RISC architecture, many instructions refer to registers. Unlike assemblers that require a programmer to encode specific register addresses in the code, Intel's microengine assembler provides a level of indirection: a programmer writes assembly code that contains *symbolic* names for registers. For example, a programmer can choose to name a register *loopindx*, and can use the symbolic name in all instructions. Symbolic names improve program readability, and help reduce errors. More important, the use of symbolic register names allows code segments to be reused easily.

Because the underlying hardware requires a numeric reference for a register, symbolic register names in a program must be translated into numbers during assembly. The process is known as *register assignment* or *register allocation*. The Intel assembler requires a programmer to choose among two distinct approaches:

- *Manual assignment:* the programmer assigns each symbolic register name to a specific hardware register.

- *Automatic assignment:* the programmer allows the assembler to assign each symbolic name to a specific register.

Manual assignment places full responsibility on the programmer. In addition to general-purpose registers, manual assignment applies to transfer registers. Figure 24.2 lists the set of directives used to assign register names and the meaning of each.

Directive	Type Of Register Assigned
.areg	General-purpose register from the A bank
.breg	General-purpose register from the B bank
.$reg	SRAM transfer register
.$$reg	SDRAM transfer register

Figure 24.2 The directives used to assign symbolic register names to specific hardware registers. Such directives are only used if the programmer decides to make the assignment manually.

The important point is that a programmer must choose between manual and automatic assignment for the entire program; the assembler does not handle a mixture of the two approaches. We can summarize:

Intel's microengine assembler uses symbolic names for registers, and then maps each name to a specific register. A programmer can use directives to specify the mapping manually or can allow the assembler to choose a mapping, but cannot mix automatic and manual assignments.

24.6 Register Types And Syntax

Recall from Chapter 20 that a microengine has general-purpose registers, SRAM transfer registers, and SDRAM transfer registers. Further recall that each type has two basic addressing modes: *context relative* and *absolute*. To distinguish among the types and modes, a programmer prepends a special character combination onto a symbolic name. For example, a single *dollar sign* ($) denotes an SRAM transfer register; a pair of dollar signs ($$) denotes an SDRAM transfer register; and an *at sign* (@) denotes an absolute register reference. Figure 24.3 lists the possible combinations.

Register Type	Relative	Absolute
General-purpose	register_name	@register_name
SRAM transfer	$register_name	@$register_name
SDRAM transfer	$$register_name	@$$register_name

Figure 24.3 The microengine assembler syntax used to denote a register type and the address mode. An at-sign always makes a name absolute.

Note that the register type mechanism is prone to errors because the assembler does not include all type information. In particular, the hardware uses separate read and write transfer registers, but assigns the same number to each. The ambiguity is especially important during debugging because it means a programmer cannot verify values — if a programmer places data in a write transfer register and then attempts to read the data back, the hardware will extract data from the corresponding read transfer register. The point is:

Separate read and write transfer registers use the same register number. A programmer must be careful to avoid confusing read and write registers because the assembler does not assign each register an I/O type and does not prevent such errors.

24.7 Local Register Scope, Nesting, And Shadowing

The microengine assembler defines the *scope* of a name to consist of the set of statements in the program over which the name is valid. In particular, Intel's assembler includes two directives that begin and terminate a scope. Directive *.local* lists a set of register names and defines the beginning of a scope; directive *.endlocal* terminates the scope. Figure 24.4 shows an example that defines three register names.

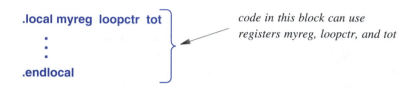

Figure 24.4 An example of the .local directive used to declare the scope of a register. The register names are only valid on code within the scope.

Local scope helps solve the problem of register constraints by allowing the assembler to reassign registers once the scope ends. In the figure above, for example, the assembler might choose to assign *myreg* to register 1, *loopctr* to register 2, and *tot* to register 3. If the programmer creates another scope following the *.endlocal*, the assembler can use registers 1, 2, and 3 for the new scope.

Local scopes can be nested, which allows some registers to be reused while others are reserved. For example, Figure 24.5 shows three local scopes that declare a total of six symbolic names. The nesting permits the assignment to be satisfied with four registers.

Intel uses *shadowing* to define the behavior of nested scopes with the same identifier. A nested scope is allowed to declare the same register name as an outer scope. In such cases, the assembler assumes the declarations refer to two different registers, and assigns priority to the inner scope. That is, if an outer scope and an inner scope both declare a register name *x*, references to *x* that occur within the inner scope all refer to the inner declaration.

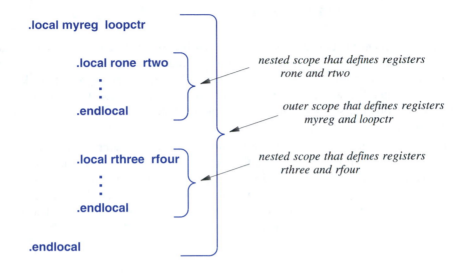

Figure 24.5 An example of nested scope declarations and the set of register names that are known in each. Although it is not required, indentation helps a programmer understand the nesting.

24.8 Register Assignments And Conflicts

Whether register assignments are handled manually or automatically, an interesting problem can arise. To understand the problem, recall that the underlying hardware mandates register bank alignment. That is, the operands for an instruction must come from opposite register banks. Consider three successive computation steps:

$$Z \leftarrow Q + R;$$
$$Y \leftarrow R + S;$$
$$X \leftarrow Q + S;$$

If Q has been assigned to bank A, the addition in the first step requires R to be assigned to bank B. Similarly, in the second step, because R is assigned to bank B, S must be assigned to bank A. The third step creates a *conflict* in the register assignment because Q and S have both been assigned to bank A.

There is no easy resolution of a register conflict — the code must be rewritten to avoid the conflict. Thus, if it encounters a conflict during automatic register assignment, the assembler simply reports the error to the programmer. The programmer must rewrite the code, and reassemble the program.

24.9 The Macro Preprocessor

Intel's microengine assembler includes a *preprocessor* that generates input for the assembler. The name is appropriate because the preprocessor can be viewed as a separate program that runs before the assembler. That is, the preprocessor reads and processes the input file, and generates an intermediate source representation without using the results of the assembly process. The intermediate representation then becomes input to the assembler.

The assembler preprocessor is derived from a traditional C preprocessor; there are both similarities and differences. Like a C preprocessor, for example, it handles *file inclusion* and definition of *symbolic constants*. Unlike a traditional C preprocessor, however, the assembler preprocessor does not allow parameters on symbolic constants. Instead, it offers a fully parameterized assembly language macro facility. The list below summarizes the preprocessor's functionality:

- File inclusion
- Symbolic constant substitution
- Conditional assembly
- Parameterized macro expansion
- Arithmetic expression evaluation
- Iterative generation of code

Recall that macro preprocessor statements are distinguished from other statements by the presence of a pound sign (*#*) as the initial character of the first token on the line. Figure 24.6 lists the preprocessor statements along with the meaning of each.

24.10 Macro Definition

Macros can be defined and invoked at any point in a program. Definitions have the form:

#macro *name* [*parameter₁, parameter₂,...*]
                   lines of text
#endm

where *name* is the name of the macro, *parameter_i* is the name of the ith formal argument, and *lines of text* consists of lines up to the next occurrence of *#endm*. For example, consider a macro to compute an expression $a = b + c + 5$. We will assume that *a*, *b*, and *c* are registers, and that the macro defines a scope to declare a temporary register, *tmp*.

Keyword	Use
#include	Include a file
#define	Definition of a symbolic constant (unparameterized)
#define_eval	Definition of a symbolic constant to be the value of an arithmetic expression
#undef	Remove a previous symbolic constant definition
#macro	Start the definition of a parameterized assembly language macro
#endm	End a macro definition started with #macro
#ifdef	Start conditional compilation if specified symbolic constant has been defined
#ifndef	Start conditional compilation if specified symbolic constant has not been defined
#if	Start conditional compilation if expression is true
#else	Terminate current conditional compilation and start alternative part of conditional compilation
#elif	Terminate current conditional compilation and start another if expression is true
#endif	Terminate current conditional compilation
#for	Start definite iteration to generate a code segment a fixed number of times
#while	Start indefinite iteration to generate a code segment while a condition holds
#repeat	Start indefinite iteration to repeat a code segment as long as a condition holds
#endloop	Terminate an iteration

Figure 24.6 The preprocessor statements available with Intel's microengine assembler. The preprocessor generates code that the assembler processes.

The code for the macro to compute $a = b + c + 5$ is:

```
/* example macro add5 that computes a=b+c+5
#macro add5[a, b, c]
        .local tmp
                alu[tmp, c, +, 5]
                alu[a, b, +, tmp]
        .endlocal
#endm
```

When a macro is invoked, actual arguments are substituted in the place of formal parameters. For example, *add5[var1, var2, var3]* expands to:

```
.local tmp
        alu[tmp, var3, +, 5]
        alu[var1, var2, +, tmp]
.endlocal
```

Because macro substitution is performed by the preprocessor, the substitution is *syntactic*. That is, the definition and invocation of macros occur before the assembler parses and checks the file. Consequently, if the code in a macro contains syntactic or semantic errors, the errors will not be detected or exposed until the macro has been expanded and the assembler processes the results. More important, a macro does not distinguish among variables and parameters. For example, if a programmer inadvertently uses the name *tmp* as an actual argument to the *add5* macro, incorrect code will be produced. For example, *add5[var1, tmp, var3]* expands to:

```
.local tmp
        alu[tmp, var3, +, 5]
        alu[var1, tmp, +, tmp]
.endlocal
```

The point is:

The macro preprocessor performs text substitution and passes the result to the assembler without checking for errors. As a result, generated code can be syntactically incorrect or may not produce the desired result.

24.11 Repeated Generation Of A Code Segment

Preprocessor iteration statements permit a programmer to generate repeated occurrences of a code segment. The primary motivation is to provide a way to iterate code rather than have a loop at run time. As an example, consider the following:

```
#defineLOOP1
#while (LOOP < 4)
        alu_shf[reg, -, B, reg, >>LOOP]
#define_eval LOOP LOOP + 1
#endloop
```

which expands to:

```
        alu_shf[reg, -, B, reg, >>1]
        alu_shf[reg, -, B, reg, >>2]
        alu_shf[reg, -, B, reg, >>3]
```

24.12 Structured Programming Directives

In addition to the macro preprocessor, Intel's microengine assembler provides directives that permit a programmer to write *structured assembly code*. Figure 24.7 lists the structured directives.

Directive	Meaning
.if	Conditional execution
.elif	Terminate previous conditional execution and start a new conditional execution
.else	Terminate previous conditional execution and define an alternative
.endif	End .if conditional
.while	Indefinite iteration with test before
.endw	End .while loop
.repeat	Indefinite iteration with test after
.until	End .repeat loop
.break	Leave a loop
.continue	Skip to next iteration of loop

Figure 24.7 The structured directives that Intel's microengine assembler provides for a programmer. The use of structured directives raises the level of the language.

The structured programming directives are patterned after the control statements found in a conventional programming language, and have the expected semantics. For example, the code below shows the general form used with the conditional execution directives.

```
.if  (   conditional_expression   )
        /* block of microcode statements */
.elif  (   conditional_expression   )
        /* block of microcode statements */
.elif  (   conditional_expression   )
        /* block of microcode statements */

        .
        .
        .

.else
        /* block of microcode statements */
.endif
```

The first expression is evaluated, and if the expression is *true*, the microcode in the first block is executed. If the first expression is *false*, the second expression is evaluated, and so on. If none of the *conditional_expressions* has the value *true*, the last block of microcode (the code associated with the *.else* directive) is executed. As in most languages, *.elif* and *.else* clauses are optional.

Other directives also resemble their counterparts in a conventional programming language. For example, indefinite iteration has the form:

```
.while  (   conditional_expression   )
        /* block of microcode statements */
.endw
```

The *conditional_expression* is evaluated repeatedly, and the block of code is executed each time the expression evaluates to *true*.

Structured directives can be nested which means that the blocks of code to be executed can contain further calls to structured directives. In particular, if the generated code contains labels, a unique label is generated for each occurrence. The generation of unique labels allows a programmer to create arbitrary compositions of structured directives at arbitrary depth. Thus, a *.if* can contain a *.while* that contains a *.if*.

Conditional expressions used with structured directives can include many of the operators used in the C language, including the integer comparison operators <, >, <=, >=, ==, !=, and the bit shift operators << and >>†. Parentheses are used to group tests, and the C operators && and || are used for left-to-right evaluation of *and* and *or*.

In addition to the C operators described above, a conditional expression can include any of the tests that Figure 24.8 lists.

---

†The ALU can perform bit shifts during a comparison.

Operator	Meaning
BIT	Test whether a bit in a register is set
BYTE	Test whether a byte in a register equals a constant
COUT	Test whether a carry occurred on the previous operation
CTX	Test the currently executing thread number
SIGNAL	Test whether a specified signal has arrived for a thread
INP_STATE	Test whether the thread is in a specified state

Figure 24.8 Tests that can be included in the conditional expression of a structured assembly language directive. Tests can be combined with conventional Boolean operators.

Note, the tests performed by *BIT*, *COUT*, *SIGNAL*, and *INP_STATE* can be inverted by prepending an exclamation mark to the name. Thus, *! COUT* tests whether a carry did not occur on the previous operation.

24.13 Instructions That Can Cause A Context Switch

Recall that although a microengine can only execute one instruction at a time, the hardware has support for four threads or contexts, and the hardware can switch from one thread to another. Control of context switching rests with the software. That is, the microengine hardware does not employ *preemption* — the programmer must specify exactly when a context switch should occur.

How does the software control hardware context switching? There are two mechanisms:

- Executing the *ctx_arb* instruction
- Executing a reference instruction

The first mechanism is easiest to understand: the *ctx_arb* instruction informs the hardware that the currently executing thread is ready to relinquish control. Usually, a thread executes *ctx_arb* to wait for an operation to complete. When the current thread executes *ctx_arb*, the hardware chooses another thread to execute. The *ctx_arb* instruction takes an argument that specifies whether the current thread is suspended or permanently terminated; parameter choices are:

voluntary	The current thread is suspended until later
signal_event	The current thread is suspended until the specified signal arrives
kill	The current thread permanently ceases execution

The second mechanism a thread uses to relinquish control is a *reference instruction*; Intel uses the term for an instruction that references memory, a FIFO, the hash unit, or another functional unit (i.e., an instruction that incurs a long delay). Each reference instruction allows the programmer to specify an additional *token* that controls context switching. The token choices are:

ctx_swap	The current thread will relinquish the processor, and not become eligible to run again until the operation completes.
sig_done	The current thread continues to run, and requests that a signal be posted when the operation completes.

The hardware defines signals for each possible functional unit or software event: *sram, sdram, fbi, pci, inter_thread, autopush, start_receive, seq_num1,* and *seq_num2*†. In the case of a reference instruction, the signal corresponds to the instruction itself (e.g., the *sram* signal corresponds to the *sram* instruction). In the case of a *ctx_arb* instruction, however, a programmer can list a specific signal. Thus, if a programmer has arranged for an *sdram* signal to arrive, the programmer can issue a *ctx_arb* instruction that specifies *sdram*. The thread will be blocked until the *sdram* signal arrives, at which time the thread becomes eligible again. Eligibility does not force a context switch — the thread will not run until a context switch occurs and the processor chooses the thread.

As an example, consider an instruction that accesses SDRAM:

$$\text{sdram} [\,\text{read, \$\$rbuf0, base, 2, 4}\,], \ \text{sig\_done}$$

The presence of *sig_done* following the instruction indicates that the thread will continue to execute while the SDRAM transfer proceeds, and instructs the hardware to raise a signal when the transfer completes.

24.14 Indirect Reference

In many cases, the size of a memory transfer is not known at compile time (e.g., the transfer may depend on the size of a packet). To handle such cases, microengine hardware includes an *indirect reference*‡ mechanism that allows the programmer to use the result of an ALU instruction to modify the reference instruction that immediately follows. Although any ALU instruction can be used, programmers usually specify an ALU instruction that does not modify state (i.e., the result is computed merely to be used in an indirect reference). The reference instruction to be modified can be one of the following: *fast_wr*, a Scratchpad memory operation (*read, write,* or *bit_wr*), an SDRAM operation (*read, write, rfifo_wr,* or *tfifo_wr*), an SRAM operation (*read, write, push,* or *pop*), or a FIFO operation (*r_fifo_rd* or *t_fifo_wr*).

---

†A *seq_num* signal occurs when the hardware increments a sequence number to enqueue an arriving packet.

‡Unlike the conventional use of the term, Intel's indirect reference mechanism does not follow pointers; the terminology is confusing at best.

To use an indirect reference, a programmer must compute an encoded value that specifies exactly what field of the next instruction to modify and what value to use for the modification. For example, consider the *scratch* instruction used to read from Scratchpad memory. Indirect reference allows a programmer to modify any of four fields:

- The microengine associated with the memory reference
- The first transfer register in a block that will receive the result
- A count of words of memory to transfer
- The thread ID of the hardware thread executing the instruction (i.e., the thread to signal upon completion)

In cases where the count of words to transfer depends on the data, a constant value will not suffice — the count must be computed at runtime. Indirect reference allows the count to be extracted from the previous ALU instruction. To do so, the programmer must specify a value for the count and a value that specifies which field of the instruction to modify. The two values are encoded into a thirty-two bit binary value. For example, bit twenty corresponds to the count field; when bit twenty is set, the new count is specified in bits sixteen through nineteen. Consider the two instructions below:

$$alu\_shf\,[\,--,\,--,\,b,\,0x13,\,<<16\,]$$
$$scratch\,[\,read,\,\$reg0,\,addr1,\,addr2,\,0\,],\,indirect\_ref$$

The ALU instruction shifts 0x13 left sixteen bits, which places *0x1* in bit twenty (i.e., turns on bit twenty), and places *0x3* in bits sixteen through nineteen. The destination is coded as two minus signs, which specifies no destination (i.e., the value is computed, but not stored). Although the *scratch* instruction is coded with a count of zero, the indirect reference token causes the value from the previous instruction to be used as a modifier. Thus, the *count* field in the *scratch* instruction will be replaced by the integer three, which means that four words will be read from Scratchpad memory†.

24.15 External Transfers

All external data transfers (e.g., to or from external memory) use *transfer registers*. To perform an external transfer, the programmer must:

---

†A value of N in the *count* field means that $N+1$ words of memory are transferred (i.e., the count is one less than the transfer size).

1. Allocate a contiguous set of transfer registers to hold the data.
2. Start a reference instruction that moves data into or out of the allocated transfer registers.
3. Arrange for the thread to wait until the operation completes.

To perform the first step, the programmer uses two assembler directives: *.local* and either *.xfer_order_rd* or *.xfer_order_wr*. The *.local* directive declares names for registers, but does not provide a way to specify that they must be contiguous. The *.xfer_order*†, *.xfer_order_rd* or *.xfer_order_wr* directive handles the task — one of the *.xfer_order* directives must immediately follow a *.local* directive to specify an ordering among registers. For example, the following two directives allocate four SRAM transfer registers and request them to be contiguous:

.local $reg1 $reg2 $reg3 $reg4
.xfer_order $reg1 $reg2 $reg3 $reg4

The second step requires the use of a reference instruction to transfer data between the external functional unit and the transfer registers. Two of the most heavily used instructions, *sram* and *sdram*, allow indirect reference, which means that the amount of data to be transferred can be specified at runtime.

The third step has been described in a previous section. The thread can execute the *ctx_arb* instruction to request that the hardware switch to another context. Alternatively, the thread can perform computation unrelated to the data being transferred. Note that the computation does not need to exceed the expected delay: a thread can start a reference instruction, request a signal, perform other (unrelated) computation, and then execute a *ctx_arb* to wait for the signal.

24.16 Library Macros And Transfer Register Allocation

Intel provides predefined library macros that allocate and deallocate transfer registers: *xbuf_alloc[]* and *xbuf_free[]*. The macros use preprocessor variables to count the number of transfer registers allocated. If a programmer tries to allocate too many transfer registers, the macros will report an error.

As an example of allocation, suppose a programmer needs to allocate SDRAM transfer registers. The following call of *xbuf_alloc[]* allocates four contiguous SDRAM transfer registers, and names them *$$buf0*, *$$buf1*, *$$buf2*, and *$$buf3*:

xbuf_alloc[$$buf, 4]

---

†The directive *.xfer_order* specifies both read and write transfer registers must be contiguous.

Because each transfer register is thirty-two bits long, the second argument to *xbuf_alloc[]* specifies the number of thirty-two bit registers. Confusion can arise because reference instructions specify an amount of data in units appropriate to the underlying device. In particular, each SDRAM data transfer is measured in sixty-four bit quantities. Thus, to handle the data from an SDRAM transfer with count N, a programmer must allocate $2N$ transfer registers.

Recall that although a microengine contains independent sets of transfer registers for input and output, both sets are numbered starting at zero. Some functional units (e.g., the hash engine) use both input and output registers. One of the disadvantages of the library macros arises because they do not distinguish between read and write transfer registers. Instead, each allocation includes both directions. That is, the macro call above internally allocates a total of eight registers: four read registers and four write registers.

Additional macros are provided that help manipulate and manage buffers. Once a set of registers is no longer needed, macro *xbuf_free* is used to release them. For example, the following code releases the registers allocated above:

xbuf_free[$$buf]

24.17 Summary

The microengine assembler provided with Intel's SDK includes features that raise the level of the language, including: a macro preprocessor, structured programming directives, symbolic register names, and automated register assignment. Symbolic register names are defined in nested scopes; if a name is reused, the inner scope has precedence. Although register assignment is automated, unresolvable conflicts can still occur because the operands for each instruction must reside in opposite banks.

Although it offers functionality such as file inclusion and conditional assembly that are found in a traditional C preprocessor, the macro preprocessor offers functions that are not provided by a C preprocessor: parameterized assembly language macro expansion, arithmetic expression evaluation, and iterative generation of code. Parameterized macros can be defined or invoked at any point in the assembly code.

When an instructions references external memory or one of the other functional units, microengine hardware can switch to another thread to keep the microengine processor executing. Reference instructions offer flags that allow a programmer to specify whether the thread should be blocked to wait for completion, another thread should run, or the microengine should continue to execute until a later instruction checks for completion.

FOR FURTHER STUDY

Intel [2001d] provides detailed information on how to program the microengines. Intel [2001e] contains the specification for assembly language macros, and Intel [2001f] describes how macros are used to modularize code for the microengines. Johnson and Kunze [2001] illustrates programming microengines in MicroC.

EXERCISES

24.1   Use structured assembly directives to write a loop that reads exactly 48 bytes of memory.

24.2   Write a loop that starts at a memory address, and finds the first occurrence of a 1 bit. Hint: an instruction exists to find the first 1 bit in a register.

24.3   What error message results if a macro attempts to use a register without declaring the register with a *.local* directive?

24.4   How does the assembler use the flag *guess_branch*?

24.5   Give an example of a circumstance in which a *ctx_arb* instruction is needed.

24.6   Given the address of a buffer in SDRAM, an offset (zero through seven) in the buffer at which a packet resides, and a packet length in bytes, write code that copies the packet to transmit registers.

Chapter Contents

25

Microengine Programming II

25.1 Introduction

Earlier chapters in this section describe the Intel IXP1200 hardware and the software architecture of Intel's SDK. The previous chapter introduces microengine programming. This chapter continues the discussion. The chapter examines a variety of hardware and software facilities, including buffer pools, locking operations, and low-level I/O. The next chapter contains example code that shows how some of the mechanisms are used in practice.

25.2 Specialized Memory Operations

Recall that memories are shared among the StrongARM and microengines. To enable efficient sharing, the hardware and software have been designed to store bulk data in SDRAM, and to use SRAM and Scratchpad memories for control information and coordination. The facilities that Intel provides include:

- Buffer pool manipulation
- Processor coordination via bit testing
- Atomic memory increment
- Processor coordination via memory locking

The next sections each discuss one of these mechanisms. They explain the intended purpose, and give the microcode instructions or macros needed for access.

25.3 Buffer Pool Manipulation

The SRAM subsystem provides a mechanism that can be used to automate buffer allocation and deallocation. Under the system, a programmer can preallocate a set of buffers, and can assign the buffers to eight linked lists (numbered zero through seven). Each linked list operates as a stack: the StrongARM or a microengine uses an SRAM *pop* operation to extract a buffer from a list or an SRAM *push* operation to insert a buffer on a list. An extraction operation has the following form:

$$\text{sram} [\text{ pop}, \$xfer, --, --, listnum\ ]$$

where *$xfer* denotes an SRAM transfer register that will hold the result (the address of the first buffer on the list), and *listnum* is a value from zero through seven that denotes the linked list from which to extract a buffer. Similarly, an insertion operation has the form:

$$\text{sram} [\text{ push}, --, addr_1, addr_2, listnum\ ]$$

As usual, operands $addr_1$ and $addr_2$ are added to produce an address in SRAM; the buffer located at the resulting address is pushed onto the list specified by *listnum*.

To use the buffer mechanism, a programmer must initialize an empty list to consist of a special end token: a single word that points to itself. Typically, a program reserves word zero in memory, and stores zero in the location. When a buffer is pushed onto a list, the first word of the buffer is assigned a pointer to the next buffer on the list, and the last buffer on the list contains a pointer to the end token.

A program uses the end token to determine whether a list is empty: the list is empty if a *pop* operation returns an address that contains a pointer to itself. Using location zero does have a disadvantage: if an error results in a null pointer, the program can confuse the value with the end of a list.

25.4 Processor Coordination Via Bit Testing

Both SRAM and Scratchpad memories offer atomic operations on individual bits of any word in memory. To perform a bit operation, a programmer specifies *bit_wr* as the first operand, and the operation to perform as the fifth operand. Because microengines use physical memory addresses, however, a conventional address can only refer to a word in memory and not to individual bits. To overcome the limitation, an instruction that operates on bits contains both the address of a word in memory and a thirty-two bit mask. The mask specifies which bits of the word to use in the instruction. For example, a bit operation in Scratchpad memory has the form:

$$\text{scratch} [\text{ bit\_wr}, \$xfer, addr_1, addr_2, op\ ]$$

where *addr₁* and *addr₂* are added to form the address of a word in Scratchpad memory, and *$xfer* specifies an SRAM write transfer register that contains a thirty-two bit mask. If a bit of the mask is set to one, the operation is performed on the corresponding bit of the word in memory; if a bit of the mask is zero, the corresponding bit of the word in memory remains unchanged.

Operand *op* specifies an operation to be performed. Figure 25.1 lists the possible bit operations and their meanings.

Operation	Meaning
set_bits	Set the specified bits to one
clear_bits	Set the specified bits to zero
test_and_set_bits	Place the original word in the read transfer register, and set the specified bits to one
test_and_clear_bits	Place the original word in the read transfer register, and set the specified bits to zero

Figure 25.1 Possible values for the fifth operand in a bit manipulation operation. Each operation is guaranteed to be atomic.

As the figure indicates, SRAM and Scratchpad memories support conventional *test-and-set* operations. Multiple processors use test-and-set for mutual exclusion (e.g., to ensure that only one processor modifies a shared data structure at any time). To implement mutual exclusion, all processors must agree on a particular bit in memory, and then use test-and-set to change the bit from zero to one. The hardware ensures that if two or more processors attempt to execute test-and-set simultaneously, exactly one processor receives an initial bit value of zero; others receive an initial value of one.

25.5 Atomic Memory Increment

Because it has the lowest latency, Scratchpad memory is ideal for storing counters that must be updated for each packet. Unfortunately, if multiple microengines use conventional instructions to increment a shared counter, an incorrect value can result. For example, suppose two microengines simultaneously load the current value of a counter into a register, increment the register, and store the result back into the counter. If the counter began with the value N, the final value will be incorrect (i.e., $N+1$ instead of $N+2$).

To enable multiple processors to update shared counter values, the Scratchpad memory hardware offers an *atomic increment* facility. The instruction has the form:

$$\text{scratch} [\text{ incr}, --, addr_1, addr_2, 1]$$

As usual, *addr₁* and *addr₂* are added to form an address in Scratchpad memory. The value at the address is incremented, and the hardware guarantees that if multiple processors simultaneously use the *incr* instruction for a given address, each increment will be performed atomically, and the resulting count will be correct.

25.6 Processor Coordination Via Memory Locking

Although atomic memory increment and test-and-set both help coordinate multiple processors, Intel provides another mechanism that a programmer can use. SRAM is designed so individual words of memory act as mutual exclusion locks. The SRAM hardware offers a *memory lock* instruction. If multiple microengines attempt to lock the same word in memory simultaneously, the hardware allows one microengine to succeed, and blocks other microengines until the lock has been released. When a microengine releases a lock, the hardware selects one of the microengines that are waiting for the lock, and allows the microengine to proceed. The StrongARM can also participate in memory locking, but uses a slightly different approach that does not block the processor. If it must deny a lock request, the hardware merely sets a bit in a Control and Status Register to inform the StrongARM. To determine when the lock has been released, the StrongARM can choose to repeatedly poll; to avoid polling overhead, the StrongARM can arrange for an interrupt to occur when the lock has been released.

The SRAM hardware combines memory locking with other SRAM operations. For example, a programmer can issue a single instruction that obtains a lock on a memory location and reads values starting at that location:

sram [read_lock, $xfer, addr₁, addr₂, count], ctx_swap

As usual, *addr₁* and *addr₂* are added to produce an address, *$xfer* specifies the first read transfer register, and *count* specifies the number of thirty-two bit words to read. The hardware acquires a lock on the first word of the data before the transfer occurs. The token *ctx_swap* is required because the microengine must block until the lock can be acquired.

Similarly, a microengine can execute a *write_unlock* operation that includes unlocking:

sram [write_unlock, $xfer, addr₁, addr₂, count], ctx_swap

As in the *read_lock* operation, the hardware performs two operations: it first deposits a value, and then unlocks the address. Also like the *read_lock* operation, the token *ctx_swap* is required because the processor can block.

When it finishes using a lock, a microengine must unlock the address to allow other microengines access. If it does not need to write a value, the processor can execute an *unlock* instruction which has the form shown below. No optional tokens are needed because unlocking is not a blocking instruction.

sram [unlock, --, *addr₁*, *addr₂*, 1]

Although a programmer can choose an arbitrary address to lock, the SRAM hardware does not allow more than eight addresses to be locked simultaneously. The SRAM controller contains a CAM that holds eight entries. When an address is locked, the address is placed in the CAM. If a microengine attempts to lock an address that is already in the CAM (i.e., previously locked), the microengine is blocked.

The implementation of memory locking has an interesting consequence for programmers. The hardware maintains a queue that is known as the *Read_lock Fail Queue*. When a microengine attempts to lock an address that is already locked or if the CAM is full, the hardware places the microengine on the Read_lock Fail Queue. When an unlock operation occurs, the hardware removes the address from CAM, and then processes the Read_lock Fail Queue sequentially. If the first request on the queue can be serviced, the hardware grants the request, and goes on to the next item on the queue. When it encounters an item that cannot be serviced, the hardware stops processing the queue. Thus, an *unlock* operation can cause multiple requests to be granted, but will only grant contiguous requests.

To understand the consequence for programmers, consider the following sequence of events:

- Thread A requests a lock on address X.
- Thread B requests a lock on address Y.
- Thread C requests a lock on address X.
- Thread D requests a lock on address Y.
- Thread B unlocks address Y.

The first two requests succeed. Both *C* and *D* are blocked, with *C* being the first entry on the Read_Fail Queue. When thread *B* unlocks address *Y*, the hardware examines the queue. Unfortunately, because the first request on the queue (i.e., thread *C*) cannot be granted, the hardware stops processing the queue, and does not grant *D*'s request to lock *Y*. We can summarize:

> *Because Intel's SRAM locking hardware uses a queue of requests that must be satisfied in order, a thread can remained blocked even if its request can be satisfied.*

25.7 Control And Status Registers

An IXP1200 has over one hundred fifty *Control And Status Registers* (*CSRs*) that allow processors to configure, monitor, interrogate, and control devices on the chip. Many CSRs are available to both the StrongARM and microengines; others are restricted to the StrongARM only.

On the StrongARM, CSRs are mapped into a single address space along with memory and devices. On a microengine, the hardware provides special instructions that are used to access CSRs. The most common access uses a *csr* instruction:

csr [*cmd, $xfer, CSR, count*]

where *cmd* specifies *read* or *write*, *$xfer* specifies a read or write SRAM transfer register, *CSR* specifies a specific control or status register, and *count* specifies the number of words to transfer to or from the CSR. Interestingly, the count is one in cases where the CSR transfers thirty-two or sixty-four bits — the only exception to a count of one occurs with a *get_cmd*, which can transfer more than sixty-four bits. If it is omitted, *count* defaults to one.

As an alternative to the *csr* command, the microengine hardware includes a fast path through the FBI to a subset of the CSRs; instruction *fast_wr* provides access through the fast path. The general form is:

fast_wr [*immediate_data, CSR*]

where *immediate_data* is a constant contained in the instruction (which is limited to ten bits), and *CSR* denotes the control or status register into which the constant should be written. The *fast_wr* instruction is needed when speed is essential (e.g., to control inter-thread communication and to prepare TFIFOs), but cannot be used for large constants.

In addition to CSRs associated with functional units on the chip, each microengine has a set of *local CSRs* that hold information on signals, event status, and current execution state. Because they are onboard the microengine, local CSRs can be accessed in a single cycle.

The *local_csr_wr* instruction, which writes a value to a local CSR, has the form:

local_csr_wr [*CSR, src*]

where *CSR* denotes a specific CSR (which must be one of the local CSRs), and *src* denotes a general purpose register or an immediate constant. A constant of zero is especially useful for clearing all bits of a CSR.

The *local_csr_rd* instruction has unusual semantics: the result of the instruction is passed directly to the next instruction, which must be an *immed* instruction. A programmer codes a sequence in which the value of an immediate constant is overridden at run time. The hardware obtains the value from the specified CSR, and stores the value in *destreg*.

local_csr_rd [*CSR*]
immed [*destreg*, 0]

25.8 Intel Dispatch Loop Macros

In addition to other facilities, Intel's SDK provides macros to automate many of the steps needed to manage I/O buffers, store state information with a packet, and move packets among ACEs. The macros store data in registers that are accessible in all code called by the dispatch loop. Figure 25.2 lists the macros related to buffer manipulation and the dispatch loop along with the purpose of each.

Macro	Purpose
Buf_Alloc	Allocate a packet buffer
Buf_GetData	Get the SDRAM address of a packet buffer (note: the name is misleading)
DL_Drop	Drop a packet and recycle the buffer
DL_GetBufferLength	Compute the length (in bytes) of the packet portion of a buffer
DL_GetBufferOffset	Compute the offset of packet data within a buffer
DL_GetInputPort	Obtain the input port over which the packet arrived
DL_GetOutputPort	Find the port over which the packet will be sent
DL_GetRxStat	Obtain the receive status of the packet
DL_Init	Initialize the dispatch loop macros
DL_MESink	Send a packet to next microblock group
DL_SASink	Send a packet to the StrongARM
DL_SASource	Receive a packet from the StrongARM
DL_SetAceTag	Specify the microblock that is handling a packet so the StrongARM will know
DL_SetBufferLength	Specify the length of packet data in the buffer
DL_SetBufferOffset	Specify the offset of packet data in the buffer
DL_SetExceptionCode	Specify the exception code for the StrongARM
DL_SetInputPort	Specify the port over which the packet arrived
DL_SetOutputPort	Specify the port on which the packet will be sent
DL_SetRxStat	Specify the receive status of the packet

Figure 25.2 Intel macros related to buffer management and the dispatch loop. Many of the macros access state information that is kept with each packet.

In addition to the macros in Figure 25.2, Intel provides macros that perform *device-independent I/O*. That is, the macros allow a programmer to send or receive packets without knowing specific details of the underlying hardware device. For example, macro *EthernetIngress* allows a programmer to obtain the next Ethernet packet without knowing whether the physical interface hardware runs at one hundred megabits per second or one gigabit per second. Similarly, macro *DL_EgressSink* allows a microengine to send a packet to an Ethernet egress port without knowing the details of the underlying hardware.

Intel also supplies macros that an egress microblock group can use to select packets to send. There are two basic approaches: a round-robin selection or a strict First-In-First-Out (FIFO) order among a set of queues. The two macros are:

> *RoundRobinSource*   Use round-robin selection
> *FifoSource*   Use FIFO selection

In practice, *RoundRobinSource* is used when an IXP1200 handles multiple 10/100 Ethernet ports, and *FifoSource* is used to handle Gigabit Ethernet.

25.9 Packet Queues And Selection

We said that a microblock group uses macro *DL_SASource* to obtain a packet that has been sent by the StrongARM. In addition, an ingress microblock group uses *EthernetIngress* to obtain incoming Ethernet frames, and an egress microblock group uses *RoundRobinSource* or *FifoSource* to select packets from queues of outgoing packets. The question arises: how does a microblock group arbitrate among packets from multiple sources?

The dispatch loop acts in a round-robin manner by repeatedly calling the macros for each of the possible input sources. If a particular source has no packets, the associated macro returns *IX_BUFFER_NULL*, which causes the dispatch loop to immediately proceed to the macro for the next input. Priority among the sources is handled by the individual macros. For example, *DL_SASource* uses constant *SA_CONSUME_NUM* to implement lower priority for packets that arrive from the StrongARM. To understand how priority operates, consider a situation in which the StrongARM is generating packets fast enough to keep the queue from becoming empty. If *SA_CONSUME_NUM* is one, each call to *DL_SASource* returns a packet. Thus, each iteration of the dispatch loop processes one packet from the StrongARM. If *SA_CONSUME_NUM* has a value *N* that is greater than one, the first call of *DL_SASource* returns a packet; the next *N−1* calls return *IX_BUFFER_NULL*, even though packets are waiting. Thus, on most iterations of the dispatch loop, no packets are processed from the StrongARM.

Macros also exist to aid in disposing of packets. Microblock code assigns a value to variable *dl_buffer_next* to mark a packet as destined either for discard, the StrongARM, the next microblock group, or for transmission over a physical network. For example, a dispatch loop invokes macro *DL_Drop* to drop the packet or *DL_SASink* to enqueue the packet as an exception for the StrongARM. Before enqueuing a packet for the StrongARM, the microengine must call macro *DL_SetAceTag* to associate the packet with a particular ACE and macro *DL_SetExceptionCode* to record the type of the exception. Finally, the dispatch loop invokes macro *DL_MESink* to enqueue a packet for another microblock group. *DL_MESink* uses the target binding specified in file *ixsys.config* to determine which microblock group should receive the packet.

How does packet flow occur in practice? A typical dispatch loop checks two possible sources of packets: the StrongARM and either a physical device or a queue from another microengine. The dispatch loop chooses among three dispositions for a packet: drop, send to the StrongARM, or send to either a physical device or enqueue for the next microengine. Figure 25.3 illustrates the dispatch loop structure.

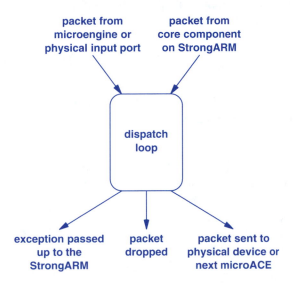

Figure 25.3 Illustration of the packet sources and sinks in a typical dispatch loop used with the Intel SDK. The dispatch loop repeatedly checks each source, processes a packet, and then chooses one of the sinks for the packet.

25.10 Accessing Fields In A Packet Header

In most computer architectures, individual fields in a packet header can be addressed as fixed offsets beyond a pointer to the packet header; the code is trivial. In a microengine, however, several steps are required before the data can be accessed. The program must allocate transfer registers to hold the packet header, compute the location of the packet within a buffer, and load the header into the transfer registers. Figure 25.4 illustrates the code.

As the figure shows, differences in the size of data items requires many conversions. For example, although macro *DL_GetBufferOffset* returns an offset measured in bytes, SDRAM references data in eight-byte units. Thus, the byte offset must be divided by eight. The code accomplishes the division by shifting. Another difference in size arises because each SDRAM transfer register holds four bytes. Thus, eight transfer registers must be allocated to hold the data fetched by an *sdram* instruction with a count of four.

```
/* Allocate eight SDRAM transfer registers to hold the packet header */
xbuf_alloc [ $$hdr, 8 ]

/* Reserve two general-purpose registers for the computation */
.local base offset

        /* Compute the SDRAM address of the data buffer */
        Buf_GetData [ base, dl_buffer_handle ]

        /* Compute the byte offset of the start of the packet in the buffer */
        DL_GetBufferOffset [ offset ]

        /* Convert the byte offset to SDRAM words by dividing by eight */
        /* (shift right by three bits) */
        alu_shf [ offset, --, B, offset, >>3 ]

        /* Load thirty-two bytes of data from SDRAM into eight SDRAM */
        /* transfer registers.  Start at SDRAM address  base + offset */
        sdram [ read, $$hdr0, base, offset, 4 ]

/* Inform the assembler that we have finished using the two */
/* registers: base and offset */
.endlocal

/* Process the packet header in the SDRAM transfer registers */
/* starting at register $$hdr */
. . .

/* Free the SDRAM transfer registers when finished */
xbuf_free [ $$hdr ]
```

Figure 25.4 Illustration of the code needed to access a packet header given
buffer handle *dl_buffer_handle*. Each word of SDRAM contains
eight bytes.

25.11 Initialization Required For Dispatch Loop Macros

Intel's dispatch loop macros require a programmer to perform five steps:

- Define three symbolic constants
- Declare registers with a *.local* directive
- Use a *.import_var* directive to name tag values (optional)
- Include the macros pertinent to the microblock
- Initialize the macros as the first part of a dispatch loop

Figure 25.5 lists the three symbolic constants that must be defined before the dispatch loop macros can be included.

Constant	Value And Meaning
SA_CONSUME_NUM	The number of packets an ingress microACE processes for each StrongARM packet. A value of N means that N-1 MAC packets will be processed each time one StrongARM packet is processed. The usual value is thirty-one.
IX_EXCEPTION	The value for macros to return when raising an exception. The usual value is zero.
SEQNUM_IGNORE	A sequence number to assign to StrongARM packets when using Gigabit Ethernet (FastPort)

Figure 25.5 The symbolic constants that must be defined before Intel's dispatch loop macros can be included in a program.

The second step is straightforward: the program must contain a *.local* directive that declares registers that will be used. The directive has the following form:

.local dl_reg1 dl_reg2 dl_reg3 dl_buffer_handle dl_next_block

If a program references thread IDs or flow IDs, the *.local* directive must also name register *dl_reg4*.

The third step is needed in any microblock that sends exceptions to the StrongARM (i.e., passes packets to the core component). The *.import_var* directive names tag values that the dispatch loop uses to direct exceptions to the correct core component. For example:

.import_var IPV4_TAG

names tag *IPV4_TAG*.

Once the first three steps have been handled, a program can include Intel dispatch loop macros and other macros pertinent to the microblock. Note that the order of statements in a program is important because the dispatch loop files have been created to assume definitions and declarations are in place. The point is:

The order of definitions and declarations is crucial — requisite constants and register declarations must occur before the include statement that references Intel's dispatch loop macros.

To include dispatch loop macros, a programmer references two files:

> DispatchLoop_h.uc
>
> DispatchLoopImportVars.h

If the microblock is a part of an ingress ACE that reads from an Ethernet device, the program should also include:

> EthernetIngress.uc

Similarly, if the microblock is a part of an egress ACE, the program should include:

> EthernetEgress.uc

A programmer must ensure that Intel's macros are initialized before they are used. The program calls *DL_Init* to initialize the basic dispatch loop macros. An ingress or egress microblock that uses Intel's ingress or egress macros must also initialize the macros. Thus, the dispatch loop for an ingress microblock begins with a series of initialization calls:

> DL_Init [ ]
>
> EthernetIngress_Init [ ]
>
> . . .   /* Other microblock initialization calls */

An egress microblock has the same structure as an ingress microblock, except that the call to *EthernetIngress_Init* is replaced by a call to *EthernetEgress_Init* and then either *RoundRobin_Init* or *Fifo_Init*.

25.12 Packet I/O And The Concept Of Mpackets

The ingress and egress macros hide many of the I/O details. For example, the physical network hardware that attaches to an IXP1200 does not operate like the interface hardware on a conventional computer because the IX bus hardware does not perform DMA to memory and does not transfer entire frames. Instead, all transfers between the network interface hardware and a microengine are limited to sixty-four octets. Thus, a large frame must be divided into blocks that are each transferred independently.

The network interface hardware on an IX bus handles the transfer of incoming frames. Once it has received a frame, the interface hardware divides the frame into sixty-four octet blocks that are known as *MAC packets* (*mpackets*)†. Acting under in-

---

†If a frame is not a multiple of sixty-four octets, the final mpacket will contain fewer than sixty-four octets.

structions from a microengine, the interface hardware performs a series of operations that each transfer one mpacket to a microengine. A microengine handles the division of an outgoing frame into mpackets. When it has a frame to send, the microengine divides the frame into mpackets, and then sends each mpacket to the MAC hardware.

On input, the interface hardware sends additional information about each mpacket. When it moves an mpacket into a Receive FIFO, the hardware places the information into an auxiliary control field in the RFIFO entry. Among other things, the additional information specifies whether the mpacket is the first mpacket of a frame or the last mpacket of a frame. The information is encoded into two bits: a *Start Of Packet* (*SOP*) bit and an *End Of Packet* (*EOP*) bit. Like an incoming mpacket, each outgoing mpacket has an SOP bit and an EOP bit to specify whether the mpacket is the first mpacket of a frame or the last mpacket of a frame. For each outgoing mpacket, the microengine also specifies details such as the mpacket size, the port over which to transmit the mpacket, and an error status.

Using separate bits to denote SOP and EOP allows arbitrary combinations. For example, consider an ATM network that delivers fifty-three octet cells. Because it requires less than sixty-four octets, an ATM cell fits into a single mpacket. For packets that occupy a single mpacket, the hardware sets both the SOP and EOP bits (i.e., declares that the mpacket corresponds to both the beginning and end of a packet).

25.13 Packet Input Without Interrupts

How does packet input occur without interrupts? The hardware uses *polling*. A hardware unit called the *Ready Bus Sequencer* is configured to periodically poll each MAC device to determine if an mpacket is available. When it determines that sixty-four bytes of data are available, the Ready Bus Sequencer sets Control And Status registers known as the *Receive Ready Registers*. Similarly, when a transfer completes, a piece of the FBI unit known as the *Receive State Machine* stores information in a CSR to specify the RFIFO into which an mpacket has been placed.

How should a programmer structure ingress threads? There are two possibilities: statically assign each ingress thread to a network interface, or use a scheduler thread to make the assignment dynamically. The static case is easiest to understand: each input thread is dedicated to a specific hardware device. The thread handles two operations: polling the device CSR to determine when a packet arrives, and moving the mpacket into SDRAM. The advantages of static assignment arise from ease of programming and lower scheduling overhead.

Dynamic assignment of ingress threads requires one microengine thread, called a *receive scheduler thread*, to be dedicated to polling and notification. The receive scheduler thread polls the Receive Ready Registers. When it finds that an mpacket is ready, the scheduler issues a command to move the mpacket into a Receive FIFO. When the transfer completes, the hardware sends a signal to the *receive thread* that will handle the mpacket. Dynamic scheduling offers a potential advantage of better resource utilization: a packet is serviced as soon as a thread is available. However, scheduling latency may negate the advantage.

25.14 Ingress Packet Transfer

A microengine can transfer data from a Receive FIFO into SRAM transfer registers or directly into SDRAM. Programmers typically choose to place the bulk of a packet in SDRAM; SRAM is usually used for forwarding tables or header data that must be accessed repeatedly during packet processing. The instruction used to move data into SDRAM has the form:

$$\text{sdram}\,[\,\text{r\_fifo\_rd},\ \$\$xfer,\ addr_1,\ addr_2,\ count\,],\ \text{indirect\_ref}$$

where $addr_1$ and $addr_2$ are added to produce an address in SDRAM, $count$ specifies the number of eight-byte words to transfer, and $\$\$xfer$ denotes the first SDRAM transfer register. The *indirect_ref* token is required — the address of the Receive FIFO for the transfer is taken from the output of the previous ALU instruction.

As an alternative to transferring an mpacket directly into SDRAM, a microengine can move parts of the mpacket into an SRAM transfer register. The instruction has the form:

$$\text{r\_fifo\_rd}\,[\,\$xfer,\ addr_1,\ addr_2,\ count\,]$$

Operand $\$xfer$ denotes a starting SRAM transfer register, and $count$ specifies the number of four-byte SRAM words to transfer. The values of $addr_1$ and $addr_2$ are added to produce an integer from zero through one hundred fifty-nine. Unlike typical memory access instructions, however, the resulting integer is not treated as a memory address. Instead, the integer specifies the starting quadword address in the RFIFO at which the mpacket resides (the range of possible values arises because a RFIFO contains sixteen entries, each of which contains ten quadwords). As with other transfer instructions, an indirect reference can be used to supply an operand at run time. For example, the program can compute a packet size, and then use an indirect reference to override the *count* operand with the computed size.

25.15 Packet Egress

Like packet ingress, packet egress can be arranged two ways: an egress microengine can be statically assigned to a specific physical interface, or the programmer can create a scheduler thread that dynamically assigns egress threads as needed. In any case, an egress thread divides the outgoing frame into sixty-four byte mpackets and handles each mpacket independently. To transfer an mpacket, the microengine performs four steps:

- Reserve a space in a Transmit FIFO (TFIFO)
- Copy the mpacket from memory into the TFIFO
- Set the SOP and EOP bits for the mpacket
- Set the *valid* flag in the *XMIT_VALIDATE* register

Copying data to a TFIFO is analogous to extracting data from an RFIFO — a microengine can copy data directly from SDRAM or from SRAM transfer registers. To copy data from SDRAM, the microengine executes a command of the form:

$$\text{sdram}\,[\,\text{t\_fifo\_wr},\,\$\$\textit{xfer},\,\textit{addr}_1,\,\textit{addr}_2,\,\textit{count}\,],\,\text{indirect\_ref}$$

where $addr_1$ and $addr_2$ are added to produce the address in SDRAM, *count* specifies the number of eight-byte words to copy, and *$$xfer* specifies a transfer register to use. Token *indirect_ref* causes the hardware to use the result of the previous ALU instruction as the address of the TFIFO buffer.

To extract data from SRAM transfer registers, a microengine executes an instruction of the form:

$$\text{r\_fifo\_rd}\,[\,\$\textit{xfer},\,\textit{addr}_1,\,\textit{addr}_2,\,\textit{count}\,]$$

where *$xfer* specifies the starting transfer register, addresses $addr_1$ and $addr_2$ are added to obtain an integer from zero through one hundred fifty-nine that specifies the starting quadword address in the TFIFO, and *count* specifies the number of four-byte words to copy.

Once it places data in a TFIFO, a microengine must mark the data as *valid*; the hardware uses the setting of a valid bit to signal the hardware to move the data to the physical device for transmission. To mark a TFIFO entry as valid, a microengine executes a *fast_wr* instruction that uses the fast path through the FBI. The instruction has the following form:

$$\text{fast\_wr}\,[\,0,\,\text{xmit\_validate}\,],\,\text{indirect\_ref}$$

where *xmit_validate* specifies the CSR used to validate data for transmission. The source operand in the instruction specifies the integer number of the TFIFO buffer to be marked valid. A value of zero is coded as the source operand in the example above. However, indirect reference must be used to override the source value. That is, the programmer must ensure that an ALU instruction precedes the *fast_wr* instruction, and the ALU instruction must compute the number of a TFIFO buffer. Token *indirect_ref* causes the hardware to replace the zero in the *fast_wr* instruction with the computed value.

If a microengine does not support interrupts, how can code in an egress microblock know when a physical device is ready to transmit a packet? As with input, the hardware uses *polling* — the Ready Bus Sequencer can be configured to poll the ports

and place the status in two Transmit Ready registers named *xmit_rdy_lo* and
xmit_rdy_hi. Fifty-six of the bits in the two registers each correspond to one port; the
bit is set to zero if the device is busy, and one if the device is ready. An egress thread
on a microengine uses the *csr* instruction to poll the Transmit Ready registers. For example, the instruction:

csr[read, $xfer, xmit_rdy_lo]

reads the CSR register *xmit_rdy_lo*, which contains the ready bits for the first thirty-two
ports, and places the result in SRAM transfer register *$xfer*.

25.16 Other I/O Details

Low-level I/O requires further details in addition to those described above. For example, after the Receive State Machine finishes delivering an incoming mpacket, the ingress thread must check the status of the mpacket to determine if errors were detected
by the hardware. To do so, the microengine executes code such as:

.local $rc
csr [read, $rc, RCV_CNTL], ctx_swap

where *$rc* specifies an SRAM transfer register, and *RCV_CNTL* denotes the CSR that
contains the status of the received packet.

A microengine must also determine if an mpacket is the first or last part of a larger
packet. To branch to label *start_of_packet#* for the first mpacket, a microengine must
determine if the low-order bit of the status is set. To do so, the microengine executes
the following code:

alu [−−, $rc, AND, 1]
br!=0 [start_of_packet#]

The *alu* instruction computes the *logical and* of SRAM transfer register *$rc* and the
constant one (i.e., turns off all bits except the low-order bit), but does not store the
result in a register. Instead, the result is used by the following instruction as the basis
for a conditional branch. The branch is taken if the bit is set.

25.17 Summary

Microengines offer hardware that aids in mutual exclusion and thread coordination. Basic facilities include buffer pool manipulation, bit testing, atomic memory increment, and memory locking. In addition, the hardware offers many Control and

Status Registers that threads use to interrogate or control physical network devices or various hardware units.

Intel's SDK offers extensive sets of macros that handle the dispatch loop, manage packet queues, and access fields in packet headers. Strict initialization of the Intel macros is required — a programmer must define constants and declare registers before including macros in a program.

Intel's SDK also provides software that handles ingress and egress; the software hides low-level details, and allows a programmer to receive and send packets without directly controlling the hardware. Programmers who do not use the Intel ingress and egress facilities must choose whether to assign threads statically or dynamically, and must handle many details. In particular, because the underlying hardware can only transfer a sixty-four byte block, a large packet must be divided into sixty-four byte units called mpackets. Status information that accompanies mpackets indicates whether a given mpacket corresponds to the first or last part of a large packet.

FOR FURTHER STUDY

Intel's Microcode Programmer's Reference Manual [Intel 2001d] provides additional information about many of the programming topics covered in this chapter; the Hardware Reference Manual [Intel 2001c] covers hardware details needed when programming.

EXERCISES

25.1 Write a set of assembly language macros that use the Scratchpad memory test-and-set operations to implement counting semaphores.

25.2 Assume that 40,960 bytes of memory are available for use at SRAM address A. Write assembly language statements that create an SRAM buffer pool of twenty buffers, each of size 2KB.

25.3 Extend the previous exercise by implementing the buffer pool in C on the StrongARM and comparing both the code size and effort.

25.4 Scratch memory test-and-set operations or SRAM memory locks can be used to implement mutual exclusion among microengine threads. Which mechanism is more efficient? Explain.

25.5 Write a sequence of assembly language instructions that extracts the destination IP address field from an IP datagram that is encapsulated in an Ethernet frame. Assume that the Ethernet frame begins with a standard fourteen byte header.

Chapter Contents

26

An Example ACE

26.1 Introduction

Previous chapters describe the architecture of the Intel IXP1200 and the programming model used by Intel's SDK. This chapter presents code for an example ACE that shows how the Intel model works in practice. Although the chapter is long, the example code is not complicated, and does not demonstrate all possible features of the SDK. Instead, wherever possible, we have avoided complexity; the example consists of a straightforward system that entails minimal code.

26.2 An Example Bump-In-The-Wire

Engineers use the informal and picturesque term *bump-in-the-wire* to refer to a network system that has two network connections and passes traffic directly from one to the other†. A bump-in-the-wire architecture is ideal for systems that passively monitor network traffic because the system can be inserted at any point in a network and appears to operate transparently — the system gathers statistics as it passes packets through. A bump-in-the-wire architecture can also be used for an active system such as a traffic policer (that ensures packets adhere to specific bounds) or a traffic shaper (that smooths the transmission rate).

We will examine code for a trivial example: a passive bump-in-the-wire system that measures Web traffic. As packets pass through, the system counts packets destined for the World Wide Web.

---

†More formally, such systems are referred to as *in-line*.

We call our example system *web wire bump* (*wwbump*). As the name implies, a wwbump system has two physical network connections, and passes traffic transparently between them. Our design uses two Ethernet connections, which allows wwbump to be inserted into any Ethernet connection. For example, Figure 26.1 shows a wwbump system placed into the connection between a router and an Ethernet switch.

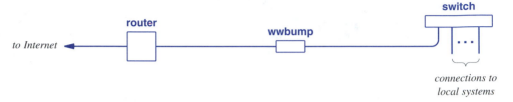

Figure 26.1 An example of a wwbump system inserted into the connection between a router and an Ethernet switch. The wwbump system passes traffic transparently.

26.3 Wwbump Design

The example code is written using Intel's SDK, and is designed to run on Intel's Bridal Veil testbed. Although the testbed has four Ethernet ports, the wwbump code only uses two of them (ports zero and one). When a packet arrives on port zero, wwbump transmits the packet on port one, and vice-versa. In addition to forwarding packets between the two ports, wwbump counts packets that are destined for the World Wide Web. We define a Web packet as a packet that has an Ethernet frame type equal to 0800_{16}, an IP type field equal to 6, and a TCP destination port equal to 80.

The example code has the following general properties:

- Accepts input from either port zero or port one.
- Forwards all traffic that is received.
- Uses the ingress and egress library ACEs supplied by Intel.
- Defines a wwbump MicroACE (i.e., both a microblock component and a core component) to handle packet processing.
- Uses the exception mechanism to pass each Web packet to the core component on the StrongARM.
- Allows access to the packet count via the crosscall mechanism.
- Uses an *ixsys.config* file to specify the binding of targets.

Figure 26.2 shows the overall structure of ACEs and the packet flow in a wwbump system. Each Web packet is sent to the core component of the wwbump ACE; other traffic is forwarded directly to the microblock of the egress ACE.

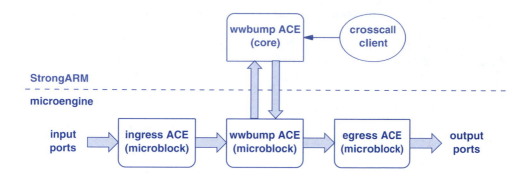

Figure 26.2 Internal structure of ACEs in the wwbump system and the packet
flow among them. Web packets are sent to the StrongARM, and
other packets flow directly through to the egress ACE.

The next sections examine the code for each piece of the system. After considering header files that contain declarations of data structures, we explore code that runs on
the microengines. Later sections in the chapter discuss code that runs on the
StrongARM, including the exception handler and the code for a crosscall.

26.4 Header Files

Following the common practice used with most large programs, symbolic constants
and other global declarations are placed in a separate file that is included in source programs as needed. For example, recall from Chapter 23 that a programmer must allocate
a control block that holds information about the ACE. File *wwbump.h*, shown on the
next page, declares a structure named *wwbump* that holds the control block for the
wwbump ACE. The file also contains *include* statements for several files that the SDK
uses.

In addition to the required *ix_ace* structure, the example wwbump control block includes five fields. Figure 26.3 lists each field, and gives the field's type and purpose.

Field	Type	Purpose
name	string	Name of the ACE in ixsys.config
tag	int	ID of ACE assigned by Resource Manager
ue	int	Bitmask of microengines running the ACE
bname	string	TAG name that the microblock uses
ccbase	ix_base_t	Handle for crosscall service

Figure 26.3 Additional fields in the control block for the wwbump ACE. The
control block begins with the *ix_ace* structure that the Intel
software requires.

```
/* wwbump.h -- global constants and declarations for wwbump */

#ifndef __WWBUMP_H
#define __WWBUMP_H

#include <ix/asl.h>
#include <ix/microace/rm.h>
#include <ix/asl/ixbasecc.h>
#include <wwbump_import.h>


typedef struct wwbump wwbump;
struct wwbump
{
        ix_ace   ace;           /* Mandatory handle for all ACEs            */

        char     name[128];  /* Name of this ACE given in ixsys.config  */
        int      tag;           /* ID assigned by RM for SA-to-ME communic. */
        int      ue;            /* Bitmask of MEs this MicroACE runs on     */
        char     bname[128]; /* Block name (need .import_var $bname_TAG) */
        ix_base_t ccbase;    /* Handle for cross call service            */
};


/* Exception handler prototype */
int     exception(void *ctx, ix_ring r, ix_buffer b);


#endif /* __WWBUMP_H */
```

The code in file *wwbump.h* is bracketed with a conditional test to ensure that the code only appears once in a program, even in cases where a programmer inadvertently includes the file multiple times. The initial *#ifndef* statement tests symbolic constant *__WWBUMP_H*. If the constant has not been defined, all code down to the closing *#endif* is added to the program (i.e., the entire file). If constant *__WWBUMP_H* has already been defined, the conditional is not executed, and the entire file is skipped.

Most of the files included by wwbump.h are part of Intel's SDK, and are required by macros that the ACE invokes. However, file *wwbump_import.h* is created by the programmer to define a common tag that links together the microblock and core components of the ACE.

File *wwbump_import.h* has an interesting structure: the file contains a mixture of assembly code and C code. To understand how such coding is possible, recall that the macro preprocessor used with the assembler follows the same general syntax as the C

preprocessor. Thus, either the assembler or C compiler can parse the basic file structure. To ensure that the preprocessor generates correct code in all cases, a programmer
uses conditional compilation — the symbolic constant *MICROCODE* is only defined
when compiling code that will run on a microengine. Thus, a programmer can use the
symbolic constant to control conditional compilation. If *MICROCODE* has been defined, the file generates an assembly language *.import* statement; otherwise, the file uses
a *#define* statement to define a string:

```
/* wwbump_import.h -- define or import tag for wwbump MicroACE */

#ifndef _WWBUMP_IMPORT_H
#define _WWBUMP_IMPORT_H

#ifdef MICROCODE

.import_var WWBUMP_TAG
#else

#define WWBUMP_TAG_STR          "WWBUMP_TAG"

#endif

#endif /* _WWBUMP_IMPORT_H */
```

As with other included files, *wwbump_import.h* uses a symbolic constant,
_WWBUMP_IMPORT_H, to ensure that the code only appears once in a program. If
the constant is defined, all the code in the file is skipped. Otherwise, the file defines
_WWBUMP_IMPORT_H, and the code in the file is processed.

26.5 Microcode For Packet Classification And Processing

The microcode for wwbump has been divided into two files: a file of code that
processes each packet and a file of code that defines the dispatch loop. File
WWBump.uc† contains the microengine assembly code for packet processing. When
reading the file, remember each *sdram* instruction requires multiple cycles and the
ctx_swap flag specifies that the thread executing the *sdram* instruction will block until
the memory access completes.

---

†Our example code follows a convention used in Intel's reference library in which macro and file names
related to microcode begin with uppercase letters.

```
/* WWBump.uc - microcode to process a packet */


#define ETH_IP          0x800           ; Ethernet type for IP
#define IPT_TCP         6               ; IP type for TCP
#define TCP_WWW         80              ; Dest. port for WWW

#macro WWBumpInit[]
        /* empty because no initialization is needed */
#endm


#macro WWBump[]
    xbuf_alloc[$$hdr,6]         ; Allocate 6 SDRAM registers

    /* Reserve a register (ifn) and compute the output port for the   */
    /* frame; a frame that arrives on port 0 will go out port 1, and  */
    /* vice versa                                                     */

    .local ifn
        DL_GetInputPort[ifn]            ; Copy input port number to ifn
        alu [ ifn, ifn, XOR, 1 ]        ; XOR with 1 to reverse number
        DL_SetOutputPort[ifn]           ; Set output port for egress
    .endlocal

    /* Read first 24 bytes of frame header from SDRAM */

    .local base off
        Buf_GetData[base, dl_buffer_handle] ; Get the base SDRAM address
        DL_GetBufferOffset[off]         ; Get packet offset in bytes
        alu_shf[off, --, B, off, >>3]   ; Convert to Quad-words
        sdram[read, $$hdr0, base, off, 3], ctx_swap ; Read 3 Quadwords
                                            ;  (six registers)
    .endlocal

    /* Classify the packet.  If any test fails, branch to NotWeb#    */

    /* Verify frame type is IP (1st two bytes of the 4th longword)    */

    .local etype
        immed[etype, ETH_IP]
        alu_shf[ --, etype, -, $$hdr3, >>16]    ; 2nd operand is shifted
        br!=0[NotWeb#]
    .endlocal
```

```
    /* Verify IP type is TCP (last byte of the 6th longword)          */

br!=byte[$$hdr5, 0, IPT_TCP, NotWeb#]

    /* Verify destination port is web (offset depends on IP header size */

.local base boff dpoff dport

        /* Get length of IP header (3rd byte of 4th longword), and     */
        /* convert to bytes by shifting by six bits instead of eight   */

        ld_field_w_clr[dpoff, 0001, $$hdr3, >>6] ; Extract header length

        /* Mask off bits above and below the IP length                 */

        .local mask
            immed[mask, 0x3c]            ; Mask out upper and lower 2 bits
            alu [ dpoff, dpoff, AND, mask ]
        .endlocal

        /* Register dpoff contains the IP header length in bytes.  Add */
        /* Ethernet header length (14) and offset of the destination   */
        /* port (2) to obtain offset from the beginning of the packet  */
        /* of the destination port.  Add to SDRAM address of buffer,   */
        /* and convert to quad-word offset by dividing by 8 (shift 3).  */

        alu[dpoff, dpoff, +, 16]                 ; Add Ether+TCP offsets
        Buf_GetData[base, dl_buffer_handle]      ; Get buffer base address
        DL_GetBufferOffset[boff]                 ; Get data offset in buf.
        alu[boff, boff, +, dpoff]                ; Compute byte address
        alu_shf[boff, --, B, boff, >>3]          ; Convert to Q-Word addr.
        sdram[read, $$hdr0, base, boff, 1], ctx_swap    ; Read 8 bytes

        /* Use lower three bits of the byte offset to determine which   */
        /* byte the destination port will be in.  If value >= 4, dest.  */
        /* port is in the 2nd longword; otherwise it's in the first.    */

        alu[ dpoff, dpoff, AND, 0x7 ]            ; Get lowest three bits
        alu[ --, dpoff, -, 4]                    ; Test and conditional
        br>=0[SecondWord#]                       ;   branch if value >=4

FirstWord#:     /* Load upper two bytes of register $$hdr0 */
        ld_field_w_clr[dport, 0011, $$hdr0, >>16] ; Shift before mask
        br[GotDstPort#]                          ; Check port number
```

```
SecondWord#:     /* Load lower two bytes of register $$hdr1 */

        ld_field_w_clr[dport, 0011, $$hdr1, >>16] ; Shift before mask

GotDstPort#:     /* Verify destination port is 80 */

        .local wprt
            immed[wprt, TCP_WWW]                ; Load 80 in reg. wprt
            alu[--, dport, -, wprt]             ; Compare dport to wprt
            br!=0[NotWeb#]                      ;  and branch if not equal
        .endlocal
    .endlocal

IsWeb#:          /* Found a web packet, so send to the StrongARM */

    /* Set exception code to zero (we must set this)              */
    .local exc                                 ; Declare register exc
        immed[exc, 0]                          ; Place zero in exc and
        DL_SetExceptionCode[exc]               ;  set exception code
    .endlocal

    /* Set tag core component's tag (required by Intel macros) */
    .local ace_tag                             ; Declare register ace_tag
        immed32[ace_tag, WWBUMP_TAG]           ; Place wwbump tag in reg.
        DL_SetAceTag[ace_tag]                  ;  and set tag
    .endlocal

    /* Set register dl_next_block to IX_EXCEPTION to cause dispatch    */
    /*   to pass packet to StrongARM as an exception                   */
    immed[dl_next_block, IX_EXCEPTION]         ; Store return value
    br[Finish#]                                ; Done, so branch to end

NotWeb#:         /* Found a non-web packet, so forward to next microblock*/
    immed32[dl_next_block, 1]                  ; Set return code to 1

Finish#:         /* Packet processing is complete, so clean up          */
xbuf_free[$$hdr]                               ; Release xfer registers
#endm
```

Although it contains many details, the code is straightforward. The file defines macro *WWBump*, which handles one packet at a time. *WWBump* performs two functions: it specifies the output port over which the packet will eventually be transmitted and classifies the packet to determine whether the packet should be sent to the StrongARM or to the next microblock (i.e., the Egress microblock).

Specifying the output port is trivial because Intel supplies macros that handle most of the work. Macro *DL_GetInputPort* obtains the port number (zero or one) over which the packet arrived, and macro *DL_SetOutputPort* allows the program to specify the port on which the packet will be sent. After obtaining the input port number, the code performs an *exclusive or* with constant one to reverse the port, and calls *DL_SetOutputPort* to record the result.

To classify a packet, macro WWbump begins by allocating six SDRAM transfer registers and reading the first twenty-four bytes of the packet header. The code then checks the Ethernet and IP type fields to verify that the frame carries IP and the datagram carries TCP. In each case, the field to be examined lies at a fixed offset from the beginning of the packet. Verifying the TCP destination port is more complex because the offset of the field depends on the IP header length. Thus, the code extracts the IP header length (the second four bits of the IP header), and multiplies by four to convert to a byte offset. The code uses *shift* and *logical and* operations to perform the extraction and conversion. After computing the byte offset, the code reads the appropriate quadword from SDRAM, and extracts the destination port field for comparison.

Once the packet has been classified, control either passes to label *IsWeb#* (for Web packets) or *NotWeb#* for other packets. In the non-Web case, the return code in *dl_next_block* is set to one, which causes the dispatch loop to forward the packet to the next microblock. In the Web case, the exception code is set to zero, the ACE tag is set to the value *WWBUMP_TAG*, and the return code is set to *IX_EXCEPTION*. In any case, the final step of macro *WWBump* releases the transfer registers.

26.6 Microcode For The Dispatch Loop

File *WWB_dl.uc* contains the code for the wwbump dispatch loop, which implements the following algorithm:

```
initialize dispatch loop macros;
do forever  {
        if (packet has arrived from the StrongARM)
                Send the packet to egress microblock;
        if (packet has arrived from Ethernet port) {
                Invoke WWBump macro to process the packet;
                if (return code specifies exception) {
                        Send packet to StrongARM;
                } else {
                        Send packet to egress microblock;
                }
        }
}
```

```
/* WWB_dl.uc - dispatch loop for wwbump program */

/* Constants */

#define IX_EXCEPTION      0       ; Return value to raise an exception
#define SA_CONSUME_NUM    31      ; Ignore StrongARM packets 30 of 31 times
#define SEQNUM_IGNORE     31      ; StrongARM fastport sequence num

/* Register declarations (as required for Intel dispatch loop macros)    */
.local  dl_reg1 dl_reg2 dl_reg3 dl_reg4 dl_buffer_handle dl_next_block

/* Include files for Intel dispatch loop macros */
#include "DispatchLoop_h.uc"
#include "DispatchLoopImportVars.h"
#include "EthernetIngress.uc"
#include "wwbump_import.h"

/* Include the packet processing macro defined previously */
#include "WWBump.uc"

/* Microblock initialization */
DL_Init[]
EthernetIngress_Init[]
WWBumpInit[]

/* Dispatch loop that runs forever */
.while(1)

Top_Of_Loop#:    /* Top of dispatch loop (for equivalent of C continue)   */

    /* Test for a frame from the StrongARM */
    DL_SASource[ ]                                  ; Get frame from SA
    alu[--, dl_buffer_handle, -, IX_BUFFER_NULL]; If no frame, go test
    br=0[Test_Ingress#], guess_branch           ;  for ingress frame
    br[Send_MB#]                                 ; If frame, go send it

Test_Ingress#: /* Test for an Ethernet frame */

    EthernetIngress[ ]                           ; Get an Ethernet frame
    alu[--, dl_buffer_handle, -, IX_BUFFER_NULL]; If no frame, go back
    br=0[Top_Of_Loop#]                           ;  to start of loop

    /* Check if ingress frame valid and drop if not */
    br!=byte[dl_next_block, 0, 1, Drop_Packet#]
```

```
        /* Invoke WWBump macro to set output port and classify the frame    */
        WWBump[]

        /* Use return value from WWBump to dispose of frame:                */
        /*    if exception, jump to code that sends to StrongARM             */
        /*    else jump to code that sends to egress                        */

        alu[ --, dl_next_block, -, IX_EXCEPTION]    ; Return code is exception
        br=0[Send_SA#]                              ;  so send to StrongARM

        br[Send_MB#]                                ; Otherwise, send to next
                                                    ;  microblock

Send_SA#:
        /* Send the frame to the core component on the StrongARM as an      */
        /* exception. Note that tag and exception code are assigned by      */
        /* the microblock WWBump.                                           */
        DL_SASink[ ]
        .continue                                   ; Continue dispatch loop

Send_MB#:
        /* Send the frame to the next microblock (egress). Note that the    */
        /* output port (field oface hidden in the internal structure) has   */
        /* been assigned by microblock WWBump.                              */
        DL_MESink[ ]
        nop
        .continue

Drop_Packet#:
        /* Drop the frame and start over getting a new frame */
        DL_Drop[ ]

.endw

nop                         ; Although the purpose of these no-ops is
nop                         ; undocumented, Intel examples include them.
nop
.endlocal
```

26.7 Code For Core Component (Exception Handler)

The central part of the core component of the wwbump ACE consists of an exception procedure that is called once for each packet that the microblock passes up as an exception. Our exception handler is trivial — it only needs to increment the count of Web packets, which is kept in a longword, *Webcnt*. However, the exception handler must perform two other steps: the Intel software requires the exception handler to call *RmGetExceptionCode* to obtain the exception code, and the exception handler must call *RmSendPacket* to forward the packet back to the microengine. Each of the two functions uses a nonzero return value to indicate that an error occurred. If an error does occur, the exception handler calls *ix_error_dump* to write an error message on *stderr*, and calls *ix_buffer_del* to delete the buffer. File *action.c* contains the code.

```
/* action.c -- Core component of wwbump that handles exceptions */

#include <wwbump.h>
#include <stdlib.h>
#include <wwbcc.h>

ix_error exception(void *ctx, ix_ring r, ix_buffer b)
{
    struct wwbump *wwb = (struct wwbump *) ctx;    /* ctx is the ACE */
    ix_error e;
    unsigned char c;
    (void) r;     /* Note:  not used in our example code */


    /* Get the exception code: Note: Intel code requires this step */
    e = RmGetExceptionCode(wwb->tag, &c);
    if ( e ) {
        fprintf(stderr, "%s:  Error getting exception code", wwb->name);
        ix_error_dump(stderr, e);
        ix_buffer_del(b);
        return e;
    }

    Webcnt++;    /* Count the packet as a web packet */

    /* Send the packet back to wwbump microblock */
    e = RmSendPacket(wwb->tag, b);
    if ( e ) {  /* If error occurred, report the error */
        ix_error_dump(stderr, e);
        ix_buffer_del(b);
        return e;
    }
```

```
    return 0;
}


/* A core component must define an ix_action_default function that is   */
/* invoked if a frame arrives from the core component of another ACE.   */
/* Because wwbump does not expect such frames, the version of the       */
/* default function used with wwmbump simply deletes any packet that    */
/* it receives via this interface.                                      */

int ix_action_default(ix_ace * a, ix_buffer b)
{
    (void) a;                       /* This line prevents a compiler warning*/
    ix_buffer_del(b);               /* Delete the frame                     */
    return RULE_DONE;               /* This step required                   */
}
```

26.8 ACE Structure

In the example code above, each web packet flows from the microblock component of the wwbump ACE to the core component and then back to the microblock component. The unusual structure was chosen to provide a compact illustration of features — a single ACE contains the code for both directions of transfer. Despite its pedagogical advantages, the example ACE structure has two drawbacks: a programmer must be careful to ensure that the code does not contain an *infinite packet loop*, and must be careful to avoid *double overhead* in which the packet passes through the entire microengine dispatch loop twice†.

26.9 Code To Initialize And Finalize The Wwbump ACE

Recall that the SDK software requires each ACE to have an *ix_init* function that performs initialization and an *ix_fini* function that performs finalization. For the wwbump ACE, *ix_init* allocates memory for the *wwbump* structure, assigns the block name *WWBUMP*, and then calls Intel functions that perform further initialization: *ix_ace_init* initializes the ACE, *RmInit* initializes a connection to the resource manager, and *RmRegister* registers with the resource manager. In addition, *ix_init* calls *cc_init* to initialize the crosscall mechanism (described below).

Finalization, which is performed by *ix_fini* complements initialization. After invoking *cc_fini* to finalize each of the crosscalls, *ix_fini* calls *RmUnRegister* to unregister from the resource manager, *RmTerm* to terminate the resource manager connection, and *ix_ace_fini* to finalize the ACE. Finally, *ix_fini* frees the memory that was allocated to hold the ACE control block. File *init.c*‡ contains the code for both *ix_init* and *ix_fini*.

---

†Intel suggests an alternative structure in which the core component of the wwbump ACE forwards a web packet to the core component of the egress ACE for transmission.

‡We follow the Intel convention of using the file name *init* for the file that contains the ACE initialization and finalization code.

```c
/* init.c -- Initialization and completion routines for the wwbump ACE  */

#include <stdlib.h>
#include <string.h>
#include <wwbump.h>
#include <wwbcc.h>

/* Initialization for the wwbump ACE */
ix_error ix_init(int argc, char **argv, ix_ace ** ap)
{
    struct wwbump *wwb;
    ix_error e;
    (void)argc;

    /* Set so ix_fini won't free a random value if ix_init fails */
    *ap = 0;

    /* Allocate memory for the WWBump structure (includes ix_ace) */
    wwb = malloc(sizeof(struct wwbump));
    if ( wwb == NULL )
        return ix_error_new(IX_ERROR_LEVEL_LOCAL, IX_ERROR_OOM, 0,
                            "couldn't allocate memory for ACE");

    /* Microengine mask is always passed as the third argument */
    wwb->ue = atoi(argv[2]);

    /* Set blockname used to associate the ACE with its microblock */
    strcpy(wwb->bname, "WWBUMP");

    /* The name of the ACE is always the 2nd argument */
    /* The first argument is the name of the executable */
    wwb->name[sizeof(wwb->name) - 1] = '\0';
    strncpy(wwb->name, argv[1], sizeof(wwb->name) - 1);

    /* Initializes the ix_ace handle (including dispatch loop, control */
    /* access point, etc) */
    e = ix_ace_init(&wwb->ace, wwb->name);
    if (e) {
        free(wwb);
        return ix_error_new(0,0,e,"Error in ix_ace_init()\n");
    }

    /* Initialize a connection to the resource manager */
    e = RmInit();
```

```
    if (e) {
        ix_ace_fini(&wwb->ace);
        free(wwb);
        return ix_error_new(0,0,e,"Error in RmInit()\n");
    }

    /* Register with the resource manager (including exception handler) */
    e = RmRegister(&wwb->tag, wwb->bname,&wwb->ace, exception, wwb,
                    wwb->ue);
    if (e) {
        RmTerm();
        ix_ace_fini(&wwb->ace);
        free(wwb);
        return ix_error_new(0,0,e,"Error in RmRegister()\n");
    }

    /* Initialize crosscalls */
    e = cc_init(wwb);
    if ( e ) {
        RmUnRegister(&wwb->tag);
        RmTerm();
        ix_ace_fini(&wwb->ace);
        free(wwb);
        return e;
    }

    *ap = &wwb->ace;
    return 0;
}

ix_error ix_fini(int argc, char **argv, ix_ace * ap)
{
    struct wwbump *wwb = (struct wwbump *) ap;
    ix_error e;
    (void)argc;
    (void)argv;

    /* ap == 0 if  ix_init() fails */
    if ( ! ap )
      return 0;

    /* Finalize crosscalls */
    e = cc_fini(wwb);
    if ( e )
        return e;
```

```
/* Unregister the exception handler and microblocks */
e = RmUnRegister(wwb->tag);
if ( e )
    return ix_error_new(0,0,e,"Error in RmUnRegister()\n");

/* Terminate connection with resource manager */
e = RmTerm();
if ( e )
    return ix_error_new(0,0,e,"Error in RmTerm()\n");

/* Finalize the ix_ace handle */
e = ix_ace_fini(&wwb->ace);
if ( e )
    return ix_error_new(0,0,e,"Error in ix_ace_fini()\n");

/* Free the malloc()ed memory */
free(wwb);
return 0;
}
```

26.10 An Example Crosscall

The wwbump example includes code that illustrates how a crosscall server can be integrated into an ACE. The wwbump crosscall server responds to a crosscall from a program running on the StrongARM†.

To create a crosscall server, a programmer must follow five basic steps:

- Define a set of functions that the crosscall server exports.
- Create an *Interface Definition Language* (*IDL*) specification for each function, and use the IDL compiler to generate the corresponding stub code.
- Write code for each exported function using the exact form of arguments needed by the generated stubs.
- Write code for an initialization function that is called once when the crosscall server is started.
- Write code for a finalization function that is called once when the crosscall server is terminated.

The next sections use the wwbump crosscall server to illustrate each step.

---

†Although it is possible to build a crosscall server that can be called from another ACE, our example cannot because we have chosen to use the *twoway* calling mechanism.

26.10.1 Definition Of An Exported Function

To keep the code easy to understand, we will examine a crosscall server that is trivial — the server exports a single function that merely returns the current value of the Web packet counter. The implementation is equally trivial because the count of packets is stored in a global variable in the ACE: a longword named *Webcnt*. Thus, our crosscall server merely returns the current value of *Webcnt* to the caller.

The programmer must choose a name for each function that a crosscall server exports. As an example, we will use the name *getcnt* for the function in our example crosscall.

26.10.2 IDL Specification

In addition to requiring a name for each individual function, IDL requires a programmer to choose a namespace for crosscall names. The programmer uses the *interface* keyword to declare the crosscall namespace, and then writes a declaration for each individual function. The syntax used for IDL function declarations resembles the syntax used to declare functions in the C programming language. A declaration specifies the type of each argument and the type of the return value. File *wwbump.idl*, shown in Figure 26.4, contains a declaration for the wwbump crosscall that exports a *getcnt* function.

```
interface wwbump
{
  twoway long getcnt();
};
```

Figure 26.4 File *wwbump.idl* that contains an IDL declaration for the wwbump ACE. The declaration uses interface name *wwbump*, and defines one function named *getcnt*.

Because IDL only requires declarations for function prototypes and not for the code itself, an IDL specification is compact. The IDL specification for our example crosscall requires only four lines to give a complete specification. The code declares that a *wwbump* interface exports exactly one function, named *getcnt*, that returns a value of type *long* and takes no arguments.

26.10.3 Files Generated By The IDL Compiler

When it runs, the IDL compiler takes an IDL specification as input and produces a series of files as output. IDL specifications in the input file determine the number of files that are generated, their names, and the contents of each. For each interface declared in the IDL file, the compiler generates eight files that contain such items as the client-side stubs and server-side skeletons. Figure 26.5 lists the files that are generated for a specification that defines a function, *FCN*, as part of an interface named *IFACE*. For each file, the figure lists the functions that appear in the file as well as included files.

As an example, consider the files that IDL generates for the specification given in Figure 26.4. Because the interface is named *wwbump*, the generated files include file *wwbump_stub_c.c*, which contains C code that the client can call. In particular, the file contains the initialization and termination functions, *init* and *fini*.

As another example, compiling the specification in Figure 26.4 also generates a file named *wwbump_stub_c.h*, which contains many declarations and constants. The file declares the types of functions such as *stub_wwbump_init*. In addition, the file defines constant *wwbump_intName* to be a string that contains the name of the interface:

#define   wwbump_intName   "wwbump"

Similarly, the file defines constant *wwbump_getcnt_opName* to be a string that contains the function name. The constant definitions are useful for debugging because they define the interface and function names as printable strings.

File Contents	Description
*IFACE*_stub_c.h	Crosscall data types and types for initialization and finalization functions
*IFACE*_intName	Interface name as a string
*IFACE_FCN*_opName	Function name as a string
stub_*IFACE*_init()	Client crosscall initialization
stub_*IFACE*_fini()	Client crosscall finalization
*IFACE_FCN*_fptr	Function pointer for FCN
stub_*IFACE_FCN*()	Client-side crosscall function
CC_VMT_*IFACE*	Crosscall Virtual Method Table structure
deferred_cb_*IFACE_IFCN*()	Client callback prototype
*IFACE_FCN*_cb_fptr	Client callback function pointer
CB_VMT_*IFACE*	Client callback VMT
getCBVMT_*IFACE*()	Find VMT for callback
*IFACE*_sk_c.h	Declarations of server-side interfaces
sk_*IFACE*_init()	Server initialization
sk_*IFACE*_fini()	Server finalization
getCCVMT_*IFACE*()	Find the VMT for the interface
invoke_*IFACE_IFCN*()	Invoke a crosscall
*IFACE*_stub_c.h	Included file
*IFACE*_cc_c.h	Prototypes for individual crosscall functions
IFACE_FCN()	Prototype for function FCN
*IFACE*_sk_c.h	Included file
*IFACE*_cb_c.h	Prototypes and Virtual Method Tables for client-side callback functions
*IFACE_FCN*_cb()	Prototype for client callback
*IFACE*_stub_c.h	Included file
*IFACE*_stub_c.c	Code for client-side initialization and finalization crosscall functions
IFACE_sk_c.c	Code for server-side initialization and finalization and VMT accessor functions
*IFACE*_cc_c.c	Default code for crosscall functions that merely return an error.
*IFACE*_cb_c.c	Default implementations of client callback functions that merely return an error.

Figure 26.5 Files generated by IDL for a function *FCN* declared in interface *IFACE*.

26.11 Code For A Crosscall Function

A programmer must supply code for each of the functions that a crosscall interface exports. Our example crosscall only exports one function, *getcnt*. According to the interface declaration, *getcnt* does not receive any arguments. In practice, however, the generated code always passes at least two arguments when invoking a crosscall function: a handle for the crosscall interface (type *ix_base_t*) and a pointer to a memory location that is used to hold the return value. To prevent a compiler warning, an explicit reference to the first argument is included in the code.

In addition to code for exported functions, a programmer must supply initialization and finalization functions that are used to start and terminate the crosscall mechanism. File *wwbcc.c* contains the initialization and finalization functions as well as the code for *getcnt*.

```
/* wwbcc.c -- wwbump crosscall functions */

#include <stdlib.h>
#include <string.h>
#include <wwbump.h>
#include <wwbcc.h>
#include "wwbump_sk_c.h"
#include "wwbump_cc_c.h"


long Webcnt;                  /* Stores the count of web packets */

/* Initialization function for the crosscall */

ix_error cc_init(struct wwbump *wwb)
{
    CC_VMT_wwbump *vmt = 0;
    ix_cap *capp;
    ix_error e;

    /* Initialize an ix_base_t structure to 0 */
    memset(&wwb->ccbase, 0, sizeof(wwb->ccbase));

    /* Get the OMS communications access point (CAP) of the ACE */
    ix_ace_to_cap(&wwb->ace, &capp);

    /* Invoke the crosscall initialization function and check for error */
    e = sk_wwbump_init(&wwb->ccbase, capp);
    if (e)
        return ix_error_new(0,0,e,"Error in sk_wwbump_init()\n");
```

```
    /* Retarget incoming crosscalls to our getcnt function */

    /* Get a pointer to the CrossCall Virtual Method Table */
    e = getCCVMT_wwbump(&wwb->ccbase, &vmt);
    if (e)
    {
        sk_wwbump_fini(&wwb->ccbase);
        return ix_error_new(0,0,e,"Error in getCCVMT_wwbump()\n");
    }

    /* Retarget function pointer in the table to getcnt */
    vmt->_pCC_wwbump_getcnt = getcnt;

    /* Set initial count of web packets to zero */
    Webcnt = 0;

    return 0;
}


/* Cross call termination function */
ix_error cc_fini(struct wwbump *wwb)
{
    ix_error e;
    /* Finalize crosscall and check for error */
    e = sk_wwbump_fini(&wwb->ccbase);
    if ( e )
        return ix_error_new(0,0,e,"Error in sk_wwbump_fini()\n");

    return 0;    /* If no error, indicate sucessful return */
}

/* Function that is invoked each time a crosscall occurs */
ix_error getcnt(ix_base_t* bp, long* rv)
{
    (void)bp;    /* Reference unused arg to prevent compiler warnings */

    /* Actual work: copy the web count into the return value */
    *rv = Webcnt;

    /* Return 0 for success */
    return 0;
}
```

The code for function *getcnt* is easiest to understand. The function obtains the current count of packets from *Webcnt*, and stores the value in the location given by the second argument, pointer *rv* (return value). The actual return value from the function is used as an error code — a value of zero indicates success.

Function *cc_init* handles initialization for the crosscall. First, the function sets the *ix_base_t* structure to zero. It then obtains the *Communication Access Process* (*CAP*) that the ACE uses to communicate with the OMS†. The function invokes the initialization function that the IDL compiler generates, *sk_wwbump_init*. Function *sk_wwbump_init* modifies the *ix_base_t* variable so it can receive crosscalls for the *wwbump* interface.

The next step of initialization consists of substituting the programmer's version of function *getcnt* for a default version generated by the IDL compiler. There are two possibilities: edit the generated file *wwbump_cc_c.c* to change function *wwbump_getcnt*, or retarget the *Virtual Method Table* (*VMT*) for crosscalls to invoke a function other than *wwbump_getcnt*. Editing the generated file is easier, but has a significant disadvantage: the file is rewritten whenever the IDL compiler runs. To avoid potential errors caused by a file being overwritten, we have selected the latter solution.

To modify the VMT, the initialization function calls *getCCVMT_wwbump* with the base address and the address of a pointer, *vmt*. Function *getCCVMT_wwbump* sets *vmt* to the address of the virtual method table, and returns an error code to indicate success or failure. If the call is successful, the code uses *vmt* as a pointer, and sets entry *_pCC_wwbump_getcnt* to the address of our example *getcnt* function.

The last step of initialization consists of storing initial values in global variables that the ACE uses. In the wwbump ACE, only one global variable needs to be initialized (the count of Web packets). Once *Webcnt* has been set to zero, the initialization function returns zero to indicate success. Finalization undoes each step of initialization by performing the steps in the reverse order and undoing the effect of each.

26.12 System Configuration

Recall that the Intel SDK uses a configuration file named *ixsys.config* to specify a set of ACEs, assign a tag to each, and associate an ACE with fast or slow ingress or egress ports. The sample configuration file supplied with the SDK, shown below, includes comments that describe each of the entries; there is no other documentation.

Especially note the last section of the file that specifies ARP entries for each of the interfaces. ARP is needed for a system that receives and processes IP datagrams directed to the IXP1200 itself; in addition to configuration file entries, such systems must also contain code to handle ARP. The entries are not needed for a system in which the IXP1200 merely passes datagrams through. In our example, the ARP specifications have been made into comments because *wwbump* does not have a local IP address. Instead, *wwbump* operates at layer 2.

---

†The CAP is stored as part of the *ix_ace* handle.

```
# *************************************************************************
#
#    Sample file for the ixconfig application
#
#    It is run at boot time and specifies
#
#    - The interfaces that are to be started at system boot time
#    - The micro aces that are to be started at system boot time
#    - The regular aces that are to be started at system boot time
#    - Bind configuration
#    - Shell commands to be run
#
#    For each microace or ace it also lets us specify another
#    configuration file that can be used to configure that ace
#
#
# *************************************************************************
#
# Specify the interfaces that the code uses
#
# For the SI board
#         --        0-15 are fast ethernet ports. 16 and 17 are gigabit ports
#
# <port number> <ip addr> <broadcast> <netmask> <mac address> <flags>
#
# Values for flags are
#
#         0x0       Unicast
#         0x1       Promiscuous Mode
#         0x2       All Multicast packets are allowed
#         0x3       Multicast packets in set only
#

interface 0 10.1.0.1 10.1.0.255 255.255.255.0 00:01:02:03:04:05 1
interface 1 10.2.0.1 10.2.0.255 255.255.255.0 00:01:02:03:04:06 1
#interface 2 10.3.0.1 10.3.0.255 255.255.255.0 00:01:02:03:04:07 1
#interface 3 10.4.0.1 10.4.0.255 255.255.255.0 00:01:02:03:04:08 1
#interface 4 10.5.0.1 10.5.0.255 255.255.255.0 00:01:02:03:04:09 1
#interface 5 10.6.0.1 10.6.0.255 255.255.255.0 00:01:02:03:04:10 1
#interface 6 10.7.0.1 10.7.0.255 255.255.255.0 00:01:02:03:04:11 1
#interface 7 10.8.0.1 10.8.0.255 255.255.255.0 00:01:02:03:04:12 1
#interface 8 10.9.0.1 10.9.0.255 255.255.255.0 00:01:02:03:04:13 1
#interface 9 10.10.0.1 10.10.0.255 255.255.255.0 00:01:02:03:04:14 1
#interface 10 10.11.0.1 10.11.0.255 255.255.255.0 00:01:02:03:04:15 1
```

```
#interface 11 10.12.0.1 10.12.0.255 255.255.255.0 00:01:02:03:04:16 1
#interface 12 10.13.0.1 10.13.0.255 255.255.255.0 00:01:02:03:04:17 1
#interface 13 10.14.0.1 10.14.0.255 255.255.255.0 00:01:02:03:04:18 1
#interface 14 10.15.0.1 10.15.0.255 255.255.255.0 00:01:02:03:04:19 1
#interface 15 10.16.0.1 10.16.0.255 255.255.255.0 00:01:02:03:04:20 1
#interface 16 10.17.0.1 10.17.0.255 255.255.255.0 00:01:02:03:04:21 1
#interface 17 10.18.0.1 10.18.0.255 255.255.255.0 00:01:02:03:04:22 1


# **********************************************************************
# Specify if debugging with the workbench and downloading code via it
#
# mode <mode>
#
# Values for mode are
#
#       0x0     No workbench.
#       0x1     Download and debug via workbench

mode 0



# **********************************************************************
# Specify the Microcode files (UOF Files)
#
# <fileType> <fileName>
#
# Values for fileType are
#
#       0x0     Slow Ingress File
#       0x1     Slow Egress File
#       0x2     Fast Ingress File for Port 1
#       0x3     Fast Ingress File for Port 2
#       0x4     Fast Egress File
#

file 0 /mnt/SlowIngressWWBump.uof
file 1 /mnt/SlowEgressRR.uof
file 2 /mnt/FastIngressWWBump-seq1.uof
file 3 /mnt/FastIngressWWBump-seq2.uof
file 4 /mnt/FastEgressFifo.uof



# **********************************************************************
#
```

```
# Specify the microaces
#
# <name of ace> <name of executable> <config file name> <runsOn> \
#        <type> <additional parameters>
#
# runsOn can be -- 0 (RUNS_ON_INGRESS_SIDE)
#                -- 1 (RUNS_ON_EGRESS_SIDE)
#
# type can be -- 0 (unknown type)
#                1 (Ingress)
#                2 (egress)
#                3 (L3)
#                4 (L2)
#                5 (input nat)
#                6 (output nat)
#
#
# The first parameter to every microace is the mask of microengines it
# runs on. This is passed automatically by the application. The <additional
# parameters> specify the rest of the command line parameters
#

# no config file for ingress and egress needed and no parameters

microace ifaceInput ./ingressAce none 0 1
microace ifaceOutput ./egressAce none 1 2

microace wwbump /mnt/wwbump none 0 0


# *********************************************************************
#
# Specify the regular aces such as stack ace, nat control ace, spanning
# tree ace, etc.
#
# <name of ace> <name of executable> <config file name> <type> <parameters>
#
#
# type can be -- 0 (unknown type)
#                1 (Spanning Tree)
#                2 (Nat control)
#                3 (Stack ace)
#
# <parameters> are any command line (argc/argv) parameters to be passed to
# the ace
```

```
#
# **********************************************************************


# **********************************************************************
#
# Specify all bind operations
#
# <static/regular> <target name> <ace name>
#
# Specify static for microace to microace static targets
#

bind static ifaceInput/default wwbump
bind static wwbump/default ifaceOutput

# **********************************************************************

# Specify any shell commands. These are executed last no matter where
# they are specified in the file. Note that these are typically used for
# operations such as adding arp entries to the linux stack.
#
# Syntax is:
#                 sh [command string to be executed]
#
#
# The following shell commands add ARP entries to the Linux ARP cache.
# Doing so is necessary if the system receives IP and the ACE code does
# not respond to ARP.  If the ACE code handles ARP, convert to comments.
#

# sh arp -s 10.1.0.2 01:02:03:04:05:06
# sh arp -s 10.2.0.2 02:02:03:04:05:06
# sh arp -s 10.3.0.2 03:02:03:04:05:06
# sh arp -s 10.4.0.2 04:02:03:04:05:06
# sh arp -s 10.5.0.2 05:02:03:04:05:06
# sh arp -s 10.6.0.2 06:02:03:04:05:06
# sh arp -s 10.7.0.2 07:02:03:04:05:06
# sh arp -s 10.8.0.2 08:02:03:04:05:06
# sh arp -s 10.9.0.2 09:02:03:04:05:06


# **********************************************************************
```

The *file* keyword defines the type of an ACE. For example, the line:

file 0 /mnt/SlowIngressWWBump.uof

defines file */mnt/SlowIngressWWBump.uof* to be a *Slow Ingress File* (i.e., type zero). Similarly, the *microace* keyword specifies whether an ACE runs on the ingress or egress side. For example, the line:

microace wwbump /mnt/wwbump none 0 0

specifies that the ACE runs on the ingress side (the first zero) and that it is of an unknown type (the second zero). The keyword *none* stands in place of the file name used in the configuration file.

File *ixsys.config* also specifies the bindings between ACEs. For example, consider the two lines:

bind static ifaceInput/default wwbump
bind static wwbump/default ifaceOutput

The first line specifies that the default binding for the ingress ACE is the ACE named *wwbump*. Similarly, the second line specifies that the default binding for output from the wwbump ACE is the ACE named *ifaceOutput*.

26.13 A Potential Bottleneck In The Wwbump Design

The example code is designed to illustrate programming facilities, and not to be especially efficient. In particular, note that all Web traffic must pass through the StrongARM, and passes through the WWBump dispatch loop twice -- once on ingress and once on egress. Although the underlying hardware offers multiple microengines that can be assigned to run a microblock in parallel, the hardware provides a single StrongARM processor that must handle all Web traffic. Thus, if a large fraction of traffic is Web traffic, the StrongARM can become a bottleneck. An exercise suggests rewriting the code to optimize it.

26.14 Summary

We have examined code for a bump-in-the-wire ACE that counts Web packets. The example code uses Intel's SDK, and relies on standard ingress and egress ACEs. Although the operation that the example ACE performs is trivial, substantial amounts of code are needed.

FOR FURTHER STUDY

Intel's SDK includes more complex examples of ACE code that demonstrate features not covered by our example.

EXERCISES

26.1   The example code assumes that each IP packet contains a complete datagram. Modify the code to ignore all IP fragments except the first.

26.2   The example code counts all packets, including retransmissions. Modify the code to keep state information and ignore retransmissions.

26.3   Modify the example code so it counts TCP connections to a Web server instead of packets (i.e., count *SYN* packets sent to port 80).

26.4   Because the code passes Web traffic to the StrongARM, packets can be reordered. Find an implementation that does not reorder packets and runs at high speed. Hint: do not simply send all packets to the StrongARM.

26.5   Modify wwbump to maintain a count of the number of currently open Web connections. Assume that the wwbump system will see all traffic and use the occurrence of *SYN* and *FIN* packets to determine when a connection opens and closes.

26.6   Read about TCP, and extend the previous exercise to handle *RESET* segments.

Chapter Contents

27

Intel's Second Generation Processors

27.1 Introduction

Previous chapters focus on the Intel IXP1200 processor. This chapter considers the next generation of Intel network processors, which have names of the form IXP2xy0, where x and y denote digits. Three second-generation models have been announced: the IXP2400 (internal name *Sausalito*), the IXP2800 (internal name *Castine*), and the IXP2850 (an IXP2800 with a processor to handle encryption). Unlike models in the first generation, which differ only in speed, models in the second generation have substantial architectural differences. For example, the IXP2800 contains more processors than the 2400, has different internal data paths, and has more onboard functional units. The next sections describe the IXP2400; a later section lists additional features of the IXP2800.

27.2 Use Of Dual Chips For Higher Data Rates

The second generation of Intel network processors can be characterized as either a one or two chip architecture. Although an IXP2400 chip contains a set of processors, coprocessors, and functional units that are capable of arbitrary packet processing, a single chip has a limited aggregate data rate. Thus, to accommodate an aggregate data rate of OC-48 or higher, a pair of IXP2400 chips is needed: one to handle ingress and the other to handle egress. Figure 27.1 illustrates the data flow through two IXP2400 chips.

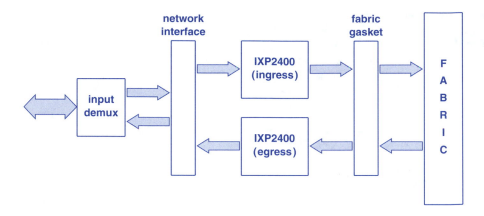

Figure 27.1 Illustration of the packet flow through two IXP2400 chips configured to handle data rates of OC-48 or higher. One chip handles ingress processing and the other handles egress.

27.3 General Characteristics

The IXP2400 follows the same general architecture as the IXP1200: an embedded RISC core plus a set of packet processing engines that operate in parallel. However, the size and power of the hardware has been increased, and additional hardware units have been added that offer new functionality. The following lists several of the facilities that are larger or faster on the IXP2400:

- XScale embedded processor (ARM compliant) with data and instruction caches
- Eight microengines running at 400 or 600 MHz
- Eight hardware threads per microengine
- Multiple microengine instruction stores with over four thousand instructions each
- Two hundred fifty-six general-purpose registers
- Five hundred twelve transfer registers
- Addressing for two gigabytes of Double Data Rate Dynamic RAM (DDR-DRAM)
- Addressing for thirty-two megabytes of Quad Data Rate Static RAM (QDR-SRAM)
- Sixteen words of Next Neighbor Registers to support software pipelining

27.4 Memory Hierarchy

As the previous list implies, the IXP2400 offers an extended memory hierarchy that includes *local memory*. In addition, memory technologies used with the IXP2400 are faster and memories can be larger than on the IXP1200. For example, the IXP2400 provides an interface to DDR-DRAM that can be used to store bulk data such as packet buffers. The maximum size of DDR-DRAM is impressive — addressing is available for up to two gigabytes. The DDR-DRAM used with the IXP2400 has a throughput of 19.2 Gbps. Similarly, the IXP2400 provides an interface for up to thirty-two megabytes of QDR-SRAM that can be used to store packet queues, forwarding tables, and other items that are accessed frequently. The QDR-SRAM controller includes a sixty-four element data structure, known as a *Q-array*, and associated logic that performs efficient enqueue and dequeue operations. Furthermore, the interface to QDR-SRAM uses two separate channels to provide over 12 Gbps of read throughput and 12 Gbps of write throughput.

In addition to the external memories listed above, the IXP2400 has sixteen Kilobytes of onboard *Scratchpad* memory that can be used for communication among the microengines and the embedded RISC core.

27.5 External Connections And Buses

The IXP2400 supports a variety of external connections. Figure 27.2 illustrates some of the connections the chip offers. For example, in addition to connections for the memories listed above, the IXP2400 has a PCI bus connection that allows communication with a host computer or devices that use a PCI interface. As in the IXP1200, the use of an external host is optional; the choice depends on the overall system design.

Unlike the IXP1200, which uses an SRAM bus to access a variety of external units, the IXP2400 has a separate *coprocessor bus* used to access non-memory functional units. For example, Figure 27.2 shows a *classification accelerator* and an ASIC coprocessor attached to the coprocessor bus. More important, the coprocessor bus can be used to connect a T-CAM to provide parallel, high-speed lookup.

27.6 Flow Control Bus

Because the IXP2400 is designed to be used in a two-chip configuration, the hardware provides an interface that the two chips can use to coordinate the flow of packets. Known as a *flow control bus*, the hardware unit provides a bandwidth of up to one gigabit per second for control information flowing between a pair of chips†. Typically, an ingress chip uses the flow control bus to provide information about packets to the egress chip.

---

†Because it is not part of the fast path through which packets flow, Figure 27.1 does not show the flow control bus connection between the two chips.

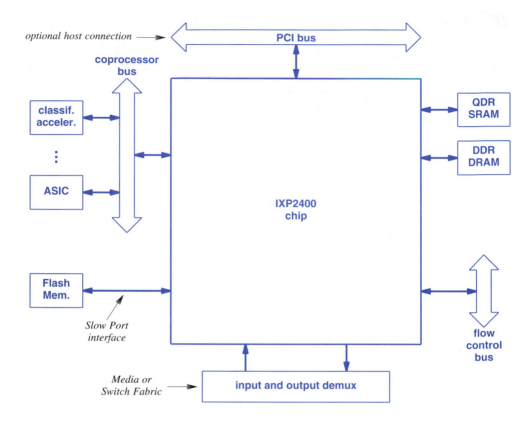

Figure 27.2 Illustration of the external connections available on Intel's IXP2400 network processor.

27.7 Media Or Switch Fabric Interface

One of the major changes between the IXP1200 and IXP2400 arises from the high-speed I/O interfaces. Unlike the IXP1200, the IXP2400 does not offer an IX bus. Instead, high-speed I/O occurs through a *Media or Switch Fabric interface* (*MSF* interface). The MSF interface is divided into separate functional units, one handles input and the other handles output. Interestingly, an MSF interface is configurable — the hardware can be configured to provide a connection to:

- A Utopia 1, 2, or 3 interface
- A CSIX-L1 fabric interface
- An SPI-3 (POS-PHY 2/3) interface

27.8 Internal Architecture

Figure 27.3 illustrates the internal architecture of an IXP2400. The figure shows the major components and their relationship to external connections.

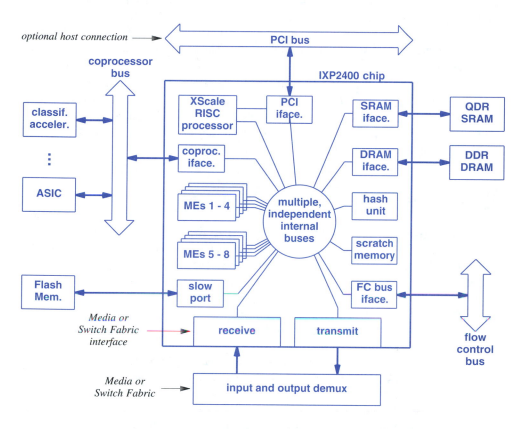

Figure 27.3 Illustration of the internal architecture of an Intel IXP2400. The chip contains additional functional units not shown.

As the figure shows, much of the internal architecture resembles the architecture of the IXP1200. As on the IXP1200, for example, the PCI interface connects directly to the embedded RISC processor. The direct connection means that the XScale processor can use the PCI bus to communicate with a host that controls and manages the IXP2400. Like its predecessor, the IXP2400 has separate interfaces for each external memory (i.e., separate SRAM and DRAM interfaces). The next sections describe some of the architectural differences, including the hardware interface used for packet I/O and the microengine enhancements.

27.9 Physical Network Interfaces And Multiplexing

Although an IXP2400 can handle an aggregate of 2.4 Gbps of traffic (i.e., an OC-48 rate), input is not restricted to a single source. Instead, a box labeled *input and output demux* is used to indicate that hardware demultiplexes connections. Multiplexing among high-speed optical connections is especially important because the OC standards are designed to allow time-division multiplexing of lower-speed connections down to the level of an individual digital telephone call. Thus, a connection that operates at OC-N speed (for some value of N) can be subdivided into lower-speed interfaces.

For example, traffic at 2.4 Gbps can be provided by a single physical connection that operates at OC-48 speed (i.e., an OC-48C connection), two connections that operate at OC-24 speed, four connections that operate at OC-12 speed, and so on. Because it handles multiplexing, the media interface hardware on the IXP2400 can be configured to accommodate a combination of high-speed connections.

27.10 Microengine Enhancements

Each microengine on the IXP2400, which is known as a *Microengine Version 2*, has more capability and can access more functional units than a microengine on the IXP1200. Figure 27.4 lists some of the enhanced capabilities and facilities that are available.

- Multiplier unit
- Pseudo-random number generator
- CRC calculator
- Integrated access to four thirty-two bit timers and timer signaling
- Sixteen entry Content Addressable Memory for inter-thread communication
- Timestamping unit
- Support for generalized thread signaling
- Six hundred forty words of local memory
- Simultaneous access to packet queues without the need for explicit mutual exclusion
- Functional units for ATM segmentation and reassembly
- Automated facilities to handle byte alignment
- Microengines divided into two clusters with independent command and SRAM buses

Figure 27.4 Enhancements in microengine functionality on the IXP2400.

27.11 Support For Software Pipelining

In the IXP2400, the hardware is designed to permit a *software pipeline* to span multiple microengines. That is, a programmer can arrange a program as a series of blocks that each perform part of the necessary packet processing and then pass the packet on to the next block. To pass control from a block on one microengine to a block on the next, the code on the first microengine must signal that it has completed processing the packet.

The hardware mechanisms used to permit efficient communication among microengines are known as *Reflector Mode Pathways*. In essence a Reflector Mode Pathway is a thirty-two bit unidirectional bus. Microengines use the pathways to share both data and global events.

In addition to Reflector Mode Pathways, the IXP2400 offers sets of *Next Neighbor Registers* that can be used to pass status information with a packet as the packet passes between microengines. Each set of registers holds up to one hundred twenty-eight words (sixteen words per thread) of information sent between microengines from one stage in a software pipeline to the next. The Next Neighbor Registers are not partitioned into input and output — a microengine has a single set of registers that are used for receiving state from a previous stage and sending state to the next stage.

27.12 The IXP2800

The IXP2800 follows the same general architecture as the IXP2400, but is designed to operate at OC-192 speed (i.e., an aggregate rate of 10 Gbps). To accommodate the higher speed, the IXP2800 has more microengines, higher-speed memory interfaces, and the processors on the chip operate at higher clock rates. Figure 27.5 lists features of the IXP2800 that are not found on the IXP2400.

- Sixteen microengines that operate at 1.4 GHz
- Two unidirectional sixteen-bit Low Voltage Differential Signaling data interfaces which can be configured to be a SPI-4 Phase 2 or a CSIX switching fabric interface
- Four QDR-SRAM interfaces that each have a bandwidth of 1.6 Gigabytes per second
- Three RDRAM interfaces that each have a bandwidth of 1.6 Gigabytes per second

Figure 27.5 Features of Intel's IXP2800 that distinguish it from the IXP2400.

27.13 Summary

Intel has announced a second generation of network processor products. The IXP2400 is designed to handle OC-48 speeds (i.e., 2.4 Gbps), and the IXP2800 is designed to handle OC-192 speeds (i.e., 10 Gbps). In each second generation model, a pair of network processors is used to achieve full duplex operation: one network processor handles ingress and the other handles egress. To provide coordination among ingress and egress, the second generation chips include a flow control bus that connects the two chips and allows them to pass information about the packets being processed.

The IXP2400 follows the same general architecture as the IXP1200: an embedded RISC processor plus parallel packet engines. Each component on the IXP2400 operates faster than the equivalent component on the IXP1200. Furthermore, the microengines on the IXP2400 have substantially more power, including the ability to multiply and compute pseudo-random numbers. The IXP2400 includes a high-speed packet interface that can be configured to handle media or switch fabric standards, local memory, and facilities to support a software pipeline that spans microengines.

Although it shares the same general architecture as the IXP2400, the IXP2800 has twice as many microengines, faster memory, and higher-speed I/O interfaces. In addition, processors and other functional units on the IXP2800 operate at higher speeds. The IXP2850 model also provides integrated functional units to handle encryption.

FOR FURTHER STUDY

Intel's web site contains a set of product briefs and white papers that describe the IXP2400, IXP2800, and IXP2850 network processors.

EXERCISES

27.1   Consider ACE code written for an IXP1200. What changes are needed to run the code on an IXP2400? an IXP2800?

27.2   What protocol processing tasks does the timestamping unit in Microengine Version 2 handle?

27.3   How can software use a CAM that has sixteen entries to perform inter-thread communication?

27.4   Study the Intel literature. Can an IXP2400 that is connected to a switching fabric be used for both ingress and egress? Why or why not?

Appendix 1

Glossary Of Terms And Abbreviations

Terminology

Anyone who ventures into networking faces a plethora of terms: names and abbreviations for products, technologies, consortia, standards, and protocols. The terminology can be daunting: difficult to learn and remember. Even after a moderate amount of exposure, readers may find specific terms confusing.

This glossary helps solve the problem by providing short definitions for terms used throughout the text and the industry. It is not designed to provide explanations or concepts. Instead, the concise definitions are intended to serve as a quick reminder for someone familiar with the basics.

A Glossary of Terms and Abbreviations
In Alphabetical Order†

10/100 hardware

Applied to any Ethernet hardware that can operate at either 10 Mbps or 100 Mbps.

10Base-T network

The standard for Ethernet hardware that operates at 10 Mbps over twisted pair copper wiring.

10GBase-X

The standard for Ethernet hardware that operates at 10 Gbps. The letter X stands for an encoding. The 8B/10B encoding represents eight bits of data by a ten-bit code group.

100Base-T

The standard for Ethernet hardware that operates at 100 Mbps over twisted pair copper wiring. See Fast Ethernet.

1000Base-CX

A standard for Ethernet hardware that operates at 1 Gbps over shielded copper cable.

1000Base-LX

A standard for Ethernet hardware that operates at 1 Gbps over single mode or multimode optical fiber.

1000Base-SX

A standard for Ethernet hardware that operates at 1 Gbps over multimode optical fiber.

1000Base-T

A standard for Ethernet hardware that operates at 1 Gbps over twisted pair copper wiring. See Gigabit Ethernet, 1000Base-LX, and 1000Base-SX.

802.11b

An IEEE standard for a popular wireless LAN technology that is also called Wi-Fi.

802.3

The IEEE standard for Ethernet. The standard defines the MAC layer for a bus network that uses CSMA/CD.

---

†Because networking terms and acronyms mix upper and lower case, the entries are alphabetized without regard to case.

AAL5

(*ATM Adaptation Layer 5*) Part of the ATM protocol standard. AAL5 is used for data, and supports variable bit rate service and large packets over the underlying connection-oriented transport.

AC '97

(*Audio Codec 1997*) An architecture developed by Intel Corporation for audio applications. The standard, which specifies using a 20-bit representation for audio, is often used on PCs.

ACE

(*Active Computing Element*) The basic unit of programming defined by Intel's Software Development Kit for their network processor. An ACE can include code that runs on packet processors as well as code that runs on the embedded RISC processor. Some Intel literature expands the acronym to *Action/Classification Engine*.

ACK

(*ACKnowledgement*) A short message sent by a receiver to inform a sender that data has arrived. Transport protocols use acknowledgements to achieve reliable transfer (i.e., to know whether a retransmission is needed).

address

An integer value used to identify a particular computer that must appear in each packet sent to the computer.

address mask

A 32-bit binary value used to specify the boundary between prefix and suffix in an IP address. A one bit in the mask corresponds to a prefix; a zero bit corresponds to a suffix. An address mask is also known as a *subnet mask*.

aggregate rate

The combined rate at which traffic can arrive simultaneously over all interfaces of a system. The aggregate data rate is measured in bits per second; the aggregate packet rate is measured in packets per second.

ALU

(*Arithmetic Logic Unit*) A hardware device, usually part of a general-purpose CPU, that performs arithmetic operations such as addition and subtraction and logical operations such as bit shifting.

AMBA

(*Advanced Microprocessor Bus Architecture*) A bus standard developed by Intel. AMBA is used with both conventional CPUs and network processors.

API

(*Application Program Interface*) The specification of the operations and services that a system makes available to a program along with exact details of how the program invokes the services.

ARM

(*ARM Limited*) A company that was previously named *Advanced RISC Machines*, ARM defined an architecture used in the StrongARM embedded processor on the Intel network processor.

ARP

(*Address Resolution Protocol*) The protocol used to dynamically bind an Internet address to a hardware address. ARP is most often used to bind an IP address to an Ethernet address.

ASI

(*Agere System Interface*) One of the three chips that comprise the 2.5G network processor sold by Agere Systems. The ASI chip gathers statistics for traffic management. See FPP and RSP.

ASIC

(*Application Specific Integrated Circuit*) A custom integrated circuit designed to fill a specific role. ASIC designs are expensive and cannot be changed once the chip has been fabricated. See network processor.

ASL (Agere)

(*Agere Scripting Language*) A programming language designed by Agere Systems that allows a programmer to create scripts for policing, packet modification, and other non-classification tasks. ASL is a subset of the C programming language.

ASL (Intel)

(*Action Service Library*) A library that Intel supplies with their Software Development Kit. Customers can incorporate items from an Action Service Library in their code.

associative store

A storage mechanism that allows retrieval of item(s) that match a specified key. See CAM.

asymmetric multiprocessing

A type of computer architecture that uses multiple, dissimilar processors. Compare to symmetric multiprocessing.

asynchronous programming

A form of programming in which a program responds to external events that occur at arbitrary times. The program writes a separate handler for each possible event.

ATM

(*Asynchronous Transfer Mode*) A connection-oriented network technology in which packets consist of 53-octet cells.

AU1X00

The series of network processor chips produced by Alchemy Semiconductor Incorporated (acquired by Advanced Micro Devices).

authentication

Any security facility used to allow a receiver to verify the sender's identity and that the message arrived without being changed. Authentication usually requires the sender to append additional information, which is encrypted.

bandwidth

A measure of the capacity of the underlying transmission system. Although bandwidth specifies frequencies of electromagnetic radiation that can be carried, engineers often use the term informally to refer to the digital throughput of a system.

Banyan switch

A multistage switching fabric architecture that is self-routing. The number of outputs on a Banyan switch is a power of two; a large Banyan switching element is composed of smaller Banyan switching elements aggregated together.

Batcher-Banyan switch

A variant of a Banyan switch that uses merge-sort hardware to avoid blocking.

big endian

A standard for storage or transmission of binary values in which the most-significant byte (bit) resides in the lowest address or is transmitted first. Compare to little endian.

binary trie

A data structure used to implement longest-prefix match lookups in which individual bits of a lookup key are used to navigate through the trie. Binary tries are most often used for IP route lookup.

blade

A single physical circuit board that contains hardware for one or more network interfaces. A blade plugs into the backplane of a network system such as a router.

bps

(*bits per second*) A measure of the rate of data transmission. See Mbps.

bridge

A network system that connects two physical network segments and forwards packets between them. A bridge makes bridged segments appear to operate as a single physical network. A bridge is also known as a layer 2 forwarder because it uses the addresses in each layer 2 frame to determine how to forward the packet.

broadcast

A transmission scheme in which a copy of a packet is delivered to all computers that attach to a given network.

broadcast address

A value used as a destination address to specify that a packet should be delivered to all stations on a network. Ethernet and IP reserve the all-1s address as a broadcast address. Compare to multicast address and unicast address.

broadcast domain

The set of stations that will receive a given broadcast (e.g., all stations attached to an Ethernet hub). A VLAN switch allows a manager to partition stations that attach to the switch into separate broadcast domains.

burst

A set of packets that arrive at nearly the same time. Data traffic is bursty, which means that instead of arriving at a steady rate, packets tend to arrive in clumps with relatively idle periods separating the clumps. A network system must be engineered to handle the highest burst rate.

bus

A hardware mechanism used to interconnect functional units in a network system, including processors and I/O devices. A bus is used to transmit address, data or control signals. Some chips contain hardware that provides a direct connection to a bus; other chips require additional logic for a bus connection.

bus arbiter

A hardware mechanism that allows multiple functional units to access a shared bus without interference. The arbiter ensures that only one unit controls the bus at any time.

bus contention

A condition in which multiple functional units desire to use a shared bus. Contention is undesirable because only one unit can control the bus at any time, which causes other units to delay. See bus arbiter.

bus width

A measure of the capacity of a bus. A bus that has a width of N bits has hardware that permits the simultaneous transfer of up to N bits.

CAM

(*Content Addressable Memory*) A memory mechanism that provides a high-speed search capability by comparing a search key to all slots in memory in parallel. Some network processors rely on CAM to achieve high-speed classification.

CAP (Intel)

(*Communication Access Process*) A mechanism that provides communication with an ACE when using a crosscall.

CAR

(*Committed Access Rate*) A synonym for CIR.

card

An informal abbreviation of NIC.

CBR

(*Constant Bit Rate*) A stream of network traffic that results from an application such as voice or video that generates data at a fixed rate. Some networks offer special facilities to transport CBR data. See UBR and VBR.

cell

A fixed-size packet; the term is usually associated with ATM technology in which a cell contains 48 octets of data and 5 octets of header. Compare to variable-size packet.

cell switch

A network system designed to forward fixed-size cells instead of variable-size packets.

cell tax

A reference to the 10% header overhead imposed by ATM.

checksum

A small, integer value used to verify that a packet arrives uncorrupted. The sending system computes a checksum for an outgoing packet; a receiving system verifies the contents of the packet by recomputing the checksum and comparing to the value sent. Although easier to compute, a checksum detects fewer errors than a CRC. See CRC.

chip set

A set of two or more integrated circuits designed to work together. A vendor may sell a chip set that consists of a processor chip plus assorted interface chips that are used to connect the processor to other devices.

CIR

(*Committed Information Rate*) The data rate that an access provider guarantees will be available on a connection. The CIR is usually part of a contract between a site and a provider. See CAR.

CISC

(*Complex Instruction Set Computer*) An architectural style for a CPU in which the CPU offers many instructions, including instructions that perform complicated operations. Compare to RISC and VLIW.

classification

A technique that extracts values from the headers of an incoming packet and uses the values to map the packet to a flow. Because it examines values across multiple layers of protocols, classification can be faster than traditional demultiplexing.

classification language

A programming language designed specifically to handle packet classification. Unlike conventional programming languages, classification languages are usually declarative.

CMOS

(*Complementary Metal Oxide Semiconductor*) A technology used to build integrated circuits that uses both PMOS (P-type Metal Oxide Semiconductor) and NMOS (N-type Metal Oxide Semiconductor) transistors. The advantage of CMOS over other technologies arises from lower power consumption. Most processor and memory chips use CMOS technology.

connection-oriented paradigm

Characteristic of a network or network protocol that requires the sender to establish a path before data can be transferred. An ATM network is classified as connection-oriented. See connectionless paradigm.

connectionless paradigm

The alternative to a connection-oriented design. A connectionless system allows packets to be sent at any time; each packet contains an identification of the destination. See connection-oriented paradigm.

contention

A situation in which two or more entities compete for access to a shared resource; a mechanism is required to prevent contending entities from interfering with one another. Contention can occur when multiple processors attempt to access a shared memory or when multiple senders attempt to transmit packets across a switching fabric to an output port. See bus contention.

context

A synonym for *threads of execution*.

context switch

A change from one program thread to another. Operating systems implement context switching in software; some network processors implement context switching in hardware.

control store

A synonym for *instruction store*.

controller hardware

A hardware mechanism that provides an interface to and control of a low-level hardware facility. For example, memory requires controller hardware.

coprocessor

A high-speed hardware device that can be used by a general-purpose processor to increase overall processing speed. Each coprocessor handles a specific task, and performs the task much faster than the general-purpose processor.

core

Any programmable processor that is part of a network processor. The term can refer to an embedded RISC processor or a packet engine.

C-Port

A brand name for network processor chips used by Motorola Corporation. Models include the C-3, C-5, and C-5e.

CP

(*Channel Processor* or *Control Point*) Used by Motorola to refer to the *Channel Processor* (i.e., packet processor) found on their network processor chip; used by IBM and other network processor vendors to refer to a *Control Point*, a general-purpose CPU that controls a network processor and handles exceptions.

CRC

(*Cyclic Redundancy Check*) A small, integer value used to verify that a packet arrives uncorrupted. The sending system computes a CRC for an outgoing packet; a receiving system verifies the contents of the packet by recomputing the CRC and comparing to the value sent. Although more expensive to compute, a CRC detects more errors than a checksum. See checksum.

crossbar

A switch or switching fabric in which any input port can be connected directly to any output port through a crossbar mechanism. Crossbar switching fabrics are much more expensive than fabrics that use a shared medium.

crosscall (Intel)

A mechanism offered by the Intel SDK that allows one ACE or a non-ACE program to make a remote procedure call to another ACE.

CSIX

A standard created by the Network Processor Forum that specifies the interconnection between a network processor and a switching fabric. The goal of defining an interface standard is to allow any vendor's network processor to connect to any vendor's switching fabric.

CSMA/CD

(*Carrier Sense Multiple Access with Collision Detection*) A technique used by Ethernet to arbitrate contention for access to a shared transmission medium. A station listens to see if the medium is idle before sending. If another station attempts simultaneous transmission, each station chooses a random backoff before attempting retransmission.

CSR

(*Control and Status Register*) A low-level hardware mechanism used to pass information from a device to a processor or to allow the processor to control a device.

cut-through

A mechanism in which a network system starts to forward data from a packet to another stage or to an output device before the entire packet has arrived.

data flow architecture

A network system architecture that treats each packet operation independently. Whenever it performs an operation on a packet, a processor stores the packet in memory with a request for the next operation. When a processor becomes available, hardware selects one of the packets that is waiting for the operation that the processor performs. Sometimes written *dataflow*.

data flow diagram

An illustration of functional units in a network system and the flow of data among them.

data rate

A measure of the data that can arrive or be sent, measured in Megabits per second (Mbps). A network system must be engineered to accommodate the aggregate data rate on all interfaces. See aggregate rate, packet rate, and Gbps.

datagram

The name given to an Internet Protocol (IP) packet. See frame.

DDR

(*Double Data Rate*) Used as a prefix for RAM technology that operates at twice the data rate of normal RAM. For example, DDR-DRAM operates twice as fast as DRAM. See QDR.

declarative language

A programming language in which the programmer provides specifications of what is to be done without specifying how it is to be done. Compare to imperative language. Also see procedural language.

default

A selection to be used when none of the explicit selections applies. Defaults arise in IP routing (a default route) and in classification (a default flow).

demultiplexing

The traditional method of handling an incoming packet when the packet has been composed using layered protocols. A protocol header is examined at each step; a type field in the header specifies the protocol that was used to compose the next layer. Compare to classification.

destination address

The address placed in a packet to specify where the packet should be delivered.

DiffServ

(*Differentiated Services*) The standard adopted by the IETF to replace the original IP Type Of Service field. DiffServ allows up to 64 possible priorities; each datagram carries an 8-bit field to specify its desired service.

DMA

(*Direct Memory Access*) A mechanism that allows a peripheral device, such as a network interface card, to move data over a bus to or from memory without using the CPU.

DNF bit

(*DO NOT FRAGMENT bit*) A bit in the IP header that a source sets to specify that the datagram must not be fragmented. If fragmentation is needed for a datagram and the DNF bit is set, the datagram is discarded and an ICMP error message is sent back to the source.

DNS

(*Domain Name System*) The system used to map human-readable machine names into IP addresses. DNS servers throughout the Internet answer requests.

dotted decimal notation

A syntactic form used to represent binary values. The value of each octet is written in base ten, with dots separating the octets. See dotted hex notation.

dotted hex notation

A syntactic form used to represent binary values. The value of each octet is written as two hexadecimal digits, with dots separating the octets. See dotted decimal notation.

DQDB

(*Distributed Queue Dual Bus*) An IEEE standard for communication in Metropolitan Area Networks (MANs) that uses a pair of unidirectional buses connecting all stations and a time-division multiplexing scheme. DQDB has not been widely adopted by industry.

DRAM

(*Dynamic Random Access Memory*) One of two broad categories used to classify random access memory technologies. Dynamic RAM stores each bit in a cell composed of a capacitor and a transistor. Dynamic RAM takes less physical space, but requires extra refresh hardware that ensures bits stay charged because the capacitor loses charge over time. Several variations of DRAM exist. Compare to SRAM. Also see DDR, QDR, and SDRAM.

dual ported memory

A memory system with hardware support that allows access by two functional units.

dynamic classification

A classification scheme in which flows are established as needed. For example, dynamic classification can create a separate flow for each TCP connection.

dynamic flow

A flow for which the classification rules depend on the history of packets. The classification rules for dynamic flows usually include the source and destination addresses.

early route binding

An optimization used to reduce route lookup times by prefetching routes and storing them in a mechanism that operates faster than conventional lookup. Early route binding can be used with classification.

ECC

(*Error Correcting Code*) A mechanism used to detect and correct bit errors. An additional binary value is computed and appended to a data item before the item is stored or transmitted. If a few bits of the item are damaged, the appended value can be used to reconstruct them.

ECN

(*Explicit Congestion Notification*) A congestion control mechanism proposed for use with IPv6 in which intermediate routers mark datagrams that experience congestion by setting the ECN bit in the header.

egress

A term used to characterize packet processing performed as a packet exits a system. Compare to ingress.

EJTAG

(*Enhanced Joint Test Action Group*) A standard interface for in-circuit testing. EJTAG extends the earlier JTAG standard adopted by IEEE.

embedded processor

A processor, usually a RISC design, that has been placed on a VLSI chip along with other functional units or memories. An embedded processor is often used on a network processor chip to control and manage other hardware units.

encapsulation

A technique used by layered protocols in which successive layers add a header to an outgoing packet. See demultiplexing and classification.

end-to-end

Characteristic of a mechanism that operates across an entire network or internet. Network applications are classified as end-to-end.

endian

See big endian and little endian.

EOP (Intel)

(*End Of Packet*) A bit set in the control information that accompanies an mpacket to indicate that the mpacket contains the last piece of a packet. See SOP.

EPC

(*Embedded Processor Complex*) A term used by IBM to refer to an area of their PowerNP network processor that contains multiple packet engines (picoengines) and an embedded PowerPC.

EPD

(*Early Packet Discard*) A technique that discards an entire packet when one piece is lost or discarded. EPD is used with ATM.

error correction

The restoration of a correct value after an error during storage or transmission corrupts one or more bits. Error correction is used by memory hardware as well as by some network protocols. See error detection.

error detection

The discovery that one or more bits of a value have been corrupted during storage or transmission. Most network protocols include a form of error detection. See error correction.

ESBGA

(*Enhanced Super Ball Grid Array*) A chip packaging technology that offers high pin counts. See HL-BGA.

Ethernet

A popular Local Area Network (LAN) technology that uses CSMA/CD for access control. Ethernet operates at 10, 100, or 1000 Mbps.

exact match lookup

A table lookup in which each bit of the search must match the corresponding bit of the key in a table entry. Compare to longest prefix match lookup.

Executive Processor

One of the coprocessors present in Motorola's network processor. The Executive Processor controls overall chip configuration and management.

fabric

See switching fabric.

Fabric Processor

A coprocessor in Motorola's network processor that provides high-speed interconnection to an external switching fabric.

fan out

The number of devices that can be connected to the output of an electronic circuit.

Fast Ethernet

A marketing term used for 100Base-T Ethernet. Fast Ethernet operates at 100 Mbps.

fast path

The path a normal packet follows through a network system. The capacity of the fast path determines the volume of traffic the system can handle; the maximum delay along the fast path provides a lower bound on the delay a packet experiences in the system. The fast path is also called the fast data path. See slow path.

FBI (Agere)

(*Functional Bus Interface*) The bus used to connect Agere's FPP and RSP chips.

FBI (Intel)

A functional unit on Intel's IXP1200 chip that provides the interface to the IX bus. Although the acronym probably arose from a descriptive phrase (e.g., Fast Bus Interface), the original phrase has been forgotten.

FCRAM

(Fast Cycle Random Access Memory) A DRAM technology that has low cycle times. The low cycle time makes FCRAM especially useful for packet storage. See RLDRAM.

FDDI

(*Fiber Distribution Data Interface*) An older network technology that uses fiber optics and token passing to control media access.

fetch-store paradigm

An approach to building hardware or software in which all operations are cast as either a fetch or store. Bus hardware uses the fetch-store paradigm.

FIB

(*Forwarding Information Base*) A term used by Cisco to refer to forwarding information (e.g., an IP routing table).

FIFO

(*First-In-First-Out*) Two meanings: a queueing policy in which items are processed in the order in which they arrive; a hardware mechanism that implements a FIFO queue. A hardware FIFO is often used as the transfer mechanism between a processor and an I/O device.

FIN

A TCP segment used to signal the end of transfer. Once each side sends a FIN segment, the connection is terminated.

FIR

(*Fast IRda*) A hardware controller that enables infrared data communications at 4 Mbps.

firewall

A security mechanism placed between a site and the Internet. An administrator configures a firewall to allow specific traffic; the firewall blocks all other traffic.

flow

A set of packets that are associated together for purposes of traffic management or forwarding. A flow can correspond to an individual session (e.g. a TCP connection) or a group of packets of one general type (e.g., all packets carrying World Wide Web traffic).

flow termination

A general term for the processing performed by an endpoint system that extracts data from an incoming flow. Flow termination usually involves transport-layer termination. See TCP termination.

forwarding

The packet processing task that chooses the next system to which a packet should be sent. In a connectionless network, forwarding requires looking up a destination address in a routing table.

FPGA

(*Field Programmable Gate Array*) A state-machine technology that allows state transitions to be reconfigured on the chip without replacing the hardware. A network system that uses an FPGA can be upgraded or changed by loading new values into the FPGA.

FPL

(*Functional Programming Language*) A classification language developed by Agere Systems. See NCL.

FPM-DRAM

(*Fast Page Mode DRAM*) A type of random access memory that allows faster access if data is on the same row or page as the data accessed previously. FPM-DRAM is optimized for large block transfers.

FPP

(*Fast Pattern Processor*) One of the three chips that comprise the 2.5G network processor sold by Agere Systems. The FPP performs packet classification and forwards packets to the RSP for processing. See ASI and RSP.

fragmentation

The process of dividing an IP datagram into smaller pieces called fragments. Fragmentation is needed when a datagram is larger than the MTU of the network over which it must travel. See segmentation.

frame

The name given to a packet recognized by the hardware. Thus, an Ethernet packet is called an Ethernet frame. See datagram.

frame alteration

Any protocol processing task that changes the contents of a packet. Tasks such as decrementing a TTL counter are included in frame alteration.

Gbps

(*Gigabit per second*) A measure of the capacity of a network. See bps and Mbps.

Gigabit Ethernet

The Ethernet technology that transmits data at 1 Gbps.

GigE

A common abbreviation for Gigabit Ethernet.

GMII

(*Gigabit Media Independent Interface*) An extension of the Ethernet Media Independent Interface to Gigabit Ethernet. See MII, PCS, PMA, and PMD.

GPIO

(*General-Purpose I/O*) A standard originally developed by Hewlett-Packard for interconnecting a processor and I/O devices. Some network processors provide a GPIO interface.

GPP

(*General-Purpose Processor*) A CPU with an instruction set that can perform most computing tasks. For example, the processor in a conventional PC is classified as a general-purpose processor. Compare to embedded processor and special-purpose processor.

GPR

(*General Purpose Register*) A small, high-speed storage mechanism in a processor used to hold intermediate results such as intermediate values for an arithmetic computation.

GPS

(*Generalized Processor Sharing*) A theoretical algorithm for fair scheduling. Although not practical, GPS is used as the underlying basis for practical scheduling schemes.

granularity

A general reference to the size of data that can be transferred across a switching fabric or across an internal bus. Hardware can use cell granularity, block granularity, or packet granularity.

hardware interrupt

A mechanism used in third-generation computer systems to allow external devices to inform the CPU when service is needed (e.g., when a packet has arrived).

header

Information carried in a packet other than the message being sent. Header information specifies the packet's source and destination as well as the contents of the data area. See payload.

HL-BGA

(*High-thermal Low-power Ball Grid Array*) A chip packaging technology that facilitates high pin counts. HL-BGA tolerates higher thermal conditions than ESBGA. See ESBGA.

HOL blocking

(*Head Of Line blocking*) A situation in which a low priority packet blocks one or more high priority packets. A low priority packet obtains a resource such as an internal communication channel that no other packets are using. If high priority packets arrive that need to use the resource, they will block until the low priority packet finishes. HOL blocking can occur in a switching fabric.

hop count

A measure of distance across an internet (or wide area network). The number of hops is equal to the number of intermediate networks (or number of wide area connections) between the source and destination.

host

An end-user system on the Internet, which can include a device such as a printer as well as conventional computers such as PCs or supercomputers.

host suffix

Each Internet address is divided into a prefix that identifies a network and a suffix that identifies a host on the network. See network prefix.

HTTP

(*HyperText Transfer Protocol*) The application-layer protocol used to access web pages. HTTP is used over a TCP connection.

hub

A hardware device that provides the illusion of a single network segment to which multiple stations attach. Hub hardware propagates incoming electrical signals to all stations. See repeater.

HyperTransport

A technology designed to provide high-speed transfer in a network system between a physical interface and the processor(s). See RapidIO, InfiniBand, PCI-X, and Utopia.

I²S

(*Inter-IC Sound*) A serial interface standard for digital audio.

ICMP

(*Internet Control Message Protocol*) A protocol in the TCP/IP suite used for control messages and to report errors. The ping program uses ICMP echo request and echo reply messages.

IDL (Intel)

(Interface Definition Language) A language used by the Intel SDK to define each crosscall. An IDL program declares a set of functions, the types of arguments for the functions, and the type of each return value.

IDS

(*Intrusion Detection System*) A security mechanism that monitors traffic and raises an alert when it detects a pattern of packets that appears to be an attack.

IEEE

(*Institute of Electrical and Electronic Engineers*) An organization that establishes standards for networking hardware.

IEEE 802.11b

An IEEE standard for wireless networks. 802.11b, also known as Wi-Fi is the most popular of the 802.11 standards.

IEEE 802.3

An IEEE standard for Ethernet.

IETF

(*Internet Engineering Task Force*) An organization that establishes standards for TCP/IP protocols and the Internet.

imperative language

A programming language in which the programmer gives an explicit sequence of instructions to specify computation. Compare to declarative language. Also see procedural language.

InfiniBand

A technology designed to provide high-speed transfer in a network system between a physical interface and the processor(s). See RapidIO, PCI-X, Utopia, and Hyper-Transport.

ingress

A term used to characterize packet processing performed as a packet enters a system. Compare to egress.

input queueing

A buffering technique that associates a packet queue with each input port. Compare to output queueing.

instruction store

A memory from which a processor fetches and executes code. See control store.

instruction-level parallelism

A performance improvement technique employed in processors that allows a processor to execute two or more instructions at the same time. Compare to task-level parallelism.

interconnect

A general term used for a hardware mechanism used to transfer data or signals between functional units. See switching fabric and bus.

internal transfer mechanism

A hardware mechanism used to transfer data (packets, cells, or blocks) within a chip or a network system.

interrupt processing

Processing that occurs as the result of an interrupt. Interrupt processing must be completed quickly because further interrupts are temporarily disabled while an interrupt is serviced.

IP gateway

A synonym for IP router.

IP router

A network system that connects to two or more networks and forwards IP datagrams among them. A router is also known as a layer 3 forwarder because it uses the IP destination address to determine how to forward each datagram.

ips

(*instructions per packet*) A measure of the maximum number of instructions a processor can execute before another packet arrives. The rate depends on the processor speed and the data rate of the network(s) to which the system attaches.

IrDA

(*Infrared Data Association*) An organization that has produced a standard for communication devices that use infrared technology.

ISO

(*International Standards Organization*) An organization that has produced standards used in computer networks.

isochronous network

A network in which the underlying hardware is built to precisely bound latency and jitter. Traditional voice telephone systems use isochronous technology.

IX-bus (Intel)

(*Intel Exchange bus*) A 64-bit bus used on Intel's IXP1200 for high-speed I/O.

IXA

(*Internet Exchange Architecture*) The marketing term Intel Corporation uses for its network processor architecture. IXA includes both hardware and software architecture. See IXP.

IXP

(*Internet Exchange Processor*) The name Intel Corporation uses for specific network processors that follow the IXA architecture. Models include the IXP1200, IXP2400, IXP2800, and IXP2850.

jitter

A measure of the variation in latency experienced by packets as they traverse a network. An isochronous network has low jitter; the Internet can have high jitter.

JTAG

(*Joint Test Action Group*) A standard interface for in-circuit testing adopted by IEEE. See EJTAG.

kernel

An abbreviation for operating system kernel.

kernel thread

A thread of execution that runs in the operating system kernel and has access to the kernel address space as well as privilege to access I/O devices.

knockout switch

An enhanced version of a crossbar switch consisting of N input ports and N output ports in which each output port can accept up to Q packets simultaneously (Q is less than N). A knockout switch can be used to build a switching fabric.

Kpps

(*Kilo packets per second*) A measure of packet rate. See Mpps.

LA-X

(*Look Aside interface*) A bus interface standard defined by the Network Processor Forum. An LA-X interface allows some of the data stream to be separated, sent through a coprocessor, and then rejoined to the original stream. A network processor can use an LA-X interface to process headers as packets are moved to memory.

label

A value in the header of a packet on a network that uses label switching. ATM and MPLS both use label switching.

LAN

(*Local Area Network*) A class of network technologies optimized for high speed and low cost. A LAN can only extend a short distance. Contrast with WAN.

latency

The technical term for delay. Transmission across a physical medium and packet processing by an intermediate system both introduce latency.

layer 2 forwarder

See bridge.

layer 3 forwarder

See IP router.

layer 5 forwarder

A load balancer that uses the content of an incoming request message as well as current loads when choosing a server.

layer 7 forwarder

A synonym for layer 5 forwarder favored by engineers who use the older OSI layering model.

layering

A technique used to construct protocols. Each layer performs a subset of the processing required.

LCD controller

(*Liquid Crystal Display controller*) A hardware controller for liquid crystal display devices.

leaky bucket

A mechanism used for traffic shaping. Leaky bucket delays outgoing packets to help eliminate bursts and smooth the packet rate. Also see token bucket.

learning bridge

A bridge that uses the source address in each incoming packet to learn which computers attach to which networks. Most bridges are learning bridges.

LINK

(*Link layer interface*) The hardware, usually a set of chips, that implements layer 2 functionality such as framing and MAC addressing.

little endian

A standard for storage or transmission of binary values in which the least-significant byte (bit) resides in the lowest address or is transmitted first. Compare to big endian.

load balancer

A network system used at web sites to equalize the load across a set of web servers. The load balancer accepts an incoming HTTP request, and chooses a server to which it should be redirected.

locality of reference

A measure of a stream of data references that refers to repetition over time (temporal locality) or close proximity (spatial locality). High temporal locality permits a cache to optimize lookups.

longest prefix match lookup

A table lookup scheme used for IP routing in which a prefix of the search must match the corresponding bits of the key in a table entry. The lookup finds the table entry for which the prefix match covers the most bits. Compare to exact match lookup.

MAC

(*Media Access Control*) A general reference to layer 2 hardware protocols used to access a particular network. The term *MAC address* often appears as a synonym for Ethernet address.

macro assembly language

An assembly language that allows complex sequences of instructions to be encoded as separate macros that the assembler expands when translating the program. Macros raise the level of the language by hiding the low-level details. Some network processor vendors offer a macro assembly language for their chip.

Mbps

(*Mega bits per second*) A measure of the data rate of a network equal to one million bits per second. See bps and compare to MBps.

MBps

(*MegaBytes per second*) A measure of the data transfer rate used with memory interfaces equal to 2^{20} bytes per second, where a byte is defined to be eight bits. Compare to Mbps.

measured service

A form of network service in which resource use (e.g., packets per second or total packets sent) is limited. An ISP that offers measured service uses traffic monitoring and policing to enforce limits.

memory access speed

A synonym for memory latency.

memory bandwidth

The rate at which data can be moved into or out of a memory. Compare to memory latency.

memory bank

A subset of memory. Memory is divided into multiple banks to improve performance. Operations on separate banks do not interfere with one another.

memory controller

A hardware mechanism that interfaces to memory and handles fetch and store operations. All memory operations go through the controller.

memory cycle time

The minimum amount of time required between successive memory operations. Memory cycle time is important for large transfers because it determines the rate at which memory accesses can be repeated. See memory latency.

memory fragmentation

A problem caused when a system dynamically allocates variable-size blocks of memory (e.g., each packet is stored in a block of memory exactly the size of the packet). After many such operations, free memory is divided into many small blocks.

memory hierarchy

A set of memories that represent a sequence of tradeoffs between high speed and low cost. Most network systems use a memory hierarchy that has a small high-speed (i.e., high-cost) memory and larger low-speed (i.e., low-cost) memories.

memory latency

The amount of time required to access a single item in memory. The latency for a fetch operation is usually slightly smaller than the latency for a store operation. See memory bandwidth and memory cycle time.

microengine

Intel's term for each of the packet processors on their network processor chip. Also see picoengine.

MII

(*Media Independent Interface*) Part of the Ethernet standard that defines a conceptual layering that hides differences in the underlying media (i.e., accommodates copper or fiber). MII is divided into three sublayers. See GMII, PCS, PMA, and PMD.

Mips

(*Millions of instructions per second*) A measure of processor speed.

MIPS

A corporation that sells a specific RISC processor. Some network processor vendors include an extended MIPS processor on their chip.

MLP

(*MultiLink PPP*) A synonym for MLPPP. Also see MPPP.

MLPPP

(*MultiLink Point-to-Point Protocol*) An extension of the Point-to-Point Protocol used with ISDN. MLPPP transfers data over two B channels to double the effective throughput from 64 Kbps to 128 Kbps. Also see MLP and MPPP.

modem

(*mo*dulator *dem*odulator) A hardware device that sends and receives digital information by encoding the information in an analog wave for transmission. The modem connects between a digital system and an analog transmission medium.

MORE FRAGMENTS bit

A bit in the IP datagram header that specifies whether the datagram contains additional data. The bit is set in all fragments except the fragment that carries the tail of the datagram.

mpacket (Intel)

The fundamental unit of data transfer used with Intel's IXP1200. Each mpacket is sixty-four bytes long, and a packet must be divided into mpackets for input or output.

MPLS

(*Multi-Protocol Label Switching*) A connection-oriented networking technology that uses label switches to forward traffic. A label switch is related to an ATM switch. MPLS includes protocols that select routes, and offers interfaces that can transfer IP, ATM, or Layer 2 protocols.

MPPP

(*Multilink PPP*) A synonym for MLPPP. Also see MLP.

Mpps

(*Millions of Packets Per Second*) A measure of packet rate.

MTU

(*Maximum Transmission Unit*) The largest amount of data that can be transferred across a network in one packet.

multicast

A technique that allows a subset of computers on a network to receive a copy of a packet. On a shared medium network like Ethernet, a single copy of a multicast is sent across the network, and stations listening for the group's multicast address receive a copy.

multicast address

A value used as a destination address to specify that a packet should be delivered to all endpoints that participate in the specified multicast group. Compare to broadcast address and unicast address.

multistage fabric

A switching fabric that is arranged as a set of stages; a transmission through the fabric passes through multiple stages. Multistage fabrics often allow larger scale.

multithreading

A mechanism in which multiple threads of execution remain ready to run; when one thread blocks (e.g., to wait for I/O), the processor is switched to another. Multithreading can be implemented by operating system software or by the processor hardware. See threads of execution and context switch.

mutual exclusion

A situation in which two or more entities contending for a shared resource agree to take turns, with only one accessing the resource at any time.

NAT

(*Network Address Translation*) A mechanism used on a connection to the Internet that allows a set of host computers at a site to share one Internet address. NAT rewrites the source addresses in outgoing datagrams and rewrites the destination address in incoming datagrams. See TCP splicing.

NCL

(*Network Classification Language*) A classification language designed by Intel. See FPL.

network byte order

A TCP/IP standard for transmission of integers that specifies the most significant byte appears first (big endian). A sender translates integers from the local integer representation to network byte order, and a receiver translates from network byte order to the local machine's representation.

network DRAM

A general reference to memory technology that can be used to store packets. Network DRAM must have low cycle times and high bandwidth. See FCRAM and RLDRAM.

network prefix

Each Internet address is divided into a prefix that identifies a network and a suffix that identifies a host on the network. See host suffix.

network processor

A programmable hardware device designed to process packets at high speed. Network processors differ from conventional processors because they have hardware that can perform protocol processing tasks quickly. See NP and NPU.

NEV

(*Network Equipment Vendor*) A company that manufactures or sells network systems or subassemblies used to construct network systems.

NIC

(*Network Interface Card*) A printed circuit board that plugs into a computer's bus and connects the computer to a network. See blade.

NP

(*Network Processor*) An abbreviation used by many vendors. Also see NPU.

NP-1

EZchip Corporation's network processor.

NP10

The name Agere Systems uses for the classification processor in their 10G network processor. See TM10.

NPF

(*Network Processor Forum*) A consortium of vendors who sell network processors. NPF attempts to achieve consensus and set standards.

NPU

(*Network Processor Unit*) A synonym for network processor. Also see NP.

OC standards

A series of standards for the transmission of data over optical fiber. The standards include OC-3, OC-48, and OC-192, which operate at 155 Mbps, 2.4 Gbps, and 10 Gbps.

octet

An eight-bit unit of data. Although many engineers use the term *byte* instead of octet, doing so is inaccurate because the size of a byte is defined by each processor.

OIF

(*Optical Internet Forum*) An organization that issues standards for the connection to optical transmission equipment, including the SFI standard.

onboard memory

A general term that refers to local memory. The memory can be located on a printed circuit board (e.g., onboard a NIC) or on a silicon chip (e.g., onboard a network processor chip).

operating system kernel

The set of procedures and data structures that reside in the kernel address space, provide services, and manage application programs, memory, and hardware devices. On a software-based network system, protocol processing software resides in the kernel.

operation chaining

A technique used to optimize I/O in which the CPU can specify a series of operations by forming a linked list. After it performs one operation, the device interface hardware automatically proceeds to perform the next operation without requiring intervention from the CPU.

OSI

(*Open System Interconnect*) A set of layered protocols defined by ISO. OSI protocols were intended to replace TCP/IP. Some engineers still refer to the OSI 7-layer model.

output queueing

A buffering technique that associates a packet queue with each output port. Compare to input queueing.

packet

A generic term used to describe the units of transmission in a packet switching network. Also see frame and datagram.

packet duplication

An error condition in a packet switching system that causes an additional copy of a packet to be transmitted.

packet filter

A mechanism found in routers and other network systems that is often used for security. A manager configures a packet filter to specify which packets are to be forwarded and which are to be rejected.

packet queue

A mechanism, usually a linked list in memory, that holds a set of packets. A typical network system places each incoming packet in a packet queue until the packet can be processed.

packet rate

A measure of the capacity needed in a network system. Some designs can only handle high data rates if the packet rate is low (i.e., packets are large). See data rate.

packet switching

A computer communication paradigm that divides data transmission into small blocks known as packets.

packet train

A set of packets that arrive with almost no delay among them. As they travel through a packet switching network, packets tend to form packet trains.

packet type field

A field in a packet header that specifies the format of the packet contents (i.e., payload). The type field is used for demultiplexing.

padding

Additional zero bits appended to a binary item to increase the length of the item. Some technologies require that short packets be padded to meet a minimum packet length.

parallel processing
An alternative to sequential processing in which the underlying hardware performs multiple computational activities at the same time. See sequential processing.

payload
The data being carried in a packet. See header.

PayLoadPlus
The brand name used by Agere Systems for their network processor architecture. Two models are the 2.5G PayLoadPlus chip set and the 10G PayLoadPlus chip set.

PCI
(*Peripheral Component Interconnect*) A standard for a bus that can interconnect processors and peripheral devices. A PCI bus is found on most PCs.

PCI-X
An extension of the PCI bus standard that can serve as a high-speed interconnect within a network system. See RapidIO, InfiniBand, Utopia, and HyperTransport.

PCMCIA
(*Personal Computer Memory Card International Association*) An organization that has developed an interface standard for connecting peripheral devices. The PCMCIA standard, which is often used in PCs, can be used to connect a variety of devices, including network devices.

PCS
(*Physical Coding Sublayer*) The top sublayer of the Ethernet Media Independent Interface. See GMII, MII, PMA, and PMD.

PDU
(*Protocol Data Unit*) A generic term for a packet or message. The terminology was originally defined by ISO. Some network processor vendors use the acronym PDU in place of *packet*.

per-packet overhead
The fixed amount of processing that a network system performs for each packet.

PGA
(*Pin Grid Array*) An implementation technique used with FPGAs.

PHY
(*PHYsical interface*) The hardware, usually a set of chips, that connects to a network device and transmits or receives packets.

picoengine

IBM's term for each of the programmable packet processors on their network processor chip. Picoengines handle fast path processing. Also see microengine.

pinout

The assignment of functions to the pins of an integrated circuit. Hardware engineers must understand the pinout when they form a printed circuit board that connects one chip to another.

pipeline

A design in which each packet passes through a sequence of processing steps, where each step is performed by a distinct processor. It is also possible to implement a pipeline in software.

PMA

(*Physical Medium Attachment*) The middle sublayer of the Ethernet Media Independent Interface. See GMII, MII, PCS, and PMD.

PMD

(*Physical Media Dependent sublayer*) The lowest sublayer of the Ethernet Media Independent Interface. See GMII, MII, PCS, and PMA.

PMM

(*Physical MAC Multiplexor*) A functional unit on IBM's network processor that transfers packets between physical interface devices and internal storage.

polling

A style of programming in which a processor repeatedly tests to determine when an event occurs. Polling can be used to determine if a packet has arrived.

port

A term with more than one meaning. Hardware engineers use the term to refer to a hardware interface device (e.g., an Ethernet port). TCP/IP protocols use the term to refer to a transport-layer abstraction known as a protocol port number.

port contention

An undesirable condition in which two or more processors attempt to transmit data to the same output port, and one must wait for the other. Port contention can occur in a switching fabric.

POS

(*Packet Over SONET*) A standard for the transmission of data packets over a network that uses the SONET framing protocol. See SONET.

POS-PHY

(*Packet Over SONET PHYsical interface*) A physical interface standard that specifies the connection from a network system to a SONET transmission system and how to transfer packets.

PowerNP

The name IBM uses for its network processor architecture.

pps

(*packets per second*) See packet rate.

PQ

(*Priority Queuing*) A queue management mechanism in which packets are selected according to their priority.

preamble

Sixty-four alternating 1s and 0s sent before an Ethernet packet to allow the receiver to synchronize its clock with the incoming signal.

preemption

A situation in which a high-priority event causes the CPU to switch from one thread of execution to another. See context switch.

prefix match

See longest prefix match lookup.

procedural language

A conventional programming language in which a programmer gives an explicit sequence of instructions to specify computation. See declarative language and imperative language.

processor hierarchy

A set of processor types arranged according to speed and capabilities. A network processor can contain a processor hierarchy that includes I/O processors, coprocessors, and an embedded RISC processor.

PROM

(*Programmable Read-Only Memory*) A memory device in which values are stored once, and afterward can only be read.

promiscuous mode

A mode that allows interface hardware to capture all frames that pass across the network. Unless it is placed in promiscuous mode, an interface usually rejects frames not intended for the local computer.

protocol

A set of message formats and the rules that must be followed to exchange those messages.

protocol port number

See port.

protocol stack

The software that forms an implementation of a protocol suite.

protocol suite

A set of protocols that have been designed to work together. The TCP/IP protocols form a suite.

provisioned

A telecommunications industry term that refers to networks or services that are configured manually.

pseudo header

Information, such as the source and destination addresses, that is sent in the IP header, but must be included in the computation of a TCP or UDP checksum.

PSM

(Programmable State Machine) A hardware technology such as an FPGA that allows an engineer to specify processing as a set of states with transitions among them. State machine implementations are often used for testing before proceeding with a silicon implementation. See FPGA.

PVC

(*Permanent Virtual Circuit*) A virtual circuit that is configured manually and lasts for long periods of time (e.g., months). Compare to SVC.

PXF

(*Parallel eXpress Forwarding*) The name used by Cisco for its network processor. The term is also used for the mechanism on the Cisco chip that performs IP forwarding.

QDR

(*Quad Data Rate*) Used as a prefix for RAM technology that operates at four times the data rate of normal RAM. For example, QDR-DRAM operates four times as fast as DRAM. See DDR.

QoS

(*Quality of Service*) A generic term that refers to network guarantees such as guarantees about loss, delay, jitter, and minimum throughput. Some proponents argue that QoS is necessary for real-time traffic.

queueing

A generic term that refers to any situation in which packets are held waiting processing or transmission.

queueing discipline

A set of rules that specify how to select a packet for processing from among a set of packets. See PQ.

RAM

(*Random Access Memory*) The generic term for main memory in a network system. See SRAM and DRAM.

RapidIO

A technology designed to provide high-speed transfer in a network system between a physical interface and the processor(s). See InfiniBand, PCI-X, Utopia, and HyperTransport.

RCU

(*Reconfigurable Communications Unit*) The term used by Cognigine for the individual processors on their network processor that have a reconfigurable instruction set. See VISC.

RDRAM

(*Rambus Dynamic Random Access Memory*) A memory technology that offers a higher data rate than DDR-DRAM. The name arises because RDRAM uses the Rambus standard for signaling levels.

real estate

An informal reference to the surface area of an integrated circuit.

reassembly

The process of collecting fragments of an IP datagram and coalescing them into an exact copy of the original datagram. The ultimate destination performs reassembly.

RED

(*Random Early Detection*) A technique a network system uses instead of tail-drop to discard packets at random. RED avoids global synchronization of multiple TCP sessions. See WRED.

reference platform

An evaluation system offered by a network processor vendor. A reference platform usually includes software as well as hardware. See SDK.

register

In a narrow sense, a set of high-speed memory devices that a CPU uses to hold temporary results. In a broadest sense, a hardware mechanism that supports the fetch-store paradigm. The registers used on many network processors follow the broadest sense of the meaning.

register bank

A subset of the registers available on a processor. Many RISC processors divide registers into two banks; optimal performance is achieved when the two operands of an instruction come from separate register banks.

repeater

A hardware device that connects two network segments and passes signals between them. See hub.

RFC

(*Request For Comments*) The name of a series of documents about TCP/IP protocols and the Internet that contain reports and jokes as well as proposed and accepted protocol standards.

RFIFO (Intel)

(*Receive First In First Out*) A set of sixteen registers on the Intel IXP1200 used as buffers to store incoming packet data.

RISC

(*Reduced Instruction Set Computer*) An architectural style for a CPU in which the CPU offers a small set of basic instructions. Compare to CISC and VLIW.

RLDRAM

(*Reduced Latency Dynamic Random Access Memory*) A DRAM technology that has low cycle times and high bandwidth, which makes RLDRAM especially useful for storing large packets. See FCRAM.

RMI

(*Remote Method Invocation*) An object-oriented language term used for remote procedure call. See RPC.

RMON

(Remote MONitoring) A standard for a set of variables used with the Simple Network Monitoring Protocol (SNMP) to permit a device to act as a packet analyzer that gathers and reports statistics about network traffic. Technically, the RMON standard specifies a Management Information Base (MIB).

ROM

(Read Only Memory) A memory technology in which values can be stored in memory once. ROM can be used in a network system to contain software or data values the system needs when it runs.

round robin

A technique for selecting packets from a set of queues in which the selection proceeds to choose one from each queue before selecting a second packet from any queue. A network system can use round robin to service packets that arrive from multiple input ports.

router

An abbreviation for IP router.

routing table lookup

One of the steps an IP router performs when forwarding a datagram. IP routing table lookup uses a longest-prefix match.

RPC

(Remote Procedure Call) A programming paradigm in which parts of a program reside on multiple computers and a procedure call causes control to pass across the network from one computer to another. Because it hides communication details, RPC raises the level of the language. Also see RMI.

RSF

(Routing Switch Fabric) The switching fabric used by Cognigine for the mechanism to interconnect the processors that comprise a network processor.

RSP

(Routing Switch Processor) One of the three chips that comprise the 2.5G network processor sold by Agere Systems. The RSP receives packets from an FPP and forwards them to an external destination. See ASI and FPP.

RTC

(Real-Time Clock) A hardware mechanism that provides regular pulses that other devices use for timing.

rule based language

A declarative programming language in which each statement specifies a rule to follow if the condition is met. See declarative language.

run to completion

A model of computation used in network processors in which a single processor or task handles all protocol processing before forwarding a packet. Contrast with task-level parallelism.

SAR

(*Segmentation And Reassembly*) The procedure a sender uses to divide an AAL5 message into cells for transmission across an ATM network, and the procedure a receiver uses to recreate the AAL5 message.

scheduling policy

A set of rules that specify how priorities are assigned and computational resources allocated. Network systems use a scheduling policy to select a packet to be processed from among the set of available packets.

Scratchpad memory (Intel)

A small, high-speed memory in the IXP1200 used for synchronization and shared values.

SDH

(Synchronous Digital Hierarchy) The European standards that correspond to SONET in the United States. See SONET.

SDK

(*Software Development Kit*) Software that a vendor supplies to accompany a hardware product. An SDK usually includes compilers, assemblers, linkers, loaders, macros, libraries, and a simulator or emulator.

SDP

(*Serial Data Processor*) One of two parallel processors that comprise the Channel Processor in Motorola's network processor. One SDP handles ingress operations; the other handles egress.

SDRAM

(*Synchronized Dynamic Random Access Memory*) A form of DRAM that achieves higher speed by synchronizing the memory clock and the CPU clock.

segment

A term with multiple meanings. When used with Ethernet, segment originally referred to a single Ethernet cable, and now refers to the functional equivalent: a single hub or a single VLAN. When used with TCP, segment refers to a single message that includes the TCP header and payload.

segmentation

An ATM term analogous to IP's fragmentation. Segmentation divides an AAL5 message into ATM cells. See reassembly.

self routing

A technique used in switching fabrics in which information prepended to a packet determines the route through the fabric.

semaphore

A mechanism used to coordinate and synchronize independent threads of execution. The two semaphore operations, *wait* and *signal*, can be used for mutual exclusion or producer-consumer coordination.

sequential processing

The chief alternative to parallel processing. Sequential processing implies that the underlying hardware can only perform a single computational activity at any time. See parallel processing.

SerDes

(*Ser*ializer/*Des*erializer) A chip that converts between parallel and serial forms of data. A SerDes chip can be used between a bus that uses parallel data paths and an optical network such as an OC-48 line which transmits data serially.

SFI

(*SerDes Framer Interface*) A standard specified by the Optical Internet Forum that specifies the interconnection between a processor and framer hardware using a parallel-to-serial converter.

shared bus

An architecture in which multiple functional units attach to a bus and contend for access. An arbiter mechanism is needed to ensure that only one unit controls the bus at any time.

shared memory

A memory to which multiple functional units attach and contend for use. Shared memory can serve as the basis for a switching fabric.

signaling

A telephony term that refers to the protocols and mechanisms that set up a circuit.

silicon spin

The process of design and fabrication used for a silicon chip. Because a typical silicon spin requires at least eighteen months, changing silicon is much more costly than changing software.

SLA

(*Service Level Agreement*) A contractual agreement between two organizations that specifies properties of the network connection between them (e.g., between an ISP and a customer). Network systems need traffic monitoring and policing facilities to enforce the terms of an SLA.

slow path

The path that exceptional packets follow through a network system. The slow path is not optimized. See fast path.

SNMP

(*Simple Network Management Protocol*) The protocol used with TCP/IP networks that allows a network administrator to configure and control network systems such as IP routers.

soft state

A technique in which stored state information times out unless it is refreshed. Soft state works well in cases where a sender and receiver become disconnected.

softswitch

A network system that serves as an interface between an internet and a traditional telephone network. A softswitch handles telephony functions such as call setup and call forwarding for digital telephone calls. See SS7.

software emulation

A technique used to allow testing of a design before a chip is fabricated. The chip design is passed to a software system that emulates the hardware. Software emulators run several orders of magnitude slower than hardware.

software interrupt

A mechanism available in some CPUs that allows a running program to generate an interrupt. Protocol software can be structured to use software interrupts.

SONET

(*Synchronous Optical NETwork*) A telecommunications industry standard for sending digitized voice calls over an optical fiber. Data networks can use SONET to send packets. See SDH and POS.

SOP (Intel)

(*Start Of Packet*) A bit set in the control information that accompanies an mpacket to indicate that the mpacket contains the first 64 bytes of a packet. See EOP.

special-purpose processor

A processor that is tailored to a specific task or tasks. Most coprocessors are special-purpose. Compare to GPP.

SPI-3

(System Packet Interface Level 3) A standard specified by the Optical Internetworking Forum for the electrical connection between a SONET/SDH physical-layer device and a link-layer device that can implement a packet protocol such as PPP. Thus, SPI-3 specifies an interface between the PHY and LINK layers.

splicing

See TCP splicing.

SRAM

(*Static Random Access Memory*) One of two broad categories used to classify memory technology. Static RAM is generally faster, but costs more than dynamic RAM. Compare to DRAM.

SS7

(*Signaling System 7*) The name of the protocol and associated mechanisms that traditional telephone systems use for functions such as call setup and call forwarding.

SSI

(*Synchronous Serial Interface*) An external hardware interface for synchronous serial communication.

SSL

(*Secure Sockets Layer*) A de facto standard for secure communication originally created by Netscape, Inc.

SSRAM

(*Synchronous Static RAM*) A type of static RAM in which fetch and store operations are synchronized with an external clock signal.

stack

See protocol stack.

stateful

Characteristic of a network system that stores information about past events and uses the stored information to determine how to process packets. Because it requires additional resources, designers avoid keeping state information whenever possible. Compare to stateless.

stateless

Characteristic of a network system that processes each packet independently without using the history of packets to determine how to handle a packet. Compare to stateful.

static classification

A classification scheme in which flows are established a priori. For example, static classification can assign a flow for each service type (e.g., a flow for all web traffic).

static flow

A flow for which the classification rules do not depend on the history of packets seen. The classification rules for typical static flows use type fields and protocol port numbers.

store and forward

A term used to describe the action of a network system that adheres to a packet switching paradigm. The network system places incoming packets in memory (the *store* aspect) until they can be processed (the *forward* aspect).

subnet mask

See address mask.

SVC

(*Switched Virtual Circuit*) A virtual circuit that is established on demand and terminated when no longer needed. Compare to PVC.

switch

A generic term for a network system that connects to two or more networks and forwards packets among them; vendors often use the term switch to imply higher performance. See bridge and IP router.

switching fabric

A hardware mechanism used to interconnect multiple functional units and allow them to exchange data. A switching fabric can be used as the internal interconnection among input and output ports in a network system.

symmetric multiprocessing

A parallel architecture in which a set of identical processors all operate at the same time. In a network system, symmetric multiprocessing usually means that an incoming packet can be handled by whichever processor becomes idle.

SYN

(*SYNchronization segment*) A segment used by TCP to establish a connection. See FIN.

system backplane

The central interconnect mechanism in a system. Printed circuit cards, known as blades, plug into the backplane. Each blade contains processors, memory, or I/O interfaces.

T-CAM

(*Ternary-CAM*) The form of Content Addressable Memory (CAM) typically used with network processors. Because it permits partial-match retrieval, T-CAM is useful for classification. See CAM.

T-series standards

A set of telecommunications industry standards for sending digitized voice calls over copper lines. Data networks can use lines that adhere to T-series standards to send packets (e.g., a T1 line or a T3 line). T1 is often used (incorrectly) as a synonym for any 1.5 Mbps connection.

tail drop

A policy that a network system can use to manage queue overflow: accept all packets that arrive until the queue fills, and then discard all successive packets. Compare to RED.

task-level parallelism

A model of computation used in network processors in which a single processor or thread handles one protocol processing task forwarding a packet. Contrast with run to completion, and compare to instruction-level parallelism. Also see pipeline.

TCP

(*Transmission Control Protocol*) The most widely used transport protocol in the Internet. In addition to providing reliability, TCP offers congestion control.

TCP splicing

A mechanism used by network systems such as NAT to interconnect two separate TCP connections. A TCP splicer changes values in the IP and TCP headers: source and destination addresses, protocol port numbers, sequence and acknowledgement numbers, and checksums.

TCP termination

A general reference to the protocol processing needed at the endpoint of a TCP connection. For example, a system running a web server must terminate many TCP connections.

termination

See TCP termination.

TFIFO (Intel)

(*Transmit First In First Out*) A set of sixteen registers on the Intel IXP1200 used as buffers to store outgoing packet data.

thread

A unit of execution that runs independently. See threads of execution and context.

thread dispatch

The process of choosing a thread to execute for a given task. In network systems, thread dispatch is often triggered by the arrival of a packet.

thread synchronization

The coordination of processing among independent threads of execution. Synchronization is required when multiple threads share data structures in memory (e.g., a linked list of packets). See semaphore.

threads of execution

A technique used to improve performance and ease programming in which independent computations proceed concurrently. Whenever one thread blocks, a processor switches to another. Some network processors offer hardware support for threads. See context.

three-way handshake

An exchange of three packets that TCP uses to reliably start or gracefully terminate a connection.

time-to-live

A mechanism used to limit the amount of time a packet can spend traversing the Internet. See TTL field.

TM10

The name for the traffic manager chip in the Agere Systems 10G network processor. See NP10.

TOE

(*TCP Offload Engine*) A network system that works in conjunction with an application server (e.g., a web server) by terminating TCP connections and extracting the data stream from each. Because it offloads TCP processing, a TOE allows a server to handle higher loads.

token bucket

A mechanism used for traffic shaping. Token bucket delays outgoing packets to help eliminate bursts and smooth the packet rate. The delay assigned to a packet depends on the packet size and the time the packet arrives. Also see leaky bucket.

token passing

A technique used for arbitration and coordination of a shared resource. Some network hardware uses token passing as do some bus arbitration mechanisms.

TOP

(*Task Optimized Processor*) A term used by EZchip Corporation to identify special-purpose processors that are part of the EZchip network processor.

TOS

(*Type Of Service*) The original name of the field in an IPv4 header that allows a sender to specify the service desired. Now replaced by DiffServ.

traffic management

The mechanisms and procedures used to establish and enforce policies related to the measurement and control of network traffic. Traffic management includes measuring, policing, and shaping; it may also include routing.

traffic measurement

The measurement of the maximums, averages, and durations of traffic patterns, including packets, data, and bursts. Accurate measurement of individual transport-layer connections is difficult for high-capacity backbone links.

traffic monitoring

The comparison of measured traffic to predetermined limits. Traffic monitoring is used to enforce service level agreements.

traffic policing

The enforcement of predefined limits on traffic: quantity, rate, or type. A policer measures incoming traffic, and discards packets that exceed the specified bounds.

traffic shaping

A function performed by a network system to assure traffic meets a set of characteristics. Typically, a traffic shaper receives packets in bursts, and emits them at a steady rate.

transfer registers

Hardware mechanisms that are used to transfer data between two functional units on a chip or between a chip and an external device. Some network processors use transfer registers to move data between the physical interface device and the chip or between the chip and external memory.

tRC

(*time for a Read Cycle*) A measure of memory hardware that specifies the minimum amount of time required between successive read operations. See memory cycle time.

TTL field

(*Time-To-Live field*) A field in an IP datagram header that specifies the maximum number of hops the datagram can take to its destination. Each router along the path decrements the TTL field, and discards the datagram if the value reaches zero.

UART

(*Universal Asynchronous Receiver and Transmitter*) A hardware device that provides serial communication according to EIA standard RS232C. Some network processor contain a UART that provides a serial line connection.

UBR

(*Unspecified Bit Rate*) A stream of network traffic that results from a data application such as email or file transfer and does not require specific performance from the network (i.e., the sender does not specify bounds on throughput, delay, or jitter). See CBR and VBR.

UDP

(*User Datagram Protocol*) An unreliable, connectionless transport-layer protocol in the TCP/IP suite. See TCP.

unicast address

A value used as a destination address to specify that a packet should be delivered to exactly one station on a network. Each station (e.g., a computer) is assigned a unique unicast address. Compare to broadcast address and multicast address.

USB

(*Universal Serial Bus*) An external hardware bus interface used to connect a processor to I/O devices.

Utopia

A technology designed to provide high-speed transfer in a network system between a physical interface and the processor(s). Compare to RapidIO, InfiniBand, PCI-X, and HyperTransport.

variable-size header

Characteristic of a network technology in which the size of a packet header is determined by the information being carried. Options in the IP datagram header make the header variable size. Variable-size headers incur more processing overhead than fixed-size headers.

variable-size packet

Characteristic of a network technology in which the size of each packet is determined by the amount of data being transferred. Variable size packets make buffer management more difficult. Compare to cell.

VBR

(*Variable Bit Rate*) A stream of network traffic that results from an application that generates bursty traffic with a fixed mean data rate. See CBR and UBR.

VC

(*Virtual Circuit* or *Virtual Connection*) A path through a network that is established by configuring switches to forward packets along the path. A VC provides the illusion of a circuit. Note: ATM uses the term *virtual connection*. See also PVC and SVC.

Verilog

A language hardware designers use to model, verify, and synthesize VLSI circuits. Verilog allows an engineer to describe designs at a high level of abstraction (e.g., architectural or behavioral) as well as at lower levels (e.g., gate and switch). See VHDL.

VHDL

(*Very high-speed integrated circuit Hardware Description Language*) A language hardware designers use to model, verify, and synthesize VLSI circuits. VHDL allows an engineer to describe designs at a high level of abstraction (e.g., architectural or behavioral) as well as at lower levels (e.g., gate and switch). See Verilog.

VISC

(*Variable Instruction Set Communications*) A technology developed by Cognigine that allows a processor's instruction set to be changed without requiring a hardware change.

VLAN switch

(*Virtual Local Area Network switch*) A configurable hardware device that connects multiple computers and allows a manager to configure the computers into subsets known as VLANs. Each VLAN corresponds to a separate broadcast domain.

VLIW

(*Very Long Instruction Word*) An architectural style for a processor in which each instruction includes bits that control separate hardware units. Compare to CISC and RISC.

VLSI

(*Very Large Scale Integrated circuit*) An integrated circuit composed of tens of thousands of transistors and other devices designed to work together. A network processor is implemented with a VLSI circuit.

VPI/VCI

(*Virtual Path Identifier/Virtual Circuit Identifier*) The label used by ATM to associate a cell with a particular VC.

VPN

(*Virtual Private Network*) A technology that provides the security of a private network at low cost. Although it sends packets across the Internet from one site to another, a VPN uses encryption to guarantee confidentiality.

WAN

(*Wide Area Network*) A class of network technologies optimized for long distance. A WAN can extend arbitrarily far. Contrast with LAN.

WFQ

(*Weighted Fair Queuing*) A technique for selecting packets from multiple queues. WFQ avoids the problem of starvation, which can arise when strict priorities are used. Also see WRR.

Wi-Fi

See 802.11b.

wire speed

A processing rate equal to the rate at which packets can arrive. Designers strive to build network systems that can run at wire speed.

WRED

(*Weighted Random Early Detection*) A variation of RED that uses weighted probabilities to handle priorities.

WRR

(*Weighted Round Robin*) A technique for selecting packets from multiple queues. Although it services all queues without starvation, WRR allows some queues to have higher priority. Also see WFQ.

ZBT-SRAM

(*Zero Bus-Turnaround SRAM*) A variation of SRAM that operates at higher speed. ZBT-SRAM allows full utilization of the bus by eliminating idle cycles between read and write operations.

zero-overhead context switch

An optimized form of context switch that occurs without delay between executing an instruction in the old context and an instruction in the new context. See thread and context switch.

Bibliography

AGERE SYSTEMS [Sept. 1999], The Challenge for Next Generation Network Processors, *White Paper*.

AGERE SYSTEMS [1999], The Case For A Classification Language, *White Paper*.

AGERE SYSTEMS [March 2002], Functional Programming Language User's And Reference Guides. For SDE Version 3.0, Austin, Texas.

AGERE SYSTEMS [Dec. 2001], PayLoadPlus Compute Engine Programming Guide Version 4, Austin, Texas.

AHMADI H. and W. DENZEL, [Sept. 1989] A Survey of Modern High-Performance Switching Techniques, *IEEE Journal on Selected Areas in Communication*, Vol. 7:7, 1091-1103.

AHO, A., R. SETHI, and J. D. ULLMAN, [1986], *Compilers, Principles, Techniques And Tools*, Addison-Wesley, Reading, Massachusetts.

AMDAHL, G., G. A. BLAAUW, and J. F. P. BROOKS, [April 1964], Architecture of the IBM System/360, *IBM Journal of Research and Development*, Vol. 8:2, 87-97

BIRREL, A.D. [1989], An Introduction to Programming with Threads, *Research Report 35*, Digital Equipment Corporation System Research Center, Palo Alto, CA.

BROOKS, F. P., [April 1987], No Silver Bullet — Essence and Accidents of Software Engineering, *IEEE Computer*, Vol. 20:4, 10-19. (Reprinted from *Proc. IFIP Congress*, Dublin, Ireland, 1986.)

BROOKS, F. P., [1995], *The Mythical Man-Month: Essays On Software Engineering,* Anniversary Edition, Addison-Wesley, Reading, Massachusetts.

BUX, W., W. E. DENZEL, T. ENGBERSEN, A. HERKERSDORF, and R.P. LUIJTEN, [Jan. 2001], Technologies and building blocks for fast packet forwarding, *IEEE Communications Magazine*, Vol. 39:1, 70-77.

CAMPBELL, A. T., S. CHOU, M. E. KOUNAVIS, V. D. STACHTOS, and J. B. VICENTE, [June 2002], NetBind: A Binding Tool for Constructing Data Paths In Network Processor-Based Routers, *IEEE Fifth International Conference on Open Architectures and Network Programming (OPENARCH '02)*.

CHIUEH, T. C. and P. PRADHAN, [1999], Cache memory design for network processors, *Proc. Sixth International Symposium on High-Performance Computer Architecture*, Vol. HPCA-6, 409-418.

CLARK, D. D. [Dec. 1985], The structuring of systems using upcalls, *Tenth ACM Symposium on Operating Systems Principles,* 171-180.

CLARK, D. D. [1988], The Design Philosophy of the DARPA Internet Protocols, *Proc. of ACM SIGCOMM '88,* 106-114.

CLARK, D. D. and D. TENNENHOUSE [September 1990], Architectural Considerations for a New Generation of Protocols, *Proc. ACM SIGCOMM '90,* Philadelphia, Pa.

COMER, D. E. [2000], *Internetworking With TCP/IP: Volume I: Principles, Protocols, And Architectures,* 4th edition, Prentice-Hall, Upper Saddle River, New Jersey.

COMER, D. E. and D. L. STEVENS [1999], *Internetworking With TCP/IP: Volume II: Design, Implementation, and Internals,* 3rd edition, Prentice-Hall, Upper Saddle River, New Jersey.

COMER, D. E. and D. L. STEVENS [2000], *Internetworking With TCP/IP Volume III – Client-Server Programming And Applications, Linux/POSIX sockets version,*, Prentice-Hall, Upper Saddle River, New Jersey.

COMER, D. E. [2001], *Computer Networks and Internets,* 3rd edition, Prentice Hall, Upper Saddle River, NJ.

CROWLEY, P., M. E. FIUCZYNSKI, J. L. BAER, and B. BERSHAD, [May, 2000], Characterizing Processor Architectures for Programmable Network Interfaces, *Proc. of the 2000 International Conference on Supercomputing,* Santa Fe, NM, 54-65.

CROWLEY, P., M. E. FIUCZYNSKI, and J. L. BAER, [2000], On the performance of multithreaded architectures for network processors. *Technical Report 2000-10-01*, Department of Computer Science & Engineering, University of Washington.

DRUSCHEL, P. [Sept. 1996], Operating System Support for High-Speed Communication, *Communications of the ACM,* Vol. 39:9, 41-51.

EZCHIP TECHNOLOGIES, [Dec. 1999], Network Processor Designs for Next-Generation Networking Equipment, *White Paper.*

FELDMEIER, D. C., [March 1988], Improving Gateway Performance with a Routing-Table Cache, *Proc. of IEEE INFOCOM'88,* New Orleans, 298-307.

GUPTA, P. and N. MCKEOWN, [March 2001], Algorithms for packet classification, *IEEE Network,* Vol. 15:2, 24-32.

HENNESSY, J. L. and D. A. PATTERSON, [2002], *Computer Architecture: A Quantitative Approach,* 3rd edition, Morgan Kaufmann Publishers, San Mateo, CA.

HINDEN, R. [June 1996], IP Next Generation Overview, *Communications of the ACM,* Vol. 39:6, 61-71.

HUSAK, D., [May 2000], Network Processors: A Definition and Comparison, *White paper,* Motorola Corporation.

HUSAK, D. and R. GOHN, [2000] Network Processor Programming Models: The Key to Achieving Faster Time-to-Market and Extending Product Life, *White paper,* Motorola Corporation.

INTEL [2001a], *IXA SDK ACE Programming Framework: IXA SDK 2.0 Reference,* Intel Corporation, Portland OR., Part number A46817-001.

INTEL [2001b], *IXA SDK ACE Programming Framework: IXA SDK 2.0 Developer's Guide,* Intel Corporation, Portland OR., Part number A71582-001.

INTEL [2001c], *IXP1200 Network Processor Family: Hardware Reference Manual,* Intel Corporation, Portland OR., Part number 278303-008.

INTEL [2001d], *IXP1200 Network Processor Family: Microcode Programmer's Reference Manual,* Intel Corporation, Portland OR., Part number 278304-009.

INTEL [2001e], *IXP1200 Network Processor: Intel Macro Library Reference Manual,* Intel Corporation, Portland OR., Part number 278390-001.

INTEL [2001f], *IXP1200 Network Processor Macro Library Style Guide,* Intel Corporation, Portland OR.

JOHNSON, E. and A. KUNZE, [2001] *IXP1200 Programming: The Microengine Coding Guide for the Intel IXP1200 Network Processor Family*, Intel Press.

KARLIN, S. and L. L. PETERSON, [2002], VERA: An Extensible Router Architecture, *Computer Networks*, Vol. 38:3, 277--293.

KENNEDY, J. and R. MELNICK, [1999], Network Processing Platforms: Minimizing Total Time-to-Market, *White paper,* MMC Networks, Incorporated.

KESHAV, S. [1997], *An Engineering Approach To Computer Networking: ATM Networks, The Internet, And The Telephone Network.* Addison-Wesley, Reading, Massachusetts.

KESHAV, S. and R. SHARMA, [May 1998], Issues and Trends in Router Design, *IEEE Communications Magazine,* Vol. 36:5, 144-151.

KNUTH, D., [1998], *The Art of Computer Programming, Volume 3: Sorting and Searching,* 2nd edition, Addison-Wesley, Reading, Massachusetts.

KOUFOPAVLOU, O., A. TANTAWY, and M. ZITTERBART, [1994], A Comparison of Gigabit Router Architectures, *High Performance Networking,* E. FDIDA (Ed.), Elsevier Science VY, Amsterdam, The Netherlands. Also in *IFIP Transactions C[Communication Systems], Vol. C-26, 107-121.*

MCKEOWN, N., [December 1997], *Fast Switched Backplane for a Gigabit Switched Router, Business Communications Review,* Vol. 27:12.

MENZILCIOGLU, O. and S. SCHLICK, [May 1991], Nectar CAB: a high-speed network processor, *Proc. of the 11th International Conference on Distributed Computing Systems,* 508-515.

NIE, X., L GAZSI, F. ENGEL, and G. FETTWEIS, [1999], A new network processor architecture for high-speed communications, *IEEE Workshop On Signal Processing Systems SiPS 99,* 548-557.

PARTRIDGE, C. [1996], Locality and route caches, *NSF Workshop on Internet Statistics Measurement and Analysis,* San Diego, CA.

PARTRIDGE, C., et. al. [Jun 1998], A Fifty Gigabit Per Second IP Router, *IEEE/ACM Trans. on Networking,* Vol. 6:3, 237-248.

PATTERSON, D. A. and J. L. HENNESSY [1997], *Computer Organization and Design: The Hardware/Software Interface,* 2nd edition, Morgan Kaufmann Publishers, San Mateo, CA.

PERLMAN, R. [2000], *Interconnections: Bridges and Routers,* 2nd edition, Addison-Wesley, Reading, Massachusetts.

PETERSON L. L. and B. DAVIE, [1999], *Computer Networks: A Systems Approach,* 2nd edition, Morgan Kaufmann Publishers, San Mateo, CA.

ROMANOW, A. and S. FLOYD, [May 1995], Dynamics of TCP Traffic over ATM Networks, *IEEE JSAC,* Vol. 13:4, 633-641.

SEAL, D. [2000], *ARM Architecture Reference Manual*, 2nd edition. Addison-Wesley, Reading, Massachusetts.

SHALABY, N., L. L. PETERSON, A. BAVIER, Y. GOTTLIEB, S. KARLIN, A. NAKAO, X. QIE, T. SPALINK, and M. WAWRZONIAK, [May 2002], Extensible Routers for Active Networks, *Proc. of the DARPA Active Networks Conference and Exposition.*

SHENKER , S. [1995], Fundamental design issues for the future internet, *IEEE Journal on Selected Areas in Communications*, Vol. 13:7, 1176-1188.

SPALINK, T., S KARLIN, L. L. PETERSON, and Y. GOTTLIEB, [October 2001], Building a Robust Software-Based Router Using Network Processors, *Proc. of the 18th ACM Symposium on Operating Systems Principles (SOSP)*, 216-229.

SPALINK, T., S KARLIN, L. L. PETERSON, [November 2000], Evaluating Network Processors in IP Forwarding, *Technical Report TR-626-00*, Princeton University.

TAYLOR, D. E., J. S. TURNER, and J. W. LOCKWOOD [April 2001], Dynamic Hardware Plugins (DHP): Exploiting Reconfigurable Hardware for High-Performance Programmable Routers, *IEEE Fifth International Conference on Open Architectures and Network Programming (OPENARCH '01)*, Washington University in Saint Louis.

WALDVOGEL M., G. VARGHESE, J. TURNER, and B. PLATTNER [November 2001], Scalable High-Speed Prefix Matching, *ACM Transactions on Computer Systems,* Vol. 19:4, 440-482.

WILLIAMS, J., [2001], Architectures for Network Processing, VLSI Technology, *Proc. Of International Symposium On Systems And Applications,* 61-64.

Index